# INFORMATICS PRACTICES
## for CBSE Class XI

# INFORMATICS PRACTICES
## for CBSE Class XI

**Reema Thareja**

Assistant Professor
Department of Computer Science
Shyama Prasad Mukherji College
University of Delhi

All rights reserved. No part of this book may be modified, reproduced or utilised in any form, or by any means, electronic or mechanical, including photocopying, recording or by any information storage and retrieval system, in any form of binding or cover other than in which it is published, without permission in writing from the publisher.

**INFORMATICS PRACTICES FOR CBSE CLASS XI**

**UNIVERSITIES PRESS (INDIA) PRIVATE LIMITED**

*Registered office*
3-6-747/1/A & 3-6-754/1, Himayatnagar, Hyderabad 500 029,
Telangana, India info@universitiespress.com; www.universitiespress.com

*Distributed by*
Orient Blackswan Private limited

*Registered office*
3-6-752 Himayatnagar, Hyderabad 500 029, Telangana, India

*Other offices*
Bengaluru, Chennai, Guwahati, Hyderabad, Kolkata,
Mumbai, New Delhi, Noida, Patna, Visakhapatnam

© Universities Press (India) Private Ltd 2022
First Published 2022
Reprinted 2022

ISBN: 978-93-89211-92-4

*Cover and book design*
© Universities Press (India) Private Ltd 2022

Typeset in Adobe Garamond Pro 10.5 by
SRS Publishing Services, Puducherry

*Printed in India by*
B.B. Press, Noida

*Published by*
Universities Press (India) Private Limited
3-6-747/1/A & 3-6-754/1, Himayatnagar, Hyderabad 500 029, Telangana, India

*Disclaimer*
Care has been taken to confirm the accuracy of information printed in this book. The author and the publisher, however, cannot accept any responsibility for errors or omissions or for consequences from the application of the information in this book and make no warranty, express or implied, with respect to its contents. This textbook does not constitute a standard, specification or regulation. The trademarks or manufacturers' names appear/are used in this book only because they are considered essential to the object of subject discussion and do not necessarily constitute endorsement of the product/standard by the author or publisher. All products and company names are trademarks[TM] or registered[®] trademarks of their respective holders. Use of them does not imply any affiliation with or endorsement by them.

*I dedicate this book to my family and my uncle Mr B L Theraja,
who is a well-known author himself.*

# Contents

Preface — xvii
About the Author — xix

## Chapter 1: Computer Systems and Organization — 1

- 1.1 What is a Computer? — 1
- 1.2 Evolution of Computing Devices — 2
  - 1.2.1 First Generation (1942–1955) — 2
  - 1.2.2 Second Generation (1955–1964) — 2
  - 1.2.3 Third Generation (1964–1975) — 3
  - 1.2.4 Fourth Generation (1975–1989) — 3
  - 1.2.5 Fifth Generation (1989–Present) — 4
- 1.3 Characteristics of Computers — 4
- 1.4 Basic Computer Organization — 5
  - 1.4.1 Input — 5
  - 1.4.2 Storage — 6
  - 1.4.3 Output — 6
- 1.5 Input Devices — 7
  - 1.5.1 Keyboard — 7
  - 1.5.2 Mouse — 8
  - 1.5.3 Touchpad — 8
  - 1.5.4 Joystick — 9
  - 1.5.5 Touchscreen — 9
  - 1.5.5 Image Scanner — 9
  - 1.5.6 Stylus — 10
  - 1.5.7 Barcode Reader — 10
  - 1.5.8 Optical Mark Recognition (OMR) — 10
  - 1.5.9 Magnetic Ink Character Reader (MICR) — 11
  - 1.5.10 Digital Camera — 11
- 1.6 Output Devices — 11
  - 1.6.1 Monitor or VDU (Visual Display Unit) — 11
  - 1.6.2 Speakers — 12
  - 1.6.3 Headphone — 12
  - 1.6.4 Printer — 13

|      |         |                                                                  |     |
|------|---------|------------------------------------------------------------------|-----|
|      | 1.6.5   | Projector                                                        | 13  |
|      | 1.6.6   | Plotters                                                         | 14  |
| 1.7  | Organization of Computer's Memory                                          | 14  |
| 1.8  | Types of Computer Memory                                                   | 14  |
|      | 1.8.1   | Cache Memory                                                     | 15  |
|      | 1.8.2   | Primary Memory                                                   | 15  |
|      | 1.8.3   | Secondary Memory                                                 | 16  |
|      | 1.8.4   | Optical Storage Discs                                            | 17  |
| 1.9  | Data Deletion and Security Concerns                                        | 18  |
|      | 1.9.1   | Risk of Data Misuse                                              | 18  |
|      | 1.9.2   | Permanently Deleting Files                                       | 18  |
| 1.10 | Recovery of Deleted Data                                                   | 19  |
|      | 1.10.1  | Recovering Deleted Files with Deleted File Recovery Software     | 19  |
|      | 1.10.2  | Restore Deleted Files from the Previous Version                  | 19  |
| 1.11 | Computer Hardware and Software                                             | 20  |
| 1.12 | Types of Computer Software                                                 | 20  |
| 1.13 | General-purpose Application Software                                       | 20  |
| 1.14 | Types of Software Based on Cost                                            | 22  |
| 1.15 | Customized Software                                                        | 23  |
|      | 1.15.1  | Generic Software Development vs. Specific-purpose Software       | 23  |
| 1.16 | Utility Software                                                           | 24  |

*Key Terms | Chapter Highlights | Review Questions | Fill in the Blanks | State True or False | Multiple Choice Questions | Answers*

## Chapter 2: Introduction to Programming Language Python — 29

|      |                                                    |     |
|------|----------------------------------------------------|-----|
| 2.1  | Features of Python                                 | 29  |
| 2.2  | Limitations of Python                              | 30  |
| 2.3  | History of Python                                  | 30  |
| 2.4  | Applications of Python                             | 31  |
| 2.5  | The Future of Python                               | 31  |
| 2.6  | Writing and Executing the First Python Program     | 32  |
| 2.7  | Interactive Python                                 | 32  |
| 2.8  | More About the `print()` Function                  | 33  |
| 2.9  | Writing Python Programs Using the Idle Editor      | 34  |
| 2.10 | Python Character Set                               | 34  |
| 2.11 | Python Tokens                                      | 34  |
| 2.12 | Literal Constants                                  | 34  |
|      | 2.12.1  Numbers                                    | 35  |
|      | 2.12.2  Strings                                    | 37  |
| 2.13 | Type Conversion                                    | 40  |

*Key Terms | Chapter Highlights | Review Questions | Fill in the Blanks | State True or False | Multiple Choice Questions | Give the Output | Answers*

## Chapter 3: Python – Building Blocks — 45

- 3.1 Variables and Indentifiers — 45
  - 3.1.1 Creating Variables — 46
  - 3.1.2 Data Types of Identifiers — 46
  - 3.1.3 Assigning or Initializing Values to Variables — 47
- 3.2 Multiple Assignments — 48
  - 3.2.1 Data Type Boolean — 48
- 3.3 Input Operation — 49
- 3.4 Comments — 49
  - 3.4.1 Multi-line Comments — 50
- 3.5 Reserved Words — 50
- 3.6 Indentation — 50
- 3.7 Operators and Expressions — 51
  - 3.7.1 Arithmetic Operators — 51
  - 3.7.2 Comparison Operators — 52
  - 3.7.3 Assignment and In-place or Shortcut Operators — 52
  - 3.7.4 Unary Operators — 52
  - 3.7.5 Bitwise Operators — 53
  - 3.7.6 Shift Operators — 53
  - 3.7.7 Logical Operators — 54
  - 3.7.8 Membership Operators — 54
  - 3.7.9 Identity Operators — 54
  - 3.7.10 Operators' Precedence and Associativity — 55
- 3.8 Expressions in Python — 56

*Programmer's Zone* — 56
*Key Terms | Chapter Highlights | Review Questions |*
*Programming Exercises | Fill in the Blanks | State True or False |*
*Multiple Choice Questions | Give the Output | Find the Error | Answers*

## Chapter 4: Decision Control Statements — 73

- 4.1 Selection/Conditional Branching Statements — 73
- 4.2 `if` Statement — 74
  - 4.2.1 Implementing `if` statement in Python — 74
- 4.3 `if-else` Statement — 75
- 4.4 Nested `if` Statements — 76
- 4.5 `if-elif-else` Statement — 76

*Programmer's Zone* — 78
*Key Terms | Chapter Highlights | Review Questions |*
*Programming Exercises | Fill in the Blanks | State True or False |*
*Multiple Choice Questions | Give the Output | Answers*

## Chapter 5: Basic Loop Structures/Iterative Statements — 89

- 5.1 `while` Loop — 89
- 5.2 `for` Loop — 90
- 5.3 The `range()` Function — 91
- 5.4 Selecting an Appropriate Loop — 92
- 5.5 Nested Loops — 92
- 5.6 The `break` Statement — 93
- 5.7 The `continue` Statement — 93
- 5.8 The `pass` Statement — 94
- 5.9 The `else` Statement Used with Loops — 94

*Programmer's Zone* — 95
*Key Terms | Chapter Highlights | Review Questions |*
*Programming Exercises | Fill in the Blanks | State True or False | Multiple Choice Questions |*
*Give the Output | Find the Error | Answers*

## Chapter 6: Functions and Modules — 113

- 6.1 Function — 113
  - 6.1.1 Need for Functions — 114
  - 6.1.2 Calling a Function — 114
- 6.2 Modules — 115
  - 6.2.1 Module Loading and Execution — 115
  - 6.2.2 The `from...import` Statement — 115
  - 6.2.3 Name of Module — 116
- 6.3 The `dir()` Function — 117
- 6.4 Packages in Python — 117
- 6.5 Python – Math Module — 117
- 6.6 Built-in Functions — 119
- 6.7 Composition — 120
- 6.8 Function Declaration and Definition — 120
- 6.9 Function Definition — 121
- 6.10 Variable Scope and Lifetime — 123
  - 6.10.1 Local and Global Variables — 123
  - 6.10.2 Resolution of Names — 124
- 6.11 The `return` Statement — 125
- 6.12 The `random` Module in Python — 126

*Programmer's Zone* — 128
*Key Terms | Chapter Highlights | Review Questions |*
*Programming Exercises | Fill in the Blanks | State True or False | Multiple Choice Questions |*
*Give the Output | Find the Error | Answers*

## Chapter 7: Strings — 137

- 7.1 String Indexing — 137
- 7.2 Finding the Number of Characters in a String — 137

| | | | |
|---|---|---|---|
| 7.3 | Traversing a String | | 138 |
| 7.4 | Concatenating, Appending and Multiplying Strings | | 139 |
| 7.5 | The `str()` Function | | 140 |
| 7.6 | Strings Are Immutable | | 140 |
| 7.7 | String Formatting Operator | | 141 |
| 7.8 | The `format()` Function | | 142 |
| 7.9 | Built-in String Methods and Functions | | 142 |
| 7.10 | Comparing Strings | | 146 |
| 7.11 | `ord()` and `chr()` Functions | | 146 |
| 7.12 | `in` and `not in` operators | | 146 |

*Programmer's Zone*     *147*
*Key Terms | Chapter Highlights | Review Questions |*
*Programming Exercises | Fill in the Blanks | State True or False |*
*Multiple Choice Questions | Give the Output | Find the Error | Answers*

## Chapter 8: Lists     161

| | | | |
|---|---|---|---|
| 8.1 | Accessing Values in Lists | | 161 |
| 8.2 | The `eval()` Function | | 162 |
| 8.3 | Updating Values in Lists | | 162 |
| 8.4 | Relational Operations on Lists | | 163 |
| 8.5 | Nested Lists | | 164 |
| 8.6 | List Aliasing and Cloning | | 164 |
| 8.7 | Deleting Elements | | 165 |
| 8.8 | Deep Copies and Shallow Copies in Python | | 165 |
| 8.9 | Basic List Operations | | 166 |
| 8.10 | List Methods | | 167 |

*Programmer's Zone*     *170*
*Key Terms | Chapter Highlights | Review Questions |*
*Programming Exercises | Fill in the Blanks | State True or False |*
*Multiple Choice Questions | Give the Output | Find the Error | Answers*

## Chapter 9: Tuple     185

| | | | |
|---|---|---|---|
| 9.1 | Creating a Tuple | | 185 |
| 9.2 | Utility of Tuples | | 186 |
| 9.3 | Accessing Values in a Tuple | | 187 |
| 9.4 | Updating Tuple | | 187 |
| 9.5 | Deleting Elements in Tuple | | 188 |
| 9.6 | Joining Tuples | | 188 |
| 9.7 | Unpacking Tuples | | 189 |
| 9.8 | Basic Tuple Operations | | 189 |
| 9.9 | Tuple Assignment | | 190 |
| 9.10 | Accessing Using Index | | 191 |
| 9.11 | Tuples for Returning Multiple Values | | 191 |

| | | | |
|---|---|---|---|
| 9.12 | | Nested Tuples | 191 |
| 9.13 | | The `count()` Method | 192 |
| 9.14 | | The `zip()` Function | 192 |
| 9.15 | | Advantages of Tuple Over List | 194 |

*Programmer's Zone*      *194*
*Key Terms | Chapter Highlights | Review Questions |*
*Programming Exercises | Fill in the Blanks | State True or False |*
*Multiple Choice Questions | Give the Output | Find the Error | Answers*

## Chapter 10: Dictionaries     205

| | | | |
|---|---|---|---|
| 10.1 | | Creating a Dictionary | 205 |
| | 10.1.1 | Creating a Dictionary using `dict()` Method | 206 |
| 10.2 | | Accessing Values in a Dictionary | 206 |
| 10.3 | | Adding an Item in a Dictionary | 207 |
| 10.4 | | Modifying an Item in a Dictionary | 207 |
| 10.5 | | Deleting Items | 207 |
| | 10.5.1 | The `pop()` Method | 207 |
| 10.6 | | Traversing a Dictionary | 209 |
| 10.7 | | Nested Dictionaries | 210 |
| 10.8 | | The `copy()` Method | 210 |
| 10.9 | | Built-in Dictionary Functions and Methods | 210 |
| 10.10 | | Difference Between a List and a Dictionary | 211 |

*Programmer's Zone*      *212*
*Key Terms | Chapter Highlights | Review Questions |*
*Programming Exercises | Fill in the Blanks | State True or False |*
*Multiple Choice Questions | Give the Output | Find the Error | Answers*

## Chapter 11: Data Handling using Numpy     225

| | | | |
|---|---|---|---|
| 11.1 | | Data and Its Purpose | 225 |
| | 11.1.1 | Importance of Data | 225 |
| 11.2 | | Structured, Semi-structured and Unstructured Data | 226 |
| 11.3 | | Data Processing | 227 |
| 11.4 | | Descriptive Statistics | 228 |
| | 11.4.1 | Measure of Central Tendency | 228 |
| | 11.4.2 | Measure of Spread/Dispersion | 228 |
| 11.5 | | The NumPy Module | 229 |
| 11.6 | | Introduction to Arrays | 229 |
| | 11.6.1 | Matrices or Two-dimensional Arrays | 230 |
| 11.7 | | The NumPy Module | 232 |
| 11.8 | | Creating NumPy Arrays | 232 |
| 11.9 | | Array Attributes | 235 |

| | | |
|---|---|---|
| 11.10 | Converting 2D NumPy Array into 1D Array | 236 |
| | 11.10.1 np.flatten() | 236 |
| | 11.10.2 np.ravel() | 236 |
| | 11.10.3 np.reshape() | 237 |
| 11.11 | Array Slicing: Accessing Subarrays | 237 |
| | 11.11.1 Subarrays as No-copy Views | 238 |
| | 11.11.2 Creating Copies of Arrays | 238 |
| 11.12 | Reshaping of Arrays | 239 |
| | 11.12.1 Unknown Dimension | 239 |
| | 11.12.2 Reshaping vs. Resizing Arrays | 240 |
| 11.13 | Array Concatenation (joining) and Splitting | 240 |
| | 11.13.1 Joining Arrays | 240 |
| 11.14 | Appending Arrays | 241 |
| 11.15 | Splitting of Arrays | 242 |
| 11.16 | How NumPy Broadcasting Works | 243 |
| 11.17 | Performing Mathematical Operations on NumPy Arrays | 243 |
| 11.18 | Transposing Arrays | 244 |
| 11.19 | Inserting and Deleting Array Elements | 245 |
| | 11.19.1 Deleting Values from an Array | 245 |
| | 11.19.2 Check if NumPy Array is Empty | 246 |
| 11.20 | Find the Index of a Value | 246 |
| 11.21 | Saving NumPy Array to CSV File | 246 |
| 11.22 | Sorting a NumPy Array | 247 |
| 11.23 | Normalize Array | 247 |
| 11.24 | Array Subsets | 247 |
| | 11.24.1 Subset an Array Based on a Boolean Condition | 247 |
| | 11.24.2 Remove a Redundant Dimension from an Array Object | 248 |
| | 11.24.3 Retrieve Diagonals from an Array | 248 |
| | 11.24.4 Sub-setting NumPy Arrays Using Indexing | 249 |
| | 11.24.5 Indexing using Index Arrays | 249 |
| | 11.24.6 Purely Integer Indexing in 2D Arrays | 249 |
| | 11.24.7 Boolean Indexing | 250 |
| *Programmer's Zone* | | *250* |
| 11.25 | Comparison of Different Data Structures | 254 |

*Key Terms | Chapter Highlights | Review Questions |
Programming Exercises | Fill in the Blanks | State True or False | Multiple Choice Questions |
Give the Output | Fill in the Blanks to Complete the Code | Find the Error | Answers*

## Chapter 12: Data Management — 269

- 12.1 Database — 270
  - 12.1.1 Advantages of a Database — 270
  - 12.1.2 Application of Database System — 271
- 12.2 Acid Property — 271
- 12.3 Components of a Database System — 272
- 12.4 Relational Databases — 273
  - 12.4.1 Advantages of Relational Databases — 273
  - 12.4.2 Disadvantages of Relational Databases — 273
- 12.5 Components of DBMS — 274
  - 12.5.1 Other Important Modules of DBMS — 274
- 12.6 Basic Terminology of Relational Database Systems — 275
- 12.7 Database Keys — 276
  - 12.7.1 Candidate Key — 276
  - 12.7.2 Primary Key — 276
  - 12.7.3 Foreign Key — 277
- 12.8 Relational Data Integrity Rules — 278

*Key Terms | Chapter Highlights | Review Questions | Fill in the Blanks | State True or False | Multiple Choice Questions | Answers*

## Chapter 13: Structured Query Language (SQL) — 285

- 13.1 MySQL Database — 285
- 13.2 Introduction to SQL — 285
  - 13.2.1 How MySQL Works — 285
  - 13.2.2 Uses of SQL — 286
  - 13.2.3 Types of SQL Queries — 286
- 13.3 SQL Data Types — 286
  - 13.3.1 Date and Time Types — 287
- 13.4 Operators in SQL — 287
- 13.5 Performing Simple Calculations with SELECT Statement — 289
- 13.6 SQL Numeric Functions — 289
- 13.7 String Functions — 291
- 13.8 Creating Database — 293
- 13.9 Removing Database — 294
- 13.10 Creating Tables — 294
- 13.11 Deleting Table — 295
- 13.12 Inserting Values in Table — 296
- 13.13 Retrieving Data from Table — 296
- 13.14 The WHERE Clause — 297
- 13.15 SQL AND and OR Operators — 298
- 13.16 The WHERE BETWEEN Clause — 299

| | | |
|---|---|---|
| 13.17 | The SQL WHERE IN Clause | 299 |
| 13.18 | The SQL SELECT DISTINCT Statement | 300 |
| 13.19 | ORDER BY Clause | 301 |
| 13.20 | Updating the Table | 302 |
| 13.21 | Deleting Rows from a Table | 303 |
| 13.22 | The WHERE LIKE Clause in SQL | 303 |
| 13.23 | SQL SELECT MIN, MAX statement | 305 |
| 13.24 | SELECT COUNT, SUM, AVG | 307 |
| 13.25 | Column Aliases | 307 |
| 13.26 | Handling Null Values | 308 |
| 13.27 | SQL Primary Key Constraint | 310 |
| 13.28 | Drop a Primary Key Constraint | 312 |
| 13.29 | Adding Foreign Key Constraint | 312 |

*Key Terms | Chapter Highlights | Review Questions | Programming Exercises | Fill in the Blanks | State True or False | Multiple Choice Questions | Give the Output | Answers*

## Chapter 14: Introduction to Emerging Trends — 321

| | | |
|---|---|---|
| 14.1 | Artificial Intelligence | 321 |
| 14.2 | Machine Learning | 321 |
| | 14.2.1 How Machine Learning Works | 323 |
| | 14.2.2 Types of Machine Learning Algorithms | 323 |
| | 14.2.3 Steps in Machine Learning | 324 |
| 14.3 | Natural Language Processing | 325 |
| | 14.3.1 Importance of NLP | 326 |
| | 14.3.2 Challenges in NLP | 326 |
| | 14.3.3 How NLP works | 326 |
| 14.4 | Immersive Experience | 327 |
| | 14.4.1 Types of Immersive Experiences | 327 |
| | 14.4.2 Applications of Immersive Experiences | 328 |
| 14.5 | Robotics | 330 |
| | 14.5.1 Types of Robots | 330 |
| | 14.5.2 Applications of Robotics | 331 |
| 14.6 | Big Data | 332 |
| | 14.6.1 History and Evolution of Big Data Analytics | 333 |
| | 14.6.2 Benefits of Big Data | 333 |
| | 14.6.3 Applications of Big Data | 334 |
| 14.7 | Internet of Things | 334 |
| | 14.7.1 Examples of Applications of IoT | 334 |
| | 14.7.2 IoT Products | 335 |
| | 14.7.3 Challenges | 336 |
| 14.8 | Sensors | 337 |

| | | |
|---|---|---|
| 14.9 | **Smart Cities** | 338 |
| | 14.9.1 Need for Smart Cities | 339 |
| | 14.9.2 Examples of Smart Cities | 340 |
| | 14.9.3 Security Objectives | 340 |
| | 14.9.4 How a Smart City Works | 341 |
| | 14.9.5 Challenges | 341 |
| 14.10 | **Cloud Computing** | 341 |
| | 14.10.1 Types of Cloud Computing | 342 |
| | 14.10.2 Types of Cloud Services: IaaS, PaaS, Serverless and SaaS | 342 |
| | 14.10.3 Uses of Cloud Computing | 343 |
| | 14.10.4 Advantages | 343 |
| 14.11 | **Grid Computing** | 344 |
| | 14.11.1 Components of Grid Computing | 344 |
| | 14.11.2 Grid Computing Applications | 345 |
| | 14.11.3 Running an Application in Grid Computing | 345 |
| | 14.11.4 Major Concern | 345 |
| 14.12 | **Blockchain Technology** | 345 |
| | 14.12.1 Key Terminology | 346 |
| | 14.12.2 Success Factors | 346 |
| | 14.12.3 Applications | 346 |
| | 14.12.4 Use of Blockchain Technology for Online Purchase | 346 |
| | 14.12.5 Pillars of Blockchain | 347 |
| | 14.12.6 Hashing in Blockchain | 348 |

*Key Terms | Chapter Highlights | Review Questions | Fill in the Blanks | State True or False | Multiple Choice Questions | Answers |*

# Preface

We all know that Information Technology (IT) is the buzzword of the 21st century. We use computers to store, retrieve, transmit and manipulate data. Today, computers are used to perform every other task such as publishing a newspaper, designing a building, coaching sports players and training pilots in flight simulators. Computers have become so widespread that almost every electrical and electronic device (like washing machines, air conditioners, etc.) has a small embedded computer within it. Even the mobile phones that we use are smart phones (phones with computing technology) that are connected to the Internet. Information technology has revolutionized our lifestyle. Thus in today's scenario, learning about computers is mandatory not only for students pursuing a career in engineering and technology but also for those in other professions like journalism, nursing, archaeology, construction and management, to name a few.

Computing skills always help one to be more productive and self-sufficient. Therefore, a basic knowledge of computers and their underlying technology will pay rich dividends in the future. In this context, Python is an open-source, excellent, easy, high-level, interpreted, interactive, object-oriented and a reliable language that uses English-like words. It is also a versatile language that supports development of a wide range of applications ranging from simple text processing to WWW browsers to games. Moreover, programmers can embed Python within their C, C++, COM, ActiveX, CORBA, and Java programs to give 'scripting' capabilities for users.

Python has a huge user base that is constantly growing. The strength of Python can be understood from the fact that this programming language is the most preferred language of companies like Nokia, Google, YouTube and even NASA for its easy syntax. The support for multiple programming paradigms, including object-oriented programming, functional Python programming, and parallel programming models makes it an ideal choice for the programmers.

However, no student can learn to program just by reading a book; rather, it is a skill that must be developed by practice. So, after learning the rudiments of program writing, students will find in this book, a number of examples and exercises that would help them learn to design efficient programs. The book presents various programming examples that have already been implemented and tested using Python 3.8.3.

## KEY FEATURES

This book is aimed at serving as a textbook for the commerce and humanities students enrolled in Class XI of CBSE. Divided into two main sections – Introduction to IT and Python Programming, it introduces the concepts of Information Technology and Python programming language so that the students can use the key ideas learnt to solve real-world problems. The book aims to acquaint the reader with the basics of computer science before introducing the Python Programming language as a multifaceted tool with diverse functions. To this end it includes several student-friendly features:

**Comprehensive Coverage:** The book provides comprehensive coverage of all important topics from the examination point-of-view.

**Easy to Understand:** The book uses very simple language to explain the concepts and breaks down technical jargons to simpler terms for the student's benefit.

**Pictorial Approach:** Numerous well-labelled diagrams are provided throughout the text for clear understanding of the concepts.

**Practical Orientation:** Replete with solved examples and chapter-end exercises in the form of objective type questions and review questions, the book's well-defined pedagogy enables students to check their understanding of the concepts.

**Glossary:** A list of key terms is provided at the end of each chapter to facilitate easy revision.

**Informative Textboxes:** Important concepts are highlighted throughout the text for a quick recap.

**Programmer's Zone** examples are used in context to help the students understand the technique of programming.

**Complementary App for CUCET:** Students can download the free mobile app Jruma from Google Play Store or Apple Store for additional learning resources. The app would help them to recapitulate and test their understanding of the concepts learnt in Classes XI and XII. The app will also be useful for the students to hone their Computer Science (CS) and Logical Reasoning (LR) skills. CS and LR is a mandatory section in the CUCET and all other entrance exams the students may take throughout their professional career.

## ACKNOWLEDGMENTS

The writing of this text book was a mammoth task for which a lot of help was required from many people. Fortunately, I have had the fine support of my family, friends and fellow members of the teaching staff at the Shyama Prasad Mukherji College.

My special thanks would always go to my father Late Sh. Janak Raj Thareja, my mother Smt. Usha Thareja, my brother Pallav and sisters Kimi and Rashi who were a source of abiding inspiration and are a divine blessing for me. I am especially indebted to my son Goransh, who has been very patient and cooperative in letting me realize my dreams. I am obliged to my uncle Mr B L Theraja for his inspiration and guidance in writing this book.

Last but not the least, my acknowledgements will always be incomplete if I do not thank the editorial team at Universities Press (India) Private Limited that gave me this brilliant opportunity to utilize my writing skills.

**Reema Thareja**
reema_thareja@yahoo.com

# About the Author

**Reema Thareja** is Assistant Professor at Shyama Prasad Mukherji College, University of Delhi. She has over 15 years of experience, teaching computer science for various courses including BA, BSc, MSc, BBA, MBA, BCA and MCA. She has authored several books, including those on Computer Fundamentals, C Programming, OOPS with C++, Data Structures, Data Warehousing and Python Programming, which are well-accepted across the globe. She has also written books on Data Science and Machine Learning in R for the current academic session.

Dr Thareja has published 17 research papers in journals of national and international repute. In addition, she has got the acceptance for four more papers. A recipient of 64 Google Scholar Citations, she has launched a Computer Science Learning and Quizzing mobile app, Jruma, for both Android and iOS devices.

A recipient of the Nobel Laureate Maria Goeppert–Mayer Inspiring Woman of the Year 2021 Award in the field of Computer Science by International Multi-disciplinary Research Foundation (IMRF), Dr Thareja was also among "India's Top 50 Women Leaders in the Education Industry" recognized by uLektz Wall of Fame for the year 2020. She has conducted several faculty development programs, student workshops and webinars in India and the US, and participated in the International Dialogue on Empowered Future – Women's Role on the eve of International Women's Day 2021.

A member of the Computer Society of India and Editorial Board and Keynote Speaker of the IMRF Conference Board, Dr Thareja is a skilled motivator who helps students utilize their untapped skills and reinvent themselves. She was recently conferred with the Knowledge Mobilization Award at the Seventh Annual Research Awards event organized by Shri Param Hans Education and Research Trust and has been invited as a speaker for the Global Virtual Summit to be held in New York this summer.

# Computer Systems and Organization

## Chapter Objectives

We all have seen computers being used in our homes, schools, offices, and in fact every other place we visit. The smartphones that we have in our hands is also an example of a small computer. Today, it is just impossible to think of our lives without this machine. The first chapter of the book will therefore give an introduction about a computer and discuss the following topics:

- Evolution of computers through five generations
- Characteristics of computers
- Applications of computers in today's digital world
- Input devices like keyboard, mouse, touch screen, touch pad, scanner, stylus, bar code reader, OMR, MICR and digital camera
- Output devices including printer, plotter, monitor, speaker and projector
- Classification of computer's memory as cache memory, primary or secondary memory
- Deleted files as a security concern
- Recovering data even after deletion
- Software and their classification based on the technique adopted to acquire them
- Utility software and customized software
- Comparing generic software with specific-purpose software

## 1.1 WHAT IS A COMPUTER?

*A computer is an electronic machine that takes data and instructions as input and performs computations on data based on the specified instructions.*

Before going into the details, let us learn some key terms that are frequently used in computers.

- *Data:* Data is a collection of raw facts or figures.
- *Information:* Information comprises of processed data to provide answers to the *who, what, where* and *when* type of questions.
- *Knowledge:* Knowledge is the application of data and information to answer the *how* part of the question (refer Fig. 1.1).
- *Instructions:* Commands given to the computer to tell what it has to do.
- *Programs:* A set of instructions in computer language is called a program.
- *Software:* A set of programs is called software.
- *Hardware:* The computer and all its physical parts are known as hardware.

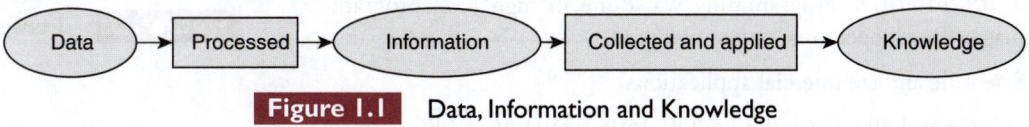

**Figure 1.1**  Data, Information and Knowledge

## 1.2 EVOLUTION OF COMPUTING DEVICES

The word *generation*, in general, indicates a state of improvement in the product development process. When applied to computing, it refers to the different advancements of new computer technology. With each new generation of computers, the circuitry becomes smaller and more advanced than that used in the previous generation. The focus of every new generation has been on miniaturization, speed, power, and efficient computer memory. Therefore, each generation of computers is characterized by a major technological development that has drastically changed the way in which computers operate. In this section, we will read about the major developments in technology that have led to the devices that we use today

### 1.2.1 First Generation (1942–1955)

*Hardware Technology:* First-generation computers were manufactured using thousands of vacuum tubes (see Fig. 1.2); a vacuum tube is a device made of fragile glass.

*Memory:* Electromagnetic relay was used as primary memory and punched cards were used to store data and instructions.

*Software Technology:* Programming was done in machine or assembly language.

*Used for* Scientific applications

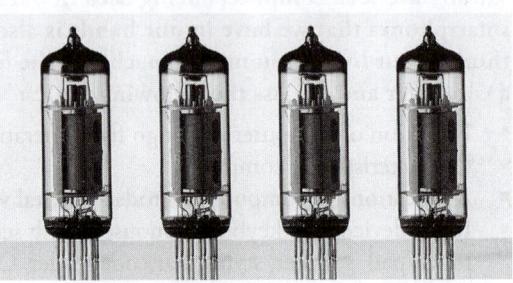

**Figure 1.2** Vacuum tubes

*Examples* ENIAC, EDVAC, EDSAC, UNIVAC I, IBM 701

*Highlights*
- They were the fastest calculating devices of those times.
- Computers were too bulky and required a complete room for storage.
- Highly unreliable as vacuum tubes emitted a large amount of heat and burnt frequently
- Required air-conditioned rooms for installation
- Costly
- Difficult to use
- Required constant maintenance because vacuum tubes used filaments that had limited life time. Therefore, these computers were prone to frequent hardware failures.

### 1.2.2 Second Generation (1955–1964)

*Hardware Technology:* Second-generation computers were manufactured using transistors (see Fig. 1.3). Transistors were reliable, powerful, cheaper, smaller and cooler than vacuum tubes.

*Memory:* Magnetic core memory was used as primary memory; magnetic tapes and magnetic disks were used to store data and instructions. These computers had faster and larger memory than the first-generation computers.

*Software Technology:* Programming was done in high level programming languages. Batch operating system was used.

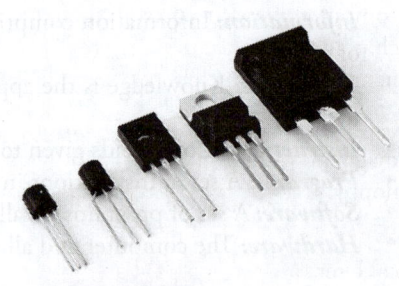

**Figure 1.3** Transistors

*Used for* Scientific and commercial applications

*Examples* Honeywell 400, IBM 7030, CDC 1604, UNIVAC LARC

*Highlights*
- Faster, smaller, cheaper, reliable, and easier to use than the first-generation computers. They consumed 1/10th the power consumed by first generation computers.
- Bulky in size and required a complete room for its installation
- Dissipated less heat than first-generation computers but still required air-conditioned rooms
- Costly
- Difficult to use

### 1.2.3 Third Generation (1964–1975)

*Hardware Technology:* Third-generation computers were manufactured using integrated chips (ICs) (shown in Fig. 1.4). ICs consist of several components such as transistors, capacitors and resistors on a single chip to avoid wired interconnections between components.

Initially, ICs contained 10–20 components. This technology was called Small Scale Integration (SSI). Later, it was enhanced to contain about 100 components. This was called Medium Scale Integration (MSI).

*Memory:* Larger magnetic core memory was used as primary memory; larger capacity magnetic tapes and magnetic disks were used to store data and instructions.

**Figure 1.4** Integrated circuit

*Software Technology:* Programming was done in high-level programming languages such as FORTRAN, COBOL, Pascal, and BASIC. Time sharing operating system was used. Software was separated from the hardware. This allowed users to invest only in the software they need.

*Used for* Scientific, commercial, and interactive online applications

*Examples* IBM 360/370, PDP-8, PADP-11, CDC6600

*Highlights*
- Faster, smaller, cheaper, reliable and easier to use than the second-generation computers
- They consumed lesser power than second-generation computers.
- Bulky in size and required a complete room for installation
- Dissipated less heat than second generation computers but still required air-conditioned rooms
- Costly
- Easier to use and upgrade.

### 1.2.4 Fourth Generation (1975–1989)

*Hardware Technology:* Fourth-generation computers were manufactured using ICs with LSI (Large-Scale Integrated) and later with VLSI technology (Very Large-Scale Integration). Microcomputers came into existence. Use of personal computers became widespread. High-speed computer networks in the form of LANs, WANs, and MANs started growing. Besides mainframes, supercomputers were also used. LSI circuits contained 30,000 components on a single chip and VLSI technology (Fig. 1.5) had about one million electronic components on a single chip.

*Memory:* Semiconductor memory was used as primary memory; large-capacity magnetic disks were used as built-in secondary memory. Magnetic tapes and floppy disks were used as portable storage devices.

**Figure 1.5** Very large scale integrated circuit

*Software Technology:* Programming was done in high-level programming languages such as C and C++. Graphical User Interface (GUI) based operating system (e.g. Windows) was introduced. It had icons and menus among other features to allow computers to be used as a general-purpose machine by all users. UNIX was also introduced as an open-source operating system. Apple Mac OS and MS DOS were also released during this period. All these operating systems had multi-processing and multiprogramming capabilities.

*Used for* Scientific, commercial, interactive online, and network applications

*Examples* IBM PC, Apple II, TRS-80, VAX 9000, CRAY-1, CRAY-2, CRAY-X/MP

*Highlights* Faster, smaller, cheaper, powerful, reliable, and easier to use than the previous generation computers.

### 1.2.5 Fifth Generation (1989–Present)

***Hardware Technology:*** Fifth generation computers are manufactured using ICs with ULSI (Ultra Large Scale Integrated) technology. The use of Internet became widespread and very powerful mainframes, desktops, portable laptops, and smartphones are being used commonly. Supercomputers use parallel processing techniques. ULSI circuits contain about 10 million electronic components on a single chip (Fig. 1.6).

***Memory:*** Semiconductor memory is used as primary memory; large-capacity magnetic disks are used as built-in secondary memory. Magnetic tapes and floppy disks were used as portable storage devices, which have now been replaced by optical disks and USB flash drives.

***Software Technology:*** Programming is done in high-level programming languages such as Java, Python, and C#. Graphical User Interface (GUI)-based operating systems such as Windows, Unix, Linux, Ubuntu, and Apple Mac are being used. These operating systems are more powerful and user friendly than the ones available in the previous generations.

**Figure 1.6** Ultra-large-scale integrated circuit

***Used for*** Scientific, commercial, interactive online, multimedia (graphics, audio, video) and network applications.

***Examples*** IBM notebooks, Pentium PCs, SUM workstations, IBM SP/2, Param supercomputer

***Highlights***
- Faster, smaller, cheaper, powerful, reliable, and easier to use than the previous generation computers
- Speed of microprocessors and the size of memory are growing rapidly
- High-end features available on mainframe computers in the fourth generation are now available on the microprocessors
- They consume lesser power than computers of prior generations
- Air-conditioned rooms are required for mainframes and supercomputers but not for microprocessors.

## 1.3 CHARACTERISTICS OF COMPUTERS

The important characteristics of a computer (as shown in Fig. 1.7) are given below:

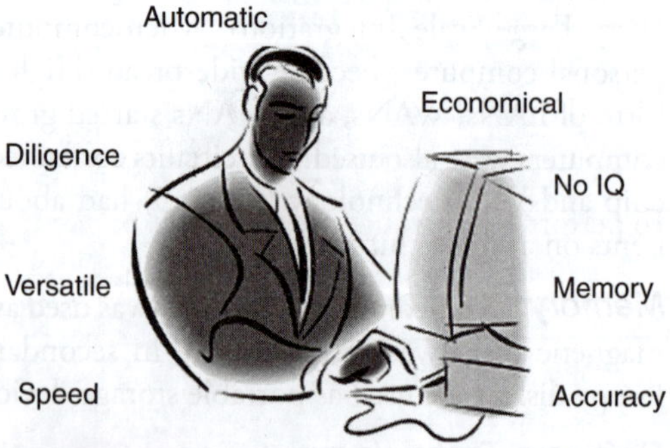

***Speed:*** Computers can perform millions of operations in a single second. This means that a computer can process data in the blink of an eye, which otherwise may take multiple days to complete. The speed of the computer is usually given in *nanosecond* and *picosecond*, where

**1 nanosecond=1*$10^{-9}$ second**
**1 picosecond=1*$10^{-12}$ second**

**Figure 1.7** Characteristics of a computer

***Accuracy:*** Computers are reliable electronic devices. They never make a mistake. They always gives accurate results, provided correct data and set of instructions are fed to it. In case of an error, only the user who had fed the incorrect data/program is responsible. If input data is wrong then the output will also be erroneous. In computer terminology, this concept is known as garbage-in garbage-out (GIGO).

***Automatic:*** Besides being very fast and accurate, computers are automatic devices which perform execution without any user intervention. The user just needs to assign the task to the computer and give the inputs, after which the computer automatically controls the different devices attached to it and executes the program instructions one by one.

***Diligence:*** Computers never get tired as the humans do. It can continually work for hours without creating any error. If a large number of executions have to be made then each and every execution will be executed in the same amount of time and with the same accuracy.

***Versatile:*** Versatile means flexible. Today computers are being used in our daily life in different fields. For example, they are used as personal computers (PCs) for home uses, for business-oriented tasks, weather forecasting, space explorations, teaching, railways, banking, medicine, etc. On the PC that you use at home, you may play a game, compose and send emails, listen to music, etc. Therefore, computers are versatile devices as they can perform multiple tasks of different nature simultaneously.

***Memory:*** Like humans, computers also have memory. Human beings cannot store everything in their own memory and need secondary media, such as a notebook to record certain important things. Similarly, computers have an internal memory (storage space) as well as external or secondary memory. While the internal memory of computers is very expensive and limited in size, the secondary storage is cheaper and bigger in size.

> When data and programs have to be used they are copied from the secondary memory into the internal memory (often known as RAM).

The computer stores large amount of data and programs in the secondary storage space. The stored data and programs can be used as and when required; the computer never forgets it. Secondary memory devices include CD, DVD, hard disk, pen drives etc.

***No IQ:*** Although the trend today is to make computers intelligent by inducing artificial intelligence (AI) in them, they still do not have any decision-making abilities of their own, that is, their IQ level is zero. They need guidance to perform various tasks.

***Economical:*** Today, computers are considered as short-term investment for achieving long-term gain. Using computers also reduces manpower requirements and leads to an elegant and efficient way for doing tasks. Hence, computers save time, energy and money. When compared to other systems, computers can do more work in lesser time. For example, using the conventional postal system to send an important document takes at least 2–3 days whereas the same information when sent using the Internet (email), will be delivered instantaneously.

## 1.4 BASIC COMPUTER ORGANIZATION

A computer performs five major operations as given below:

1. Accepts data or instructions (input)
2. Stores data
3. Process data
4. Displays results (output) and
5. Controls and co-ordinates all operations inside a computer.

To perform these functions, different parts of a computer interact with each other as shown in the Fig. 1.8.

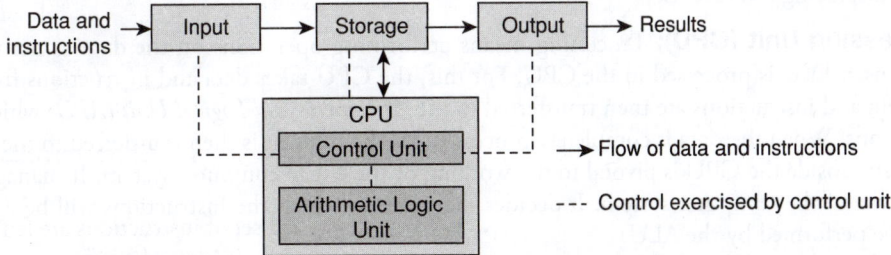

**Figure 1.8** Interaction between different parts of a computer system

### 1.4.1 Input

The process of entering data and instructions in to the computer system is known as input. Users can provide input to the computer using different input devices like keyboard, mouse, scanner, trackball, etc.

> The computer understands only binary language, which consists of only two symbols (0s and 1s); so it is the responsibility of the input devices to convert the input data into binary codes.

## 1.4.2 Storage

Storage is the process of saving data, instructions and results of processing in the computer's memory for future use. Once our work is stored in a computer, we can use it at any time. A computer has two types of storage areas:

**Primary storage:** Primary storage or the main memory is that storage area of the computer which is directly accessible by the CPU at a very fast speed. It can be used to store data, instructions and recently generated results of processing. However, the primary storage is very expensive and therefore limited in capacity. Another drawback of main memory is that it is volatile in nature, i.e., as soon as the computer is switched off, the information stored in it gets erased. Hence, it cannot be used as a permanent storage of useful data and programs for future use. Example, RAM (Random Access Memory).

**Secondary storage:** Secondary storage is also known as the secondary memory or auxiliary memory. It is cheaper and can therefore be used in large capacity. Secondary memory is non-volatile. This means that it can be used to permanently store all our data and instructions, irrespective of whether or not they are currently being used by the CPU. For example, the hard disk (you store your files in C drive, D drive), pen drive, etc. are used to store data for future use. Table 1.1 lists some important differences between primary and secondary memory.

**Table 1.1** Difference between primary and secondary memory

| Primary Memory | Secondary Memory |
| --- | --- |
| • It is more expensive | • It is cheaper |
| • It is faster to access | • It is slower to access |
| • Directly accessed by the CPU | • Cannot be accessed directly by the CPU |
| • It is volatile in nature | • It is non-volatile in nature |
| • Storage capacity is limited | • Large storage capacity |
| • Consumes less power | • Consumes more power |
| • Stores data temporarily | • Stores data permanently |
| • Holds instructions and data when a program is executing. | • The secondary memory holds data and programs that are not currently being executed by the CPU. |

## 1.4.3 Output

Output is the reverse of input. It is the process of giving the result of data processing to the outside world (external to the computer system). The results are given through output devices like monitor, printer, etc. Now that the computer accepts data only in binary form and the result of processing is also in the binary form, the result cannot be directly given to the user. The output devices therefore convert the results available in binary codes into a human readable language before displaying it to the user.

**Central Processing Unit (CPU):** Processing means performing operations on the data as per the instructions specified by the user. Data is processed in the CPU. For this, the CPU takes data and instructions from the primary memory. The data and instructions are then transferred to the *Arithmetic and Logical Unit (ALU)* which performs the necessary operations. When the data is completely processed, the final result is then transferred to the main memory.

The *control unit* inside the CPU is pivotal to the working of the entire computer system. It manages and controls all the components of the computer system. It decides the order in which the instructions will be executed and the operations will be performed by the ALU.

CPU (Central Processing Unit) is a combination of the ALU and the Control Unit. It is known as the brain of the computer system as the entire processing of data is done with the help of ALU and the control unit. While the entire processing of data is done in the ALU, CU on the other hand, activates and monitors the operations of other units (such as input, output, and storage) of the computer system. The two units of the CPU are detailed as follows.

*Arithmetic and logic unit:* The ALU performs all kinds of calculations, such as arithmetic (add, subtract, multiply, divide, etc.), comparison (less than, greater than, or equal to), and other operations. The intermediate results of processing may be stored in the main memory, as they might be required again. When the processing completes, the final result is transferred to the main memory. Hence, the data may move from main memory to the ALU multiple times before the processing is over.

*Control unit:* The main function of the CU is to direct and coordinate the computer operations. It interprets the instructions (program) and initiates action to execute them. The CU controls the flow of data through the computer system and directs the ALU, input/output (I/O) devices and other units. It is therefore called the central nervous system of the computer system. In addition, the CU is responsible for fetching, decoding, executing instructions, and storing results.

## 1.5 INPUT DEVICES

We have read that data and instructions that we enter into the computer are called *input*. And devices that help us to give input to the computer are called *input devices*.

Some commonly used input devices are keyboard, mouse, microphone, web camera, scanner, joystick, etc.

### 1.5.1 Keyboard

A keyboard (Fig. 1.9) is the main input device for computers. With a keyboard, a user can type a document, use keystroke shortcuts, access menus, play games, and perform numerous other tasks. Most keyboards have between 80 and 110 keys, which include the following:

*Alphabetic keys* include the letters of the English alphabet. The layout of the keyboard is known as QWERTY for its first six letters. The QWERTY pattern has been a standard right from the time computer keyboards were introduced.

*Numeric keys* include Arabic numerals (0–9), arranged in the same configuration found on calculators to speed up data entry of numbers. When the Num Lock key is set to ON, the user can type numbers, dot, or input the symbols /, *, –, and +. When the Num Lock key is set to OFF, the numeric keys can be used to move the cursor on the screen. A set of numeric keys are also present at the top of alphabet keys.

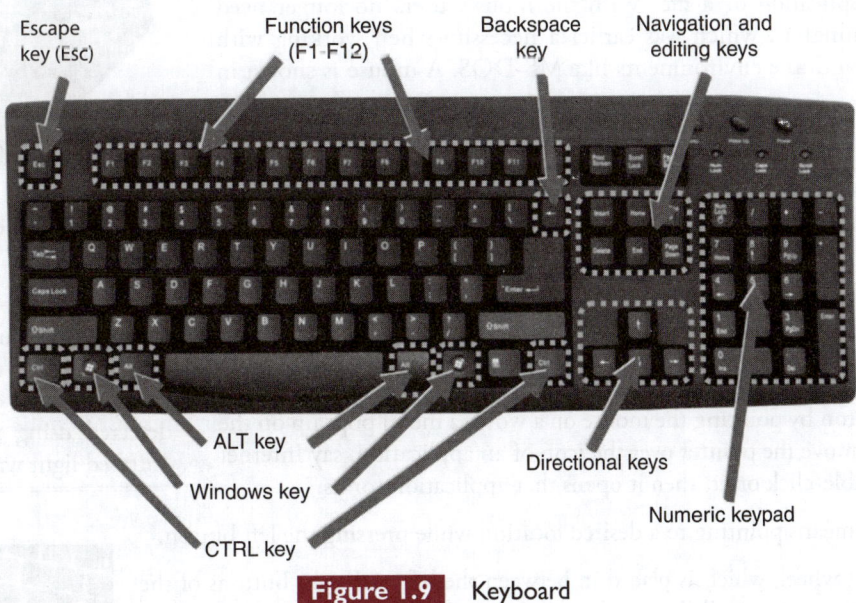

**Figure 1.9** Keyboard

*Function keys* are used by computer programs (or software) and operating systems to input specific commands. They are often placed on the top of the keyboard in a single row. Function keys can be programmed so that their functionality varies from one program to another. For example, the ALT and F4 keys, when pressed together, will close the current window.

*Arrow keys* arranged in an inverted T-type fashion between the alphabetic and the numeric keys, and are used to move the cursor on the screen in small increments.

*Home and End keys* are used to move the cursor to the beginning and end of the current line, respectively.

***Page Up and Page Down*** move the cursor up and down by one screen at a time, respectively.

***Insert key*** is used to enter a character between two existing characters.

***Delete key*** deletes a character at the cursor position.

***Shortcut key*** is used to access the options available by pressing the right mouse button.

***Esc key*** cancels the selected option.

***Pause key*** suspends a command/process in progress.

***Print Screen key*** captures everything on the screen as an image. The image can be pasted into any document.

> Keys such as Shift, Ctrl, and Alt are called *modifier keys* because they are used to modify the normal function of a key. For example, Shift + character (lowercase) makes the computer display the character in uppercase.

***Wireless Keyboard*** can be operated without connecting it to the computer through a physical wire. It is powered by a battery and allows users to work up to 10 feet from its receiver. This is especially desirable when we want to keep our desk uncluttered without wires. However, on the downside, greater the distance between the wireless keyboard and the receiver monitor, more is the delay in receiving the keystrokes.

> Many a time, a few keystrokes get dropped from input.

***Bluetooth wireless keyboard:*** Bluetooth is one of the most popular methods of syncing a wireless keyboard with a computer. Such a keyboard is well-suited for offices as it creates a reliable connection without cluttering the desk.

### 1.5.2 Mouse

Mouse is an input device that was invented by Douglas Engelbart in 1963. It is the key input device used in a graphical user interface (GUI). Mouse can be used to handle the pointer on the screen to perform various functions such as opening an application or a file. With the mouse, users no longer need to memorize commands, which was earlier a necessity when working with text-based command line environments like MS-DOS. A mouse is shown in Fig. 1.10.

A mouse has two buttons and a scroll wheel. It can be held in the hand and easily moved, without lifting, along a hard-flat surface to move the cursor to the desired location—up, down, left, or right. Once the mouse is placed at an appropriate position, a user may perform the following operations:

**Figure 1.10** Computer mouse

***Point:*** Placing the pointer over a word or an object on the screen by moving the mouse on the desk is termed as pointing.

***Click:*** Pressing either the left or the right button of the mouse is known as clicking. Clicking a mouse button initiates some action; for example, when we click the right button by pointing the mouse on a word, a menu pops up on the screen. When we move the pointer over the icon of an application, say Internet Explorer, and double-click on it, then it opens that application for us.

> A cordless or wireless mouse is not connected to a computer. The movement of the mouse is detected using radio waves or infrared light waves.

***Drag:*** Dragging means pointing to a desired location while pressing the left button.

***Scroll:*** The scroll wheel, which is placed in between the left and right buttons of the mouse, is used to vertically scroll through long documents.

### 1.5.3 Touchpad

Touchpad or a trackpad, as shown in Fig. 1.11, is a small, flat, rectangular stationary pointing device with a sensitive surface of 1.5–2 square inches. A user has to slide his or her fingertips across the surface of the pad to point to a specific object on the screen. The surface translates the motion and position of the user's fingers to a relative position on the screen.

**Figure 1.11** Touchpad

## 1.5.4 Joystick

Joystick is a cursor control device widely used in computer games and computer-aided design (CAD)/computer-aided manufacturing (CAM) applications. It consists of a hand-held lever that pivots on one end and transmits its coordinates to a computer as shown in Fig. 1.12.

The joystick has one or more push buttons, called switches, whose position can also be read by the computer. The lever of a joystick moves in all directions to control the movement of the pointer on the computer screen. The function of a joystick is similar to that of a mouse, but with the mouse, the cursor stops moving as soon as we stop moving the mouse. However, in the case of the joystick, the pointer continues moving in the direction to which the joystick is pointing. To stop the pointer, the user must return the joystick to its upright position.

**Figure 1.12** Joystick

## 1.5.5 Touchscreen

Touch screen (shown in Fig. 1.13) is a display screen that can identify the occurrence and position of a touch inside the display region. A user can touch the screen by using either a finger or a stylus. Such touchscreen displays are available on computers, laptops, Personal Device Assistants (PDAs), and mobile phones.

Touchscreen monitors are an easy way of entering information into computers (or mobile phones). They have become more and more commonplace as their price has steadily dropped over the past decade. These days, touchscreen monitors are widely used in different applications including point-of-sale (POS) cash registers, automated teller machines (ATMs), car navigation screens, mobile phones, gaming consoles, and any other type of appliance that requires users to input and receive information instantly.

**Figure 1.13** Touchscreen

## 1.5.5 Image Scanner

Image Scanner (shown in Fig. 1.14) is a device that captures images, printed text, and handwritten text, from different sources such as photographic prints, posters, and magazines and converts them into digital images for editing and display on computers.

Some scanners have graphics software such as Adobe Photoshop to help users resize or modify captured images.

The scanners that we see in our colleges or offices are flatbed scanners. In this type, the document to be scanned is placed on a glass pane and an opaque cover is lowered over it. A sensor and light moves along the pane, reflecting off the image placed on the glass. The reflected image is scanned onto a computer for further processing.

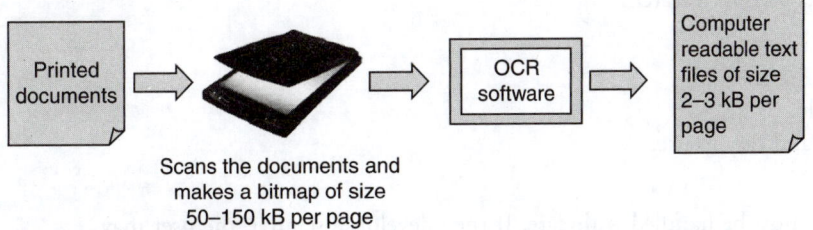

**Figure 1.14** Image scanner with OCR software

### Advantages
- Any printed or handwritten document can be scanned and stored in a computer for further processing.
- The scanned and stored document will never deteriorate in quality with time. The document can be displayed and printed whenever required.
- There is no fear of loss of documents. Users can scan important documents and store them permanently in the computer.

### Disadvantages

- Scanners are usually costlier than other input devices.
- The documents that are scanned and stored as images are bigger in size as compared to other equivalent text files. Text documents are scanned and stored as images. Therefore, they occupy more space and are also un-editable because computers cannot interpret individual characters in images.

To make these documents occupy lesser space, the scanned document can be passed through optical character recognition (OCR) software (see Fig. 1. 14) where the images of individual characters are recognised and stored as a doc file. However, this method cannot be used for documents where illustrations or mathematical equations are present.

### 1.5.6 Stylus

Stylus (Fig. 1.15) is a pen-shaped input device used to enter information or write on the touchscreen of a handheld device. It is a small stick that can also be used to draw lines on a surface as input into a device, choose an option from a menu, move the cursor to another location on the screen, take notes, and create short messages. The stylus usually slides into a slot built into the device for that purpose.

**Figure 1.15** Stylus

### 1.5.7 Barcode Reader

Barcode Reader (also price scanner or POS scanner), as shown in Fig. 1.16, is a handheld input device that is used to capture and read information stored in a barcode. It consists of a scanner, a decoder, and a cable used to connect the reader to a computer. The function of the barcode reader is to capture and translate the barcode into numerals and/or alphabets. It is connected to a computer for further processing of the captured information.

A barcode reader works by directing a beam of light across the barcode and measuring the amount of light reflected back.

The scanner converts this light energy into electrical energy. The decoder then converts these signals into data and sends it to the computer for processing. These days, barcode readers are widely used in following areas:

- Supermarkets and retail stores as POS devices
- To take inventory in retail stores
- To check out books from a library
- To track manufacturing and shipping movement
- To keep track of employee login
- To identify hospital patients
- To tabulate the results of direct mail marketing returns
- To tag honeybees used in research.

**Figure 1.16** Barcode reader

### Advantages

- Barcode readers are cheap.
- They are portable.
- They are handy and easy to use.

### Disadvantages

- Barcode readers must be handled with care. If they develop a scratch, the user may not be able to read the code.
- They can interpret information using a limited series of thin and wide bars. To interpret other unique identifiers, the bar display area must be widened.

### 1.5.8 Optical Mark Recognition (OMR)

OMR is the process of electronically extracting data from marked fields, such as checkboxes and fill-in fields, on printed forms. The optical mark reader, as shown in Fig. 1.17, is fed with an OMR sheet that has pen or pencil marks in pre-defined positions to indicate each selected response (such as answers for multiple-choice questions in an entrance examination).

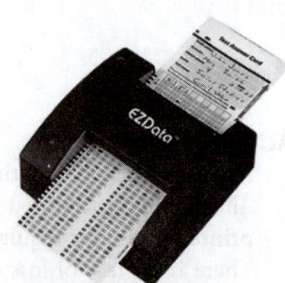

**Figure 1.17** Optical mark reader

The OMR sheet is scanned by the reader to detect the presence of a mark by measuring the reflected light levels. The dark or the marked areas reflect less light than the unmarked ones. The OM reader interprets this pattern marks and spaces, and stores the interpreted data in a computer for storage, analysis, and reporting. The error rate for OMR technology is less than 1%. For this reason, OMR is widely used for applications in which large numbers of hand-filled forms have to be quickly processed with great accuracy, such as surveys, reply cards, questionnaires, ballots, or sheets for multiple-choice questions.

**Advantage**
Optical mark readers work at very high speeds. They can read up to 9,000 forms per hour.

**Disadvantages**
- It is difficult to gather large amounts of information using an OMR.
- Some data may be missing in the scanned document.
- It is a sensitive device that rejects the OMR sheet if it is folded, torn, or crushed.

### 1.5.9 Magnetic Ink Character Reader (MICR)

MICR is used to verify the legitimacy of paper documents, especially bank checks. It consists of magnetic ink printed characters that can be recognized by high-speed magnetic recognition devices (refer Fig. 1.18). The printed characters provide important information (such as check number, bank routing number, checking account number, and, in some cases, the amount on the check) for processing to the receiving party.

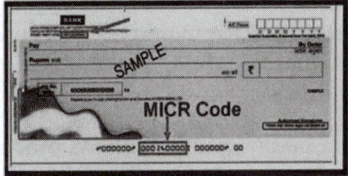
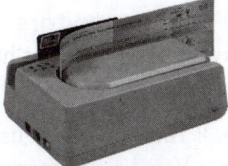

**Figure 1.18** MICR code and MICR reader

### 1.5.10 Digital Camera

Digital camera (Fig. 1.19) is used to click photographs and record videos. These pictures and videos are stored in a small memory chip placed inside the camera. To transfer all the pictures and videos in the computer, you simply need to connect the digital camera with the computer.

**Figure 1.19** Digital camera

## 1.6 OUTPUT DEVICES

Devices that give the output are called *output devices.* Some commonly used output devices are monitor, printer, speakers, headphone, etc.

### 1.6.1 Monitor or VDU (Visual Display Unit)

Monitor looks like a TV screen. Whatever we type on the keyboard can be seen on the monitor as output. Monitors are available in different sizes like 15, 17, 21 inches. You must use a bigger-size monitor as it causes less strain to your eyes. There are three types of monitors: Cathode Ray Tube (CRT) monitor, Liquid Crystal Display (LCD) monitor and Plasma monitor (Figs 1.20 a, b and c).

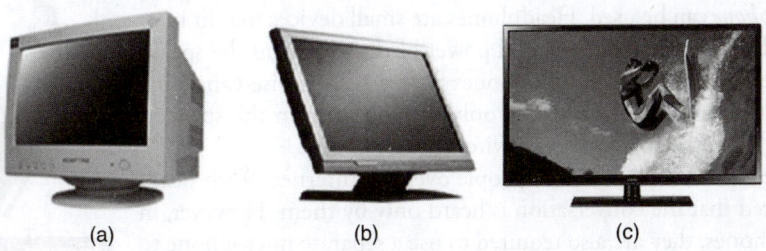

**Figure 1.20** (a) Cathode ray tube, (b) Liquid crystal display and (c) Plasma monitors

The output seen on the monitor is called **soft copy** output because we can see it for the time the computer is switched on.

CRT monitors are the traditional type of monitors used in computers and televisions. These are the first type of monitors that were used in the early days of computers are now being gradually phased out in favour of the more efficient and less power consuming LCD monitors. However, CRT monitors are still used by graphics professionals because of their accurate rendering of colours. The difference between CRT and LCD monitors is presented in Table 1.2.

**Table 1.2** Comparison of CRT and LCD monitors

| Cathode Ray Tube (CRT) Monitor | Liquid Crystal Display (LCD) Monitor |
| --- | --- |
| Very big in size | Light weight |
| Difficult to carry from one place to another | Easy to carry from one place to another |
| Consumes more electricity | Consumes less electricity |

**Plasma monitors** are thin and flat monitors widely used in televisions and computers. The plasma display contains two glass plates that have hundreds of thousands of tiny cells filled with xenon and neon gases.

### Advantages
- The technology used in plasma monitors allows producing a very wide screen using extremely thin materials.
- Very bright images are formed which look good from almost every angle.
- These monitors are not heavy and are thus easily portable.

### Disadvantages
- These monitors are very expensive.
- They have a high-power consumption.
- Since the images are phosphor-based, at times, they may suffer from flicker.

### 1.6.2 Speakers

Speakers help us to listen to music. Other sounds from the computer can also be heard from speakers. For example, when you switch on your computer a welcome sound is heard. Usually two speakers are attached to a computer (Fig. 1.21 (a)).

*These days, monitors also have a speaker fitter inside them.*

### 1.6.3 Headphone

Headphones are used to listen to music from the computer. We can also use headphones while chatting with our friends through a computer (Fig. 1.21 (b)). With speakers, users can enjoy music, movie, or a game, and the voice will be spread through the entire room. With good-quality speakers, the voice will also be audible even to people sitting in another room or even to neighbours!

However, in case the user wants to enjoy loud music without disturbing the people nearby, a *headphone* can be used. Headphones are small devices that fit in or on the ear, and give about the same quality and power of the sound, as the speakers, only to the listener. Most of today's headphones feature some noise-cancelling technologies, so that the listener may listen to only the sound from the speakers and not anything else from the surrounding environment.

Users often use headphones to chat with people over the Internet. With headphones, they are assured that the conversation is heard only by them. However, in addition to the headphones, they are also required to use a separate microphone to

**Figure 1.21** (a) Speaker

**Figure 1.21** (b) Headphone

## 1.6.4 Printer

A printer is a device that takes the text and graphics information from a computer and prints it on to a paper. Printers are available in the market in various sizes, speeds, sophistication, and costs (Fig. 1.21 (c)). High-quality printers are used for enhanced resolution in color printing and are usually more expensive.

*Colour* printouts are needed for presentations, maps, and other pages where colour is part of the information. Colour printers can also be set to print only in monochrome. These printers are more expensive, so if the users do not have a specific need for colour and usually take lot of printouts, they will find a black-and-white printer cheaper to operate.

*Resolution of a printer* means the sharpness of text and images rendered on paper. It is usually expressed in dots per inch (dpi). Even the least expensive printer provides sufficient resolution for most purposes at 600 dpi.

**Figure 1.21** (c) Printer

*Speed* means number of pages that are printed in one minute. The speed of a printer is an important factor for users who have a large number of pages to print. While high-speed printers are quite expensive, the inexpensive printers, on the other hand, can print only about 3–6 sheets per minute. Colour printing is even slower.

*Memory* Most printers have a small amount of memory (for example, 1 MB), which can be expanded by the user. Having more memory enhances the speed of printing.

## 1.6.5 Projector

A projector (Fig. 1.22) is a device that takes an image from a video source and projects it onto a screen or another surface. These days, projectors are used for a wide range of applications, varying from home theatre systems for projecting movies and television programs onto a screen much larger than even the biggest available television, to organizations for projecting information and presentations onto screens large enough for rooms filled with many people.

Projectors also allow users to change/adjust some features of the image such as brightness, sharpness, and colour settings, similar to the features available in a standard television. Projectors are now available in a variety of different shapes and sizes, and are produced by many different companies.

**Figure 1.22** Projector

Projectors can be broadly classified into two categories depending on the technology they use.

*LCD projector* These projectors make use of their own light to display the image on the screen/wall. They are based on LCD technology. To use these projectors, the room must be first darkened, else the image formed will be blurred.

*Digital light processing (DLP) projector* uses a number of mirrors to reflect the light. When using the DLP projector, the room may or may not be darkened because it displays a clear image in both situations.

### 1.6.6 Plotters

A plotter is a printing device that is usually used to print vector graphics with high print quality (Fig. 1.23). They are widely used to draw maps, in scientific applications, and in CAD, CAM, and computer aided engineering (CAE).

Architects use plotters to draw blueprints of the structures they are working on. A plotter is basically a printer that interprets commands from a computer to make line drawings on paper with one or more automated pens. Since plotters are much more expensive than printers, they are used only for specialized applications.

Hewlett–Packard is the leading vendor of plotters worldwide.

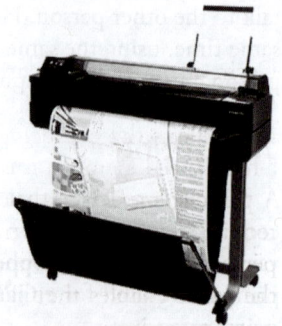

Figure 1.23 Plotter

## 1.7 ORGANIZATION OF COMPUTER'S MEMORY

A computer is an electronic machine that is made of many electronic components. These components work in two states – either on or off. ON means 1 and OFF means 0. Computers understand only these two digits and every data and instruction that we give to the computer are converted and stored as a series of 1s and 0s.

The memory of the computer is therefore divided into a large number of cells where each cell can store one digit – either 0 or 1. More the number of cells, more data can be stored and therefore higher will be the storage capacity of memory. The storage capacity of a computer's memory is measured in units like Bytes, Kilo Bytes, Giga Bytes, Tera Bytes, etc. as shown in Table 1.3.

Table 1.3 Units for measurement of computer's memory

| Smaller Unit | Larger Unit | Symbol |
|---|---|---|
| 8 Bits | 1 Byte | B |
| 1024 Bytes | 1 Kilo Byte | KB |
| 1024 Kilo Bytes | 1 Mega Byte | MB |
| 1024 Mega Bytes | 1 Giga Byte | GB |
| 1024 Giga Bytes | 1 Tera Byte | TB |
| 1024 Tera Bytes | 1 Peta Byte | PB |
| 1024 Peta Bytes | 1 Exa Byte | EB |
| 1024 Exa Bytes | 1 Zeta Byte | ZB |
| 1024 Zeta Bytes | 1 Yotta Byte | YB |

## 1.8 TYPES OF COMPUTER MEMORY

We have read that the computer's memory is used to store data and instructions either temporarily or permanently. It can be broadly divided into three groups: cache memory, primary (main) memory and secondary memory as shown in Fig. 1.24.

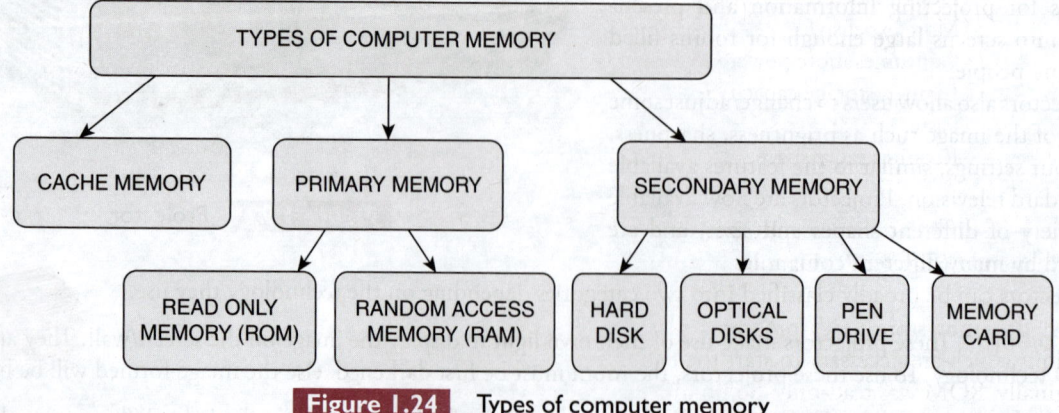

Figure 1.24 Types of computer memory

Computer Systems and Organization 15

### 1.8.1 Cache Memory

Cache memory is a volatile, small-sized and high-speed memory which is used to speed up the work of CPU. The cache memory stores those parts of data and instructions that are being repeatedly used by the CPU. Since cache memory is a high-speed memory, it is very expensive and therefore used in small quantity.

Cache memory is used to store instructions and data that are repeatedly required to execute programs thereby improving the overall system speed and performance of the computer. Keeping frequently used data and instructions in the cache enables the CPU to access them quickly instead of using the slower primary memory.

Figure 1.25  Cache memory

### 1.8.2 Primary Memory

We have seen the difference between primary and secondary memories in Table 1.1. Let us now study the types of memory in detail. There are two types of primary memory: RAM and ROM.

**Random Access Memory (RAM):** RAM is a volatile (stores data only when the power is on) storage area within the computer. It stores data temporarily so that it can be accessed by the CPU. The information stored in RAM is loaded from the computer's hard disk or any other secondary memory (like optical drive, pen drive, magnetic tape). These days, computers have 8GB to 16GB of RAM. *More the RAM, more is the number of programs/applications that can be run and shorter is the time taken to execute an instruction.* There are two types of RAM—SRAM and DRAM.

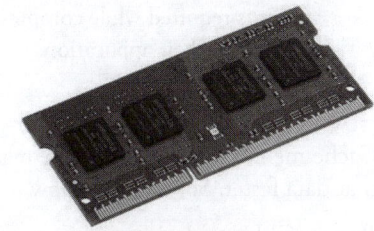

Figure 1.26  RAM

*SRAM (Static RAM)* This type of RAM holds data without an external refresh as long as it is powered. This is in striking contrast with the DRAM which must be refreshed multiple times in a second to hold its data contents.

However, SRAM is faster and more reliable than DRAM. SRAM is often used as cache memory. Static RAM chips are also used in cars, household appliances, and handheld electronic devices.

*DRAM (Dynamic RAM )* SRAM and DRAM are both types of RAM and store data as long as power is supplied to its circuits. DRAM is the most common type of memory used in personal computers, workstations, and servers today. Table 1.4 illustrates the difference between SRAM and DRAM.

Table 1.4  Comparison of SRAM and DRAM

| SRAM | DRAM |
|---|---|
| • Design based on transistor technology | • Design based on capacitor technology |
| • More expensive | • Cheaper than SRAM |
| • Consumes more power | • Consumes less power |
| • Limited storage capacity | • Storage capacity is more than SRAM |
| • Faster | • Slower than SRAM |
| • Requires more space | • Requires less space |

**Read Only Memory (ROM):** ROM is that part of the main memory which stores data permanently (Fig. 1.27). Data or instructions once written in ROM can never be changed.

ROM does not store user's programs, data or instructions. Rather, it stores those instructions which are necessary to start the computer and load the operating system.

Originally, ROM was read-only. So, in order to update the programs stored in ROM, the ROM chip had to be removed and physically replaced by the ROM chip that has new version of the program. However, today ROM chips are not literally *read-only*, as updates to the ROM chip are possible. Rewritable ROM chips include PROMs, EPROMs and EEPROMs.

Figure 1.27  ROM

*Programmable read-only memory (PROM)* also called one-time programmable ROM can be written to or programmed using a special device called a PROM programmer.

*Erasable programmable read-only memory (EPROM)* is a type of ROM that can be erased and re-programmed. The EPROM can be erased by exposing the chip to strong ultraviolet light typically for 10 minutes or longer and then rewritten.

*Electrically erasable programmable read-only memory (EEPROM)* allows its entire or selected contents to be electrically erased and rewritten electrically. The process of writing an EEPROM is also known as flashing.

**Table 1.5** Difference between RAM and ROM

| RAM | ROM |
| --- | --- |
| • Data can be read as well as written<br>• Stores data temporarily<br>• Stores the data of user while computer is being used<br>• It is required while computer is being used by users to run their applications | • Data can only be read<br>• Stores data permanently<br>• Data is stored during the time of fabrication<br>• It is required for starting the computer and storing important programs |

### How it all works together

Cache memory is faster than the main memory. So, if CPU gets data and instructions at a faster speed, it can process that data faster. So, let us see how it works.

**Step 1:** CPU needs data and instructions, so it requests these inputs from the cache memory.
**Step 2:** If cache memory has the required data and instruction, it gives them to CPU.
If cache memory does not have that data and instruction, it then asks for them from the RAM.
**Step 3:** If the RAM has the data and instruction, it sends them to cache. The cache memory gives them to CPU. The cache memory also stores a copy of this data and instruction in itself so that in future if CPU asks for it again, it does not have to ask from the RAM.

If RAM also does not have the data and instruction, it takes the information from the secondary memory that stores all data and instructions permanently. After getting the data and instructions, it gives the information to the cache memory and also stores a copy of it. The interaction between the CPU and the different types of memories is shown in Fig. 1.28

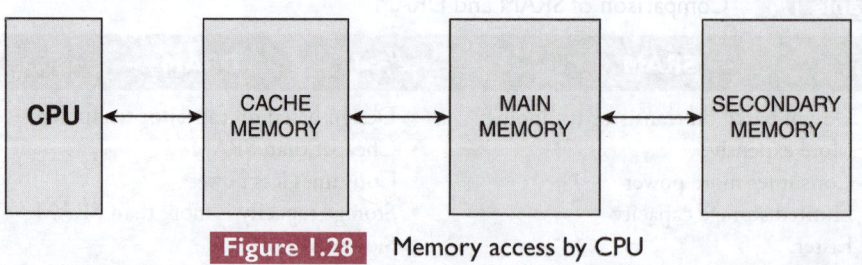

**Figure 1.28** Memory access by CPU

### 1.8.3 Secondary Memory

The secondary memory or the external memory is non-volatile memory that stores user's data, instructions and programs permanently. It is slower than the main memory. CPU cannot directly access the secondary memory. So, whenever we open a program or file stored on secondary memory, it is copied from there to the main memory.

**Hard Disk:** Every computer has a hard disk installed in it (Fig. 1.29). Hard disk is the main storage device of any computer. It has the highest storage capacity. The hard disk is placed inside the CPU box. As compared to other secondary storage devices, hard disk is the fastest device. It is more expensive and heavier than other storage devices.

**Figure 1.29** Hard disk

# Computer Systems and Organization

All the programs that we use on computer like MS Paint, WordPad, MS Word, Games, Calculator, etc. are stored on the hard disk. Apart from these, operating system files and other system software are also stored on the hard disk. Moreover, all the files that we create or download are stored in the hard disk.

The C: drive (and D:, E: drives on some computers) that we see in the File Explorer actually refers to the hard disk of the computer. These days, hard disks can store several Tera Bytes (TB) of data and every year with improved technology the storage capacity of hard disk increases many times.

> Anything you save to your computer, such as a picture, file, program or video. is sent to your hard drive for storage.

### 1.8.4 Optical Storage Discs

Optical storage discs use light to store data. They are very light, weighing around 15–20 grams and are thus portable. Because of their portability, they are widely used to transfer data from one computer to another.

The only limitation of these devices is that they are fragile (delicate) and prone to scratches. Scratches can affect the readability of data.

*CD (Compact Disc):* CDs are small circular plastic discs on which music, games, movies and computer programs are stored (Fig. 1.30 (a)). A CD can store up to 700 MB of data. This means that an audio CD can store 80 minutes of audio.

There are two types of CDs – CD-R and CD-RW. CD-R stands for CD – Read only. Data once written can only be read. You cannot write on the CD again. CD-RW are those CDs that can be read as well as written on.

*DVD (Digital Versatile Disc):* DVD is also a circular plastic disc which looks exactly like a CD. A DVD can store data either on one side or on both sides (Fig. 1.30 (b)). DVD that can store data only one side can store 4.7 GB data and the one that can store data on both sides can store 9.4 GB data.

Like CDs there are two types of DVDs – DVD-R and DVD-RW. DVD-R stands for DVD – Read only. Data once written can only be read. You cannot write on the DVD again, you just read it multiple times. DVD-RW are those DVDs that can be read as well as written on.

> A CD player can read a CD. But a DVD player can read both CD and DVD.

*Blu Ray Disc:* A Blu Ray Disc looks exactly similar to a DVD but it can store five times more data than a DVD can store (Fig. 1.30 (c)). Moreover, the quality of video, audio and pictures stored on a Blu Ray disc is much better than the quality that stored on a CD or a DVD. Therefore, these days Blu Ray discs are replacing the use of CDs and DVDs for storing music, games, movies and computer programs.

A single sided Blu-ray disc can hold up to 25 GB of data. Blu-ray player can read Blu-ray discs, DVDs, and CDs. But a DVD Player or a CD Player cannot read a Blu Ray Disc.

*Pen Drive:* A pen drive is a light-weight key chain like storage device that is used to transfer files from one computer to another. A pen drive can store much more data than a CD, DVD or a Blu Ray Disc. These days, Pen drives with storage capacity 1 TB are available in the market.

Though pen drives are little expensive than CDs and floppy disks (which were used till 2005), they have still succeeded in replacing the disks because of their capability of storing more data and transferring the data at a faster speed. A pen drive is also called a USB Drive because it is plugged into the USB port of the computer.

The main advantage of pen drive is that unlike a CD, DVD or Blu Ray disc, it is not affected by scratches.

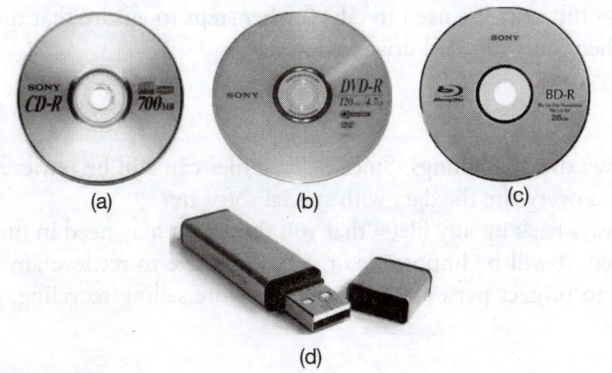

**Figure 1.30** (a) CD, (b) DVD, (c) Blu Ray Disc, (d) Pen Drive

**Figure 1.31** Fitting a pen drive in a laptops's USB port

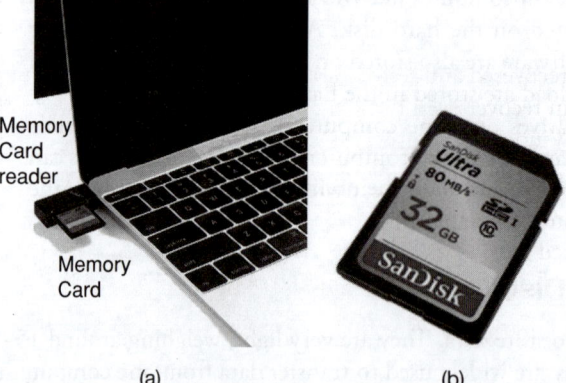

**Figure 1.32** (a) Memory card in a Memory Card Reader is connected to the Laptop's USB Port, (b) Memory Card

**Memory Card** Memory card, also known as a flash card or multimedia card, is a storage device that is used to store pictures, files, videos, programs and games. It is used to transfer these data and files between two computers, smartphones, tablets or digital cameras. For example, we can plug in the memory card in our phone to store our pictures and videos. To transfer these files to a computer, we can use a card reader and connect it to the USB port of the computer. This will help us to transfer files just in the same way we transfer files between a computer and pen drive.

> Did you know that you have a USB port in your car? You can enjoy your favorite music and songs by storing them on a pen drive and plugging it into that USB port.

> We insert SD card in our smart phones to increase its storage capacity. These SD cards are nothing but memory cards.

## 1.9 DATA DELETION AND SECURITY CONCERNS

Many a time, when we intentionally or accidentally delete one or more files, they may not be deleted permanently. If it was an accidental deletion, then the user need not worry as the deleted files can still be recovered. And in case it was an intentional deletion, the main concern is that someone with malicious intentions can still recover them.

When we delete a file or a folder, it goes in the Recycle Bin. But if we had pressed the Shift button along with the Delete button to delete the file/folder or if the file or folder size is too large to fit in the Recycle Bin then in both the cases, the file or the folder does not goes to the Recycle Bin and is deleted permanently.

### 1.9.1 Risk of Data Misuse

Cybercriminals and hackers can access our deleted files containing pictures, videos, personal, financial or other vital information stored in it. Therefore, before selling, recycling, donating or destroying your computer, you must properly clean your hard drive to ensure that it does not have any file – not even the deleted ones.

Files which do not contain any confidential or personal data, or those that are deleted just to free up used space can be ignored as they would be of no use to the hacker. But if the deleted files have personal, confidential, financial or business data, then simply deleting them is not sufficient. We need to take further steps to ensure that the files are irretrievable and that cybercriminals cannot find them on your hard drive in any way.

### 1.9.2 Permanently Deleting Files

Formatting a hard drive and wiping it clean are two different things. Since deleted files can still be retrieved from a formatted hard drive, you must take an extra step to overwrite the data with special software.

But in case of wipe-cleaning the hard drive, always back up any file(s) that you think you may need in future. This is important because once the drive is wipe-cleaned, it will be impossible or very expensive to retrieve any lost data later. Wipe-cleaning the hard drive must be done to protect personal information before selling/recycling, giving or donating a computer.

## 1.10 RECOVERY OF DELETED DATA

Data once deleted can be easily recovered and restored back from the Recycle Bin or data backup storage. In fact, there are file recovery software that can recover even those files that have been permanently removed without any backup.

To recover a file deleted in Windows, follow the steps given below.

*Step 1:* Right-click on the Recycle Bin icon on the desktop.
*Step 2:* Select the file(s) to restore.
*Step 3:* Right click on the selected files.
*Step 4:* Click the Restore option from the pop-up menu (as shown in Fig. 1.33).

This will retrieve deleted files back to their original location. After restoration, you can move the files to any other drive or folder as you like.

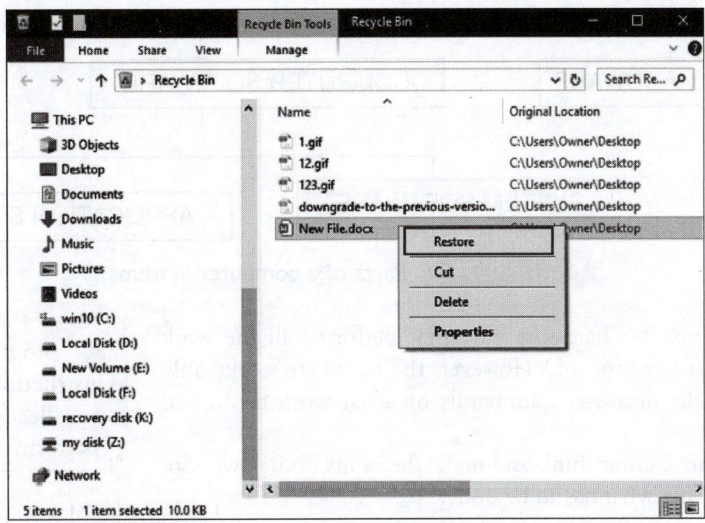

**Figure 1.33** Restoring files/folders from recycle bin

### 1.10.1 Recovering Deleted Files with Deleted File Recovery Software

If you have permanently deleted the files (by pressing Shift + Delete keys) then the deleted files do not go to the Recycle Bin. To restore such files to a previously saved version, you must use a third-party data recovery software. Such software are specifically designed for dealing with all complicated data loss situations that could arise due to accidental deletion or deletion due to system format, malware attack, system crash, etc. Recovery software help users in retrieving deleted files from their computers, external hard drives, memory cards or USB drives.

In such software, the user just has to select a local hard drive disk or a removable storage device and the exact location from which the files were deleted and click the "Scan" button.

The Scan process will show a list of deleted files. Select the file(s) from the list and press the Recover button to restore the selected file(s).

### 1.10.2 Restore Deleted Files from the Previous Version

If the deleted file is not in the Recycle Bin, or if you have already emptied the Recycle Bin and do not want to use third-party software to retrieve those deleted files, then Windows allow users to recover an older version of the deleted or lost file by using the free backup and restore feature that is already built into it. Follow the steps given below to restore deleted files in Windows 10.

*Step 1:* Open the folder from which the file(s) was/were deleted.
*Step 2:* Click on the "History" button in the ribbon.
*Step 3:* File History will display all the files contained in the most recent backup of that folder.
*Step 4:* Click the "Previous" button to locate and select the file you want to retrieve.
*Step 5:* Click on the "Restore" button to get it back.

## 1.11 COMPUTER HARDWARE AND SOFTWARE

The TV sets that we have at home is just a dumb box if it is unable to show any program. Similarly, a computer is just a dumb box if it does not allow users to work with any applications. Thus, TV and programs are two separate things, as are computers and their applications. The easiest way to distinguish between them is that one is the hardware that can be touched (like the TV set and the computer) and the other which cannot be touched (like program and applications) is the software.

**Hardware:** All the physical parts that can be touched is called hardware (refer Fig 1.34). For example, all input, output and memory devices form the computer hardware.

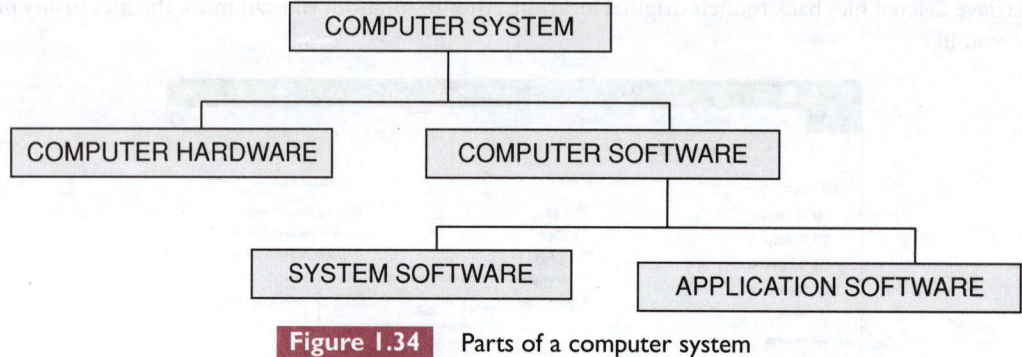

Figure 1.34  Parts of a computer system

**Software:** It is the computer's hardware part that performs all the work (input, output, storage, processing, etc.) However, the hardware works only when the software gives the necessary commands on what work to do and how to do it.

The computer hardware cannot think and make decisions on its own. So, it needs a software to instruct what has to be done.

> A program is a set of instructions. And a software is a collection of programs that performs a specific task.

## 1.12 TYPES OF COMPUTER SOFTWARE

Computer software can be broadly classified into two groups: system software and application software.

**Application software:** Application software is designed to solve a particular problem for users. Examples of application software include MS Word, MS PowerPoint, MS Excel, games, web browser, etc.

**System software:** System software represents programs that enable the hardware to run properly. It acts as an interface between the hardware of the computer and the application software. System software provides an environment in which users can create and/or run their applications. Table 1.5 illustrates the difference between application and system software

## 1.13 GENERAL-PURPOSE APPLICATION SOFTWARE

While using smartphones, your parents must have used the term app frequently. Basically, an app, or the short form of application is a type of software that allows you to perform a particular task.

An app or application for desktop or laptop computers is known as desktop application. Correspondingly, an app or application for a smartphone is known as mobile app. When you open an app, it runs using the operating system until you close it.

Some general-purpose application software that we frequently use are given below.

 **Word Processor:** It is the most commonly used software. A word processor is used to type documents, letters, memos, etc. On Windows, MS Word is the most popularly used word processor.

### Table 1.5 Difference between application and system software

| System Software | Application Software |
| --- | --- |
| It is a collection of programs that enables the users to interact with hardware components efficiently. | It is a collection of programs written for a specific application. |
| It controls and manages the hardware. | It uses the services provided by the system software to interact with hardware components. |
| System software is machine dependent. | It is machine independent. |
| The programmer must understand the architecture of the machine and hardware details to write a system software. | The programmer ignores the architecture of the machine and hardware details to write an application software. |
| Writing a system software is a complicated task. | Writing application programs is relatively very easy. |
| Example: compiler, operating system. | Example: MS-WORD, PAINT. |
| Created to provide a base on which application software is used. | Created to perform a specific task. |
| System software are used to manage hardware devices and other software. | Application software are used to solve real-world problems. |
| System software allow computers to work more efficiently. | Application software focuses on allowing a particular task work efficiently. |
| System software directly interacts with the hardware. | Application software cannot directly interact with the hardware. |

**Presentation Software:** A presentation software is used to display information in the form of a slide show. In a slide you can easily insert, edit and format text or images. The slides can be presented one after the other and animation effects can be added while displaying the information. You can also add audio and videos in your slides.

 **Spreadsheet Software:** A spreadsheet is a software that arranges data using rows and columns. It is used to make report cards, record expenses, salaries, balance sheets, etc. On Windows, MS Excel is the most popularly used spreadsheet software.

**Database Software:** It is used to create and manage records. For example, in a school, a database of all the students is created that stores the details about each student such as class, address, phone number, fees submitted, etc. On Windows, MS Access is the most popularly used database software.

 **Desktop Publishing Software (DTP):** It allows users to design books, newspapers, magazines to give them a professional look. These days, Photoshop, GIMP and Corel Draw are popularly used DTP software.

**Entertainment Software:** This software allows users to play audio and video files on the computer. Windows Media Player, VLC Media Player and Real Player are some examples of entertainment software.

 **Multimedia and Animation Software:** This software is used to combine text, pictures and sounds to make an animated video. Example of such a software is Adobe Flash.

**Communication Software:** The communication software allows users to connect their computer to the Internet. Once connected, you can search for information, send emails, chat with your friends, download apps and shop online. Examples of communication software include Google Chrome, Opera Safari, Internet Explorer, etc.

## 1.14 TYPES OF SOFTWARE BASED ON COST

Software can also be categorized based on the cost to acquire (or get) it. Different categories based on this classification are given below:

**Shareware:** A shareware software is usually distributed on a free or trial basis for few days. After that period, user has to buy it to use it further.

**Liteware:** It is a type of shareware software with limited functions. This means that in a liteware software, some functionalities can be used only when the full version is purchased.

**Freeware:** A freeware software can be downloaded for free but with some restrictions. Also, users are not allowed to make any changes in the software.

**Public Domain Software:** Public domain software can be downloaded for free without restriction.

**Figure 1.35** (a) Open-source software, (b) Proprietary software

**Table 1.6** Comparison of open-source and proprietary software

| Feature | Open-source Software | Proprietray Software |
|---|---|---|
| Ownership | No owner as software is developed and tested through open collaboration. | Software owned by the individual or company that had developed it. |
| Right to use | Anyone can use the code | Only the individual or the company who has paid a license fee to the owner can use it |
| Right to modify | Anyone having a good understanding of the code can modify the software | Only the individual or the company who owns the software can modify it |
| Availability of source code | Yes | No |
| Maintenance and support | Community support and commercial support (if available) | Commercial support |
| Bug/Error Fixing | Can be done anyone having a good understanding of the code | Can be done only by the company who owns that software |
| Flexibility | Due to less restrictions more people can join, collaborate and innovate | More restrictions limit the scope of innovation |
| Example | GIMP, GAMBAS, Open Office, Python | MacOS, MS Office Suite, Java, Adobe Photoshop |

***Open-source Software*** A type of software which can be freely downloaded and even distributed to others. Also, its source code (or set of instructions) is also available for free so that anybody in the world can see how the software was created and also make changes in it to improve it further.

***Proprietary Software:*** Software that has to be purchased before use. For example, Microsoft Office that includes Microsoft Word, Microsoft Excel, Microsoft PowerPoint, etc. is a proprietary software created by Microsoft Company. We have to first pay a fee to use this software.

## 1.15 CUSTOMIZED SOFTWARE

Have you ever gone to a tailor? Why do you go to him? The answer is either to get a dress stitched exactly according to your measurements or to get the dress altered to make it fit as per your measurements. So, we can say that we go to a tailor get a customized dress (according to us, the customer). Similarly, we have customized software, that is, a software that is customized exactly according to the user's needs.

A company opts for customized software when the pre-written software (already written software) available does not meet its requirements. In such cases, the company can get the customized software made in two ways.

- First, create the customized software ***in-house*** (if the organization has an IT team)
- Second, ***outsource*** it to another company.

Continuing with our example, you can customize the dress either by anyone in your family if someone knows stitching; otherwise, you can give your dress to a tailor. In the same way, a company can get it done in their own company if they have a team of IT professionals or get it done by another company.

### 1.15.1 Generic Software Development vs. Specific-purpose Software

From the above discussion, it can be seen that we can also categorize software as generic or specific-purpose software. A generic software product is developed to suit all types of business needs. They are expected to have a huge demand in the market over a duration of time. Software development companies develop generic software and distribute it to a group of customers having a similar need.

***Custom Software Development:*** A **specific-purpose software** is the one which a company develops for an individual client. The client may be a company or a group of individuals. The specific-purpose software has a limited use for a very specific purpose and for a limited duration of time. Software development companies developing such software charge the cost of development from the client. Table 1.7 highlights the difference between generic and specific-purpose software.

**Table 1.7** Comparison between generic and specific-purpose software

| Generic Software | Specific-purpose Software |
| --- | --- |
| It is developed for general use by a large number of people. | It is developed to suit the needs of a particular customer. |
| Software requirements have to be depicted by software developers. | Software requirements have to be collected from the end-users by software developers. |
| Software must be properly marketed so that it can be used by a large number of people. | Software need not be marketed as it is developed for a specific client who needs it and is paying for it. |
| Users have to pay less to use the software as the cost of development is shared among all the users. | Client has to pay more because the entire cost of development has to be paid. |
| Example, Word processing software | Example, Employee recruitment system |

## 1.16 UTILITY SOFTWARE

Utility software is used to analyze, configure, optimize and maintain the computer system. Utility programs may be requested by application programs during their execution for multiple purposes. Some of them are listed below.

*Disk defragmenters* can be used to detect computer files whose contents are broken across several locations on the hard disk, and move the fragments to one location in order to increase storage efficiency.

*Disk checkers* scan the contents of a hard disk to find files or areas that are corrupted in some way. This helps the hard drive to operate more efficiently.

*Disk cleaners* can be used to locate files that are either not required for computer operation, or take up considerable amounts of space. Disk cleaner helps users to decide what to delete when their hard disk is full.

*Disk space analyzers* is used for visualizing the disk space usage by getting the size for each folder (including sub-folders) and files in folder or drive.

*Disk partitions* are used to divide an individual drive into multiple logical drives, each with its own file system. Each partition is then treated as an individual drive.

*Backup utilities* can be used to make a copy of all information stored on a disk. In case a disk failure occurs, backup utilities can be used to restore the entire disk. Even if a file gets deleted accidentally, the backup utility can be used to restore the deleted file.

*Disk compression* is used to enhance the capacity of the disk by compressing/uncompressing the contents of a disk

*File managers* allow users to conveniently perform tasks like deleting, renaming, cataloging, moving, copying, merging, generating and modifying files.

*System profilers* provides detailed information about the software installed and hardware attached to the computer.

*Anti-virus utilities* are used to scan for computer viruses and other malware (software with malicious intentions).

*Data compression utilities* are used to reduce the size of a file.

*Cryptographic utilities* encrypt and decrypt files to prevent unauthorized users from reading them.

*Launcher applications* can be used as a convenient access point for application software.

*Registry cleaners* can be used to clean and optimize the Windows registry by deleting the old registry keys that are no longer in use.

*Network utilities* can be used to analyze the computer's network connectivity, configure network settings and check data transfer or log events.

### Key Terms

**Computer:** A computer is an electronic machine that takes data and instructions as input and performs computations on data based on the specified instructions.

**Input:** The process of entering data and instructions in to the computer system is known as input.

**Storage:** Storage is the process of saving data, instructions and results of processing permanently in the computer's memory.

**Primary storage:** Storage area of the computer which is directly accessible by the CPU at a very fast speed.

**Secondary storage:** Storage area of the computer which permanently stores the user's files.

**Output:** Output is the process of giving the result of data processing to the outside world.

**Processing:** Performing operations on the data as per the instructions specified by the user.

**Soft copy:** The output seen on the monitor is called soft copy output.

**Hard copy:** The printed copy of information from the computer on a sheet of paper is called a printout or the hardcopy.

**Flashing:** The process of writing an EEPROM is also known as flashing.

**Hardware:** All the physical parts that can be touched is called hardware.

**Program:** A set of instructions which direct hardware devices what work to perform.

**Software:** A collection of programs that performs a specific task.

**Shareware:** A shareware software is usually distributed on a free or trial basis for few days. After that period, user has to buy it to use it further.

**Liteware:** It is a type of shareware software with limited functions. This means that in a liteware software, some functionalities can be used only when the full version is purchased.

**Freeware:** A freeware software can be downloaded for free but has some restrictions. Also, users are not allowed to make any changes in the software.

**Public Domain Software:** Public Domain software can be downloaded for free and does not have any restriction.

**Open-source Software:** A type of software which can be freely downloaded and even distributed to others.

**Data:** Data is a collection of raw facts or figures.

**Information:** Information comprises of processed data to provide answers to *who, what, where* and *when* type of questions.

**Knowledge:** Knowledge is the application of data and information to answer *how* part of the question.

**Instructions:** Commands given to the computer that tells what it has to do.

**Programs:** A set of instructions in computer language is called a program.

**Software:** A set of programs is called software.

**Hardware:** Computer and all its physical parts are known as hardware.

## Chapter Highlights

- The control unit inside the CPU manages and controls all the components of the computer system.
- In a computer, ON means 1 and off means 0. Like any other machine, computer understands only these two digits.
- Memory of the computer is divided into a large number of cells where each cell can store one digit – either 0 or 1.
- The cache memory stores those parts of data and instructions that are being repeatedly used by the CPU.
- SRAM holds data without an external refresh as long as it is powered. This is in striking contrast with the DRAM which must be refreshed multiple times in a second to hold its data contents.
- ROM is that part of the main memory which stores data permanently. Data or instructions, once written in ROM, can never be changed.
- The secondary memory or the external memory is non-volatile memory that stores the user's data, instructions and programs permanently. It is slower than the main memory.
- Application software is designed to solve a particular problem for users.
- System software represents programs that enable the hardware to run properly.
- A company opts for customized software when the pre-written software available does not meet its requirements.
- Utility software is used to analyze, configure, optimize and maintain the computer system.
- When we delete a file or a folder, it goes in the Recycle Bin. But if we had pressed the Shift button along with the Delete button to delete the file/ folder or if the file or folder size is too large to fit in the Recycle Bin then in both the cases, the file or the folder does not goes to the Recycle Bin and is deleted permanently.

## Review Questions

1. Define a computer and explain its basic organization.
2. Write a short note on generation of computers.
3. List some basic features of computers.
4. What do you understand by GIGO principle?
5. Differentiate between the terms data, information and knowledge with the help of a relevant example.
6. How is an instruction related to software?
7. Differentiate between primary and secondary storage.
8. Explain the different parts of CPU.
9. Write a short note input devices.
10. Briefly explain any three output devices.
11. Differentiate between CRT and LCD.
12. Explain the different types of memory in a computer.
13. Differentiate between SRAM and DRAM.
14. What are the different types of ROM?
15. Differentiate between RAM and ROM.
16. Write a short note on secondary storage devices of the computer.
17. Compare the different types of optical discs.
18. Differentiate between computer hardware and software.
19. Differentiate between system software and application software.
20. Differentiate between proprietary and open-source software.
21. Write a short note on utility software.
22. In what two ways can a software be customized?
23. How can we restore deleted files?
24. Differentiate between generic software and specific-purpose software.

## Fill in the Blanks

1. _____ is a collection of raw facts or figures.
2. High-level programming languages started to be used in the _____ generation of computers.
3. Speed of a computer is measured in _____ or _____.
4. _____ storage area of the computer is directly accessible by the CPU at a very fast speed.
5. Data is processed based on _____ given.
6. Data processing is done by _____ of the _____.
7. _____ decides the order in which the instructions will be executed and the operations that will be performed by the ALU.
8. _____ is used instead of a mouse on the laptop computers.
9. The output seen on the monitor is called _____.
10. Speed of a printer is measured in _____.
11. Memory of the computer is divided into a large number of _____.
12. _____ is a type of primary memory that stores data permanently.
13. Optical storage discs use _____ to store data.
14. To transfer files to a computer, a memory card reader is connected to the _____ port of the computer.

15. A _____ software that arranges data using rows and columns.
16. A _____ software is usually distributed on a free or trial basis for few days.
17. A company opts for a _____ software when the pre-written software (already written software) available does not meet its requirements.
18. _____ scans the contents of a hard disk to find files or areas that are corrupted in some way.
19. _____ provide detailed information about the software installed and hardware attached to the computer.
20. Once the drive is _____, it will be impossible or very expensive to retrieve any lost data later.

## State True or False

1. Second generation computers were manufactured using thousands of vacuum tubes.
2. The process of entering data and instructions into the computer system is known as output.
3. RAM is an example of secondary memory.
4. Touch screen is an input as well as output device.
5. ON means 0 and OFF means 1.
6. SRAM must be refreshed multiple times in a second to hold its data contents.
7. PROM can be erased by exposing the chip to strong ultraviolet light typically for 10 minutes or longer.
8. CPU cannot directly access the secondary memory.
9. A single-sided CD can hold up to 25 GB of data.
10. Latest pen drives can store more data than a BD.
11. In liteware software, some functionalities can be used only when the full version is purchased.
12. Disk defragmenters are used to detect computer files whose contents are broken across several locations on the hard disk, and move the fragments to one location in order to increase efficiency.
13. Data compression utilities are used to increase the size of a file.
14. Disk partitions are used to make a single drive in the hard disk.
15. When we delete a file/ folder, it always goes to the Recycle Bin.

## Multiple Choice Questions

1. Which of the following is not a first-generation computer?
   a. ENIAC		b. EDVAC		c. PARAM		d. EDSAC
2. In which generation of computers were _____ used?
   a. First		b. Second		c. Third		d. Fourth
3. _____ is a set of instructions in computer language.
   a. Software		b. Program		c. Instruction		d. Knowledge
4. A computer can be used to perform a variety of tasks. This means that computer is a/an _____ machine.
   a. automatic		b. accurate		c. versatile		d. diligent
5. A computer takes _____ as input.
   a. data		b. instructions		c. Both of these.		d. None of these.
6. Storage involves storing _____ .
   a. data		b. instructions		c. results of processing		d. All of these.
7. Which of the following is not a feature of main memory?
   a. Limited		b. Expensive		c. Volatile		d. Slow

8. Monitor, printer, speakers and headphone are examples of _____ devices.
   a. input  b. output  c. processing  d. memory
9. Which of the following devices can be used to hear sound from the computer?
   a. Speaker  b. Headphone  c. Headset  d. All of these.
10. 1024 MB = 1 ____.
    a. KB  b. TB  c. GB  d. ZB
11. Which type of memory is used to store those parts of data and instructions that are being repeatedly used by the CPU?
    a. Main memory  b. Cache memory  c. Secondary memory  d. All of these.
12. Which of the following is used for cache memory?
    a. SRAM  b. DRAM  c. PROM  d. EEPROM
13. Instructions which are necessary to start the computer and load the operating system are stored in _____.
    a. RAM  b. ROM  c. Cache memory  d. Secondary memory
14. The fastest of the given memories is _____.
    a. Cache  b. RAM  c. ROM  d. Hard Disk
15. Which of the following memory has the highest storage capacity?
    a. Cache  b. RAM  c. ROM  d. Hard Disk
16. MS Access is an example of _____ software.
    a. Word Processor  b. Spreadsheet  c. Database  d. DTP
17. _____ is a software which can be freely downloaded and even distributed to others.
    a. Open-source Software  b. Liteware
    c. Shareware  d. Freeware
18. Which software is used to analyze, configure, optimize and maintain the computer system?
    a. Application  b. Open-source  c. Utility  d. Shareware
19. Which utility software is used to locate files that are either not required for computer operation, or take up considerable amounts of space?
    a. Disk cleaner  b. Disk checker  c. Disk space analyser  d. Backup
20. Cryptographic utilities are used to _____ files to prevent unauthorized users?
    a. encrypt  b. decrypt  c. Both of these.  d. None of these.

## Answers

### Fill in the Blanks
1. Data
2. Third
3. nano second, pico second
4. Primary
5. instructions
6. ALU, CPU
7. Control unit
8. Touch Pad
9. Soft copy output
10. Pages Per Minute (PPM)
11. cells
12. ROM
13. light
14. USB
15. spreadsheet
16. shareware
17. customized
18. Disk checkers
19. System profilers
20. Wipe-cleaned

### State True or False
1. False   2. False   3. False   4. True   5. False   6. False   7. False   8. True   9. False   10. True   11. True   12. True   13. False   14. False   15. False

### Multiple Choice Questions
1. c   2. b   3. b   4. c   5. c   6. d   7. d   8. b   9. d   10. c   11. b   12. a   13. b   14. a   15. d   16. b   17. a   18. c   19. a   20. c

# Introduction to Programming Language Python

## Chapter Objectives

The chapter aims to introduce Python as a programming language. To arouse interest in the language and enhance the reader's computational skills, the following topics will be discussed:

- Understanding the relationship between computational thinking and programming skills
- Basic features, historical background, future scope, advantages, applications and limitations of Python
- Working with Python in interactive mode
- Writing Python scripts in IDLE
- Executing programs or rather scripts
- Introduction to Python character set, tokens, literals, numbers, strings, escape sequences
- Formatting numbers and understand basic errors that may pop up while working with floating-point values
- Strings, escape sequences and string operations
- Type conversion

Python is a powerful programming language with the right combination of performance and features that makes programming fun and easy. It is a high-level, interpreted, interactive, object-oriented and reliable language that uses English-like words. It has a vast library of modules to support integration of complex solutions from pre-built components. In this chapter, we will start with a basic introduction of Python.

## 2.1  FEATURES OF PYTHON

Python is an open-source project, supported by many individuals. It can be used on any operating system. Some features which make Python a complete programming language are given below.

***Simple:*** Python is a small and simple language. Reading a program written in Python feels almost like reading English.

***Easy to Learn:*** A Python program is easy to read and understand. It uses a few keywords and a clearly defined syntax. This makes it easy for just anyone to pick up the language quickly.

***Versatile:*** Python supports development of a wide range of applications ranging from simple text processing to games.

***Free and Open Source:*** Python is an example of an open-source software. Therefore, anyone can freely distribute it, read the source code, edit it and even use the code to write new (free) programs.

***High-level Language:*** When writing programs in Python, the programmers do not have to worry about the hardware related details. They just need to concentrate on writing solutions for the current problem at hand.

***Interactive:*** Programs in Python work in interactive mode. Users can give input and get the results accordingly. In this way, users feel as if they are directly communicating with the program.

***Portable:*** Python is a portable language. Hence, the programs behave the same on a wide variety of hardware platforms. The programs work on a wide range of operating systems without requiring any change.

> Python is being continuously improved by a community of users who strive hard to take the language to the next level.

***Object Oriented:*** Python supports object-oriented as well as procedure-oriented style of programming. While object-oriented technique encapsulates data and functionalities within objects, *procedure-oriented* technique, on the other hand, builds the program around procedures or functions which are nothing but reusable pieces of programs.

*Interpreted:* Python program is processed at runtime by the interpreter. In junior classes, we have learnt that an interpreter is a software that is used to convert the instructions written in programming language into the machine language of 0s and 1s. Machine language is the only language that the computer understands and processes. The interpreter translates an instruction and executes it, then translates the next instruction and executes it, and so on.

*Dynamic:* Python program executes dynamically. They can be copied and used for flexible development of applications. If there is any error, it is reported at run time to allow interactive program development.

*Extensible:* Since Python is an open-source software, anyone can add modules to the Python interpreter. These modules enable programmers to add to or customize their tools to work more efficiently.

*Embeddable:* Programmers can embed Python programs within their C, C++, COM, ActiveX, CORBA, and Java programs for added functionality.

*Extensive Libraries:* Python has a huge library that allows programmers to perform a wide range of applications varying from text processing, maintaining databases to GUI programming.

Besides the above stated features, Python has a big list of good features, such as

*Easy Maintenance:* Code written in Python is easy to maintain.

*Secure:* The Python language environment is secure from tampering.

*Robust:* Python programmers cannot manipulate memory directly. Moreover, errors can be easily handled by the program code itself through exception handling procedures. For every syntactical mistake, a simple and easy-to-interpret message is displayed. All these things make the language robust.

*Multi-threaded:* Python supports multi-threading, that is, executing more than one process (or copy) of a program simultaneously.

*Garbage Collection:* Python performs garbage collection of all objects that are no longer used.

## 2.2 LIMITATIONS OF PYTHON

- *Parallel processing* can be done in Python but not as elegantly as done in some other languages (like JavaScript and Go Lang).
- Being an interpreted language, Python is *slow* as compared to C/C++. Python is not a very good choice for those developing a high-graphic 3d game that takes up a lot of CPU.
- As compared to other languages, Python is evolving continuously and there is little substantial *documentation* available for the language.
- As of now, there are only a *few users* of Python as compared to those using C, C++ or Java.
- It lacks true *multiprocessor support*.
- It has very limited *commercial support* point.
- Python is slower than C or C++ when it comes to computation of heavy tasks and desktop applications.
- It is difficult to pack up a big Python application into a single executable file. This makes it difficult to distribute Python to *non-technical users*.

> BitTorrent, YouTube, Dropbox, Deluge, Cinema 4D and Bazaar are a few globally-used applications based on Python.

## 2.3 HISTORY OF PYTHON

Python was developed by Guido van Rossum in the late 80's and early 90's at the National Research Institute for Mathematics and Computer Science in the Netherlands. It has been derived from many languages like ABC, Modula-3, C, C++, Algol-68, SmallTalk, Unix shell and other scripting languages. Since the early 90's Python has been improved on tremendously. Version 1.0, released in 1991, introduced several new functional programming tools. Version 2.0, which brought list comprehensions in 2000, was released by the BeOpen Python Labs team. Python 2.7 which is still used today will be supported until 2020. But there will be no 2.8, instead, the support team will continue to support version 2.7 and concentrate on further development of Python 3.

Python 3.8.x is already available. The newer versions have better features. These days, from data to web development, Python has emerged as a very powerful and popular language.

## 2.4 APPLICATIONS OF PYTHON

Since its origin in 1989, Python has grown to become part of a plethora of web-based, desktop-based, graphic design, scientific and computational applications. Some of the key applications of Python include:

- Python is used to develop a wide range of applications including *image processing, text processing, web*, and enterprise-level using scientific, numeric and data from network.
- 3D software like Maya includes Python, which can be used for *automating* small user tasks.
- Python is a popular language for *web development*. For example, websites like Quora, Odoo and Google App engine have their codes written in Python. For web development, Python has frameworks such as Django, Pyramid, Flask and Bottle.
- *GUI-based Desktop Applications* can be easily developed in Python.
- Python is used to make *2D imaging software* such as Inkscape, GIMP, Paint Shop Pro and Scribus. It is also used to make *3D animation* packages, like Blender, 3ds Max, Cinema 4D, Houdini, Lightwave and Maya.
- Features like high speed, productivity and availability of tools such as Scientific Python and Numeric Python, have made Python a preferred language to perform *computation and processing of scientific data*. 3D modeling software, such as FreeCAD, and finite element method software, like Abaqus, are coded in Python.

Moreover, SciPy is a collection of packages for mathematics, science, and engineering; Pandas is a data analysis and modelling library and IPython is a powerful interactive shell that supports ease of editing and recording a work session. In addition to this, IPython supports visualizations and parallel computing.

- Python has various modules, libraries and platforms that support development of *games*. While PySoy is a 3D game engine, PyGame, on the other hand, provides functionality and a library for game development. Games like Civilization-IV, Disney's Toontown Online, Vega Strike, etc., are coded using Python.
- Python is a suitable coding language for *customizing business applications*. For example, Reddit which was originally written in Common Lips, was rewritten in Python in 2005. A large part of YouTube code is also written in Python.
- Python is also used for *writing codes for operating system*. For example, Ubuntu's Ubiquity Installer, and Fedora's and Red Hat Enterprise Linux's Anaconda Installer are written in Python. Gentoo Linux uses Python for Portage – its package management system.
- Python is used to develop other *languages*. For example, Boo language uses an object model, syntax and indentation, similar to Python. Apple's Swift, CoffeeScript, Cobra, and OCaml all have syntax similar to Python.
- Since Python is very easy to learn and an open-source language, it is widely used for *prototype development*.
- Python is used for *network programming* as it has easy-to-use socket interface, functions for email processing and support for FTP, IMAP and other Internet protocols.
- Python is a perfect language for teaching programming skills at the introductory as well as advanced level.

## 2.5 THE FUTURE OF PYTHON

Python has a huge user base that is constantly growing. It is a stable language that is going to stay for long. The strength of Python can be understood from the fact that this programming language is the most preferred language of companies, such as Nokia, Google, and YouTube, as well as NASA for its easy syntax. Python has a bright future ahead of it supported by a huge community of OS developers. The support for multiple programming paradigms including object-oriented Python programming, functional Python programming, and parallel programming models makes it an ideal choice for programmers. Based on the data from Google Trends (Fig. 2.1), Python is amongst the top five most preferred languages in academics as well industry.

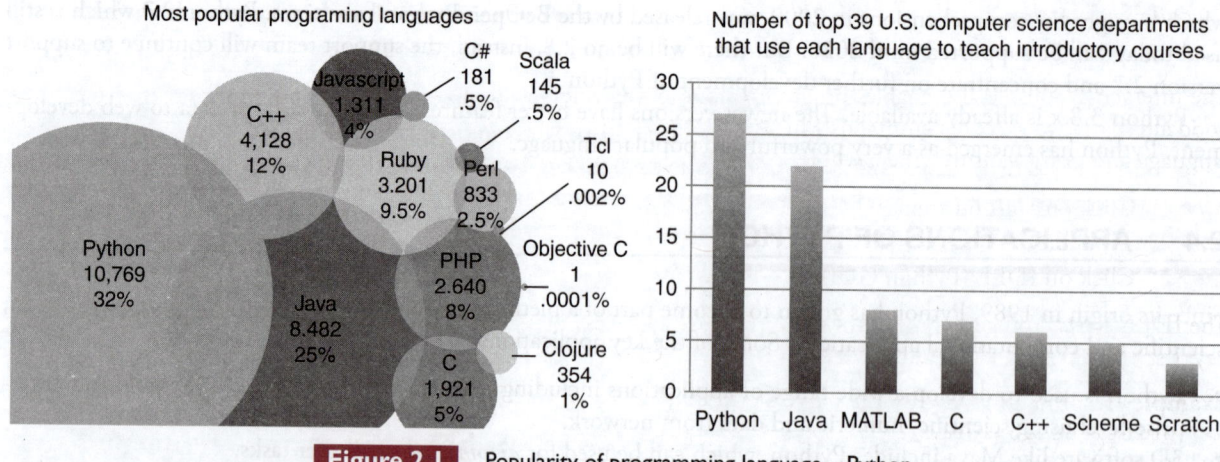

**Figure 2.1** Popularity of programming language – Python

Python is a high-speed dynamic language. Therefore, it works well in applications like photo development and has been embedded in programs such as GIMP and Paint Shop Pro. In fact, the YouTube architect, Cuong Do, has appreciated this language for the record speed with which the language allows them to work. The best part is that more and more companies have started using Python for a broad range of applications ranging from social networks, through automation to science calculations.

## 2.6 WRITING AND EXECUTING THE FIRST PYTHON PROGRAM

From here onwards, we will be using Python, via the Python console. For this, you will need to first download Python from www.Python.org. The codes in this book have been developed on Python 3.7.3.

Once installed, the Python console can be accessed in several ways. We will discuss only two of them here. First, using the command line and running the Python interpreter directly. Second, using a GUI software that comes installed with Python called IDLE (as shown in Fig. 2.2).

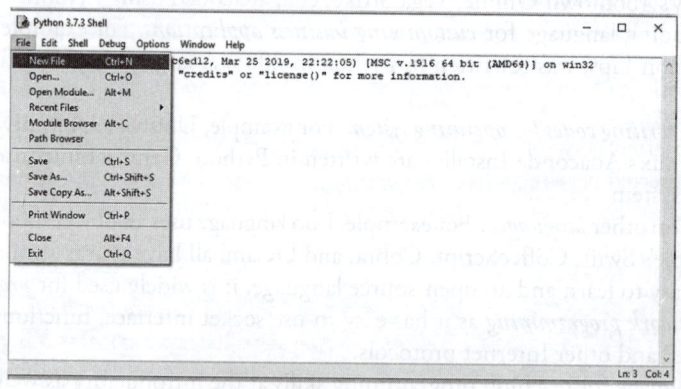

**Figure 2.2** Python IDLE

## 2.7 INTERACTIVE PYTHON

The Python interactive console, also known as the Python interpreter or Python shell, provides programmers a quick way to execute commands without creating a Python file (with a .py extension). For the convenience of users, it provides support for everything including,

- all of Python's built-in functions
- pre-installed modules

- command history
- auto-completion feature.

The interactive console also enables programmers to paste code into programming files as and when required. It is a good alternative to execute commands when programmers want to quickly test some basic functionality of the Python language and don't want to write a whole script. To get the interactive interpreter, follow the steps given below.

*Step 1:* Click on Start button.
*Step 2:* Type Idle.
*Step 3:* Click on IDLE (Python GUI).

The IDLE starts. You get a prompt of three right arrows. Type in your instructions at the prompt and press the enter key. Let us print **Hello World!!!** on the screen. For this, simply type the following line on the IDLE.

**Example:** To print a message on the screen
```
>>> print("Hello World!!!")
Hello World!!!
```

> The >>> symbol denotes the Python prompt.

## 2.8 MORE ABOUT THE print() FUNCTION

The print() function prints one or more literals (or values) followed by a newline. If you don't want to print on a new line then write end = ' ' after a comma as shown below.

| # printing strings | # printing strings on the same line |
|---|---|
| print("Python") | print("Python", end = ' ') |
| print("Programming") | print("Programming") |
| OUTPUT | OUTPUT |
| Python | Python Programming |
| Programming | |

### Key points to remember

- To print more than one value, you can use comma to separate those values or use the + sign.
  ```
  print("HELLO","GOOD MORNING")
  print("PYTHON" + " PROGRAMMING")
  OUTPUT
  HELLO GOOD MORNING
  PYTHON PROGRAMMING
  ```
- By default, a space is inserted between two or more values that are to be printed. Therefore, in the above code, a space is automatically inserted between HELLO and GOOD MORINING in the output.
- The default separator between values is the space, which can be changed to any other character using the sep argument in the print() function as shown below. We shall discuss more about argument in a later chapter.
  ```
  print("HELLO","GOOD MORNING","INDIA", sep = '#')
  OUTPUT
  HELLO#GOOD MORNING#INDIA
  ```
- The print() function prints a string (i.e., a group of characters). If any non-string value is specified in the print() function, the fuction automatically converts it to a string before printing.
  ```
  print("Neha's Total Marks = ",98)
  OUTPUT
  Neha's Total Marks =  98
  ```
- The print() function automatically inserts a new line. So, in case we have multiple print() functions in the same program, then output of each print() function will be displayed on the next line or the new line.
  ```
  print("HELLO")
  print("GOOD MORNING")
  OUTPUT
  HELLO
  GOOD MORNING
  ```

## 2.9 WRITING PYTHON PROGRAMS USING THE IDLE EDITOR

In general, the standard way to save and run a Python program is as follows:

*Step 1:* Open an editor.
*Step 2:* Write the instructions.
*Step 3:* Save it as a file with the file name having the extension .py.
*Step 4:* Run the interpreter with the command python program_name.py or use IDLE to run the programs.

To execute the program in the *command prompt*, simply change your working directory to C:\Python37 (or move to the directory where you have saved Python) and then type python program_name.py.

If you want to execute the program in Python shell, then just press **F5** key (Fig. 2.3) or click on Run Menu and then select **Run Module**.

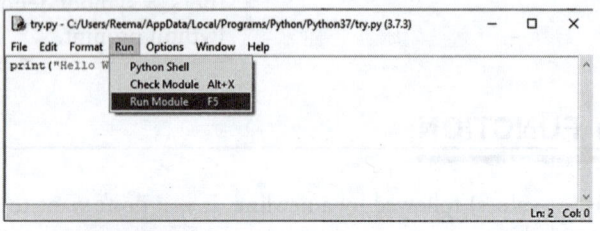

**Figure 2.3** Executing Python code in IDLE

To exit from the IDLE, click on File→Exit, or, press Ctrl + Q keys or type quit() at the command prompt.

## 2.10 PYTHON CHARACTER SET

The character set of a language is a set of valid characters that the language can recognize. Such characters may be digits, alphabets, or any other symbol. Python supports Unicode encoding. The character set of Python includes:

- Lowercase English letters *a* through *z*.
- Uppercase English letters *A* through *Z*.
- Special symbols like $, !, &, ,, ', " etc.
- Punctuation symbols like , ; ?
- Whitespace characters which include a space (" "), tab, newline, etc.
- Non-printable characters like backspace ("\b") that cannot be printed but have a specific meaning.

## 2.11 PYTHON TOKENS

Tokens are small units of the programming language (Fig. 2.4). Python supports the following types of tokens: Literals, Keywords, Identifiers and Operators. In this chapter, we will read about literals in detail.

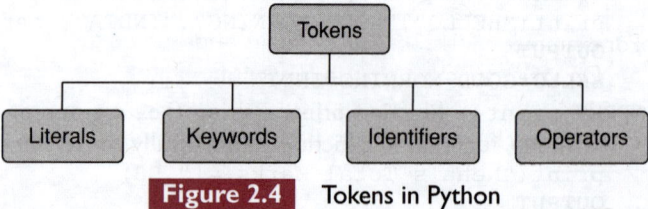

**Figure 2.4** Tokens in Python

## 2.12 LITERAL CONSTANTS

The word "literal" has been derived from literally. The value of a literal constant can be used directly in programs. For example, 7, 3.9, 'A', and "Hello" are examples of literal constants. The number 7 always represents itself and nothing else. Moreover, it is a constant because its value cannot be changed. Hence, it is known as *literal constant*. In this section, we will read about number and string constants in Python.

### 2.12.1 Numbers

Number, as the name suggests, refers to a numeric value. You can use four types of numbers in Python programs. These include integers, long integers, floating-point and complex numbers.

> **Programming Tip:** You can specify integers in octal as well as hexadecimal number system.

- Numbers like 5 or other whole numbers are referred to as *integers*. Integers can be positive or negative or even equal to zero. They do not have any decimal point.
  Bigger whole numbers are called *long integers*. For example, 535633629843L is a long integer. Note that a long integer must have 'l' or 'L' as the suffix.
- Numbers like are 3.23 and 91.5E–2 are termed as *floating-point numbers*. They are real numbers with a decimal point dividing the integer and fractional parts. The real part of the number can be either negative or positive or even equal to zero.

> The 'E' notation indicates powers of 10. In this case, 91.5E–2 means $91.5 \times 10^{-2}$.

- Numbers of $a + bi$ form (like $-3 + 7i$) are *complex numbers*, where $a$ is the real part and $b$ is the imaginary part of the number. Both $a$ and $b$ are floating-point numbers and i represents square root of $-1$.

*Remember that commas are never used in numeric literals or numeric values. Therefore, numbers like 3,567 1,23.89, –8,904 are not allowed in Python.*

**Types of Integer Literals:** There are three types of integer literals – decimal, octal and hexadecimal integer literal.

***Decimal Integer Literal:*** Any integer literal that does not start with a zero (0) is a decimal integer literal. Example, +17, –26,1234, –89072.

***Octal Integer Literal:*** Any integer literal that starts with digit zero followed by letter o is treated as an octal integer literal in Python. Example, 0o12, 0o7654. Type the following statements in IDLE and see the output.

```
>>>0o12        >>>0o12        >>>0o7654
10             -10            4012
```
Note that decimal equivalent of the octal value is displayed

```
>>>0o1789
SyntaxError: invalid Syntax
Digits 8 and 9 are not there
in octal number system
```

***Hexadecimal Integer Literal:*** Any integer literal that starts with digit zero followed by letter x is treated as a hexadecimal integer literal in Python. Example, 0x1234, 0xA7B6F. Type the following statements in IDLE and see the output.

```
>>>0x1234      >>>0xABCD      >>>0x7B9CF1
4660           43981          8101105
```
Note that decimal equivalent of the hexadecimal value is displayed.

```
>>>0xTG1F
SyntaxError: invalid token
Digits T and G are not there
in hexadecimal number system
```

**Large Floating-point Numbers:** Large floating-point numbers are efficiently represented in scientific notation. For example, $5.0012304*10^6$ (6 digits of precision) can be written as 5.0012304e+6 in scientific notation.

Do you remember that in a scientific notation, we have two parts – exponent and the mantissa? The mantissa appears before e and the exponent part follows e. While mantissa can be an integer or a floating-point number, the exponent is always an integer. Both mantissa and exponent can be either negative or positive.

**Errors When Dealing with Floating-point Values:** Although floating-point numbers are very efficient at handling large numbers, there are some issues while dealing with them as they may produce the following errors.

- **The Arithmetic Overflow Problem:** When two very large floating-point numbers are multiplied, it may result in an *arithmetic overflow*. Arithmetic overflow is a condition that occurs when a calculated result is too large. For example, try to multiply 2.7e200 * 4.3e200. You will get result as inf, which means infinity. Infinity denotes that an arithmetic overflow has occurred.
- **The Arithmetic Underflow Problem:** Arithmetic underflow occurs when one floating-point number is divided by another. It is a condition that occurs when a calculated result is too small in magnitude to be represented. For example, try to divide 3.0e-400/5.0e200. You will get the result as 0.0. The value 0.0 indicates that an arithmetic underflow has occurred.

- **Loss of Precision Problem:** When you divide 1/3 you know that the results is .33333333..., where 3 is repeated infinitely. Since any floating-point number has a limited precision and range, the result is just an *approximation* of the true value. Python automatically displays a rounded result to keep the number of digits displayed manageable. For most applications, this slight loss in accuracy is of no practical concern but in scientific computing and other applications in which precise calculations are required, it may be a big issue.

**Built-in `format()` Function:** Any floating-point value may contain an arbitrary number of decimal places, so it is always recommended to use the built-in `format()` function to produce a string version of a number with specific number of decimal places. Observe the difference between the following outputs.

```
# Without using format()         # Using format()
>>> float(16/(float(3)))         >>> format(float(16/(float(3))), '.2f')
5.333333333333333                '5.33'
```

Here, .2f in the `format()` function rounds the result to two decimal places of accuracy in the string produced. For very large (or very small) values, 'e' can be used as a *format specifier*. The `format()` function can also be used to format floating-point numbers in scientific notation. Look at the result of the expression given below.

```
>>> format(3**50,'.5e')
'7.17898e+23'
```

The result is formatted in scientific notation with five decimal places of precision. This feature is especially useful when displaying results in which only a certain number of decimal places is needed. Finally, the `format()` function can also be used to insert a comma in the number as shown below.

```
>>> format(123456.8901,',.2f')
'123,456.89'
```

## Simple Operations on Numbers

Python can carry out simple operations on numbers. To perform a calculation, simply enter the numbers and the type of operations that need to be performed on them directly into the Python console and it will print the answer, as shown below.

```
>>> 17 + 56      >>> 90 + 50 - 40     >>> 35 * 15     >>> 108 / 12     >>> -10 * 14
73               100                  525             9.0              -140
```

Dividing a number by zero in Python generates an error and no output is produced, as shown below.

```
>>> 117 / 0
Traceback (most recent call last):
  File "<pyshell#7>", line 1, in <module>
    117 / 0
ZeroDivisionError: division by zero
```

> The spaces around the plus and minus signs here are optional. They are just added to make the statement more readable. The code will execute even if you remove the spaces.

*When two numbers are divided, a floating-point number is always produced.*

```
>>> 15 / 5       >>> 75 / 15.0        >>> 39.0 / 3    >>> 24.0 / 2.0
3.0              5.0                  13.0            12.0
```

You can easily work with a floating-point number and an integer because Python automatically converts the integer to a float. This is known as **implicit conversion or type coercion**. An implicit conversion is performed by the compiler without programmer's intervention.

*Quotient and Remainder:* When dividing a number by another, if you want to know the quotient and remainder, use the floor division (//) and modulo operator (%), respectively. These operators can be used with both floats and integers. Observe the following statements and their output. When we divide 78 by 5 we get a quotient of 15 and a remainder of 3.

```
>>> 18 // 4      >>> 18 % 4           >>> 324.0 // 6.0     >>> 234.567 % 6.5
4                2                    54.0                 0.5670000000000073
```

*Exponentiation:* Besides, +, -, *, / Python also supports ** operator. The ** operator is used for exponentiation, i.e., raising of one number to the power of another. Consider the statements given below and observe the output.

## 2.12.2 Strings

A *string* is a group of characters. We have already printed a string in our first program in which we had printed "HELLO WORLD !!!". In Python, there are three ways in which a string can be used.

```
>>> 11 ** 3
1331
```
```
>>> 5.25 ** 4
759.69140625
```

- **Using Single Quotes (')**: For example, a string can be written as 'HELLO'.
- **Using Double Quotes (")**: Strings in double quotes are exactly same as those in single quotes. Therefore, 'HELLO' is same as "HELLO".
- **Using Triple Quotes (''' ''')**: A multi-line string is specified using triple quotes. We can use as many single quotes and double quotes as required in a string within triple quotes. An example of a multi-line string can be given as,

```
>>> ''' HELLO WORLD !!!
'GOOD MORNING'
"WELCOME TO THE WORLD OF 'PYTHON PROGRAMMING' "
HAPPY LEARNING....'''
' HELLO WORLD !!!\n\'GOOD MORNING\'\n"WELCOME TO THE WORLD OF \'PYTHON PROGRAM-
MING\' "\nHAPPY LEARNING....'
```

> All spaces and tabs within a string are preserved in quotes (single quote as well as double).

Note that all the characters, spaces, tabs, new lines, and quotes (single as well as double) are preserved within triple quotes.

```
>>> 'Hello'          >>> "HELLO"          >>> '''HELLO'''
'Hello'              'HELLO'              'HELLO'
```

*Irrespective of the way in which a string is specified, all strings are* **mutable**. *This means that once you have created a string, you cannot change it.*

**String Literal Concatenation:** Python concatenates two string literals that are placed side by side. Consider the code below wherein Python has automatically concatenated the two string literals.

```
>>> 'HELLO' 'WORLD'
'HELLOWORLD'
```

**Unicode Strings:** Unicode is a standard way of writing international text. That is, if you want to write some text in your native language like Hindi, then you need to have a Unicode-enabled text editor. Python allows you to specify Unicode text by prefixing the string with a u or U. For example,

```
>>> u"Shubh Prabhat"
'Shubh Prabhat'
```

> The 'U' prefix specifies that the file contains text written in a language other than English.

**Escape Sequences:** Some characters (like , ", \) cannot be directly included in a string. Such characters must be escaped by placing a backslash before them as given below.

```
>>> print('How's life?')
    SyntaxError: invalid syntax
>>> print('How\'s life?')
How's life?
```

The reason for the error was that Python got confused as to where the string starts and ends. So, we need to clearly specify that this single quote does not indicate the end of the string. This indication can be given with the help of an *escape sequence* as specified in the second string – *a single quote preceded by a backslash*.

Similarly, to print a double quote in a string enclosed within double quotes, we must precede the double quotes with a backslash as given below.

```
>>> print("Sheena asked,"Will you come with me?"")
SyntaxError: invalid syntax
>>> print("Sheena asked,\"Will you come with me?\"")
Sheena asked, "Will you come with me?"
```

> When a string is printed, the quotes around it are not displayed.

Other useful escape sequences are given in Table 2.1.

> An escape sequence is treated as a single character.

**Table 2.1** Some of the escape sequences used in Python

| Escape Sequence | Purpose | Example | Output |
|---|---|---|---|
| `\\` | Prints backslash | `print("\\")` | `\` |
| `\'` | Prints single-quote | `print("\'")` | `'` |
| `\"` | Prints double-quote | `print("\"")` | `"` |
| `\a` | Rings bell | `print("\a")` | Bell rings |
| `\f` | Prints form feed character | `print("Hello\fWorld")` | Hello<br>    World |
| `\n` | Prints newline character | `print("Hello\nWorld")` | Hello<br>World |
| `\t` | Prints a tab | `print("Hello\tWorld")` | Hello   World |
| `\o` | Prints octal value | `print("\o56")` | . |
| `\x` | Prints hex value | `print("\x65")` | e |

**Multi-line Strings:** When specifying a string, if a single backslash (\) at the end of the line is added then it indicates that the string is continued in the next line, but no new line is added otherwise. For example,

```
>>> print("Hello World,\
Good Morning !!!")
Hello World, Good Morning !!!
```

**Raw Strings:** If you want to specify a string that should not handle any escape sequences and want to display exactly as specified, then you need to specify that string as a *raw string*. A raw string is specified by prefixing r or R to the string.

> Raw strings are not processed in any special way, not even the escape sequences.

```
>>> R"How\'s life at your end?"
"How\\'s life at your end?"
```

**String Formatting:** We have already used the built-in `format()` function to format floating-point numbers. The same function can also be used to control the display of strings. The syntax of `format()` function is given as,

```
format(value, format_specifier)
```

where, `value` is the value or the string to be displayed, and `format_specifier` can contain a combination of formatting options.

**Example:** Commands to display 'PYTHON' left-justified, right-justified and centre-aligned in a field width of 30 characters.

```
>>> format('PYTHON','<30')      >>> format('PYTHON','>30')      >>> format('PYTHON','^30')
'PYTHON                    '    '                    PYTHON'    '           PYTHON             '
```

Here, the `'<'` symbol means to left justify. Similarly, to right justify the string use the `'>'` symbol and the `'^'` symbol to centrally align the string.

```
>>> print('PYTHON',format('-','<10'),'PROGRAMMING'
PYTHON---------- PROGRAMMING
```

We have seen above that `format()` function uses blank spaces to fill the specified width. But you can also use the `format()` function to fill the width in the formatted string using any other character as shown below.

## Introduction to Programming Language Python

**String Concatenation:** Like numbers, we can also add two strings in Python. The process of combining two strings is called *concatenation*. Two strings, whether created using single or double quotes, are concatenated in the same way.

| | |
|---|---|
| `>>> 'HI...and.....' + 'BYE'`<br>`HI...and.....BYE` | `>>>'''PYTHON'''+'''PROGRAMMING'''`<br>`'PYTHONPROGRAMMING'` |
| `>>>'''PYTHON'''+''' PROGRAMMING'''`<br>`'PYTHON PROGRAMMING'` | |

**Slice a String:** A substring of a string is called a **slice**. You can extract subsets of strings by using the slice operator (`[ ]` and `[:]`). You need to specify index or the range of index of characters to be extracted. The index of the first character is 0 and the index of the last character is $n - 1$, where $n$ is the number of characters in the string.

```
Index from     P    Y    T    H    O    N
the start      0    1    2    3    4    5    Index from
              -6   -5   -4   -3   -2   -1    the end
```

The syntax of slice operation is s[start:end:stride], where start specifies the beginning index of the sub-string and end is the index of the last character of the string s. *Omitting either start or end index, by default, takes the start or end of the string. Omitting both means the entire string is taken.*

If you want *to extract characters starting from the end of the string, then you must specify the index as a negative number.* For example, the index of the last character is –1.

***Specifying Stride while Slicing Strings:*** In the slice operation, you can specify a third argument as the ***stride***. The stride specifies the number of characters to move forward after the first character is retrieved from the string. By default, the value of stride is 1, which means that every character between two index numbers is retrieved. If stride is 2, then every second character is accessed, if stride is 3 then every third character is accessed, and so on.

```
#Slice operation on string
>>> str = "Python Programming is Fun"
>>> str[0]           #prints the first character
P
>>> str[4:10]        #prints characters from 4 to 9
on Pro
>>> str[5:]          #prints all characters staring from fifth character
n Programming is Fun
>>> str[-1]          # prints the last character
n
>>> str[:-1]         #prints all except the last character
Python Programming is Fu
>>> str[-7:]         #prints last seven character
is Fun
>>> str[3:15:2]      #prints every 2nd character from 3rd - 15th character
'hnPorm'
```

Did you notice that when we use the slice operator, elements are accessed from left towards right? For any index $n$ (positive or negative), s[:n] + s[n:] = s. This means that the slice operation always partitions the string into two parts in such a way that all characters are conserved.

Even the whitespace characters are skipped as they are also a part of the string. *If you omit the first two arguments and only specify the third one, then the entire string is used in steps.* We can even have a negative value in the stride. For example, if the value of stride is –1, then the string is printed in reverse order.

| `#print every third character`<br>`str ="Python programming is fun"`<br>`print(str[::3])`<br>`OUTPUT`<br>`Ph oai n` | `#print string in reverse`<br>`str = "Python programming is fun"`<br>`print(str[::-1])`<br>`OUTPUT`<br>`nuf si gnimmargorp nohtyP` |
|---|---|

```
#print every second character in the
#reversed string
str ="Python programming is fun"
print(str[::-2])
OUTPUT
nfs nmagr otP
```

## 2.13 TYPE CONVERSION

In Python, it is not possible to complete certain operations that involve different types of data. For example, it is not possible to perform "4" + 7 since one operand is an integer and the other is of string type.

Another situation in which type conversion is a must is when you want to accept a non-string value (integer or float) as an input. The input() function which accepts input(s) from the user takes it as a string. In case you want the user to enter a numeric value then the string value must be explicitly type-casted to numbers (integers or floats) so that calculations can be performed on them. In such situations, you must perform conversions between data types.

```
>>> "7" + "4"        >>> int("7") + int("3")
'74'                 10
```

```
x = input("Enter the first number : ")        x = int(input(" Enter the first number : "))
y =input("Enter the second number : ")        y = int(input("Enter the second number : "))
print(x + y)                                  print(x + y)
OUTPUT                                        OUTPUT
Enter the first number : 7                    Enter the first number : 7
Enter the second number : 4                   Enter the second number : 4
74                                            11
```

Python provides several built-in functions to convert a value from one data type to another. These functions return a new object representing the converted value. Some of them are given in Table 2.2.

**Table 2.2** Some commonly used built-in functions in Python

| Function | Description | Example |
|---|---|---|
| `int(x)` | Converts x to an integer | `int(3.5) gives 3` |
| `float(x)` | Converts x to a floating point number | `float('123') gives 123.0` |
| `str(x)` | Converts x to a string | `str(123.45) gives '123.45'` |
| `tuple(x)` | Converts list x to a tuple | `tuple([1,2,3]) gives (1, 2, 3)` |
| `list(x)` | Converts tuple x to a list | `list((1,2,3)) gives [1, 2, 3]` |
| `set(x)` | Converts x to a set | `set([1,2,3]) gives {1, 2, 3}` |
| `ord(x)` | Converts a single character to its integer value. | `ord('D') gives 68` |
| `oct(x)` | Converts an integer to an octal string. | `oct(9) gives 'Oo11'` |
| `hex(x)` | Converts an integer to a hexadecimal string. | `hex(1234) gives '0x4d2'` |
| `chr(x)` | Converts an integer to a character. | `chr(70) gives 'F'` |
| `complex(x)` | Converts to a complex number | `complex(3,-8) gives (3-8j)` |

However, before using type conversions to convert a floating-point number into an integer number, remember that int() converts a float to an integer by truncation (discarding the fractional part) and not by rounding to the nearest whole number. The round() works more appropriately by rounding a floating-point number to the nearest integer as shown below. The round() can even take a second, optional argument which is usually a number that indicates the number of places of precision to which the first argument should be rounded.

```
>>> int(3.7)        >>> round(3.7)        >>> round(1234.56789012,2)
3                   4                     1234.57
```

Note that each argument passed to a function has a specific data type. If you pass an argument of the wrong data type to a function, it will generate an error. For example, you cannot find the square root of a string. If you don't know what type of arguments a function accepts, you should use the `help()` before using the function.

## Key Terms

**Statement:** A statement in Python is an instruction given to the computer to perform any kind of action.
**String:** A string is a group of characters.
**String concatenation:** The process of combining two strings.
**Slice:** A sub-string of a string is called a slice.

## Chapter Highlights

- GIGO stands for 'Garbage-In–Garbage-Out'. It means that if we give incorrect data or instructions, then the computing system will give wrong results.
- Python is a high-level, interpreted, interactive, object-oriented and a reliable language.
- Once installed, the Python console can be accessed in several ways. First, using the command line and running the Python interpreter directly and second, using a GUI software that comes installed with Python called IDLE.
- If you want to execute a program in Python shell, press **F5** key or click on Run Menu and then select **Run Module**.
- The character set of a language is a set of valid characters that the language can recognize. Such characters may be digits, alphabets, or any other symbol.
- Tokens are the small units of the programming language. Python supports literals, keywords, identifiers and operators as tokens.
- Number, as the name suggests, refers to a numeric value. You can use four types of numbers in Python programs. These are integers, long integers, floating-point and complex numbers.
- When two very large floating-point numbers are multiplied, it may result in an *arithmetic overflow*. Arithmetic overflow is a condition that occurs when a calculated result is too large.
- Arithmetic underflow occurs when one floating-point number is divided by another. It is a condition that occurs when a calculated result is too small in magnitude to be represented.
- Any floating-point value may contain an arbitrary number of decimal places, so it is always recommended to use the built-in `format()` function to produce a string version of a number with a specific number of decimal places. It can also be used to control the display of strings.
- A raw string does not handle any escape sequence. It is specified by prefixing r or R to the string.

## Review Questions

1. Explain the features of Python.
2. Give some applications of Python.
3. What do you understand by the term 'Python character set'?
4. Write a short note on literals in Python.
5. What problems can pop up while dealing with floating-point numbers?
6. With the help of an example, explain the use of `format()` function.
7. What is a string in Python? Explain the different ways in which you can define a string.
8. Differentiate between implicit conversion and type conversion.
9. What is an escape sequence? Give examples. Why are they called so?

10. Write the commands to display the text "I love programming" in a width of 50 characters when the text is left-justified, right justified and centre aligned.
11. Write a command to print a string in reverse.
12. Justify the statement, "Python is a free and open-source programming language."
13. Which of the following expressions would result in overflow or underflow error? Justify your answer.
    a. `1.23e+150*4.56e+100`      b. `6.78e-100/4.67e+200`
14. Identify the expressions which will involve coercion and the ones which will involve explicit type conversion.
    a. `5.0+2`    b. `6.5*3.0`    c. `7.0+float(8)`    d. `6.2*5.0`    e. `5.7+int(9.0)`
15. Find and correct the error (if any).
    a. `>>> print('It is Teacher's Daty today ')`
    b. `>>> print("Rohan knows "Hindi","English","Punjabi"")`

## Fill in the Blanks

1. A _____ in Python is an instruction given to the computer to perform any kind of action.
2. _____ means that if we give incorrect data or instructions, then it will give wrong results.
3. _____ means looking for patterns in the puzzles and categorizing them.
4. Python files are stored with a _____ extension.
5. The _____ function prints one or more literals (or values) followed by a newline.
6. To execute Python script file, _____ key is pressed.
7. _____ are the small units of the programming language.
8. Large floating-point numbers are efficiently represented in _____ notation.
9. _____ denotes that an arithmetic overflow has occurred.
10. _____ function is used to produce a string version of a number with specific number of decimal places.
11. The ____ prefix specifies that the file contains text written in language other than English.
12. A _____ is specified by prefixing r or R to the string.
13. The process of combining two strings is called _____.
14. The _____ specifies the number of characters to move forward after the first character is retrieved from the string.

## State True or False

1. Python is an interpreted programming language.
2. Python is an open-source programming language.
3. Programmers can embed Python programs within their C, C++ codes.
4. Parallel processing can be done in Python.
5. Integers can be specified as octal and hexadecimal numbers also.
6. Arithmetic underflow is a condition that occurs when a calculated result is too large.
7. Strings are mutable in Python.
8. When specifying a string, if a single backslash (\) at the end of the line is added then it indicates that the string is continued in the next line, but no new line is added otherwise.
9. A Unicode string does not handle any escape sequences. It is specified by prefixing r or R to the string.
10. `format()` function can be used to control the display of strings.
11. The default value of stride is 0.
12. Whitespace characters are also counted as a character in the string.
13. Computational thinking means thinking like a computer or to give instructions to a computer.

14. Coding is not a part of computational thinking.
15. Computational thinking involves considering different options carefully before deciding upon the best one.
16. \r represents a newline.
17. An escape sequence is treated as a single character.

## Multiple Choice Questions

1. Python is a _____ language.
   a. high-level     b. interpreted     c. object-oriented     d. all of these
2. Python programs work on any of the operating system without requiring any change. This means that Python is _____.
   a. interactive     b. simple     c. portable     d. dynamic
3. Which of the following is not a valid token in Python?
   a. Character set     b. Literals     c. Identifiers     d. Keywords
4. Which of the following is not a valid literal constant in Python?
   a. 1.2     b. 5     c. H5     d. "H5"
5. Which of the following is not a valid number in Python?
   a. 50000000000L     b. 5E10
   c. 5000000000.123455D     d. 3 – 8i
6. The value _____ indicates that an arithmetic underflow has occurred.
   a. -inf     b. inf     c. 0.0     d. All of these.
7. Which of the following is known as the exponentiation operator?
   a. %     b. //     c. **     d. ^
8. By default, the format() function uses ____ character to fill the specified width.
   a. blank space     b. >     c. <     d. ^
9. A string can be sliced using which of the following operators?
   a. []     b. [:]     c. both a and b     c. None of these.
10. The index of the first character is ____ and the index of the last character is ____, where *n* is the number of characters in the string.
    a. 0, *n*     b. 0, *n* – 1     c. 1, *n*     d. 1, *n* – 1
11. The index of the last character is _____.
    a. –1     b. 0     c. *n* – 1     d. *n*
12. Which of the following statements is syntactically not correct.
    a. a = input ( )
    c. a = input (enter a number)
    b. a = input ("enter a number")
    d. a = INPUT ("enter a number")
13. Which of the following statement is correct?
    a. a = 10 * 5     b. 50 = 10 * 5     c. 15 + 60 = y     d. print 3 * 4
14. Identify the invalid string literal.
    a. 'PYTHON'     b. «PYTHON»     c. "PYTHON"     d. «»PYTHON»»
15. Identify the valid floating-point value.
    a. 9     b. 23/4     c. 123,456.67     d. 1.2
16. Which of the following is a valid long floating-point value.
    a. 1.2e     b. 1.2e2.3     c. 1.2e01     d. 1,234e9
17. Which of the following is not a valid integer literal in Python?
    a. 0o123     b. 0x123     c. 0X123     d. 0123

## Give the Output

1. ```
   print("Hello")
   print("My Dear Students", end = ' ')
   print("Let us learn Python")
   print("Programming")
   ```
2. `>>> format(10**25,'.2e')`
3. `>>> format(987654321.315978,',..3f')`
4. `>>> 'PYTHON'`
5. `>>> "PROGRAMMING IN PYTHON"`
6. `>>> ''' I ENJOY PROGRAMMING`
   `IN`
   `PYTHON'''`
7. `>>> 'PYTHON' "PROGRAMMING"`
8. `>>> print("Python Programming \ is FUN !!!!")`
9. `>>> print(R'It is Teacher's Day today ')`
10. `>>> "I" + 'LOVE' + '''PROGRAMMING'''`
11. ```
    str = "I Love Programming in Python"
    print(str[0])
    print(str[7])
    print(str[-5])
    print(str[7:10])
    print(str[::2])
    print(str[3:11:3])
    print(str[:-7])
    print(str[-6:])
    ```
12. `>>> print(type(int('10')))`
13. `>>> str(print())+»abc»`
14. `>>> print(print(«abc»))`
15. `>>> str(print(«abc»))+»xyz»`
16. `>>> print(print("abc",end=" "))`
17. `(10<20) and (20 < 10) or (5 < 30) and not (15 < 40)`

## Answers

### Fill in the Blanks
1. statement
2. GIGO
3. Pattern recognition
4. .py
5. print()
6. F5
7. Tokens
8. scientific
9. Infinity (inf)
10. `format()`
11. 'U'
12. raw string
13. string concatenation
14. stride

### State True or False
1. False
2. True
3. True
4. True
5. True
6. False
7. True
8. True
9. False
10. True
11. False
12. True
13. False
14. True
15. True
16. False
17. True

### Multiple Choice Questions
1. d
2. c
3. a
4. c
5. c
6. c
7. c
8. a
9. c
10. b
11. a
12. c
13. a
14. d
15. d
16. c
17. d

### Give the Output
1. ```
   Hello
   My Dear Students Let us learn Python
   Programming
   ```
2. `'1.00e+25'`
3. `'987,654,321.316'`
4. `'PYTHON'`
5. `'PROGRAMMING IN PYTHON'`
6. `' I ENJOY PROGRAMMING\nIN\nPYTHON'`
7. `'PYTHONPROGRAMMING'`
8. `Python Programming is FUN !!!!`
9. `It is Teacher's Day today`
10. `'ILOVEPROGRAMMING'`
11. ```
    I
    P
    y
    Pro
    ILv rgamn nPto
    o o
    I Love Programming in
    Python
    ```
12. `<class 'int'>`
13. `'Noneabc'`
14. ```
    abc
    None
    ```
15. ```
    abc
    'Nonexyz'
    ```
16. ```
    abc
    None
    ```
17. False
    ```

# Python – Building Blocks

## 3

### Chapter Objectives

This chapter allows readers to understand the basic building blocks of Python. The topics listed below are discussed here in detail.

- Variables and identifiers
- Creating, initializing and assigning values to variables
- Multiple assignments that is unique to Python
- Relevance of comments in program code
- Data types, operators and expressions
- Indentation that may change the logic of the program altogether

We have already seen that a statement in Python is an instruction that performs an action. A statement may or may not display a value. For example, the statement, sum = 2 + 3, adds two values but does not display any value. But the statement, print(sum) displays the value that we obtain after adding 2 and 3.

In Python, no symbol is used to terminate a statement. Users just have to press the Enter key after typing the statement. Although we can type multiple statements in a single line using semi-colon (;) between the two statements, it is always better to type one statement in a single line for more clarity. So, avoid writing the two statements as,

> A line in Python can contain maximum 79 characters.

```
>>> sum = 2 + 3; print(sum)
5
```

In the last chapter, we started learning about tokens in Python. We have already covered literals. In this section, we will read about other tokens like keywords, identifiers and operators.

## 3.1 VARIABLES AND INDENTIFIERS

Using just literal constants, nothing much can be done in programs. For developing complex programs, we must store information to manipulate it as and when required. This is where *variables* can help.

Variable, in simple terms, means something that may change. We can store any piece of information in a variable and this information may change. For example, a variable `today_temp` may have value = 30 today but tomorrow it may be 29 or 31.

Thus, we see that in Python, variable represents a named location that has a value which can be processed as and when required (as for calculating values).

To be identified easily, each variable is given an appropriate name. Variable names are examples of **identifiers**. *Identifiers*, as the name suggests, are names given to identify something. This something can be a variable, function, class, module or other objects. For naming any identifier, there are some basic rules that you must follow. These rules are:

- The first character of an identifier must be an underscore ('_') or a letter (upper or lowercase).
- The rest of the identifier name can be underscores ('_'), letters (upper or lowercase), or digits (0–9).
- Identifier names are case-sensitive. For example, myvar and myVar are **not** the same.
- Punctuation characters such as @, $, and % are not allowed within identifiers.

**Remember:** Python is a case-sensitive language.

*Examples of valid identifier names* are sum, __my_var, num1, r, var_20, First, etc.

*Examples of invalid identifier names* are 1num (starting with a digit), my-var (punctuation and special characters not allowed), %check (first character should be an alphabet or an underscore), Basic Sal (space not allowed), H#R&A (special characters not allowed), etc.

## 3.1.1 Creating Variables

To create a variable in Python, just assign a value to the identifier using the 'equal to' sign (also known as the assignment operator). For example, the following statements create variables with different values in Python.

```
num = 7
float_num = 12.34
ch = 'A'
str = "ABC"
print(num)
print(float_num)
print(ch)
print(str)
```

**OUTPUT**
```
7
12.34
A
ABC
```

When we create a variable, Python creates labels referring to those values as shown in Fig. 3.1.

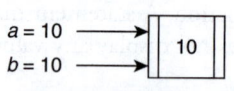

Here, both variables *a* and *b* have the same value. A label with value 10 is created and both variables point to the same label.

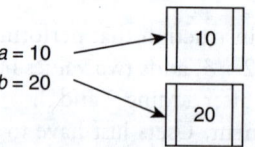

Here, the value of the variables are changed. Both variables *a* and *b* have differrent values. A label with label 20 is created and both variables point to their label.

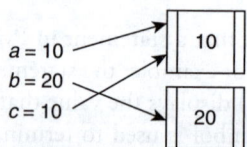

Here, both variables *a* and *b* have different values. A label with value 10 and another with label 20 are created and both variables point to their respective labels. When the variable *c* is created with same value as that of *a*, it points to the label to which *a* is pointing.

**Figure 3.1** Creating labels

Do you know that Python IDLE remembers variables and their values? Just type the following lines in the command console of IDLE and observe the output.

```
>>> x = 10
>>> y = 20
>>> str1 = "HELLO"
>>> print(str1)
HELLO
>>> print(x * y)
200
```

## 3.1.2 Data Types of Identifiers

In any programming language, data type is a classification that specifies which type of value a variable has. It also specifies the type of mathematical, relational or logical operations that can be applied to it without causing an error. For example, a string data type is used to hold textual data. An integer is a data type that can store whole numbers.

Python has various standard data types that are used to define the operations possible on them and the storage method for each of them. Based on the data type of a variable, the interpreter reserves memory for it and also determines the type of data that can be stored in the reserved memory.

*The five standard data types supported by Python include numbers, string, list, tuple, and dictionary.* We can even create our own data types in Python (like classes). In this chapter, we will learn about numbers and strings. Other data types will be explored in subsequent chapters.

> **Remember:** Python is a purely object-oriented language. It refers to everything as an object including numbers and strings.

### 3.1.3 Assigning or Initializing Values to Variables

In Python, programmers need not explicitly declare variables to reserve memory space. The declaration is done automatically when a value is assigned to the variable using the equal sign (=). The operand on the left side of equal sign is the name of the variable and the operand on its right side is the value to be stored in that variable.

**Program to Display Data of Different Types using Variables and Literal Constants**

```
age = 27
salary = 1234567
gender = 'M'
name = "Siva"

print("NAME:"+name)             # To convert integer to a string
print("AGE:"+str(age))
print("SALARY:"+str(salary))
print("GENDER:"+gender)         # To concatenate or to join two strings
```

OUTPUT

```
NAME : Siva
AGE  : 27
SALARY : 1234567
```

To run this program, type the code in IDLE. Save it with a suitable name with an extension .py. Press F5 or click on *Run* and then on *Run Module*.

In the code, the program assigns literal constant 27 to the variable age using the assignment operator (=). Similarly, we have assigned literal constants to other variables and then printed their values.

*In Python, you can reassign variables as many times as you want to change the value stored in them. You may even store value of one data type in a statement and then a value of another data in a subsequent statement.* This is possible because Python variables do not have specific types; so you can assign an integer to a variable, and later assign a string to the same variable.

**Program to Reassign Values to a Variable**

```
age = 27 = 1              # age is an integer
print("AGE: ", age)

age = 'TWELVE'            # age is a string
print("AGE: ", age)

age = 15.6                # age is a floating point number
print("AGE: ", age)
```

**OUTPUT**

```
AGE: 27
AGE :TWELVE
AGE: 15.6
```

While re-assigning values to variables, be cautious about ensuring that the right type of value is used in operations. This is very much evident from the code given below.

```
a = 10
a = a*10
print(a)
a = "PYTHON"
a = a/10
print(a)
```

**OUTPUT**
```
100
Traceback (most recent call last) :
  File "C : \Python37\try .py" , line 5, in <module>
    a = a/10
TypeError: unsupported operand type(s) for /:
' str ' and ' int'
```

**The type() Function** The type() function having the syntax type(object) is used to determine the data type of the object. This function should be used to ensure that the right type of values is used in the expressions.

```
num = 10
print (type (num))
val = 3 . 4
print (type (val))
ch = ' a'
print (type (ch))
str = "abc"
print (type (str))
```

**OUTPUT**
```
<class 'int'>
<class 'float'>


<class 'str'>
<class 'str'>
```

**lvalue and rvalue** As the name suggests, expressions that come on the left side of the assignment operator are known as the lvalue. Correspondingly, expressions that come on the right side of the assignment operator are known as the rvalue.

This means that, lvalues are those objects to which values can be assigned. And rvalues are the literals. That is, they are expressions that evaluate a value and come on the right-hand side of the assignment operator.

Remember that

- literals or expressions that evaluate a value cannot come on the left-hand side of the assignment operator.
- variable names can come on the left-hand side of the assignment operator.

| Valid lvalue and rvalue | Invalid lvalue and rvalue |
|---|---|
| a = 10 | 10 = a |
| B = 1*20 | a*20 = b |

## 3.2 MULTIPLE ASSIGNMENTS

Python allows programmers to assign a single value to more than one variable simultaneously. For example,

```
sum = flag = a= b = 0
```

In the above statement, all four integer variables are assigned a value 0. You can also assign different values to multiple variables simultaneously as shown below.

```
sum, a, b, mesg = 0, 3, 5, "RESULT"
```

Here, variable sum, *a*, and *b* are integers (numbers) and mesg is a string. sum is assigned a value 0, *a* is assigned 3, *b* is assigned 5 and mesg is assigned "RESULT".

Remember that *trying to reference a variable that has not been assigned any value causes an error*. This may happen if you have mistakenly used a variable without assigning it a value prior to its use or have deliberately deleted or removed a variable using the del statement and then tried to use it later in your code. The examples given below illustrate this concept.

Also remember that the right-hand side expression is evaluated before assignment is done and if there are multiple expressions in a statement separated by commas, then expressions on the RHS are evaluated from *left to right* and assigned in the same order.

```
x,y = 10,20
y,y = y+5, y-20   # last value of y persists
print("x = ",x, " y = ",y)
```

**OUTPUT**
x = 10 y = 0

*Programs to assign and access variables*

```
>>>name= "Kartik"
>>>age= 15
>>> print(name)
Kartik
>>> print(grade)
Traceback (most recent call last):
  File "<pyshell#8>", line 1, in <module>
    print(grade)
NameError: name 'grade' is not defined
```

*Variable not declared prior to use*

```
>>>name= "Kartik"
>>>age= 15
>>> grade = 'O'
>>> print(name)
Kartik
>>>del age
>>> print(age)
Traceback (most recent call last):
  File "<pyshell#14>", line 1, in <module>
    print( age)
NameError: name 'age' is not defined
```

*Variable being used after it is deleted*

### 3.2.1 Data Type Boolean

Boolean is another data type in Python. A variable of Boolean type can have one of the two values – *True* or *False*. Similar to other variables, the Boolean variables are also created while we assign a value to them or when we use a relational operator on them.

**Remember:** Boolean variables are also created by comparing values using the == operator.

| `>>>Boolean_ var =True`<br>`>>>Boolean_var`<br>`True` | `>>> 30 ==50`<br>`False` | `>>>"HELLO" == 'HELLO'`<br>`True` |
|---|---|---|
| `>>> 10 !=10`<br>`False` | `>>"Python3.7" != "Python3.4"`<br>`True` | `>>>50>80`<br>`False` |
| `>>> 20 <=20`<br>`True` | `>>> 13 == 13.0`<br>`False` | `>>>13>=13.0`<br>`True` |

## 3.3 INPUT OPERATION

Real-world programs need to be interactive. By interactive, we mean that you need to take some sort of input or information from the user and work on that input to get the desired result.

*To take input from the users, Python makes use of the* `input()` *function.* The `input()` function prompts the user to provide some information on which the program can work and give the result. However, we must always remember that the *input function takes user's input as a string.* So, whether you input a number or a string, it is treated as a string only.

### Program to Read Variables from the User

```
name= input("What's your name?")
age = input("Enter your age:")
print(name+ ",you are" +age+ " years old")
```

OUTPUT
What's your name? Goransh
Enter your age : 13
Goransh, you are 13 years old

**To read integers or floating-point numbers using the `input()` function**, you must use the `int()` and the `float()` function respectively. The `int()` function is used to convert a non-integer value to an integer. Similarly, the `float()` function is used to convert a non-floating-point value into a floating-point value. Hence, the output of the `input()` function which returns a string value can be passed to the `int()` or `float()` function to get a numeric value.

```
a = int (input ("Enter a number : "))
a = a + 10
print(a)
```

OUTPUT
Enter a number : 10
20

```
marks = float(input("Enter your total marks : "))
avg = marks/5.0
print (avg)
```

OUTPUT
Enter your total marks : 495
99.0

## 3.4 COMMENTS

Comments are added in a program to describe the statements in the program code. They make the program easily readable and understandable by the programmer as well as other users who are seeing the code. In Python, a hash sign (#) that is not inside a string literal begins a comment. *All characters following the # and up to the end of the line are part of the comment.*

### Program to use Comments

```
#Program to find the cost of a dozen pens
price_1 = int(input("Enter the price of 1 pen : "))
price_12 = price_1 * 12  # dozen means 12
print("Price of a dozen pens= ", price_12)
```

OUTPUT
Enter the price of 1 pen : 10
Price of a dozen pens = 120

### Some important points to remember about comments are:
- Comments are the non-executable statements in a program.
- The interpreter simply ignores the comments.
- When the program is run, comments are not displayed.
- Comments can be either typed in a new line or on the same line after a statement or expression.
- A program can have any number of comments.

## 3.4.1 Multi-line Comments

In Python, multi-line comments are also known as docstrings. They can be specified in two ways. First, by using three single quotes (or apostrophe). Second, by using three double quotes. They are used when explanation of the statements cannot be sufficiently given in one line. The code given below demonstrates the use of multi-line comments.

```
''' adding two
numbers'''
sum = 2 + 3
print(sum)
"""calculating average
of the two numbers
"""
avg = sum/2.0
print(avg)
```

**OUTPUT**
5
2.5

Did you notice that comments are not printed?

## 3.5 RESERVED WORDS

In every programming language there are certain words which have a pre-defined meaning. These words also known as reserved words or keywords that cannot be used for naming identifiers. Table 3.1 shows a list of Python keywords.

> All the Python keywords contain lowercase letters only.

**Table 3.1** Reserved words in Python

| and  | assert  | break | class | continue | def    | del    | elif  | else | except |
|------|---------|-------|-------|----------|--------|--------|-------|------|--------|
| exec | finally | for   | from  | global   | if     | import | in    | is   | lambda |
| not  | or      | pass  | print | raise    | return | try    | while | with | yield  |

## 3.6 INDENTATION

Whitespace at the beginning of the line is called *indentation*. These whitespaces or indentations are very important in Python. In a Python program, the leading whitespace including spaces and tabs at the beginning of the logical line determines the indentation level of that logical line.

The level of indentation groups statements to form a block of statements. This means that statements in a block must have the same indentation level. Python checks the indentation level very strictly and gives an error if indentation is not correct.

In the code below, there is a tab at the beginning of the second line. The error indicated by Python tells us that there is an indentation error. Python does not allow you to arbitrarily start new blocks of statements.

```
a= 10
    a=a+1      #Indentation Error
print(a)
```

```
a = 10
a = a + 1
print(a)
```

**OUTPUT**
11

> **Remember:** Use a single tab for each indentation level.

Like other programming languages, Python does not use curly braces ({...}). Therefore, to indicate blocks of code for class and function definitions or for flow control (discussed later in the book), it uses only indentation to form a block. *All statements inside a block should be at the same indentation level.*

## 3.7 OPERATORS AND EXPRESSIONS

Operators are the constructs that are used to manipulate the value of operands. Some basic operators include +, −, * and /. An expression in a programming language is any valid combination of tokens that represents a value. There are two types of expressions:

**Simple expressions** in which there are only values. For example, 29.

**Complex expression** in which one or more operators are used on operand(s) to generate a value. For example, in the expression sum = 2 + 4. Here, 2 and 4 are operands and + is the operator. 10 * 8 / 2 is another example of a complex expression.

> Operands are values on which operators are applied to generate a value.

However, expressions can also be classified as arithmetic expressions, logical expressions, string expressions and relational expressions, where

- Arithmetic expressions consist of numbers and arithmetic operators.
- Logical expressions have literals or variables and logical operators.
- Relational expressions have literals or variables and relational operators.
- String expressions have string operands and string operators (like, * and +).

*Different operators supported by Python include:*
a. Arithmetic operators
b. Comparison (Relational) operators
c. Assignment operators
d. Logical operators
e. Unary operators
f. Bitwise operators
g. Membership operators
h. Identity operators

### 3.7.1 Arithmetic Operators

Some basic arithmetic operators are +, −, *, /, %, ** and //. You can apply these operators on numbers as well as on numeric variables to perform corresponding operations. For example, if *a* = 10 and *b* = 20, then the result of the operations can be shown as given in Table 3.2.

**Table 3.2** Arithmetic operators

| Operator | Description | Example | Output |
|---|---|---|---|
| + | Addition – Adds the operands | >>> print(a + b) | 30 |
| − | Subtraction – Subtracts operand on the right from the operand on the left of the operator | >>> print(a - b) | -10 |
| * | Multiplication – Multiplies the operands | >>> print(a * b) | 200 |
| / | Division – Divides operand on the left side of the operator with the operand on its right. The division operator returns the quotient. | >>> print(b / a) | 2.0 |
| % | Modulus – Divides operand on the left side of the operator with the operand on its right. The modulus operator returns the remainder. | >>> print(b % a) | 0 |
| // | Floor Division – Divides the operands and returns the quotient. It also removes the digits after the decimal point. If one of the operands is negative, the result is floored (rounded away from zero towards negative infinity). | >>> print(24//5)<br>>>> print( 24.0//5.0)<br>>>> print(-37//4)<br>>>> print(-17.0//3) | 4<br>4.0<br>-10<br>-5.0 |
| ** | Exponent – Performs exponential calculation. That is, it raises operand on the right side to the operand on the left of the operator. | >>> print(a**b) | $10^{20}$ |

## 3.7.2 Comparison Operators

Comparison operators, also known as *relational operators*, are used to compare the values on its either side and determine the relation between them. For example, assuming $a = 10$ and $b = 20$, we can use the comparison operators on them as specified in Table 3.3.

**Table 3.3** Comparison operator

| Operator | Description | Example | Output |
|---|---|---|---|
| == | Returns true if the two values are exactly equal. | `>>> print(a == b)` | False |
| != | Returns true if the two values are not equal. | `>>> print(a != b)` | True |
| > | Returns true if the value at the operand on the left side of the operator is greater than the value on its right side. | `>>> print(a > b)` | False |
| < | Returns true if the value at the operand on the right side of the operator is greater than the value on its left side. | `>>> print(a < b)` | True |
| >= | Returns true if the value at the operand on the left side of the operator is either greater than or equal to the value on its right side. | `>>> print (a >= b)` | False |
| <= | Returns true if the value at the operand on the right side of the operator is either greater than or equal to the value on its left side. | `>>> print (a <= b)` | True |

## 3.7.3 Assignment and In-place or Shortcut Operators

Assignment operator, as the name suggests, assigns value to the operand. In-place operators, also known as *shortcut operators*, that include +=, -=, *=, /=, %=, //= and **= allow you to write codes like num = num + 10 more concisely, as num += 3. Different types of assignment and in-place operators are given in Table 3.4.

> Remember that <, > operators can also be used to compare strings lexicographically.

**Example 3.1** Application of the += operator on strings

```
>>> str1 = "PYTHON"
>>> str2 = "PROGRAMMING"
>>> str1 += str2
>>> print(str1)
PYTHONPROGRAMMING
```

**Table 3.4** Assignment and In-place Operator

| Operator | Example |
|---|---|
| = | c = a, assigns value of a to c |
| += | a += b is same as a = a + b |
| -= | a -= b is same as a = a - b |
| *= | a *= b is same as a = a * b |
| /= | a /= b is same as a = a / b |
| %= | a %= b is same as a = a % b |
| //= | a //= b is same as a = a // b |
| **= | a **= b is same as a = a ** b |

## 3.7.4 Unary Operators

Unary operators act on single operands. Unary minus operator is strikingly different from the arithmetic operator that operates on two operands and subtracts the second operand from the first operand. When an operand is preceded by a unary minus sign, its value is negated.

For example, if a number is positive, it becomes negative when preceded with a unary minus operator. Similarly, if the number is negative, it becomes positive after applying the unary minus operator. Consider the given example.

> Remember that unlike other programming languages, Python does not support prefix and postfix increment or decrement operators.

```
>>>a = -5          >>>a = -5
>>>b = -a          >>>b = -a
>>>print(b)        >>>print(b)
OUTPUT             OUTPUT
5                  -5
```

## 3.7.5 Bitwise Operators

As the name suggests, bitwise operators perform operations at bit level. These operators include bitwise AND, bitwise OR, bitwise XOR, and shift operators. Bitwise operators expect their operands to be integers and treat them as a sequence of bits.

*Bitwise AND (&):* When we use the bitwise AND operator, the bit in the first operand is ANDed with the corresponding bit in the second operand. The bitwise-AND operator compares each bit of its first operand with the corresponding bit of its second operand. If both bits are 1, the corresponding bit in the result is 1 and 0 otherwise.

*Bitwise OR (|):* When we use the bitwise OR operator, the bit in the first operand is ORed with the corresponding bit in the second operand. The bitwise-OR operator compares each bit of its first operand with the corresponding bit of its second operand. If one or both bits are 1, the corresponding bit in the result is 1 and 0 otherwise.

*Bitwise XOR (^):* When we use the bitwise XOR operator, the bit in the first operand is XORed with the corresponding bit in the second operand. That is, the bitwise-XOR operator compares each bit of its first operand with the corresponding bit of its second operand. If one of the bits is 1, the corresponding bit in the result is1 and 0 otherwise.

*Bitwise NOT (~):* The bitwise NOT, or complement, is a unary operation that performs logical negation on each bit of the operand. By performing negation of each bit, it actually produces the ones' complement of the given binary value. Bitwise NOT operator sets the bit to 1, if it was initially 0 and sets it to 0, if it was initially 1.

The truth tables of these Bitwise operators are summarized in Table 3.5.

**Table 3.5** Truth tables for bitwise operators

| A | B | A&B | A | B | A\|B | A | B | A^B | A | !A |
|---|---|-----|---|---|------|---|---|-----|---|----|
| 0 | 0 | 0 | 0 | 0 | 0 | 0 | 0 | 0 | 0 | 1 |
| 0 | 1 | 0 | 0 | 1 | 1 | 0 | 1 | 1 | 1 | 0 |
| 1 | 0 | 0 | 1 | 0 | 1 | 1 | 0 | 1 | | |
| 1 | 1 | 1 | 1 | 1 | 1 | 1 | 1 | 0 | | |

```
>>> x = 6          >>> x = 6          >>> x = 6          >>> x = 6
>>> y = 8          >>> y = 8          >>> y = 8          >>> print(~x)
>>> print(x&y)     >>> print(x|y)     >>> print(x^y)     -7

OUTPUT             OUTPUT             OUTPUT
0                  14                 14
```

You can check the result of bitwise operator by converting a number into binary using the **bin() function**. For example, >>> bin(15) will give '0b1111'. >>> bin(7) gives '0b111'. >>> 15 & 7 gives 7, as 1 1 1 1 & 0 1 1 1 gives 0 1 1 1.

```
1111
0111
0111
```

## 3.7.6 Shift Operators

Python supports two bitwise shift operators. They are shift left (<<) and shift right (>>). These operations are used to shift bits to the left or to the right. The syntax for a shift operation can be given as: **operand op num,**

where the bits in operand are shifted left or right depending on the operator (left if the operator is << and right if the operator is>>) by number of places denoted by num.

If we left shift 01011101, then after first left shift we will get, 10111010. After second left shift, we will get, 01110100.

If we right shift 01011101, then after first right shift we will get, 00101110, After second left shift, we will get, 00010111.

```
>>> x = 5      >>> x= 80
>>> y = 4      >>> y = 4
>>> x >> y     >>>x >> y
80             5
```

When we apply a left shift, every bit in x is shifted to the left by one place. Therefore, the MSB (most significant bit) of x is lost and the LSB of x is set to 0.

If you observe carefully, you will notice that *shifting once to the left multiplies the number by 2*. On the contrary, when we apply a right shift, every bit in x is

> Remember that Bitwise operators cannot be applied to float or double variables.

shifted to the right by one place. Therefore, the LSB (least significant bit) of x is lost and the MSB of x is set to 0. *When we shift once to the right, it divides the number by 2.*

### 3.7.7 Logical Operators

Python supports three logical operators—logical AND, logical OR, and logical NOT. As in case of arithmetic expressions, the logical expressions are evaluated from left to right.

- *Logical AND:* Logical AND operator is used to simultaneously evaluate two conditions or expressions with relational operators. If expressions on both the sides (left and right side) of the logical operator are true, then the whole expression is true; else it is false. For example, (a > b) and (a > c), will return TRUE only if the value of a is greater than the values of b and c.
  *The AND operator tests the second operand only if the first operand is true.*

  > Remember that the Truth table of logical and, or and not is exactly same as that of Bitwise AND, OR and NOT operators.

- *Logical OR:* Logical OR operator is used to simultaneously evaluate two conditions or expressions with relational operators. If one or both the expressions of the logical operator is true, then the whole expression is true. This means that the expression is false only if both the expressions are false. For example, (a > b) or (a != b) will return TRUE if a is either greater than b or less than b. It will return FALSE if a is equal to b.
- *Logical NOT:* The logical NOT operator takes a single expression and negates the value of the expression. Logical NOT produces a zero if the expression evaluates to a non-zero value and produces a 1 if the expression produces a zero. In other words, it just reverses the value of the expression. For example,

```
>>> a = 10                          >>> a = 0
>>> b = not a   a is non-zero (or   >>> b = not a   a is zero (or FALSE) so
>>> print(b)    TRUE) so b is FALSE >>> print(b)    b is TRUE
False                               True
```

It can be noted that the *logical expressions operate in a shortcut (or lazy) fashion and stop the evaluation when it knows the final outcome for sure.* For example, in a logical expression involving logical AND, if the first operand is false, then the second operand is not evaluated as it is certain that the result will be false. Similarly, for a *logical expression involving logical OR, if the first operand is true, then the second operand is not evaluated as it is certain that the result will be true.*

### 3.7.8 Membership Operators

Python supports two types of membership operators – **in** and **not in**. These operators, as the name suggests, test for membership in a sequence such as strings, lists, or tuples that will be discussed in later chapters and are listed below.

```
>>> str1="HELLO"            >>> str1="HELLO"
>>> 'L' in str1             >>> 'e' not in str1
True                        True
>>> 'T' in str1             >>> 'E' not in str1
False                       False
```

- *in operator:* The operator returns True if a variable is found in the specified sequence and False otherwise.
- *not in operator:* The operator returns True if a variable is not found in the specified sequence and False otherwise.

```
>>> a = "r"
>>> str = "Good Morning"
>>> a in str
True
>>> 'R' in str
False
```

### 3.7.9 Identity Operators

Python supports two types of identity operators. These operators compare the memory locations of two objects and are given as follows.

> The id() function returns a unique id of the object. Every object in Python has its own unique id which is assigned to the object when it is cleared. This id is the object's memory address, and will be different for each time you run the program.

- **is Operator:** Returns True if operands or values on both sides of the operator point to the same object and False otherwise. For example, if *a* is *b* returns TRUE if id(a) is same as id(b).
- **is not Operator:** Returns True if operands or values on both sides of the operator do not point to the same object and False otherwise. For example, if *a* is not *b* returns TRUE if id(a) is not same as id(b).

***We have learnt that Python creates labels when a variable is created.*** Two variables with the same value refer to the same label and thus have the same id. This concept can be understood by the following example.

```
>>> a = 10
>>> b = 10
>>> a is b
True
>>> a = 20
>>> b = 10
>>> a is b
False
```

***When the is operator returns True, it also indicates that the equality operator will also return True. But this is not always applicable the other way.*** That is, two objects having the same value and returning True with equality operator may return False with the is operator. This generally happens in three cases.

- First, when input is taken from the user
- Second, with integer literals having several digits
- Third, with floating-point and complex numbers.

In all the cases, Python creates two different objects even if they have same value. This is illustrated below.

```
CASE 1:
>>> s1 = "HELLO"
>>> s2 = input("Enter a string:")
Enter a string : HELLO
>>> s1 == s2
True
>>> s1 is s2
False
```

```
CASE 2:
>>> s1="HELLO"
>>> n2 = 1234567
>>> n1 == n2
True
>>> n1 is n2
False
```

```
CASE 3:
>>> n1 = 1.23
>>> n2 = 1.23
>>> n1 == n2
True
>>> n1 is n2
False
```

## 3.7.10 Operators' Precedence and Associativity

Table 3.6 lists all operators from highest precedence to lowest. When an expression has more than one operator, then it is the relative priorities of the operators with respect to each other that determine the order in which the expression will be evaluated.

**Remember that,**

Operators are associated from left to right. This means that operators with same precedence are evaluated in a left-to-right manner.

Parentheses can change the order in which an operator is applied. The operator in parenthesis is applied first even if there is a higher priority operator in the expression.

```
>>>5*6+3
33
>>>5+6*3
23
```

*\* has higher precedence than +. Hence, first the operands will be multiplied and then addition will be performed.*

**Table 3.6** Operator precedence chart

| Operator | Description |
| --- | --- |
| () | Parenthesis (for grouping) |
| ** | Exponentiation |
| -, +,- | Complement, unary plus and minus |
| *, /, %, // | Multiply, divide, modulo and floor division |
| +,- | Addition and subtraction |
| >>, << | Right and left bitwise shift |
| & | Bitwise 'AND' |
| ^\| | Bitwise exclusive 'OR' and regular 'OR' |
| <=, <, >, >= | Comparison operators |
| <>, ==, != | Equality operators |
| =, %=, /=,\|/=, -=, +=,*=, **= | Assignment operators |
| Is, is not | Identity operators |
| In, not in | Membership operators |
| Not, or, and | Logical operators |

Let us try some more codes to see how operator precedence works in our expressions.

```
>>> (50 + 40) * 10 / 20
45.0
>>> 50+ (40 * 10) / 20
70.0
>>> 50*100/5//4
250.0
>>> ((50+ 40) * 20) / 10
180.0
>>> (False==False) or True
True
>>> ((50*100)/15)//4)
250.0
>>> (50+ 40) * (20 / 1o)
180.0
>>> False==(False or True)
False
>>> 50*(100/(5//14))
5000.0
```

## 3.8 EXPRESSIONS IN PYTHON

In any programming language, an expression is any legal combination of symbols (like variables, constants and operators) that represents a value. Every language has its own set of rules that define whether an expression is valid or invalid in that language. *In Python, an expression must have at least one operand (variable or constant) and can have one or more operators. On evaluating an expression, we get a value.*

Operand is the value on which the operator is applied. These operators use constants and variables to form an expression. A * B + C – 5 is an example of an expression, where, +, *, – are operators; A, B and C are variables and 5 is a constant. Some valid expressions in Python are: x = a / b, y = a * b, z = a^ b, x = a > b, etc. When an expression has more than one operator, then the expression is evaluated using the operator precedence chart.

An example of an illegal expression can be a+ –b or <y++. When the program is compiled, the validity of all expressions is checked. If an illegal expression is encountered, an error message is displayed.

In Python, we can categorize expressions based on the data type of the result obtained on evaluating an expression. These types of expressions include,

- *Constant Expressions* that involve only constants. Example: 8 + 9 – 2
- *Integral Expressions* that produce an integer result. Example:
  a = 10, b = 5
  c = a * b
- *Floating-point Expressions* produce floating-point results. Example: a * b / 2
- *Relational Expressions* return either *true* or *false* value. Example: c = a > b
- *Logical Expressions* combine two or more relational expressions and return a value as *true* or *false*. Example: a > b and y! = 0.
- *Bitwise Expressions* manipulate data at bit level. Example: x = y & z.
- *Assignment Expressions* assign a value to a variable. Example: c = 10.

> Remember that deleted variables can be used again in the code if and only if you reassign them some value.

## PROGRAMMER'S ZONE

1. **Write a program to enter a number and display its hex and octal equivalent and its square root.**
   ```
   num = int(input("Enter a number : "))
   print("Hexadecimal of " + str(num) + " : " + str(hex(num)))
   print("Octal of " + str(num) + " : " + str(oct(num)))
   print("Square root of " + str(num) + " : " + str(num**0.5))
   ```
   **OUTPUT**
   ```
   Enter a number : 17
   Hexadecimal of 17 : 0x11
   Octal of 17 : 0o21
   Square root of 17 : 4.123105625617661
   ```

2. **Write a program to read and print values of variables of different data types.**
   ```
   num = int(input("Enter Roll Number : "))
   fees = float(input("Enter Fees : "))
   ```

```
grade = input("Enter the grade : ")
name = input("Enter the name : ")
#Print the values of variables
print(ROLL NUMBER = ,num)
print(NAME = ,name)
print(FEES = ,fees)
print(GRADE = ,grade)
```

**OUTPUT**
```
Enter Roll Number : 1
Enter Fees : 99999
Enter the grade : A
Enter the name : Priya
ROLL NUMBER = 1
NAME = Priya
FEES = 99999.0
GRADE = A
```

3. **Write a program to calculate area of a triangle using Heron's formula.**
   (**Hint:** Heron's formula is given as: area = sqrt(S*(S-a)*(S-b)*(S-c)))
   ```
   a = float(input("Enter the first side of the triangle : "))
   b = float(input("Enter the second side of the triangle : "))
   c = float(input("Enter the third side of the triangle : "))
   print(a,b,c)
   S = (a+b+c)/2
   area = (S*(S-a)*(S-b)*(S-c))**0.5
   print("Area = ",area)
   ```

   **OUTPUT**
   ```
   Enter the first side of the triangle : 6
   Enter the second side of the triangle : 8
   Enter the third side of the triangle : 10
   6.0 8.0 10.0
   Area = 24.0
   ```

4. **Write a program to calculate the distance between two points.**
   ```
   x1 = (int(input("Enter the x coordinate of the first point : ")))
   y1 = (int(input("Enter the y coordinate of the first point : ")))
   x2 = (int(input("Enter the x coordinate of the second point : ")))
   y2 = (int(input("Enter the y coordinate of the second point : ")))
   distance = ((x2-x1)**2+(y2-y1)**2)**0.5
   print("Distance = ", distance)
   ```

   **OUTPUT**
   ```
   Enter the x coordinate of the first point : 1
   Enter the y coordinate of the first point : 1
   Enter the x coordinate of the second point : 5
   Enter the y coordinate of the second point : 5
   Distance = 5.656854249492381
   ```

5. **Write a program to perform addition, subtraction, multiplication, division, integer division, and modulo division on two integer numbers.**

```
num1 = int(input("Enter two numbers : "))
num2 = int(input("Enter two numbers : "))
add_res = num1+num2
sub_res = num1-num2
mul_res = num1*num2
idiv_res = num1//num2
modiv_res = num1%num2
fdiv_res = float(num1)/num2
print(num1, " + ", num2," = ", add_res)
print(num1, " - ", num2, " = ", sub_res)
print(num1, " * ", num2, " = ", mul_res)
print(num1," / ",num2," = ",idiv_res," (Integer Division)")
print(num1," // ",num2," = ",fdiv_res," (Float Division)")
print(num1," % ", num2," = ",modiv_res," (Modulo Division)")
```

**OUTPUT**
```
Enter two numbers : 25
Enter two numbers : 4
25 + 4 = 29
25 - 4 = 21
25 * 4 = 100
25 / 4 = 6 (Integer Division)
25 // 4 = 6.25 (Float Division)
25 % 4 = 1 (Modulo Division)
```

6. **Write a program that demonstrates the use of relational operators.**

```
x = 30
y = 10
print(x, " < ", y, " = ", x<y)
print(x, " == ", y, " = ", x==y)
print(x, " != ", y," = ", x!=y)
print(x, " > ", y," = ", x>y)
print(x, " >= ", y," = ", x>=y)
print(x, " <= ", y," = ", x<=y)
```

**OUTPUT**
```
30 < 10 = False
30 == 10 = False
30 != 10 = True
30 > 10 = True
30 >= 10 = True
30 <= 10 = False
```

7. **Write a program to calculate the volume of a cylinder.**

```
radius = float(input("Enter the radius : "))
height = float(input("Enter the height : "))
volume = 3.14*radius*radius*height
print("VOLUME = %.2f"%volume)
```

**OUTPUT**
```
Enter the radius : 7
Enter the height : 14
VOLUME = 2154.04
```

8. **Write a program to print the digit at one's place of a number.**
    ```
    num = int(input("Enter any number : "))
    digit_at_ones_place = num%10
    print("The digit at ones place is : ",digit_at_ones_place)
    ```

    **OUTPUT**
    ```
    Enter any number : 12345
    The digit at ones place of 12345 is 5
    ```

9. **Write a program to swap two numbers without using a temporary variable.**
    ```
    n1 = int(input("Enter the first number : "))
    n2 = int(input("Enter the second number : "))
    n1, n2 = n2, n1
    print("The first number is = ",n1," and the second number = ",n2)
    ```

    **OUTPUT**
    ```
    Enter the first number : 6
    Enter the second number : 9
    The first number is = 9 and the second number = 6
    ```

10. **Write a program to calculate the average of two numbers. Print their deviation.**
    ```
    n1 = int(input("Enter the two numbers : "))
    n2 = int(input("Enter the two numbers : "))
    avg = (n1+n2)/2
    dev1 = n1-avg
    dev2 = n2-avg
    print("AVERAGE = ",avg)
    print("Deviation of first num =",dev1)
    print("Deviation of second num =",dev2)
    ```

    **OUTPUT**
    ```
    Enter the two numbers : 10
    Enter the two numbers : 20
    AVERAGE = 15.0
    Deviation of first num = -5.0
    Deviation of second num = 5.0
    ```

11. **Write a program to convert degrees Fahrenheit into degrees Celsius.**
    ```
    Fahrenheit = float(input("Enter the temperature in Fahrenheit : "))
    Celsius = (0.56)*(Fahrenheit-32)
    print("Temperature in degrees Celsius = %.2f"%Celsius)
    ```

    **OUTPUT**
    ```
    Enter the temperature in Fahrenheit : 100
    Temperature in degrees Celsius = 38.08
    ```

12. **Write a program to calculate the total amount of money in the piggybank, given the coins of Rs 10, Rs 5, Rs 2, and Re 1.**

    ```
    num_of_10_coins = int(input("Enter the number of 10Rs coins in the piggybank : "))
    num_of_5_coins = int(input("Enter the number of 5Rs coins in the piggybank : "))
    num_of_2_coins = int(input("Enter the number of 2Rs coins in the piggybank : "))
    num_of_1_coins = int(input("Enter the number of 1Re coins in the piggybank : "))
    total_amt = num_of_10_coins*10+num_of_5_coins*5+num_of_2_coins*2+num_of_1_coins
    print("Total amount in the piggybank =",total_amt)
    ```

    **OUTPUT**
    ```
    Enter the number of 10Rs coins in the piggybank : 5
    Enter the number of 5Rs coins in the piggybank : 20
    Enter the number of 2Rs coins in the piggybank : 30
    Enter the number of 1Re coins in the piggybank : 50
    Total amount in the piggybank = 260
    ```

13. **Write a program to calculate the bill amount for an item, given its quantity sold, value, discount, and tax.**

    ```
    qty = float(raw_input("Enter the quantity of item sold : "))
    val = float(raw_input("Enter the value of item : "))
    discount = float(raw_input("Enter the discount percentage : "))
    tax = float(raw_input("Enter the tax : "))
    amt = qty*val
    discount_amt = (amt*discount)/100
    sub_total = amt-discount_amt
    tax_amt = (sub_total*tax)/100
    total_amt = sub_total + tax_amt
    print "**********BILL***********"
    print " Quantity sold : \t ",qty
    print "Price per item : \t",val
    print "\n \t \t ---------------"
    print "Amount : \t\t",amt
    print "Discount : \t\t-",discount_amt
    print " \t \t -----------------"
    print "Discounted Total : \t",sub_total
    print "Tax : \t\t\t + «",tax_amt
    print " \t \t -----------------"
    print "Total amount to be paid ",total_amt
    ```

    **OUTPUT**
    ```
    Enter the quantity of item sold : 10
    Enter the value of item : 100
    Enter the discount percentage : 15
    Enter the tax : 8
    **********BILL***********
     Quantity sold :    10.0
    Price per item :    100.0
            ---------------
    Amount :     1000.0
    ```

```
Discount :            - 150.0
                  ------------------
Discounted Total :   850.0
Tax :              + 68.0
                  ------------------
Total amount to be paid 918.0
```

14. **Write a program to calculate a student's result based on two examinations, 1 sports event and 3 activities conducted. The weightage of activities = 30 per cent, sports = 20 per cent, and examination = 50 per cent.**

```
ACTIVITIES_WEIGHTAGE = 30.0
SPORTS_WEIHTAGE = 20.0
EXAMS_WEIGHTAGE = 50.0
EXAMS_TOTAL = 200.0
ACTIVITIES_TOTAL = 60.0
SPORTS_TOTAL = 50.0
exam_score1 = int(input("Enter the marks in first examination (out of 100) : "))
exam_score2 = int(input("Enter the marks in second examination(out of 100) : "))
sports_score = int(input("Enter the score obtained in sports activities (out of 50) : "))
activities_score1 = int(input("Enter the marks in first activity (out of 20) : "))
activities_score2 = int(input("Enter the marks in second activity (out of 20) : "))
activities_score3 = int(input("Enter the marks in third activity (out of 20) : "))
exam_total = exam_score1 + exam_score2
activities_total = activities_score1 + activities_score2 + activities_score3
exam_percent = float(exam_total * EXAMS_WEIGHTAGE / EXAMS_TOTAL)
sports_percent = float(sports_score * SPORTS_WEIHTAGE / SPORTS_TOTAL)
activities_percent  =   float(activities_total  *  ACTIVITIES_WEIGHTAGE / ACTIVITIES_TOTAL)
total_percent = exam_percent + sports_percent + activities_percent
print("\n\n ********************** RESULT**************************")
print("\n Total percent in examination :", exam_percent)
print("\n Total percent in activities :",activities_percent)
print("\n Total percent in sports", sports_percent)
print("\n --------------------------------------------------------")
print("\n Total percentage", total_percent)
```

**OUTPUT**

```
Enter the marks in first examination (out of 100) : 89
Enter the marks in second examination(out of 100) : 80
Enter the score obtained in sports activities (out of 50) : 35
Enter the marks in first activity (out of 20) : 17
Enter the marks in second activity (out of 20) : 19
Enter the marks in third activity (out of 20) : 16
 ********************** RESULT**************************
Total percent in examination : 42.25
Total percent in activities : 26.0
Total percent in sports 14.0
--------------------------------------------------------
Total percentage 82.25
```

## Key Terms

**Variable:** Variable means something that may change. In Python programs, any piece of information can be stored in a variable and the information may change.

**Identifiers:** Names given to identify a variable, function, class, module or any other object.

**Lvalue:** Expressions that come on the left side of the assignment operator

**Rvalue:** Expressions that come on the right side of the assignment operator.

**Docstring:** In Python, multi-line comments are also known as docstring.

**Keywords:** Reserved words in a programming language that have a pre-defined meaning.

**Operators:** Constructs used to manipulate the value of operands.

**Operands:** Values on which the operator is applied.

**Expression:** An expression in a programming language is any valid combination of tokens that represents a value.

**Unary operator:** Operator applied on a single operand.

## Chapter Highlights

- To create a variable in Python, just assign a value to the identifier using the equal to sign.
- When we create a variable, Python creates labels referring to those values.
- Variables can hold values of different types called data types.
- Based on the data type of a variable, the interpreter reserves memory for it and also determines the type of data that can be stored in the reserved memory.
- The five standard data types supported by Python include – numbers, string, list, tuple, and dictionary.
- In Python, you can reassign variables as many times as you want to change the value stored in them. You may even store the value of one data type in a statement and then the value of another data in a subsequent statement.
- The `type()` function is used to determine data type of an object.
- Python allows programmers to assign a single value to more than one variable simultaneously.
- Trying to reference a variable that has not been assigned any value causes an error. This may happen if you have mistakenly used a variable without assigning it a value prior to its use or have deliberately deleted or removed a variable using the del statement and then tried to use it later in your code.
- A variable of Boolean type can have one of the two values – True or False.
- Comments are added in a program to describe the statements in the program code. They make the program easily readable and understandable by the programmer as well as other users who are seeing the code.
- To take input from the users, Python makes use of the `input()` function.
- Whitespace at the beginning of the line is called indentation. These whitespaces at the beginning of the logical line determines the indentation level of that logical line.
- Comparison operators, also known as relational operators, are used to compare the values on its either side and determine the relation between them.
- Unary operators act on single operands. When an operand is preceded by a unary minus sign, its value is negated.
- Python supports two bitwise shift operators. They are shift left (<<) and shift right (>>). These operations are used to shift bits to the left or to the right. The syntax for a shift operation can be given as: operand op num
- Python supports two types of membership operators – in and not in. These operators test for membership in a sequence such as strings, lists or tuples.

## Review Questions

1. What are identifiers? List some rules that must be kept in mind while naming an identifier.
2. With the help of a diagram explain what happens when a variable is created in Python.
3. With the help of an example explain how variables can be re-assigned values in Python.
4. Can we re-assign a value of another data type to a variable? If yes, why?
5. Differentiate between lvalue and rvalue.
6. What do you understand by the term multiple assignment?
7. What are Boolean variables? How are they created?
8. What are comments? How are they written in Python?
9. What is a docstring? How is it defined in a Python program?
10. Why is indentation necessary in Python?
11. Logical expressions operate in a shortcut (or lazy) fashion. Justify this statement.
12. Will the statement, print "Python # Programming" be executed? If yes, justify its output.
    **Hint:** The # is inside a string, so it is just considered as a character and not as comment.
13. Differentiate between = and ==.
    **Hint:** The = is used to assign value but the == is used to test if two things have the same value.
14. Which data type will you use to represent the following data values?
    a. Number of days in a week
    b. The circumference of a circle
    c. You school fees
    d. Distance between moon and the earth
    e. Your favorite book
    f. Whether or not you will take the entrance exam.
15. Which type of value will you use for storing the following information?
    a. Employee ID    b. Employee Name    c. Employee Salary    d. Phone Number
16. Which of the following are correct type conversions?
    a. int (8.2+6.3)
    b. str (5.6 * 6.7)
    c. float ("12"+"3.4")
    d. str ( 6/4 )
17. Express the following floating-point numbers in scientific notation:
    a. 123.456789    b. 0.000123456    c. 1.234567
18. Evaluate the following arithmetic expressions using the rules of operator precedence in Python.
    a. 4+5*10    b. 6+7*2+5    c. 20//4*2    d. 5*6**3    e. 24//6//3
    f. 4**2**3   g. 100-(15*3)   h. 50%7   i. -(100/6)+5
19. Write the following values in the exponential notation.
    a. 1230.4567    b. 0.00000056009    c. 7000809.000000000003
20. Evaluate the following expressions:
    a. True and False
    b. (100<10) and (100>50)
    c. True or False
    d. (100<10) or (100>200)
    e. not(True) and False
    f. not (100<10) or (100>50)
    g. not(True and False)
    h. not (100<10 or 100>50)
    i. not True and False
    j. 100<10 and not 100>50
    k. not True and False or True
    l. not (100<10 or 50<200)
21. Which of the following results in True?
    a. >>>90 == 90 and 11==11   b. >>>31==51 and 71==31   c. >>>72!=12 and 25==25
    d. >>>54<51 and 61>86   e. 15<20 or 20

22. Identify the correct arithmetic expression in Python:
    a. `10(13+76)`     b. `(15*16)(47+18)`   c. `14*(33-52)`   d. `15***2`

23. Give an appropriate Boolean expression for each of the following.
    a. Check if variable var is greater than or equal to 10, and less than 100.
    b. Check if variable var is less than 100 and greater than or equal to 10, or it is equal to 50.
    c. Check if either the name 'Kalam' or 'Azad' appears in a list of names assigned to variable names.
    d. Check if the name 'Abdul' appears and the name 'Maulana' does not appear in a list of names assigned to variable names.

23. Write the data types of the following:
    a. `type(5+4)`   b. `(20*345)`   c. `type(987/45)`   d. `type(2345//12)`   e. `type(123%34)`

24. Identify the data types of the following literals: 9, 29.4, 5j, 3+7i

25. Write the following expressions in Python:

    $\dfrac{-b \pm \sqrt{b^2 - 4ac}}{2a}$     $\sqrt{a^2 + b^2}$     $\dfrac{\pi}{2} rh$     $(a-b)^2 = a^2 - 2ab + b^2$     $d = a^{mn}/a^{-3}$     $(e^m)^n = e^{mn}$

26. Differentiate between a. `bool('0')` and `bool('')` b. `bool(0k)` and `bool('0k')`

## Programming Exercises

1. Write a program to calculate the Body Mass Index (BMI) of a person. (BMI = kg/m², where kg is the person's weight and m is his/her height in metres).

2. Write a program to perform string concatenation.

3. Write a program to demonstrate printing a string within single quotes, double quotes and triple quote.

4. Write a program to print the ASCII value of a character.

5. Write a program to read a character in upper case and then print it in lower case.

6. Write a program to swap two numbers using a temporary variable.

7. Write a program to read the address of a user. Display the result by breaking it in multiple lines.

8. Write a program to calculate simple interest and compound interest.

9. Write a program that prompts users to enter two integers x and y. The program then calculates and displays $x^y$

10. Write a program that prompts user to enter his first name and last name and then displays a message `"Greetings!!! First name Last name"`.

11. Write a program to calculate salary of an employee given his basic pay (to be entered by the user), HRA = 10 per cent of basic pay, TA = five per cent of basic pay. Define HRA and TA as constants and use them to calculate the salary of the employee.

12. Write a program to prepare a grocery bill. Enter the name of the items purchased, quantity in which it is purchased and its price per unit. Then display the bill in the following format.
    ```
    *************** B I L L ***************
    Item Quantity              Price Amount
    ****************************************
    Total Amount to be paid
    ****************************************
    ```

13. Energy is calculated as, $e = mc^2$, where *m* is the mass of the object and *c* is its velocity. Write a program that accepts an object's mass (in kilograms) and velocity (in metres per second) and displays its energy.

14. Write a program that calculates the number of seconds in a day.
15. Write a program to read and display the details of a student. While printing use '-' to separate two values.
16. Write a program that prompts the user to enter the first name and the last name. Then display the following message.
    ```
    Hello firstname lastname
    Welcome to Python!
    ```

## Fill in the Blanks

1. A line in Python can have maximum _____ characters.
2. _____ are used to store values.
3. Names given to identify a variable, function, class, module or any other object are generally known as _____.
4. >>>not 10 ==10 gives the answer _____.
5. >>>not 100>700 gives _____.
6. A variable in Python is assigned a value by using the _____ operator.
7. When we create a variable, Python creates _____ referring to those values.
8. Variables can hold values of different types called _____.
9. _____ are those objects to which values can be assigned.
10. To take input from the users, Python uses the _____ function.
11. The _____ function is used to convert a non-integer value to an integer.
12. In Python, multi line comments are also known as _____.
13. The level of _____ groups statements to form a block of statements.
14. Value on which the operator is applied is called _____.
15. _____ operator is used to negate the value of the operand on which it is applied.
16. _____ expressions operate in a shortcut (or lazy) fashion and stop the evaluation when it knows the final outcome for sure.
17. If a is b returns TRUE, then _____.
18. _____ can change the order in which an operator is applied.
19. Literals of the form a + bi are called _____.
20. 123.45E-9 is equal to _____.
21. _____ converts an integer to a floating-point number.
22. The ___ operator returns the quotient after division.
23. To find $x^y$, you will use _____ operator.
24. _____ is a group of characters.
25. Variable names can contain only _____, _____ and _____.
26. >>>90 != 70 gives output _____.
27. 29%0 = _____.

28. int("10"+"20") will give _____.
29. _____ operator treats operand as a sequence of bits.
30. >>> print (format(12356.265901, '.3f')) will result in the value _____.

## State True or False

1. In Python, a semi-colon is used to terminate every statement.
2. Python allows writing multiple statements in a single line.
3. The first character of an identifier must be a dollar sign ($).
4. Python is a case-sensitive language.
5. Based on the data type of a variable, the interpreter reserves memory.
6. While re-assigning values to a variable, the data type must not change.
7. Python variables do not have specific data types.
8. Comments are written to make the program easily readable and understandable.
9. Comments are the executable statements in a program.
10. When a program is run, comments are not displayed.
11. All keywords are written in uppercase characters.
12. Statements in a block must have the same indentation level.
13. Arithmetic operators are also known as relational operators.
14. Relational operators can be used to compare strings.
15. Python does not support prefix and postfix increment/decrement operators.
16. Bitwise OR operator produces the ones' complement of the given binary value.
17. Shifting once to the right multiplies the number by 2.
18. The is operator returns true if operands or values on both sides of the operator do not point to the same object and false otherwise.
19. INT = 2; print(INT) will give an error.
20. The id() function can be used to print the address of the variable.

## Multiple Choice Questions

1. Which of the following is a valid identifier in Python?
   a. _AaBb          b. 1A_Bb          c. @AaBB          d. Aa-Bb
2. Which of the following can be the first character of a valid identifier in Python?
   a. #              b. @              c. _              d. -
3. Which of the following is known as the string concatenation symbol?
   a. +              b. *              c. ,              d. -
4. Which function is used to is determine data type of an object?
   a. data()         b. type()         c. val()          d. str()

5. A variable can be removed by using the _____ statement.
   a. Remove    b. erase    c. del    d. delete

6. Boolean variables are created using which of the following operator(s)?
   a. Equality    b. assignment    c. Both a and b.    d. None of these.

7. The input function takes user's input as a/an _____.
   a. integer    b. floating-point    c. string    d. None of these.

8. All characters following the _____ symbol and up to the end of the line are part of the comment.
   a. #    b. _    c. %    d. @

9. Which operator is used for integer division?
   a. /    b. %    c. //    d. \

10. If both bits are 1, the corresponding bit in the result is 1 and 0 otherwise. This is a feature of which bitwise operator?
    a. AND    b. NOT    c. OR    d. XOR

11. Which operator returns TRUE if a variable is found in the specified sequence and FALSE otherwise?
    a. is    b. not is    c. in    d. not in

12. Identify valid assignment statements.
    a. x = y + 2    b. a = a++    c. x + y = 10    d. x + 10 = y

13. Which line of code produces an error?
    a. "one" + "2"    b. 'one' + 2    c. 1 + 2    d. "1" + "two"

14. abc ="AABBCC"; print(abc*3)
    a. abcabcabc    b. "abcabcabc"    c. ABCABCABC    d. AABBCCAABBCCAABBCC

15. Identify the correct variable creation statement.
    a. my_var =7    b. 123my_var =10    c. my var = 12    d. 10 = myvar

16. Bitwise operator can be applied on which data type?
    a. Integer    b. Float    c. String    d. Complex number

17. Which operator is also known as string repetition operator?
    a. +    b. *    c. &    d. ^

18. The following statement will produce __ lines of output.
    print('Python \n Programming \n is\n ---Fun')
    a. 1    b. 2    c. 3    d. 4

19. Identify the expression that may result in arithmetic overflow.
    a. a*b    b. a**b    c. a/b    d. a+b

20. Which operations do not result in 9?
    a. 95 // 10    b. 130 % 11    c. 3 **3    d. 81 ** 0.5

## Give the Output

1. ```
   x,y,z = 10,20,30
   y,z,x = x+5, y+7, z-3
   print("x = ",x, " y = ",y, "z = ",z)
   ```
   ```

2. ```
x,y = 10,20
y,z = x+5, y-20
print("x = ",x, " y = ",y,» z = ",z)
```

3. ```
>>> 350 + 230 - 170
```

4. ```
>>> (51 + 9.7 - 4) * 100
```

5. ```
>>> 110%(95//3)
```

6. ```
>>> 'Python Programming is fun… '
```

7. ```
>>>"Python Programming is fun…"
```

8. ```
>>>'''Python… \n Programming?'''
```

9. ```
>>> print("Python \n Programmiung")
```

10. ```
>>> print("PYTHON !!!!"*3)
```

11. ```
>>>x = 100 ; x *= 3 ; print(x)
```

12. ```
>>> s1 = "HELLO"     ;     s1 += "WORLD"     ;     print(s1)
```

13. ```
days = "Mon Tue Wed Thu Fri Sat Sun"
months = "Jan\nFeb\nMar\nApr\nMay\nJun\nJul\nAug"
print("Days are : "+ days)
print("Months are: "+ months)
print(""" There's a new dream today.
I'll tell you some other day.
Come on, let's enjoy. """)
```

14. ```
# print ABCD
Nothing
```

15. ```
>>> num1 = "7"
>>> num1 += "10"
>>> num2 = int(num1) + 3
>>> print (float(num2))
```

16. ```
name = input("Enter a word :")
print ('HELLO' + name)
```

17. ```
>>> abs(100-200) * 3
```

18. ```
>>>float("5678" * int(input("Enter a number:")))
```

19. ```
>>> int = 2;  print(int)
```

20. ```
a,b = 10,20
b,a = a *5, b /2
print("a = ",a, " and b = ", b)
```

21. ```
a,b = 10,20
a,b,a = a*10, b*5,a*20
print("a = ",a, " and b = ", b)
```

22. ```
    x =10
    print(id(x))
    x = x + 10
    print(id(x))
    x = x - 10
    print(id(x))
    ```

23. `0 or 10`

24. `10 or 0`

25. `0 or 0`

26. `"abc" or ""`

27. `'' or ''`

28. `'k' or 'r'`

29. `10 ** 3 ** 2`

30. `7 -5 -12 > -5 *3 +8`

31. `len(str(7 -5 -12 > -5 *3 +8)) == len('true')`

32. `bool('0') and (10 < 20)`

33. `23%5 is 23%5`

34. `20 or len(20)`

35. `10 == 10.0`

36. `10 == int(10)`

37. `str(10)==str('10.0')`

38. `'R' == 'R'`

39. `70/(7-(2+4))or 4<5`

40. `5 < 9 or 60/(10-(6+4))`

41. `len("abcd") == 30/6 or 30/10`

42. `2 * (5 *(len("007")))`

43. `30 < 70 and 40 > 50`

44. `N = 1 + 1 + 1 == 0.3; print(N)`

45. ```
    a = True;      b = 0<5
    a==b     ;     a is b
    ```

46. ```
    print(bool(int('0')))
    print(bool(str(0)))
    print(bool(float('0.0')))
    print(bool(str(0.0)))
    ```

47. ```
    a,b,c = 12,13,16
    d = a + b *c/b
    print(d)
    ```

## Find the Error

1. ```
   >>>10+'20'+30+'40'
   ```

2. ```
   >>>'10'*'20'
   >>>'PYTHON'*7.0
   ```

3. ```
   x = 10
   print(x)
   ```

4. ```
   x = 123.456
   print('%'+x)
   ```

5. ```
   x = 1; y = 2;
   print(x+y+z)
   ```

6. ```
   if = 5; print(if)
   ```

7. ```
   a = 10; b = 20; print(a;b)
   ```

8. ```
   x =10
   y = x * 30
   x = "PYTHON"
   z = x/10
   ```

9. ```
   name = int(input("Enter your name : "))
   print("HELLO", name)
   ```

10. ```
    print(len(bool(0)))
    ```

11. ```
    >>> print("HELLO"/2)
    ```

12. ```
    >>> print(type(int("HELLO")))
    ```

13. ```
    >>>n1 = 20
    >>>n2 = 30
    >>>del num1
    >>>n2 = 40
    >>>n1 = 50
    >>>print(num1 - num2)
    ```

14. ```
    n1 = 90
    n2 = n1 + 50
    n2 = int(str(n2) + "40")
    print(num2)
    ```

## Answers

### Fill in the Blanks
1. 79
2. Variables
3. identifiers
4. False
5. True
6. assignment
7. labels
8. data types
9. lvalues
10. input()

11. `int()`
12. docstring
13. indentation
14. operand
15. Unary minus
16. Logical
17. id(a) is same as id(b).
18. Parentheses
19. complex numbers
20. 0.00000012345

21. `float()`
22. / or //
23. **
24. String
25. underscore, upper case, lower case character
26. True
27. ZeroDivisionError
28. 1020
29. Bitwise
30. 12356.266

## State True or False

1. False
2. True
3. False
4. True
5. True
6. False
7. False
8. True
9. False
10. True

11. False
12. True
13. False
14. True
15. True
16. False
17. False
18. False
19. False
20. True

## Multiple Choice Questions

1. a
2. c
3. a
4. b
5. c
6. c
7. c
8. a
9. c
10. a

11. c
12. a
13. b
14. d
15. a
16. a
17. b
18. d
19. b
20. c

## Give the Output

1. x = 27 y = 15 z = 27
2. x = 10 y = 15 z = 0
3. 410
4. 5670.0
5. 17
6. 'Python Programming is fun...'
7. 'Python Programming is fun...'
8. 'Python... \n Programming?'
9. Python
   Programmiung
10. PYTHON !!!!PYTHON !!!!PYTHON !!!!
11. 300
12. HELLOWORLD
13. Days are : Mon Tue Wed Thu Fri Sat Sun
    Months are: Jan
    Feb
    Mar
    Apr
    May
    Jun
    Jul
    Aug
    There's a new dream today.
    I'll tell you some other day.
    Come on, let's enjoy.
14. No output
15. 713.0
16. HELLO(input)

17. 300
18. 5678567856785678.0 (if input = 4)
19. 2
20. a = 10.0 and b = 50
21. a = 200 and b = 100
22. 140705644503984
    140705644504304
    140705644503984
23. 10
24. 10
25. 0
26. 'abc'
27. ''
28. 'k'
29. 1000000000
30. False
31. False
32. True
33. True
34. True
35. True
36. True
37. False
38. True
39. 70.0
40. True
41. 3.0
42. 30

43. False
44. False
45. True    True

46. False    True    False    True
47. 28.0

## Find the Error

1. `TypeError: unsupported operand type(s) for +: 'int' and 'str'`
2. `TypeError:can't multiplay sequence by non-int of type 'str'`
   `TypeError: can't multiply sequence by non-int of type 'float'`
3. `Error! Tab at the start of the line`
4. `TypeError: cannot concatenate 'str' and 'float' objects`
5. `NameError: name 'z' is not defined`
6. `SyntaxError: invalid syntax`
7. `SyntaxError: invalid syntax`
8. `TypeError: unsupported operand type(s) for /: 'str' and 'int'`
9. `ValueError: invalid literal for int() with base 10: 'ABC'`
10. `TypeError: object of type 'bool' has no len()`
11. `TypeError: unsupported operand type(s) for /: 'str' and 'int'`
12. `ValueError: invalid literal for int() with base 10: 'HELLO'`
13. `NameError: name 'num1' is not defined`
14. `NameError: name 'num2' is not defined`

# Decision Control Statements

**Chapter Objectives**

The chapter discusses a very crucial set of statements that may alter the sequence of program flow. These statements include conditional branching statements such as:

- The `if` statement
- The `if-else` statement
- The nested `if` statement
- The `if-elif-else` Statement

Until now, we have executed simple statements in Python. Such statements are executed sequentially from the first line of the program to the last. That is, the second statement is executed after the first; the third statement is executed after the second, and so on. This way of execution is known as **sequential control flow**.

However, in some cases we may want to either execute only a selected set of statements (i.e., selection control) or execute a set of statements repeatedly (i.e., iterative control). In such cases, decision control system comes into picture.

A *decision control statement* is a statement that determines the flow of control in a program. Flow of control means deciding on which instruction would next be executed. A decision control statement can skip either one or more instructions. The three fundamental methods of control flow in a programming language are *sequential, selection, and iterative control*.

Selection and iterative control are a part of decision control system. Thus, a decision control statement can alter (change) the flow of a sequence of instructions. And this type of conditional processing helps users to extend the usefulness of programs.

Programmers can make programs that determine which statements of the code should be executed and which should be ignored in certain circumstances. Figure 4.1 shows the categorization of decision control statements.

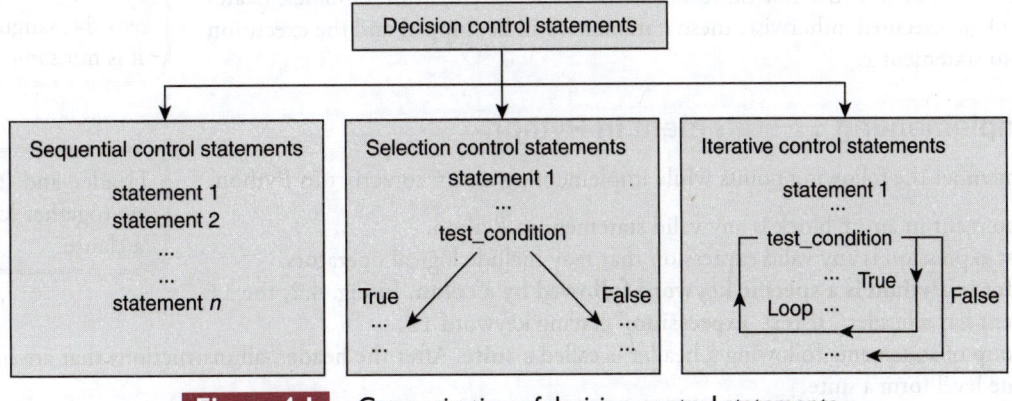

**Figure 4.1** Categorization of decision control statements

## 4.1 SELECTION/CONDITIONAL BRANCHING STATEMENTS

The decision control statements usually jump from one part of the code to another depending on whether a particular condition is satisfied or not. That is, they execute statements selectively based on certain decisions. Such type of decision control statements is known as **selection control statements** or *conditional branching statements*. Python language supports different types of conditional branching statements which are as follows:

- `if` statement
- Nested `if` statement
- `if-else` statement
- `if-elif-else` statement

## 4.2 `if` STATEMENT

An `if` statement is the simplest form of decision control statement that is frequently used in decision making. An `if` statement is a selection control statement based on the value of a given Boolean expression. The general form of a simple `if` statement is shown in Fig. 4.2.

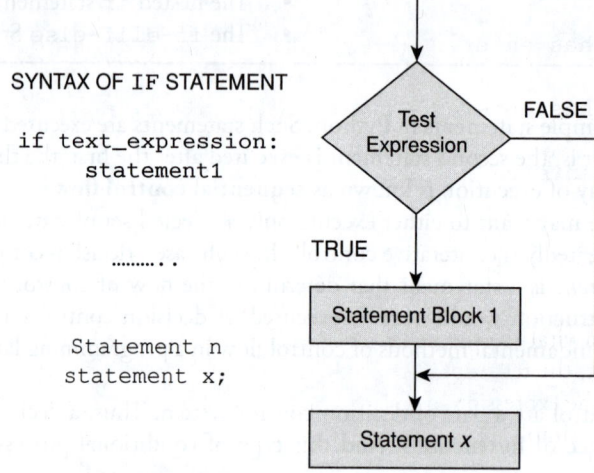

```
SYNTAX OF IF STATEMENT
if text_expression:
    statement1
    
    ……..
    
Statement n
statement x;
```

**Figure 4.2** `if` statement construct

The `if` block may include 1 or more statements. According to the figure, first the test expression is evaluated. If the test expression is true, the statement of `if` block (statement 1 to *n*) are executed; otherwise, these statements will be skipped and the execution will jump to statement x.

> Python is a case sensitive language. So, if is not same as IF.

### 4.2.1 Implementing `if` statement in Python

Always remember the following points while implementing an `if` construct in Python.

- The statement in an `if` block is any valid statement in Python.
- The test expression is any valid expression that may include logical operators.
- **A header in Python is a specific keyword followed by a colon.** In Fig. 4.2, the `if` statement has a header, "**if text_expression:**" having keyword `if`.
- The group of statements following a header is called a **suite**. After the header, all instructions that are indented at the same level form a suite.
- While four spaces are commonly used for each level of indentation, any number of spaces may be used.

> Header and its suite are together known as a clause.

**Example 4.1** **Program to increment a number if it is positive.**

```
x = 10    #Initialize the value of x
if(x>0):  #test the value of x
    x = x+1   #Increment the value of x if it is > 0
print(x)  #Print the value of x
```

**OUTPUT**
```
x = 11
```

> Remember to properly indent the statements that are dependent on the previous statements.

In the above code, we take a variable *x* and initialize it to 10. In the test expression, we check if the value of *x* is greater than 0 or not. If the test expression evaluates to true, then the value of *x* is incremented and is printed on the screen. Note that the print statement will be executed even if the test expression is false.

*Python uses indentation to form a block of code. Other languages such as C and C++, use curly braces to accomplish this.*

**Example 4.2** Write a program to determine whether a person is eligible to vote.

```
age= int(input("Enter the age :"))
if(age>=18):
    print("You are eligible to vote")
```

OUTPUT
Enter the age : 35
You are eligible to vote

**Example 4.3** Write a program to determine the character entered by the user.

```
char= input("Press any key : ")
if(char.isalpha()):
    print("The user has entered a character")
if( char.isdigit()):
    print("The user has entered a digit")
if(char.isspace()):
    print("The user entered a white space character" )
```

OUTPUT
Press any key : 7
The user has entered a digit

## 4.3 if-else STATEMENT

Although `if` statement plays a vital role in conditional branching, its usage is very limited. Its simplicity is also its drawback. In the `if` statement, the test expression is evaluated; if the result is true, the statement(s) followed by the expression is executed. But, if the expression is false, nothing useful happens. Using an `if-else` statement solves this problem. The general form of a simple `if-else` statement is shown in Fig. 4.3.

SYNTAX OF IF-ELSE STATEMENT

```
if test_expression:
        statement block 1

else:
        statement block 2

statement x;
```

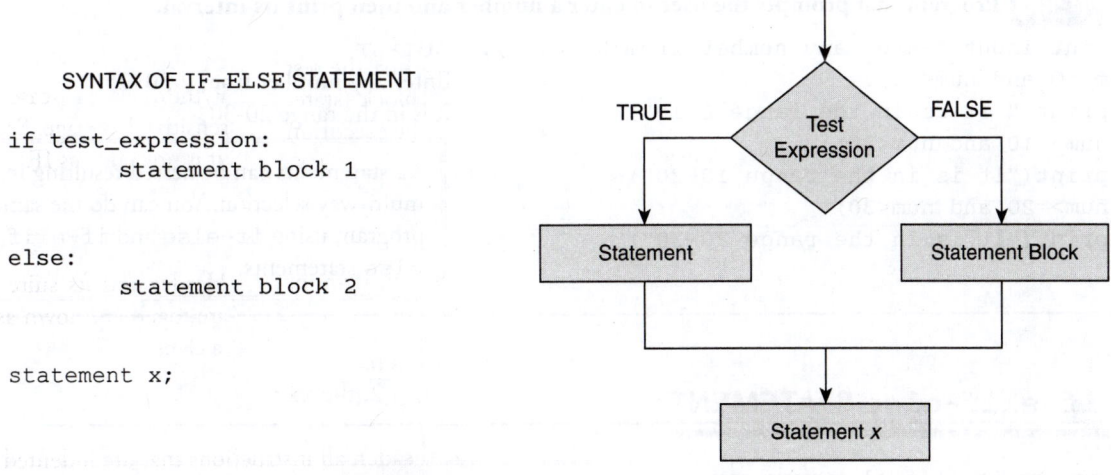

**Figure 4.3** `if-else` statement construct

In the above syntax, we have written the statement block. A statement block may include one or more statements. According to the if–else construct, first the test expression is evaluated. If the expression is true, statement block 1 is executed and statement block 2 is skipped. Otherwise, if the expression is false, statement block 2 is executed and statement block 1 is ignored. In any case, after the statement block 1 or 2 gets executed the control will pass to statement *x*. Therefore, statement *x* is executed in every case.

**Example 4.4** Write a program to determine whether a person is eligible to vote or not. If he is not eligible display how many years are left to be eligible.

```
age = int(input("Enterthe age : " ))
if(age>=18):
    print("You are eligible to vote")
else:
    yrs = 18 - age
    print("You have to wait for " + str(yrs) +" years")
```

**OUTPUT**
Enter the age : 10
You have to wait for 8 years

**Example 4.5** Write a program to find larger of two numbers.

```
a = int(input("Enter the value of a : "))
b = int(input("Enter the value of b : "))
if(a>b):
    large = a
else:
    large = b
print("Large= ",large)
```

**OUTPUT**
Enter the value of a: 50
Enter the value of b : 30
Large= 50

## 4.4 NESTED `if` STATEMENTS

A statement that contains other statements is called a ***compound statement***. To perform more complex checks, `if` statements can be nested, that is, it can be placed one inside the other. In such a case, the inner `if` statement is the statement part of the outer one. Nested `if` statements are used to check if more than one condition is satisfied. Consider the code given below to understand this concept.

**Example 4.6** Program that prompts the user to enter a number and then print its interval.

```
num = int(input("Enter any number from 0-30: "))
if(num>=0 and num<10):
    print(" It is in the range 0-10")
elif(num>=10 and num<20):
    print("lt is in the range 10-20")
elif(num>=20 and num<30):
    print("lt is in the range 20-30")
```

**OUTPUT**
Enter any number from 0-30: 25
It is in the range 20-30

> if statements can be nested resulting in multi-way selection. You can do the same program using if-else and if-elif-else statements.

## 4.5 `if-elif-else` STATEMENT

Python supports `if-elif-else` statements to test additional conditions apart from the initial test expression. The `if-elif-else` construct works in the same way as a usual `if-else` statement. If-elif-else construct is also known as **nested-if construct**. The `elif` (short for `else if`) statement is a shortcut to `if` and `else` statements. *A series of `if` and `elif` statements have a final else block, which is executed if none of the `if` or `elif` expressions is True.* Its syntax is given in Fig. 4.4.

> **Comparing Floating-point Numbers**
> Never test floating-point numbers for exact equality. This is because floating-point numbers are just approximations, so it is always better to test floating-point numbers for 'approximately equal' rather than testing for exactly equal. We can test for approximate equality by finding the difference between the two floating-point numbers (that are to be tested) and comparing their absolute value of the difference against a very small number, epsilon.

## Decision Control Statements

SYNTAX OF **IF-ELIF-ELSE** STATEMENT

```
if ( test expression 1)
        statement block 1
elif ( test expression 2)
        statement block 2
..........................

elif (test expression N)
        statement block N
else
        statement block x
statement y
```

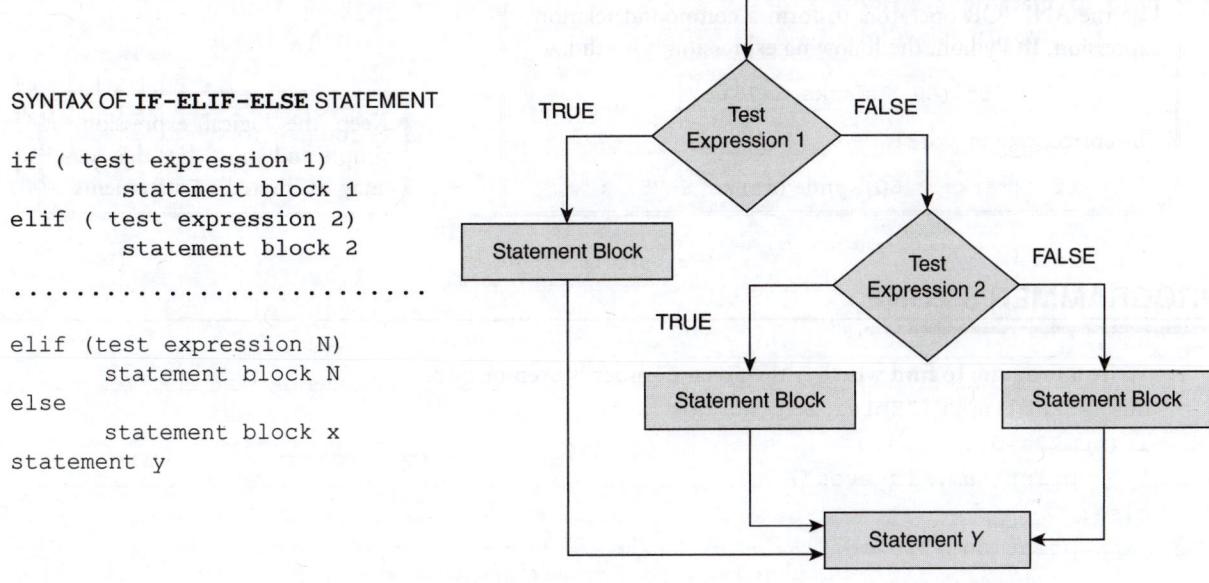

**Figure 4.4** if-elif-else syntax

Note that it is not necessary that every `if` statement should have an `else` block as Python supports simple `if` statements also. After the first test expression or the first `if` branch, the programmer can have as many `elif` branches as he wants depending on the expressions that have to be tested. The final `else` block is called if none of the `if` or `elif` expressions is True.

> Remember that the `elif` and `else` part are optional.

**Example 4.7** To test whether a number entered by the user is negative, positive or equal to zero.

```
num = int(input("Enter any number : "))
if(num==0):
    print("The value is equal to zero" )
elif(num>0):
    print("The number is positive")
else:
    print("The number is negative")
```

**OUTPUT**
Enter any number : -10
The number is negative

**Example 4.8** Write a program to determine whether the character entered is a vowel or not.

```
ch = input("Enter any character : ")
if(ch=="A" or ch=="E" or ch=="I" or ch=="O" or ch=="U"):
    print ch,"is a vowel")
elif(ch=="a" or ch=="e" or ch=="i" or ch=="o" or ch=="u"):
    print(ch,"is a vowel")
else:
    print(ch, "is not a vowel")
```

**OUTPUT**
Enter any character: h
h is not a vowel

In the program to test whether a number is positive or negative, note that if the first test expression evaluates a true value, then the rest of the statements in the code will be ignored and after executing the `print` statement that displays "The value is equal to zero", the control will jump to `return 0` statement.

Python assumes any non-zero and non-null values as TRUE. Similarly, all values that are either zero or null are assumed as FALSE value.

> Use the AND/OR operators to form a compound relation expression. In Python, the following expression is invalid.
>
> $$\text{if } (60 \leq \text{marks} \leq 75) :$$
>
> The correct way to write is,
>
> $$\text{if } ((\text{marks} \geq 60) \text{ and } (\text{marks} \leq 75) :$$

> Keep the logical expressions simple and short. For this, you may use nested if statements.

## PROGRAMMER'S ZONE

1. **Write a program to find whether the given number is even or odd.**
   ```
   num = int(input("Enter any number : "))
   if(num%2==0):
        print(num,"is even")
   else:
        print(num,"is odd")
   ```
   **OUTPUT**
   ```
   Enter any number:125
   125 is odd
   ```

2. **Write a program to enter any character. If the entered character is in lower case then convert it into upper case and if it is an upper case character then convert it into lower case.**
   ```
   ch = input("Enter any character : ")
   if(ch >= 'A' and ch <='Z'):
        ch = ch.lower()
        print("The entered character was in upper case. In lower case it is : " + ch)
   else:
        ch = ch.upper()
        print("The entered character was in lower case. In upper case it is : " + ch)
   ```
   **OUTPUT**
   ```
   Enter any character: c
   The entered character was in lower case. In upper case it is:C
   ```

3. **A company decides to give bonus to all its employees on Diwali. A 5% bonus on salary is given to the male workers and 10% bonus on salary to the female workers. Write a program to enter the salary of the employee and sex of the employee. If the salary of the employee is less than Rs 10,000 then the employee gets an extra 2% bonus on salary. Calculate the bonus that has to be given to the employee and display the salary that the employee will get.**
   ```
   ch = input("Enter the sex of the employee (m or f) : ")
   sal = int(input("Enter the salary of the employee : "))
   if (ch=='m'):
        bonus = 0.05*sal
   else :
        bonus = 0.10*sal
   amt_to_be_paid = sal+bonus
   print(" Salary = ",sal)
   print(" Bonus = ",bonus)
   print(" *******************************")
   print("Amount to be paid : ",amt_to_be_paid)
   ```

**OUTPUT**
```
Enter the sex of the employee (m or f) : f
Enter the salary of the employee : 50000
Salary = 50000
Bonus = 5000.0
*******************************
Amount to be paid : 55000.0
```

4. **Write a program to find whether a given year is a leap year or not.**
    ```
    year = int(input("Enter any year : "))
    if((year%4==0 and year %100!=0) or (year%400 == 0)):
        print("Leap Year")
    else:
        print("Not a Leap Year")
    ```

    **OUTPUT**
    ```
    Enter any year: 2000
    Leap Year
    ```

5. **Write a program to find the greater of two numbers.**
    ```
    x = int(input("Enter the first number : "))
    y = int(input("Enter the second number : "))
    if(x==y):
        print("The two numbers are equal")
    elif(x>y):
        print(x,"is greater than",y)
    else:
        print(x,"is less than",y)
    ```

    **OUTPUT**
    ```
    Enter the first number: 6
    Enter the second number: 3
    6 is greater than 3
    ```

6. **Write a program to find the greatest number from three numbers.**
    ```
    num1 = int(input("Enter the first number : "))
    num2 = int(input("Enter the second number : "))
    num3 = int(input("Enter the third number : "))
    if(num1>num2):
        if(num1>num3):
            print(num1,"is greater than",num2,"and",num3)
        else:
            print(num3,"is greater than",num1,"and",num2)
    elif(num2>num3):
        print(num2,"is greater than",num1,"and",num3)
    else:
        print("The three numbers are equal")
    ```

    **OUTPUT**
    ```
    Enter the first number: 13
    Enter the second number: 43
    Enter the third number: 25
    43 is greater than 13 and 25
    ```

7. **Write a program that prompts the user to enter a number between 1 and 7 and then displays the corresponding day of the week.**

```
num = int(input("Enter any number between 1 to 7 : "))
if(num==1): print("Sunday")
elif(num==2): print("Monday")
elif(num==3): print("Tuesday")
elif(num==4): print("Wednesday")
elif(num==5): print("Thursday")
elif(num==6): print("Friday")
elif(num==7): print("Saturday")
else :
print("Wrong input")
```

**OUTPUT**

```
Enter any number between 1 to 7: 5
Thursday
```

8. **Write a program to calculate tax, given the following conditions:**
   If income is less than 1,50,000 then no tax
   If taxable income is 1,50,001 - 300,000 then charge 10% tax
   If taxable income is 3,00,001 - 500,000 then charge 20% tax
   If taxable income is above 5,00,001 then charge 30% tax

```
MIN1 = 150001
MAX1 = 300000
RATE1 = 0.10
MIN2 = 300001
MAX2 = 500000
RATE2 = 0.20
MIN3 = 500001
RATE3 = 0.30
income = int(input("Enter the income : "))
taxable_income = income - 150000
if(taxable_income <= 0):
    print("No tax")
elif(taxable_income>=MIN1 and taxable_income<MAX1):
    tax = (taxable_income - MIN1) * RATE1
elif(taxable_income>=MIN2 and taxable_income<MAX2):
    tax = (taxable_income - MIN2) * RATE2
else:
    tax = (taxable_income-MIN3)*RATE3
print("TAX = ",tax)
```

**OUTPUT**

```
Enter the income: 2000000
TAX = 404999.7
```

9. **Write a program to take input from the user and then check whether it is a number or a character. If it is a character, determine whether it is in upper case or lower case.**

```
ch = input("Enter the character : ")
if(ch>="A" and ch<="Z"):
    print("Upper case character was entered")
```

```
    elif(ch>='a' and ch<='z'):
        print("Lower case character was entered")
    elif(ch>='0' and ch<='9'):
        print "A number was entered"
```

**OUTPUT**

```
Enter any character: C
Upper case character was entered
```

10. Write a program to enter the marks of a student in four subjects. Then calculate the total, aggregate and display the grade obtained by the student. If the student scores an aggregate greater than 75%, then the grade is Distinction. If aggregate is 60>= and <75, then the grade is First Division. If aggregate is 50>= and <60, then the grade is Second Division. If aggregate is 40>= and <50, then the grade is Third Division. Else, the grade is Fail.

```
marks1 = int(input("Enter the marks in Mathematics : "))
marks2 = int(input("Enter the marks in Science : "))
marks3 = int(input("Enter the marks in Social Science : "))
marks4 = int(input("Enter the marks in Computers : "))
total = marks1+marks2+marks3+marks4
avg = float(total)/4
print("Total = ",total,"\t Aggregate = ",avg)
if(avg>=75):
    print("Distinction")
elif(avg>=60 and avg<75):
    print("First Division")
elif(avg>=50 and avg<60):
    print("Second Division")
else:
   print("Fail")
```

> While forming the conditional expression, try to use positive statements rather than using compound negative statements.

**OUTPUT**

```
Enter the marks in Mathematics: 90
Enter the marks in Science: 91
Enter the marks in Social Science: 92
Enter the marks in Computers: 93
Total = 366     Aggregate = 91.5
Distinction
```

11. Write a program to calculate the roots of a quadratic equation.

```
a = int(input("Enter the values of a : "))
b = int(input("Enter the values of b : "))
c = int(input("Enter the values of c : "))
D = (b*b)-(4*a*c)
deno = 2*a
if(D>0):
    print("REAL ROOTS")
    root1 = (-b + D**0.5)/deno
    root2 = (-b - D**0.5)/deno
    print("Root1 = ",root1,"\tRoot2 = ",root2)
    print "EQUAL ROOTS"
    root1 = -b/deno
    print("Root1 and Root2 = ",root1)
else:
    print("IMAGINARY ROOTS")
```

> Do not use floating-point numbers to check for equality in the test expression.

**OUTPUT**
```
Enter the values of a, b and c : 3 4 5
IMAGINARY ROOTS
```

12. **Write a program that prompts the user to enter three angles. Check whether the angles are that of a triangle or not.**

```
ang1= int(input("Enter the first angle : "))
ang2= int(input("Enter the first angle : "))
ang3= int(input("Enter the first angle : "))
if (ang1 + ang2 + ang3) == 180:
    print("The angles are angles of a triangle")
else:
    print("The angles are not the angles of a triangle")
```

**OUTPUT**
```
Enter the first angle: 120
Enter the first angle: 40
Enter the first angle: 20
The angles are angles of a triangle
```

## Key Terms

**Sequential control flow:** A programming style in which the statements in a program are executed one after the other.

**Flow control:** Flow control means control on which statement would be executed next.

**Decision control flow:** A type of flow control in which either a selected set of statements is executed or a particular set of statements is executed repeatedly.

**Selection control statements:** Decision control statements that allow the flow control to jump from one part of the code to another depending on whether a particular condition is satisfied or not. Since they execute statements selectively based on certain decisions, such type of decision control statements is known as selection control statements or *conditional branching statements*.

**Clause:** Combination of a header and its suite.

**Suite:** Group of statements following the header.

**Nested (or compound) statement:** A statement that contains other statements is called a compound statement.

## Chapter Highlights

- A test expression is any valid expression that may include logical operators.
- After the header, all instructions that are indented at the same level form a suite.
- Python uses indentation to form a block of code.
- An `if-else` statement specifies what has to be done if the statement is true as well as when it is false.
- Nested `if` statements are used to check if more than one condition is satisfied.
- A series of `if` and `elif` statements have a final `else` block, which is executed if none of the `if` or `elif` expressions is True.

## Review Questions

1. What is flow control?
2. Differentiate between sequential control flow and selection control flow.
3. Why do we need decision control statements?

4. With the help of a flowchart, explain the syntax of the following statements:
   a. if      b. if-else      c. if-el-if      d. nested if
5. What are conditional branching statements? How does Python support such statements?
6. How will you identify the suite of an `if` statement?
7. With the help of an example explain why `if-else` statement is better than a simple `if` statement.
8. What do you mean by a nested `if` statement? How is it implemented In Python?
9. Why should we not use floating-point numbers to test for exact equality?
10. Change the indentation to make the code syntactically correct.
    ```
    if condition1:
    statement1
    elif condition2:
    statement2
    elif condition3:
    statement3
    elif condition4:
    statement4
    ```
11. Under what conditions, Programming will be printed?
    ```
    if a < 10:
       print("Python")
    elif a < 20:
       print("Programming")
    else:
       print("is fun..")
    ```

## Programming Exercises

1. Write a program to check whether a number is divisible by 10 or not. If the number is not divisible, then print how much should be added to it to make it completely divisible by 10.
2. Write a program to verify whether a candidate is eligible to appear for an exam or not. The minimum and maximum age of person appearing for the exam is 21 and 35 respectively.
3. Write a program that prompts the user to enter an angle and then prints its quadrant.
4. Write a program that prompts the user to enter a number between 1–12 and then display the corresponding month of the year.
5. Write a menu-driven program that prompts the user to enter the two sides of a rectangle. The user can then choose from a given set of options, if he/she needs to calculate perimeter, area or diagonal of the rectangle.
6. Write a program that prompts users to enter a character (A, B, C, D, E). Then using `if-elif-else` construct, display Outstanding, Very Good, Good, Average and Fail respectively.
7. Write a program that determines whether a student is eligible for PG course or not. To be eligible, the student must have obtained more than 80% in X and XII examination, and 70% plus marks in Graduation. If the student changes his stream (Science, Commerce, Arts), then deduct 5% from his Graduation score.
8. Write a program to read a floating-point number and an integer. If the value of the floating-point number is greater than 3.14 then multiply the value of the integer with 100.
9. Write a program that prompts the user to enter two integers. Divide the greater number with the smaller one and print the remainder and quotient thus obtained.
10. What output will be generated when the expression 5 or 100/0 is evaluated? What change can you do so that Python reports a Divide-by-Zero Error?

11. Write a program that accepts the current date and the date of birth of the user. Then calculate the age of the user and display it on the screen. Note that the date should be displayed in the format specified as dd/mm/yy.
12. Write a code to calculate the amount to be paid by a customer by considering the following points.
    If the amount_to_be_paid >=30000, then discount = 30%.
    If the amount_to_be_paid >=20000, then discount = 20%.
    If the amount_to_be_paid >=10000, then discount = 10%.
    Otherwise, discount = 5%
13. Write a program that prompts the user to enter his/ her age (15–18 years) and then display the perfect height and weight for that age.

    | Age | Weight (kg) | Height (cm) |
    |---|---|---|
    | 15 | 56 | 170 |
    | 16 | 60 | 173 |
    | 17 | 64 | 175 |
    | 18 | 66 | 176 |

14. Write a program that prompts the user to enter his/her body temperature. Check and display whether the user has normal body temperature, high fever or low fever.
15. Write a program that prompts the user to enter a number. Display the square root of the number. Remember that square root of negative numbers is not defined.
16. Write a program that prompts the user to enter the lengths of three sides. Check whether these are the sides of a triangle.
    **Hint:** Sides of a triangle follow the rule, a + b > c. Similarly, b + c > a and a + c > b.
17. Write a program that prompts the user to enter the angles of a triangle. Check whether the triangle is acute-, obtuse- or right-angled.
18. Write a program to check whether a number entered by the user is positive, negative or equal to zero.
19. Write a program that prompts users to enter status code 'S', 'M', 'D', or 'U' and returns the string 'Separated', 'Married', 'Divorced', or 'Unmarried', respectively. In case an inappropriate letter is passed, print an appropriate message.
20. An employee's total weekly pay is calculated by multiplying the hourly wage and number of regular hours plus any overtime pay, which in turn is calculated as total overtime hours multiplied by 1.5 times the hourly wage. Write a program that takes as inputs the hourly wage, total regular hours, and total overtime hours and prints an employee's total weekly pay.
21. Write a program to calculate electricity bill based on the following information.

    | Consumption Unit | Rate of Charge |
    |---|---|
    | 0 – 150 | Re 3 per unit |
    | 151 – 350 | Rs 100 plus Rs 3.75 per unit exceeding 150 units |
    | 301 – 450 | Rs 250 plus Rs 4 per unit exceeding 350 units |
    | 451 – 600 | Rs 300 plus Rs 4.25 per unit exceeding 450 units |
    | Above 600 | Rs 400 plus Rs 5 per unit exceeding 600 units |

## Fill in the Blanks

1. _____ means control on which statement would be executed next.
2. _____ is the simplest form of decision control statements.
3. Header and its suite together form a _____.

4. Python uses _____ to form a block of code.
5. A _____ statement contains other statements.
6. A series of `if` and `elif` statements have a final _____ block.
7. _____ and _____ operators are used to form a compound relational expression.
8. _____ is a short form of `else if` statement. Ans
9. Python uses _____ to form a block of code.
10. A series of if `elif` statements have a final _____ block, which is executed if none of the `if` or `elif` expressions is True.
11. Python assumes any non-zero and non-null values as _____.
12. _____ begins with a keyword and ends with a colon.
13. ```
    x = 10
    y = 20
    __x>y__
    print print("In if")
    _____
            print ("In else")
    ```
14. Fill the blanks to print *Python* on the screen.
    ```
    x = 10
    y = 50
    if x>10 __ y<100:
    ___ ("Python")
    ```

## State True or False

1. A sequential control program can skip one or more statements.
2. In selection control statements, all the statements are executed from the first one to the last.
3. A group of statements following the header is known as a clause.
4. After the header, all instructions that are indented at the same level form a suite.
5. It is mandatory to use four spaces to define each level of indentation. Ans
6. The final `else` block in an `if-elif-else` statement is executed when none of the `if` or `elif` expressions is True.
7. You can use floating point numbers for checking for equality in the test expression.
8. Indentation identifies a statement block.
9. Statements within a suite can be indented at different levels.
10. `elif` and else blocks are optional.

## Multiple Choice Questions

1. Which part of `if` statement should be indented?
   a. The first statement   b. All the statements   c. Statements within the `if` block   d. None of these.
2. A programming style in which the statements in a program are executed one after the other.
   a. Sequential         b. Decision control     c. Iterative control    d. None of these.
3. A test expression must have a/an _____ operator.
   a. arithmetic         b. logical              c. unary                d. assignment
    ```

4. In an `if` statement, which of the following headers are optional?
   a. If
   b. elif
   c. else
   d. Both b and c

5. A logical expression should not be _____
   a. simple
   b. long
   c. positive
   d. Both b and c

6. Which of the following is placed after the if condition?
   a. ;
   b. .
   c. :
   d. ,

## Give the Output

1. ```
   if(5.0 < 9.0):
   print("DONE")
   ```

2. ```
   years = 99
   if(years == 100):
        print("Century")
   elif(years == 75):
        print("Platinum Jublee")
   elif(years == 50):
        print("Half Century")
   elif(years == 25):
        print("Silver Jublee")
   elif(years == 10):
        print("Decade")
   else:
        print("Long way to go….")
   ```

3. ```
   years = 99
   if years > 30:
        print("30")
   if years < 50:
        print("50")
   if years == 7:
        print("70")
   ```

4. ```
   num = int((10*6 + 10 - 20) > 0)
   if num == 50:
        print("You win...")
   else:
        print("Try Again")
   ```

5. ```
   num = 3
   if (num ** 3) > (5%2 - 3 * 4 /2):
      if (num // 4) >= 2:
         print("You win")
      else:
         print("Try Again")
   ```

6. ```
   num = 3
   if num == 2:
        print("Yes")
   elif num == 4:
        print("Yes")
   elif num == 8:
        print("Yes")
   else:
        print("Number is not an even number")
   ```

## Decision Control Statements

7. ```
   if(10 == 100) and (100 + 200 > 300):
        print("Win Win..")
   else:
        print("Oh No !!!")
   ```

8. ```
   if not True:
        print("WRONG")
   elif not((10+10 - 20 * 3) == 30):
        print("Really !")
   else:
        print("May Be")
   ```

9. ```
   if (10 << ((41 - 40 // 2 + 1)%2)) == 60:
        print("WoW")
   else:
        print("Gosh")
   ```

10. ```
    a = 5
    b = 70
    if not 10 + 10 == b or a == 40 and 70== 80:
         print("Yeah")
    elif a != b:
         print("Nope")
    ```

11. ```
    num = 10
    if num > 30:
         if num > 40:
              print("Python")
         else:
              print("Programming")
    elif num < 20:
         if(num!=0):
              print("is fun..")
    print("Isnt it !!!")
    ```

12. ```
    weather = 'foggy'
    if weather == 'sunny':
         print("Take your shades")
    elif weather == 'raining':
         print("Take your umbrella")
    else:
         print("Stay at home")
    ```

## Answers

### Fill in the Blanks

1. Flow control
2. If statement
3. clause
4. indentation
5. compound/nested
6. else
7. and, or
8. elif
9. indentation
10. else
11. True
12. Header
13. if, :, else:
14. or, print

### State True or False

1. False
2. False
3. False
4. True
5. False
6. True
7. True
8. True
9. False
10. True

## Multiple Choice Questions

1. b
2. a
3. b
4. d
5. b
6. c

## Give the Output

1. Done
2. Long way to go….
3. 30
4. Try Again
5. Try Again
6. Number is not an even number
7. Oh No !!!
8. Really !
9. Gosh
10. Yeah
11. is fun..
    Isnt it !!!
12. Stay at home

# Basic Loop Structures/Iterative Statements

# 5

**Chapter Objectives**

This chapter elucidates the concept of iterative statements in Python. Like decision control statements, the iterative statements may also change the flow of program control. Here, we shall learn about:

- while loop
- for loop
- The range() function
- Nested loops
- The technique to choose an appropriate loop for the given situation
- Path breaking statements like break, continue, pass and else

In the last chapter, we had read about decision-controlled statements and covered conditional branching statements including if, if-else and if-elif-else statements. In this chapter, we will study iterative statements through which Python supports basic loop structures. Iterative statements are used to repeat the execution of one or more statements. In Python, iterative statements are implemented through while loop and for loop.

## 5.1 while LOOP

The while loop provides a mechanism to repeat one or more statements while a particular condition is true. Figure 5.1 shows the syntax and general form of representation of a while loop.

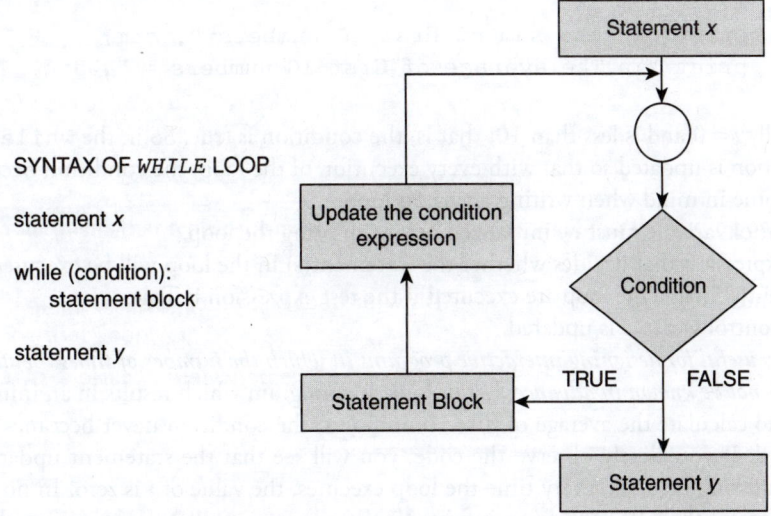

**Figure 5.1** The while loop construct

Note that in the while loop, the condition is tested before any of the statements in the statement block is executed. If the condition is true, only then the statements will be executed; otherwise if the condition is false, the control will jump to statement y, which is the immediate statement outside the while loop block.

> Iterative statements are used to repeat the execution of a list of statements, depending on the value of an integer expression.

We must update the condition with every iteration of the loop. This is necessary because it is this condition which determines when the loop will end. If we do not update the condition, then it will never become false. This will result in an infinite loop which is never desirable.

A `while` loop is also referred to as a top-checking loop since control condition is placed as the first line of the code. If the control condition evaluates to False, then the statements enclosed in the loop are never executed. Look at the following example code.

**Example 5.1** **To print the first 10 numbers using a `while` loop.**

```
i = 0
while(i< =10):
      print(i,end=' ')
      i = i+1
```

**OUTPUT**
0 1 2 3 4 5 6 7 8 9 10

**Example 5.2** **Write a program to calculate the sum and average of first 10 numbers.**

```
i = 0
s = 0
while(i<=10):
   s = s+i
   i=i+1
avg = float(s)/10
print("The sum of first 10 numbers is : ",s)
print("The average of first 10 numbers is :",avg)
```

**OUTPUT**
The sum of first 10 numbers is : 55

```
i = 0
sum=0
avg= 0.0
while(i<=10):
    sum = sum + i
avg = sum/10
print("\n The sum of first 10 numbers=", sum)
print("\n The average of first 10 numbers = ", avg)
```

> The infinite loop is a loop which never stops running. Its condition always True.

In the program, initially *i* = 0 and is less than 10; that is, the condition is true. So in the `while` loop, the value of *i* is printed and the condition is updated so that with every execution of the loop, the condition becomes more approachable. This has to be borne in mind when writing a `while` loop,

First, the loop control variable must be initialized before entering the loop.
Second, the test expression that decides whether the statement(s) in the loop will be executed or not, is evaluated.
Third, the statement(s) inside the loop are executed if the test expression is True.
Fourth, the loop control variable is updated.

*while* loop is very useful for designing interactive programs in which the number of times the statements in loop has to be executed may or may not be known in advance. Let us look at a program which results in an infinite loop. Though the program is supposed to calculate the average of first 10 numbers, the condition never becomes false, and the desired output is *not* generated. If you clearly observe the code, you will see that the statement updating the value of loop control variable (*i*) is missing here. So, every time the loop executes, the value of *i* is zero. In no way, will the value of *i* become equal to or greater than 10. Hence, an infinite loop – a loop that never ends is entered.

Once you get stuck in an infinite loop, either press Ctrl + C keys on the keyboard or press the close button of the Python shell window.

## 5.2 for LOOP

Like the `while` loop, the `for` loop provides a mechanism to repeat a task until a particular condition is true. The `for` loop is usually known as a determinate or definite loop because the programmer knows exactly how many times the loop will repeat. The number of times the loop has to be executed can be determined mathematically by checking the logic of the loop.

The for..in statement is a looping statement used in Python to iterate over a sequence of objects, i.e., go through each item in a sequence. Here, by sequence we mean just an ordered collection of items. The flow of statements in a for loop can be given as in Fig. 5.2.

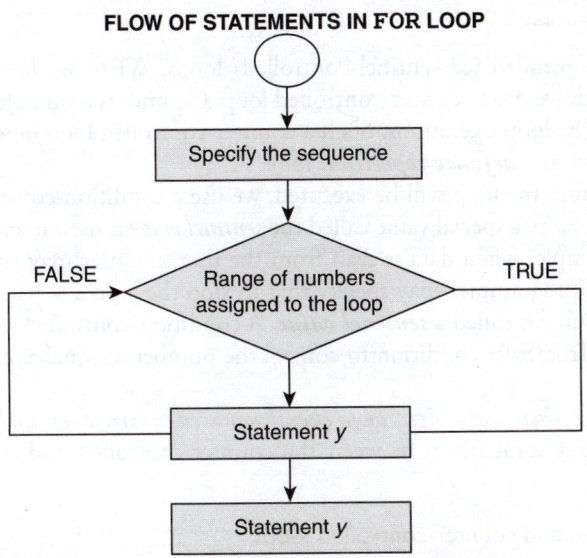

**SYNTAX OF FOR LOOP**
```
for loop_contol_var in sequence:
    statement block
```

**Figure 5.2**  for loop construct

When a for loop is used, a range of sequence is specified (only once). The items of the sequence are assigned to the loop control variable one after the other. The for loop is executed for each item in the sequence. With every iteration of the loop, a check is made to ensure if the loop control variable has been assigned all the values in the sequence. If all the values have not been assigned, the statement block of the loop is executed; else, the statements comprising the statement block of the for loop are skipped and the control jumps to the immediate statement following the for loop body. Note that every iteration of the loop must make the loop control variable closer to the end of the sequence.

Let us print all the characters in a string using the for loop. We know that a string is a sequence of characters. So, the for loop statement(s) will be executed for each character in the string.

```
for i in "PYTHON":
    print(i, end = ' ')
P Y T H O N
```

## 5.3  THE range() FUNCTION

The range() is a built-in function in Python that is used to iterate over a sequence of numbers. The syntax of range() is **range(beg, end, [step])**

The **range()** generates a sequence of numbers starting with **beg** (inclusive) and ending with one less than the number **end**. The **step** argument is optional (hence, written in brackets). By default, every number in the range is incremented by 1 but we can specify a different increment using step. It can be both negative and positive, but not zero.

> Step can be either positive or negative but cannot be zero.

**Program to print first n numbers using the range() in a for loop.**

```
for i in range(1, 5):
    print(i, end= ' ')
```
**OUTPUT**  Print numbers in the same line
1 2 3 4

```
for i in range(1, 10, 2):    [beg] [step]
    print (i, end= ' ')      [end]
```
**OUTPUT**
1 3 7 9

The `range()` function has produced values 1, 2, 3 and 4. Did you notice that the statement(s) of the `for` loop is executed for each value of the loop control variable (which is *i*, here). Initially, *i* is 1, in the next iteration it is 2, and so on. The loop continues until all the values in the sequence are processed.

## 5.4 SELECTING AN APPROPRIATE LOOP

Loops can be either counter-controlled or condition-controlled (or sentinel-controlled) loops. When we know in advance the number of times the loop should be executed, we use a counter-controlled loop. Counter is a variable that must be initialized, tested, and updated for performing the loop operations. Such a counter-controlled loop in which the counter is assigned a constant or a value is also known as a ***definite repetition loop***.

When we do not know in advance the number of times the loop will be executed, we use a condition-controlled (or sentinel-controlled or indefinite loop) loop. In such a loop, a special value called the *sentinel value* is used to change the loop control expression from True to False. For example, when data is read from the user, the user may specify when they want the execution to stop. For example, the programmer may specify that to stop the loop a – 1 (or any other value) should be entered, they may enter –1. This value is called a ***sentinel value***. A condition-controlled loop is often useful for indefinite repetition loops as they use a True/False condition to control the number of times the loop is executed.

If your requirement is to have a *counter-controlled loop, then choose* `for` *loop; else, if you need to have a sentinel-controlled loop then go for a* `while` *loop*. Table 5.1 shows a comparison between the counter-controlled and condition-controlled loops.

**Table 5.1** Comparison between condition-controlled and counter-controlled loops

| Attribute | Counter-controlled Loop | Condition-controlled Loop |
|---|---|---|
| Number of execution | Used when number of times the loop has to be executed is known in advance. | Used when number of times the loop has to be executed is not known in advance. |
| Condition variable | In counter-controlled loops, we have a counter variable. | In condition-controlled loops, we use a sentinel variable. |
| Value and limitation of variable | The value of the counter variable and the condition for loop execution, both are strict. | The condition for loop execution is strict but the value of the sentinel variable may vary. |

```
i = 0                    i = 0                         for i in range(11):
while(i<=10):            while(1):                         print(i, end = ' ')
    print(i, end=' ')        print(i, end = ' ')      Counter-controlled
    1+=1                     i+=1
Counter-controlled           if(i==11):
                                break
                         Condition-controlled
```

## 5.5 NESTED LOOPS

Nested loop means that a loop is placed inside another loop. Although both `for` and `while` loop can be nested, we usually use nested `for` loops as they are easiest to control. In such a case, the inner `for` loop can be used to control the number of times a particular set of statements will be executed and the outer `for` loop can be used to control the number of times the inner loop is repeated. In Python, loops can be nested to any desired level.

## Basic Loop Structures/Iterative Statements

| Example 5.3 | Write a program to print the following pattern. |
|---|---|

Pass 1- 1 2 3 4 5
Pass 2- 1 2 3 4 5
Pass 3- 1 2 3 4 5
Pass 4- 1 2 3 4 5
Pass 5-1 2 3 4 5

```
for i in range(1,6):
    print{"PASS",i,"- ",end='')
    for j in range{1,6):
        print(j, end=' ')
    print()
```

| Example 5.4 | Write a program to print the following pattern. |
|---|---|

\*\*\*\*\*\*\*\*\*\*
\*\*\*\*\*\*\*\*\*\*
\*\*\*\*\*\*\*\*\*\*
\*\*\*\*\*\*\*\*\*\*
\*\*\*\*\*\*\*\*\*\*

```
for i in range(5):
    print()
    for j in range{5):
        print "*",end='')
```

## 5.6 THE break STATEMENT

The break statement is used to terminate the execution of the nearest enclosing loop in which it appears. The break statement is widely used with for loop and while loop. When the compiler encounters a break statement, the control passes to the statement that follows the loop in which the break statement appears. Its syntax is quite simple, just type the keyword **break**.

Note that the code is meant to print first 10 numbers using a while loop, but it will actually print only numbers from 0 to 4. As soon as i becomes equal to 5, the break statement is executed and the control jumps to the statement following the while loop.

*Hence, the **break** statement is used to exit a loop from any point within its body, bypassing its normal termination expression.* When the break statement is encountered inside a loop, the loop is immediately terminated, and program control is passed to the next statement following the loop. Figure 5.3 shows the transfer of control when the break statement is encountered.

**Program to demonstrate the break statement**
```
i = 1
while i <= 10:
    print(i, end=' ')
    if i==S:
        break
    i = i+1
print("\n Done")
```
**OUTPUT**
1 2 3 4 5
Done

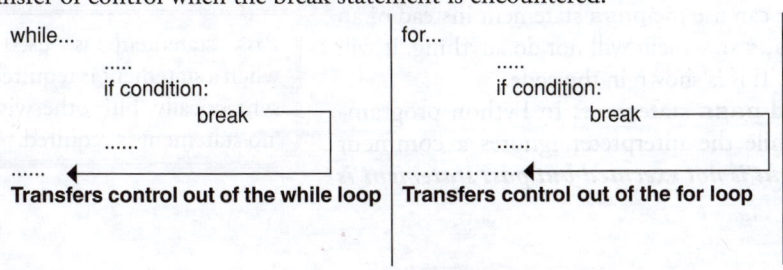

**Figure 5.3** The break statement

## 5.7 THE continue STATEMENT

Like the break statement, the continue statement can only appear in the body of a loop. When the compiler encounters a continue statement then the rest of the statements in the loop are skipped and the control is unconditionally transferred to the loop-continuation portion of the nearest enclosing loop. Its syntax is quite simple, just type the keyword **continue**.

When the continue statement is encountered in the while and for loop, the control is transferred to the statement that tests the controlling expression. However, if placed with a for loop, the continue statement causes a branch to the code that updates the loop variable.

**Program to demonstrate the continue statement**
```
for i in range(1,11):
    if(i==S):
        continue
    print(i, end=' ')
print("\n Done")
```
**OUTPUT**
1 2 3 4 6 7 8 9 10
Done

Note that the code is meant to print numbers from 0 to 10. But as soon as *i* becomes equal to 5, the continue statement is encountered, so rest of the statement(s) in the `for` loop are skipped. In the output, there is no 5 (5 could not be printed as continue caused early increment of *i* and skipping of statement that printed the value of i on screen). Figure 5.4 illustrates the use of `continue` statement in loops.

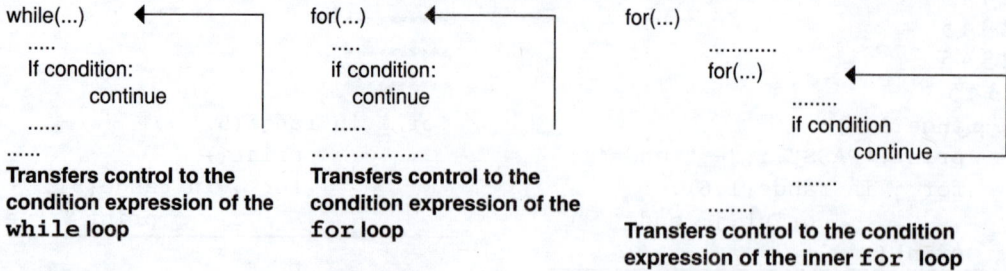

Figure 5.4  The `continue` statement

Hence, the `continue` statement is the opposite of the `break` statement. It forces the next iteration of the loop thereby skipping any statements that were a part of the loop. The `continue` statement is usually used to restart a statement sequence when an error occurs.

## 5.8  THE pass STATEMENT

Pass statement is used when a statement is required syntactically but no instruction has to be executed. It specifies a *null* operation or simply **No Op**eration (NOP) statement. Nothing happens when the `pass` statement is executed. Syntax of pass statement is simple, just type the keyword **pass**.

The `pass` statement is used as a placeholder for future statements. For example, if we have a loop that is not implemented yet, in which we may wish to write some code in the future. Then, we can use the `pass` statement instead of an empty body of the loop. Though the `pass` statement will not do anything, it will make the program syntactically correct. This is shown in the code.

**Difference between comment and pass statements** In Python programming, pass is a null statement. While the interpreter ignores a comment entirely, pass is not ignored. *Comment is not executed but pass statement is executed but nothing happens.*

**Program to demonstrate pass statement**
```
for i in range(5):
    pass  #The statement is doing nothing
    print(i,end = ' ')
print("Done")
```
**OUTPUT**
0 1 2 3 4 Done

> Pass statement is used when a statement is required syntactically but otherwise no statement is required.

## 5.9  THE else STATEMENT USED WITH LOOPS

We have studied `if-else` block in the previous chapter. We can also have an `else` statement associated with loop statements. *If the `else` statement is used with a `for` loop, the `else` statement is executed when the loop has completed iterating. But when used with the `while` loop, the `else` statement is executed when the condition becomes false.*

```
for i in range(3):
    print(i, end=' ')
else:
    print("Done")
```
**OUTPUT**
0 1 2 3 Done

```
i = 10
while(i<0):
    print(i)
    i = i + 1
else:
    print(i, "is not negative so loop did not execute")
```
**OUTPUT**
i is not negative so loop did not execute

# PROGRAMMER'S ZONE

1. **Write a program to print 10 horizontal hyphens(-).**
   ```
   i = 1
   while(i<=10):
       print("-",end=' ')
       i = i+1
   ```
   **OUTPUT**
   _ _ _ _ _ _ _ _ _ _

2. **Write a program to calculate the sum of numbers from *m* to *n*.**
   ```
   m = int(input("Enter the value of m : "))
   n = int(input("Enter the value of n : "))
   s = 0
   while(m<=n):
           s = s+m
           m = m+1
   print("SUM = ",s)
   ```
   **OUTPUT**
   ```
   Enter the value of m : 3
   Enter the value of n : 9
   SUM =   42
   ```

3. **Write a program to read the numbers until −123 is encountered. Also count the negative, positive and zeroes entered by the user.**
   ```
   negatives = positives = zeroes = 0
   print("Enter -1 to exit...")
   while(1):
      num = int(input("Enter any number : "))
      if(num==-123):
          break
      if(num==0):
          zeroes = zeroes+1
      elif(num>0):
          positives = positives+1
      else:
          negatives = negatives+1
   print("Count of positive numbers entered : ",positives)
   print("Count of negative numbers entered : ",negatives)
   print("Count of zeroes entered : ",zeroes)
   ```
   **OUTPUT**
   ```
   Enter -1 to exit...
   Enter any number : 17
   Enter any number : 19
   Enter any number : 11
   Enter any number : 13
   Enter any number : -30
   Enter any number : -60
   Enter any number : -70
   ```

```
Enter any number : 40
Enter any number : 50
Enter any number : 0
Enter any number : -15
Count of positive numbers entered :   6
Count of negative numbers entered :   3
Count of zeroes entered :   1
```

4. **Write a program to read the numbers until −123 is encountered. Find the average of positive numbers and negative numbers entered by the user.**

```
neg_count = 0
neg_s = 0
pos_count = 0
pos_s = 0
print("Enter -1 to exit....")
num = int(input("Enter the number : "))
while(num!=-123):
    if(num<0):
        neg_count=neg_count+1
        neg_s=neg_s+num
    else:
        pos_count=pos_count+1
        pos_s=pos_s+num
    num = int(input("Enter the number : "))
neg_avg = float(neg_s)/neg_count
pos_avg = float(pos_s)/pos_count
print("The average of negative numbers is : ",neg_avg)
print("The average of positive numbers is : ",pos_avg)
```

> if statement is run once if condition is True, and never if it is False. A while statement is similar, except that it can be run more than once.

**OUTPUT**
```
Enter -1 to exit....
Enter the number : 1
Enter the number : 2
Enter the number : 3
Enter the number : -4
Enter the number : -5
Enter the number : -6
Enter the number : 8
Enter the number : -9
Enter the number : 10
Enter the number : -123
The average of negative numbers is :  -6.0
The average of positive numbers is :  4.8
```

5. **Write a program to calculate the average of numbers entered by the user.**

```
s = 0
count = 0
print "Enter -1 to stop...."
num = 0
while(num != -1):
    s = s+num
```

```
    num = int(input("Enter the marks : "))
    count = count+1
avg = float(s)/count
print "TOTAL MARKS : ",s,"\tAVERAGE MARKS : ",avg
```

**OUTPUT**
```
Enter -1 to stop....
Enter the marks : 90
Enter the marks : 98
Enter the marks : 97
Enter the marks : 89
Enter the marks : 79
Enter the marks : 96
Enter the marks : -1
TOTAL MARKS :   549    AVERAGE MARKS :    78.4285714286
```

6. **Write a program to find whether the given number is an Armstrong number or not.**
   **Hint:** An Armstrong number of three digits is an integer such that the sum of the cubes of its digits is equal to the number itself. For example, 371 is an Armstrong number since 3**3 + 7**3 + 1**3 = 371.
   ```
   n = int(input("Enter the number : "))
   s = 0
   num = n
   while(n>0):
           r = n%10
           s = s+(r**3)
           n = n/10
   if(s==num):
           print("The number is Armstrong")
   else:
           print("The number is not Armstrong")
   ```

   **OUTPUT**
   ```
   Enter the number : 373
   432 is not an Armstrong number
   ```

7. **Write a program to enter a decimal number. Calculate and display the binary equivalent of this number.**
   ```
   decimal_num = int(input("Enter the decimal number: "))
   binary_num = 0
   i = 0
   while(decimal_num!=0):
           remainder = decimal_num%2
           binary_num = binary_num+remainder*(10**i)
           decimal_num = decimal_num/2
           i = i+1
   print("The binary equivalent =",binary_num)
   ```

   **OUTPUT**
   ```
   Enter the decimal number : 8
   The binary equivalent = 1000
   ```

8. **Write a program to enter a binary number and convert it into decimal number.**
   ```
   binary_num = int(input("Enter the binary number : "))
   decimal_num = 0
   ```

```
i = 0
while(binary_num!=0):
        remainder = binary_num%10
        decimal_num = decimal_num+remainder*(2**i)
        binary_num = binary_num/10
        i = i+1
print("The decimal equivalent is",decimal_num)
```

**OUTPUT**

```
Enter the binary number : 1010
The decimal equivalent is 10
```

9. **Write a program to enter a number and then calculate the sum of its digits.**
```
sumOfDigits = 0
num = int(input("Enter the number : "))
while(num!=0):
        temp=num%10
        sumOfDigits = sumOfDigits+temp
        num=num/10
print("The sum of digits is :",sumOfDigits)
```

**OUTPUT**

```
Enter the number : 456
The sum of digits = 15
```

10. **Write a program to calculate the GCD of two numbers.**
```
num1 = int(input("Enter the two numbers : "))
num2 = int(input("Enter the two numbers : "))
if(num1>num2):
        dividend = num1
        divisor = num2
else:
        dividend = num2
        divisor = num1
while(divisor!=0):
        remainder = dividend%divisor
        dividend = divisor
        divisor = remainder
print("GCD of",num1,"and",num2,"is",dividend)
```

> To stop an infinite loop, press Ctrl + C keys or close the IDLE.

**OUTPUT**

```
Enter the first number : 40
Enter the second number : 10
GCD of 64 and 14 is = 10
```

11. **Write a program to print the reverse of a number.**
```
num = int(input("Enter the number : "))
print("The reversed number is :",)
while(num!=0):
        temp = num%10
        print(temp, end=' ')
        num = num/10
```

**OUTPUT**
```
Enter the number : 678
The reversed number is : 8 7 6
```

12. **Write a program using for loop to calculate the average of first *n* natural numbers.**
    ```
    n = int(input("Enter the value of n : "))
    avg = 0.0
    s = 0
    for i in range(1,n+1):
        s = s+i
    avg = s/i
    print("The sum of first",n,"natural numbers is",s)
    print("The average of first",n,"natural numbers is",avg)
    ```

    **OUTPUT**
    ```
    Enter the value of n : 10
    The sum of first n natural numbers = 55
    n The average of first n natural numbers = 5.500
    ```

13. **Write a program to print the multiplication table of *n*, where *n* is entered by the user.**
    ```
    n = int(input("Enter any number : "))
    print("Multiplication table of",n)
    print("*********************************")
    for i in range(1,11):
        print(n,"X",i,"=",n*i)
    ```

    **OUTPUT**
    ```
    Enter any number : 5
    Multiplication table of 5
    **********************
    5 X 0 = 0
    5 X 1 = 5
    …..
    5 X 20 = 100
    ```

14. **Write a program using for loop to print all the numbers from *m* to *n*, thereby classifying them as even or odd.**
    ```
    m = int(input("Enter the value of m : "))
    n = int(input("Enter the value of n : "))
    for i in range(m,n+1):
        if(i%2==0):
            print(i,"is even number")
        else:
            print(i,"is odd number")
    ```

    **OUTPUT**
    ```
    Enter the value of m : 10
    Enter the value of n : 15
    10 is even number
    11 is odd number
    12 is even number
    13 is odd number
    14 is even number
    15 is odd number
    ```

15. **Write a program using `for` loop to calculate the factorial of a number.**

    ```
    num = int(input("Enter the number : "))
    if(num==0):
            fact = 1
    fact = 1
    for i in range(1,num+1):
            fact = fact*i
    print("Factorial of",num,"is",fact)
    ```

    **OUTPUT**
    ```
    Enter the number : 6
    Factorial of is : 720
    ```

16. **Write a program to classify a given number as prime or composite.**

    ```
    number = int(input('Enter number : '))
    isComposite = 0
    for i in range(2,(number-1)/2):
       if(number%i == 0):
           isComposite = 1
           break
    if(isComposite == 1):
       print("Number is Composite")
    else :
       print("Number is prime")
    ```

    **OUTPUT**
    ```
    Enter the number : 17
    17 is a prime number
    ```

17. **Write a program using `while` loop to read the numbers until −1 is encountered. Also count the number of prime numbers and composite numbers entered by the user.**

    ```
    total_prime = 0
    total_composite = 0
    while(1):
       num = int(input("Enter no. "))
       if(num == -1):
          break
       is_composite = 0
       for i in range(2,(num-1)/2):
           if(num%i == 0):
               is_composite = 1
               break
       if(is_composite):
           total_composite+=1
       else:
           total_prime+=1
    print("total composite : ",total_composite)
    print("total prime : ",total_prime)
    ```

**OUTPUT**
```
Enter no. 12
Enter no. 17
Enter no. 15
Enter no. 27
Enter no. 39
Enter no. 29
Enter no. 37
Enter no. -1
total composite : 4
total prime : 3
```

18. **Write a program that prints whether every number in a range is prime or composite.**
```
n = int(input("Enter the value of n : "))
i=2
print("1 is neither prime nor composite")
while i<n:
  flag = 0
  for j in range(2,i-1):
    if(i%j==0):
      flag=1
      print(i,"is a composite number")
      break
  if(flag==0):
    print(i,"is a prime number")
  i = i+1
```

**OUTPUT**
```
Enter the value of n : 10
1 is neither prime nor composite
2 is a prime number
3 is a prime number
4 is a composite number
5 is a prime number
6 is a composite number
7 is a prime number
8 is a composite number
9 is a composite number
```

19. **Write a program to calculate pow(*x*,*n*).**
```
num = int(input("Enter the number : "))
n = int(input("Till which power to calculate?"))
result = 1
for i in range(n):
     result = result*num
print(num,"raised to the power",n,"is",result)
```

**OUTPUT**
```
Enter the number : 3
Till which power to calculate : 5
3 raised to the power 5 is 243
```

20. **Write a program that displays all leap years from 2000–2050.**
    ```
    print("Leap Years from 2000-2050 are : ")
    for i in range(2000,2051):
            if(i%4==0):
                    print(i,end=' ')
    ```
    **OUTPUT**
    ```
    Leap Years from 2000-2050 are :
    2000 2004 2008 2012 2016 2020 2024 2028 2032 2036 2040 2044 2048
    ```

21. **Write a program to sum the series – $1 + 1/2 + \dots + 1/n$.**
    ```
    n = int(input("Enter the number : "))
    s = 0.0
    for i in range(1,n+1):
            a = 1.0/i
            s = s+a
    print("The sum of 1,1/2......1/"+str(n)+" is "+str(s))
    ```
    **OUTPUT**
    ```
    Enter the number : 7
    The sum of 1,1/2......1/5 is  2.5928571428571425
    ```

22. **Write a program to sum the series – $1/1^2 + 1/2^2 + \dots + 1/n^2$.**
    ```
    n = int(input("Enter the number : "))
    s = 0.0
    for i in range(1,n+1):
            a = 1.0/(i**2)
            s = s+a
    print("The sum of series is",s)
    ```
    **OUTPUT**
    ```
    Enter the number : 7
    The sum of series is  1.511797052154195
    ```

23. **Write a program to sum the series – $1/2 + 2/3 + \dots + n/(n+1)$.**
    ```
    n = int(input("Enter the number : "))
    s = 0.0
    for i in range(1,n+1):
            a = float(i)/(i+1)
            s = s+a
    print("The sum of 1/2+2/3......n/(n+1) is",s)
    ```

    > Using break or continue statement outside a loop caused an error.

    **OUTPUT**
    ```
    Enter the number : 7
    The sum of 1/2+2/3......n/(n+1) is  5.2821428571428575
    ```

24. **Write a program to sum the series – $1/1 + 2^2/2 + 3^3/3 + \dots + n^2/n$.**
    ```
    n = int(input("Enter the value of n : "))
    s = 0.0
    for i in range(1,n+1):
            a = float(i**i)/i
            s = s+a
    print("The sum of the series is",s)
    ```

**OUTPUT**
```
Enter the value of n : 7
The sum of the series is  126126.0
```

25. **Write a program to calculate sum of cubes of numbers 1–n.**
```
n = int(input("Enter the value of n : "))
s = 0
for i in range(1,n+1):
     a = i**3
     s = s+a
print("The sum of cubes is",s)
```

**OUTPUT**
```
Enter the value of n : 4
The sum of cubes is 100
```

26. **Write a program to find the sum of squares of odd numbers.**
```
n = int(input("Enter the number : "))
s = 0
for i in range(1,n+1):
     if(i%2!=0):
          term = i**2
     else:
          term = 0
     s = s+term
print("The sum of squares of odd number less than",n,"is",s)
```

**OUTPUT**
```
Enter the number : 10
The sum of squares of even number less than 10 is 165
```

27. **Write a program to print the following pattern.**
```
*
* *
* * *
* * * *
* * * * *
for i in range(1,6):
     print()
for j in range(i):
     print("*", end=' ')
```

> The continue statement is used to stop the current iteration of the loop and continue with the next one.

28. **Write a program to print the following pattern.**
```
1
1 2
1 2 3
1 2 3 4
1 2 3 4 5
```
```
for i in range(1,6):
    print()
    for j in range(1,i+1):
        print(j, end=' ')
```

29. Write a program to print the following pattern.

```
    1
   2 2
  3 3 3
 4 4 4 4
5 5 5 5 5
```

```
for i in range(1,6):
    print()
    for j in range(1,i+1):
        print(i, end=' ')
```

30. Write a program to print the following pattern.

```
   0
  1 2
 3 4 5
6 7 8 9
```

```
count = 0
for i in range(1,5):
    print()          #prints a new line
    for j in range(1,i+1):
        print(count, end=' ')
        count = count+1
```

31. Write a program to print the following pattern.

```
A
AB
ABC
ABCD
ABCDE
ABCDEF
```

```
for i in range(1,7):
    ch = 'A'
    print()
    for j in range(1,i+1):
        print(ch, end=' ')
        ch = chr(ord(ch)+1)
```

32 Write a program to print the following pattern.

```
    1
   12
  123
 1234
12345
```

```
N = 5
for i in range(1,N+1):
    for k in range(N,i,-1):
        print(" ", end=' ')
    for j in range(1,i+1):
        print(j, end=' ')
    print()
```

33. Write a program to print the following pattern.

```
        1
      1 2 1
    1 2 3 2 1
  1 2 3 4 3 2 1
1 2 3 4 5 4 3 2 1
```

```
N = 5
for i in range (1 , N+1) :
    for k in range(N,i,-1) :
        print( " " , end=' ' )
    for j in range(1,i+1):
        print(j, end=' ')
    for 1 in range(i-1 , 0 ,-1) :
        print(1 , end= ' ' )
    print()
```

**34.** Write a program to print the following pattern.

```
                         N = 5
         1               for i in range(1 , N+1) :
       2 2                   for k in range(N,i , -1):
     3 3 3                       print("", end=' ')
   4 4 4 4                   for j in range(1,i+1) :
 5 5 5 5 5                       print(i , end=' ')
                             print()
```

**35.** Write a program to calculate the square root of all positive numbers entered by the user.

```
import math
while(1):
    num = int(input("Enter no. "))
    if(num == -111):
        break
    elif num < 0:
      print("Square root of negative numbers cannot
    be calculated")
        continue
    else:
        print("Square root of ", num, " = ", math.sqrt(num))
```

> When the complier encounters a continue statement then the rest of the statements in the loop are skipped and the control is unconditionally transferred to the loop-continuation portion of the nearest enclosing loop.

**OUTPUT**
```
Enter no. 169
Square root of  169  =  13.0
Enter no. 64
Square root of  64  =  8.0
Enter no. 625
Square root of  625  =  25.0
Enter no. -16
Square root of negative numbers cannot be calculated
Enter no. -111
```

> break statement terminates the loop and transfers execution to the statement immediately following the loop.

## Key Terms

**Iterative statement:** Statements that repeat the execution of a block of statements depending on the value of an integer expression.

**Definite repetition loop:** A counter-controlled loop in which the counter is assigned a constant or a value is also known as a definite repetition loop.

**Nested loop:** A loop that is placed inside another loop.

## Chapter Highlights

- In Python, iterative statements are implemented through `while` loop and `for` loop.
- The `while` loop provides a mechanism to repeat one or more statements while a particular condition is true.
- The value of the loop control variable is updated with every iteration of the loop.
- The `for` loop provides a mechanism to repeat a task until a particular condition is true.
- The `for..in` statement is a looping statement used in Python to iterate over a sequence of objects.
- The `range()` is a built-in function in Python that is used to iterate over a sequence of numbers.
- Loops can be either counter-controlled or condition-controlled (or sentinel-controlled) loops.

- When we do not know in advance the number of times the loop will be executed, we use a condition-controlled loop.
- The `break` statement is used to terminate the execution of the nearest enclosing loop in which it appears.
- When the compiler encounters a `continue` statement then the rest of the statements in the loop are skipped and the control is unconditionally transferred to the loop-continuation portion of the nearest enclosing loop.
- `Pass` statement is used when a statement is required syntactically but no instruction has to be executed. It specifies a null operation or simply No Operation (NOP) statement.
- If the `else` statement is used with a `for` loop, the `else` statement is executed when the loop has completed iterating. But when it is used with the `while` loop, the `else` statement is executed when the condition becomes false.

## Review Questions

1. With the help of a flowchart, explain the construct of a `while` loop.
2. Why is the value of the loop control variable updated with every iteration of the loop?
3. With the help of a flowchart, explain the construct of a `for` loop.
4. With the help of an example explain the use of `range()` function.
5. Differentiate between a condition-controlled and a counter-controlled loop.
6. With the help of an example, explain the use of `break` statement.
7. What happens when the pass statement executes?
8. Differentiate between the comment and the pass statements.
9. When is the else statement with loops executed?
10. What will happen if we replace the break statement in the code with a `continue` statement?
11. Fill in the blanks to complete the code:

    a. create a loop that increments the value of x by 3 and prints the odd values from 0–100.
    ```
    x = 0
    ___x <= ___
    ___(x)
    x += 2
    ```
    b. to create a for loop that prints only the even values in the range 0–50:
    ```
    ____ i in range(_____):
        print(___)
    ```

12. Identify the definite and indefinite loop.
    ```
    n = input('Enter a number: ')        x = 0
    while n != -1:                       while x<10:
        n = input('Enter a number: ')        print 10**num
                                             n = n+1
    ```

13. Correct the code to produce the desired output.
    ```
    for i in range(10,0):    i=10                    i=10 ;  result = 1
        print(i)             while(i>0):             while(i>0):
                                 print(i)                result = result + i**2
                                 i-1                     i = i+1
                                                     print(result)
    ```

14. The following for loops are written to print numbers from 1 to 10. Are these loops correct? Justify your answer.
    ```
    for i in range(10):      for i in range(10):     for i in range(10):
        print(i)                 num = i+1               print(i)
                                 print(num)              i = i+1
    ```

15. Write the following piece of code using for loop.
    ```
    i = 20
    while i>0:
        print(i)
        i = i-2
    ```

## Programming Exercises

1. Write a program that converts a decimal number into its equivalent octal value.
2. Write a program that converts an octal number into its equivalent decimal value.
3. Write a function that accepts two positive numbers n and m where m<=n, and returns numbers between 1 and n that are divisible by m.
4. Write a program to convert time in hours into minutes and vice-versa.
5. Write a program to calculate conveyance charges to be paid by the users. Enter the type of car as a character (like s for sedan, p for prime, m for mini) and distance in km. Calculate charges as given below: sedan – 17 Rs per km, prime – 12 Rs per km, mini – 10 Rs per km.
6. Modify the above program to calculate the conveyance charges. Read the km when the user sits in the car and the time of his/her exit. Calculate the difference between the two readings and calculate the charges based on following rules.

| Car Type | Rate up to First 5 km | Rate after First 5 km |
| --- | --- | --- |
| Mini | 10 | 10 |
| Prime | 20 | 12 |
| Sedan | 30 | 17 |

7. Write a program to sum the series $1^2/1 + 2^2/2 + 3^2/3 +.....+n^2/n$.
8. Write a program that prints cube of numbers in the range (1,n).
9. Write a program that prompts user to enter the distance between his/her home and school. If the distance is in kilometers, display it in meters and vice versa.
10. Write a program that displays Python Programming as:
    a. python programming      b. PYTHON PROGRAMMING      c. pYTHON pROGRAMMING
11. Write a program that prompts users to enter numbers. Once the user enters -1, it displays the count, sum and average of even numbers and that of odd numbers.
12. Write a program to display the sin(x) value where x ranges from 0 to 360 in steps of 45.
13. Write a program that displays all the numbers from 1-100 that are not divisible by 7 as well as by 11.
14. Write a program that accepts any number and prints the number of digits in that number.
15. Write a program that prints numbers from 100 to 1 in steps of 4.
16. Write a program to generate the following pattern:
    ```
    * * * *
    *     *
    *     *
    *     *
    * * * *
    ```

17. Write a program to generate the following pattern:
    ```
    $ * * * *
    * $     *
    *   $   *
    *     $ *
    * * * * $
    ```
18. Write a program to generate the following pattern:
    ```
    $ * * * $
    * $   $ *
    *   $   *
    * $   $ *
    $ * * * $
    ```
19. Write a program that reads integers until the user wants to stop. When the user stops entering numbers, display the largest of all the numbers entered.
20. Write a program to generate the Fibonacci series.
21. Write a program to print first 20 even numbers in descending order.
22. Write a program to print the sum of the following series:
    a. $-x + x^2 - x^3 + x^4 + ...$
    b. $1 - x + x^2/2! - x^3/3! + ...$
23. Write a program to print the following pattern:
    a.
    ```
        *
       * *
      * * *
       * *
        *
    ```
    b.
    ```
    *
    * *
    * * *
    * *
    *
    ```
    c.
    ```
      *
     * *
    *   *
     * *
      *
    ```
    d.
    ```
    *
    * *
    *   *
    * *
    *
    ```
    e.
    ```
          A
         A B A
        A B C B A
       A B C D C B A
    ```
    f.
    ```
        1
       2 1 2
      3 2 1 2 3
    ```
    g.
    ```
    12345
    2345
    345
    45
    5
    ```
    h.
    ```
    1
    12
    123
    1234
    12345
    ```

## Fill in the Blanks

1. _____ statements are used to repeatedly execute one or more statements in a block.
2. In Python, iterative statements are implemented through _____ and _____ loops.
3. An _____ loop will occur if the condition of `while` loop never becomes false.
4. The `for` loop provides a mechanism to repeat a task until a particular condition is _____.
5. The _____ function in Python is used to iterate over a sequence of numbers.
6. When we know in advance the number of times the loop should be executed, we use a _____ -controlled loop.
7. When we do not know in advance the number of times the loop will be executed, we use a _____ -controlled loop.
8. When _____ statement is encountered, the rest of the statements in the loop are skipped and the control is unconditionally transferred to the loop-continuation portion of the nearest enclosing loop.
9. The _____ statement specifies a null operation.
10. The _____ statement is executed when the for loop has completed iterating.

## Basic Loop Structures/Iterative Statements

### State True or False

1. The `while` loop repeats one or more statements while a particular condition is false.
2. Iterative statement repeats the execution of a block of statements depending on the value of an expression that evaluates to an integer value only.
3. In the `while` loop, the condition is tested after the statement block is executed at least once.
4. The value of the loop control variable is updated with every alternate iteration of the loop.
5. An infinite loop will occur if the condition of `while` loop is always false.
6. The `for` loop is executed for each item in the sequence.
7. Every iteration of the loop must make the loop control variable farther from the end of the sequence.
8. The step argument in the `range()` function is optional.
9. Sentinel value is used in counter-controlled loop.
10. Both `for` and `while` loop can be nested. Ans
11. The `break` and `continue` statements can only appear in the body of a loop.
12. In a `for` loop, the `continue` statement causes a branch to the code that updates the loop variable.
13. The `pass` statement is a non-executable statement that is ignored by the compiler.
14. The number of times the loop control variable is updated is equal to the number of times the loop iterates.
15. In a `while` loop, the loop control variable is initialized in the body of the loop.

### Multiple Choice Questions

1. Which keys are not pressed to exit from the infinite loop?
   a. Alt + C
   b. Ctrl + C
   c. Alt + F4
   d. Ctrl + Q
2. The step argument in the `range()` function cannot be _____.
   a. less than zero
   b. greater than zero
   c. zero
   d. none of these
3. `range(1,5)` will generate numbers _____.
   a. 0, 1, 2, 3, 4, 5
   b. 0, 1, 2, 3, 4
   c. 1, 2, 3, 4
   d. 1, 2, 3, 4, 5
4. By default, every number in the range is incremented by ____.
   a. 0
   b. 1
   c. 2
   d. 3
5. In a counter-controlled loop, the counter must be _____.
   a. initialized
   b. tested
   c. updated
   d. All of these.
6. A loop within another loop is also known as a _____ loop.
   a. sentinel-controlled
   b. condition-controlled
   c. counter-controlled
   d. nested
7. Which statement is used to terminate the execution of the nearest enclosing loop in which it appears?
   a. `break`
   b. `continue`
   c. `pass`
   d. `else`
8. In a `while` loop, if the body is executed n times, then the test expression is executed ____ times.
   a. n – 1
   b. n
   c. n + 1
   d. 2n
9. ```
   i = 1
   while i > 0:
       print("loop")
   ```
   The above loop is best example of _____ loop.
   a. nested
   b. infinite
   c. counter-controlled
   d. condition-controlled
   ```

10. How many numbers will be printed?
    ```
    i = 5
    while i>=0:
        print(i)
        i=i-1
    ```
    a. 5            b. 6            c. 4            d. 0

11. How many numbers will be printed?
    ```
    i = 10
    while True:
        print(i)
        i = i - 1
        if i<=7:
            break
    ```
    a. 1            b. 2            c. 3            d. 4

12. How many lines will be printed by this code?
    ```
    while False:
        print("Hello")
    ```
    a. Hello        b. 0            c. 10           d. Countless

## Give the Output

1. ```
   for i in range(1,20):
       if i%5==0:
           break
       else:
           print(i)
   ```

2. ```
   for i in range(1,20):
       if i%5==0:
           continue
       else:
           print(i)
   ```

3. ```
   while(4>5):
       print("DONE")
   else:
       print("NOT DONE")
   ```

4. ```
   for i in range(1,5):
       for j in range(1,i):
           print('#',end = ' ')
       print()
   ```

5. ```
   while(5*2 > 10):
       print("JUST DO IT")
   else:
       print("DONE")
   ```

6. ```
   a = 10; b = 0
   while(a>b):
       print(a,b)
       a=a-1
       b=b+1
   ```

7.  ```
    run = True
    a = 100
    while run == True:
        print(a)
        a = a - 10
        if a < 40:
            run = False
    ```

8.  ```
    for i in range(100,50,-10):
        print(i)
    ```

9.  ```
    for i in range(100,50,-10):
        print(i)
    ```

10. ```
    x = 10; y = 5
    for i in range(x-y*2):
        print("%")
    ```

11. ```
    for letter in "HELLO":
        pass
    ```

12. ```
    i=1
    while i<=6:
        print(i),
        i=i+1
    print("Done")
    ```

13. ```
    i=0
    while i<10:
        i = i + 1
        if(i == 5):
            print("\n Continue")
            continue
        if(i==7):
            print("\n Breaking")
            break
        print(i),
    print("\n Done")
    ```

14. ```
    for i in range(5):
        print("hello!", end= " ")
    ```

15. ```
    for i in range(10):
        if not i%2==0:
            print(i+1)
    ```

16. ```
    for i in range(10,0,-1):
        print(i, end = ' ')
    ```

17. ```
    for i in range(5,25,3):
        print(i, end = ' ')
    ```

18. ```
    for i in "PYTHON":
        print(i,'-',end='')
    ```

19. ```
    for i in range(10):
        pass
    print(i)
    ```
    ```

**20.**
```
while True:
    str = input("Enter a string (Bye to exit) : ")
    if str == "bye":
        break
    print(str)
else:
    print("Exiting......")
```

## Find the Error

**1.**
```
while(i<10):
    print(i)
```

## Answers

### Fill in the Blanks
1. Flow control
2. while, for.
3. infinite
4. true
5. range()
6. counter
7. condition
8. continue
9. pass
10. else

### State True or False
1. False
2. True
3. False
4. False
5. False
6. True
7. False
8. True
9. False
10. True
11. True
12. True
13. False
14. True
15. False

### Multiple Choice Questions
1. a
2. c
3. c
4. b
5. d
6. d
7. a
8. c
9. b
10. b
11. c
12. b

### Give the Output
1. 1,2,3,4
2. 1
3. NOT DONE
4. #
   ##
   ###
5. DONE
6. 10 0
7. 100 90 80 70 60 50 40
8. 100 90 80 70 60
9. No output
10. No output
11. No output on the screen.
12. 1 2 3 4 5 6 Done
13. 1 2 3 4 Continue 6 Breaking Done
14. hello! hello! hello! hello! hello!
15. 2 4 6 8 10
16. 10 9 8 7 6 5 4 3 2 1
17. 5 8 11 14 17 20 23
18. P -Y -T -H -O -N -
19. 9
20. No output when bye is entered.

### Find the Error
1. NameError: name 'i' is not defined

# Functions and Modules

## Chapter Objectives

This chapter helps the reader to think like computer professionals and engineers by breaking big complex problems into smaller and simpler ones. It illustrates how to create building blocks on which solution of real-world problems can be fabricated. The topics covered in this chapter include:

- Defining, calling and re-defining functions
- Working with built-in modules
- Creating own customized packages
- Using popular built-in functions
- Variable lifetime and scope
- Vital statements like `return` and `global`
- Function composition

In the previous chapters, we have used Python to write many useful programs. To further extend the usability of our programs, we must learn about the concept of functions. To understand functions, consider a scenario. If you are a project manager working on a very big project, then will you give the entire project to a single person or divide the project into *n* pieces and allocate each person an individual piece?

Of course, you will divide and allocate. Same is the case with programs. Instead of writing the entire code in one place, we must break the program into different functions or modules. Each module should then be coded individually. Whenever the functionality of these modules is required, it can just be called. In a program, you can call a function any number of times depending on the requirements.

## 6.1 FUNCTION

***A function is a block of organized and reusable program code that performs a single, specific, and well-defined task.*** Consider Fig. 6.1, which explains how a function `func1()` is called to perform a well-defined task. As soon as `func1()` is called, the program control is passed to the first statement in the function. All the statements in the function are executed and then the program control is passed to the statement following the one that called the function.

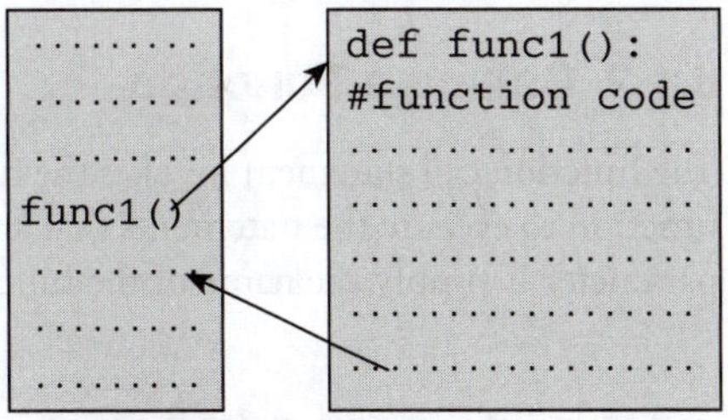

In Fig. 6.2, we see that `func1()` calls another function named `func2()`. Therefore, `func1()` is known as the **calling function** and `func2()` is known as the **called function.** The moment the compiler encounters a function call, instead of executing the next statement in the calling function, the control jumps to the statements that are a part of the called function. After the called function is executed, the control is returned to the calling program.

**Figure 6.1** Calling a function

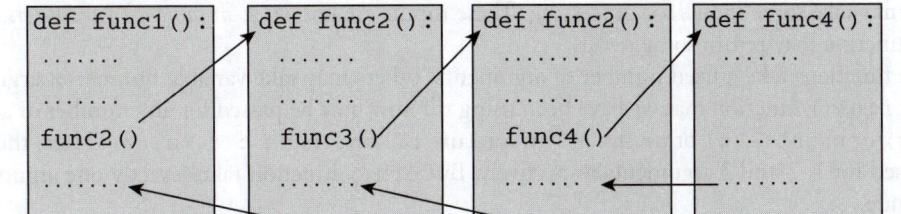

**Figure 6.2** Calling a function from another function

There is no rule that the `func1()` can call only one function; it can call as many functions as it wants and as many times as it wants. For example, a function call placed within `for` loop or `while` loop may call the same function multiple times until the condition holds true.

### 6.1.1 Need for Functions

Functions are needed to facilitate *each function to be written and tested separately*. This simplifies the process of getting the total program to work.

Moreover, if a big program has to be developed without the use of any function, then there will be countless lines in the code and maintaining that program will be quite messy.

In fact, *all the libraries in Python* contain a set of functions that the programmers can use in their programs. These functions have been pre-written and pre-tested, so the programmers use them without worrying about their code details. In this chapter, we will be using some libraries in our programs.

Functions or modules *speed up program development* as the programmer needs to concentrate only on the code that he/she has to write. Also, when a big program is broken into multiple functions and then written by different programmers, the workload gets divided and program development gets speeded up.

Besides Python libraries, programmers can themselves *make their own functions* and modules to be used in other programs as well.

Thus, *code reuse* is one of the most prominent reasons to use functions. Large programs usually follow the DRY principle, that is, **Don't Repeat Yourself** principle. In the absence DRY principle, the programmer has to re-write the same piece of code multiple times thereby not only increasing the size and complexity of the code but also making it more prone to errors. For example, you have been using the `print()` function so often. Just imagine if you had to yourself write the code to display output of a variable without using the `print()` function, then even a small 2–3 line code will have many more lines of complex instructions.

Once a function is written it can be called multiple times wherever its functionality is required (as shown in Fig. 6.3). This not only saves us from rewriting the same instructions but also reduces the complexity of programs. Even a beginner can easily write codes for solving his/her problems without getting bogged down by unnecessarily writing instructions which are pre-written to do a particular task.

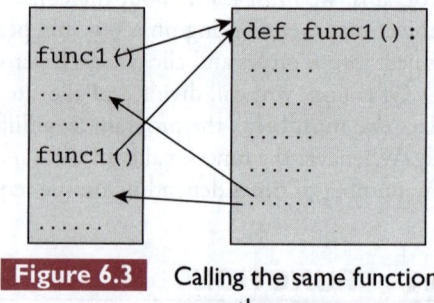

**Figure 6.3** Calling the same function more than once

### 6.1.2 Calling a Function

The function call statement invokes the function. When a function is invoked, the program control jumps to the called function to execute the statements that are a part of that function. The syntax of calling a function that does not accept parameter is simply the name of the function followed by parentheses, which is given as,

```
function_name()
```

Function call statement has the following syntax when it accepts parameters.

```
function_name(variable1, variable2, ...)
```

Also, remember certain points that must be remembered while calling a function.

- A function that is called or invoked to use its functionality is known as the *called function*.
- A function may take some inputs for processing. These inputs are known as *arguments/parameters*.
- The called function may return some result.
- While some functions take a fixed number of arguments, others may take variable number of arguments. For example, the `print()` function that we have been using till now may be passed for any number of arguments, such as `print(a)` or `print(a,b)` or `print("The value of and b is : ", a, b)`. Here, the same function is being passed for 1, 2 and 3 arguments respectively. But `ord()` function takes exactly one argument and prints its ASCII value.
- When the function is called, the interpreter checks if the correct number and type of parameters are passed in the function call. It also checks the type of the returned value (if it returns a value).

## 6.2 MODULES

In the previous section, we have seen that functions help us to reuse a particular piece of code. Modules go a step ahead. They allow you to reuse one or more functions in your programs, even in the programs in which those functions have not been defined.

Simply put, *module is a file with a .py extension that has definitions of all functions and variables that you would like to use even in other programs.* The program in which you want to use functions or variables to be defined in a module will simply import that particular module (or .py file).

> Modules are pre-written pieces of code that are used to perform common tasks like generating random numbers, performing mathematical operations, etc.

The basic way to use a module is to add **import module_name** as the first line of your program and then write **module_name.var** to access functions and values with the name var in the module. Let us first use the standard library modules.

**Program to print the PATH variable**

```
import sys          ← Importing a module named sys
print("\n PYTHONPATH = \n", sys.path)
```
Using the path variable defined in sys module

**OUTPUT**
```
PYTHONPATH =
['C:\\Users\\Reema\\AppData\\Local\\Programs\\Python\\Python37\\Lib\\idlelib',
'C:\\Users\\Reema\\AppData\\Local\\Programs\\Python\\Python37\\python37.zip',
'C:\\Users\\Reema\\AppData\\Local\\Programs\\Python\\Python37\\DLLs',
'C:\\Users\\Reema\\AppData\\Local\\Programs\\Python\\Python37\\lib',
'C:\\Users\\Reema\\AppData\\Local\\Programs\\Python\\Python37',
'C:\\Users\\Reema\\AppData\\Local\\Programs\\Python\\Python37\\lib\\
site-packages']
```

In the above code, we *import* the sys module (short form of system) using the `import` statement to use its functionality related to the Python interpreter and its environment. When the import sys statement is executed, Python looks for the sys.py file in one of the directories listed in its sys.path variable. If the file is found, then the statements in the module are executed.

### 6.2.1 Module Loading and Execution

A module imported in a program must be located and loaded into memory before it can be used. Python first searches for the modules in the current working directory. If the module is not found there, it then looks for the module in the directories specified in the PYTHONPATH environment variable. If the module is still not found or if the PYTHONPATH variable is not defined, then a Python installation-specific path (like C:\Python37\Lib) is searched. If the module is not located even there, then an **ImportError** exception is generated.

Once a module is located, it is loaded in memory. A compiled version of the module with file extension **.pyc** is generated. Next time when the module is imported, this .pyc file is loaded rather than the .py file, to save the time of recompiling.

A new compiled version of a module is again produced whenever the compiled version is out of date (based on the dates when the .pyc file was created/modified). Even the programmer can force the Python shell to reload and recompile the .py file to generate a new .pyc file by using the **reload()** function.

### 6.2.2 The `from...import` Statement

A module may contain definition for many variables and functions. *When you import a module, you can use any variable or function defined in that module.* But if you want to use only selected variables or functions, then you can use the `from...import` statement. For example, in the given program you are using only the path variable in the sys module, so you could have better written **from sys import path**.

To import more than one item from a module, use a comma separated list. For example, to import the value of PI and sqrt() from the math module you can write

```
from math import pi, sqrt
```

If all the identifiers in the sys module are to be imported, you can use the from sys import * statement. However, you should avoid using the import * statement as it would consume a lot of memory.

You can also import a module with a different name using the **as** keyword. This is particularly more important when a module has either a long or confusing name.

For example,

```
from math import sqrt as square_root
......
print(square_root(81))
```

> #Program that uses the
> #from ... import statement
> ```
> from math import pi
> print(" PI=",+ pi)
> ```
> **OUTPUT**
> 3.141592653589793

Python also allows you to pass **command line arguments** to your program, which will be required for execution. This can be done using the **sys** module. The **argv** variable in this module keeps a track of command line arguments passed to the .py script. To understand this, just open a new file, save it as main.py (or any other name) and write the following code in it.

```
import sys
print(sys.argv)
```

> This imports * statement imports all names except those beginning with an underscore(_).

To execute this program code, go to Command Prompt (in Windows), write

```
C:\ Python37>python main.py Python programming is fun
```

In the above statement, did you notice that apart from program name, you passed some information to the program? The program may use this information in any way for processing it. Here, we have just accepted the command line arguments and printed them on the screen using sys.argv. You will get the output as,

```
['try.py', 'Python', 'programming', 'is', 'fun']
```

```
# Program to demonstrate sys.exit
import sys
print("Python Programming is Easy and Fun ... ")
sys.exit("Exiting Program ........")
```
**OUTPUT**
Python Programming is Easy and Fun ...

We can also use the **sys.exit([arg])** to exit from Python. Here, **arg** is an optional argument, which can either be an integer giving the exit status or another type of object.

If it is an integer, zero signifies successful termination and any nonzero value indicates an error or abnormal termination of the program. Generally, **sys.exit("Error Message")** is a quick way to exit a program when an error occurs.

### 6.2.3 Name of Module

Every module has a name. You can find the name of a module by using the __**name**__ attribute of the module.

```
#Program to print name of a module
print("Python Programming is Easy and Fun ... ")
print("Name of this module is:", _name_)
```
**OUTPUT**
Python Programming is Easy and Fun ...
Name of this module is : _main_

Observe the output and always remember that for every standalone program written by the user the name of the module is __main__.

## 6.3 THE `dir()` FUNCTION

`dir()` is a built-in function that lists the identifiers defined in a module. These identifiers may include functions, classes and variables. If you mention the module name in the `dir()` function as given below, it will return the list of the names defined in that module.

```
dir(module_name)
```

If no name is specified, the `dir()` will return the list of names defined in the current module.

## 6.4 PACKAGES IN PYTHON

A package is a hierarchical file directory structure that *has modules and other packages within it*. Like modules, you can very easily create packages in Python.

Remember that *every package in Python is a directory which must have a special file called __init__.py*. This file may not even have a single line of code. It is simply added to indicate that this directory is not an ordinary directory and contains a Python package. In your programs, you can **import a package** in the same way as you import any module.

> By convention, modules are named using lower case letters and optional underscore.

For example, to create a package called MyPackage, create a directory (or folder) called MyPackage having all the modules and the __init__.py file. Now, to use a module named m1 in a program, you must first import it. This can be done in two ways.

```
import MyPackage.m1
or
from MyPackage import m1
```

The `import` statement first checks if the item is defined in the package. If it is unable to find it, an **ImportError** exception is raised.

> Though you can write the import statement anywhere in the code before using the module, it is always recommended to write all `import` statements at the top of the program code.

## 6.5 PYTHON – MATH MODULE

Python has a standard library that has many important and useful built-in functions (like `print()`, `ord()`, `int()`, etc). Besides these built-in functions, the library also has various modules that have functionalities for specified actions.

```
#Program to print the value of PI and e
import math
print("PI = ", math.pi)
print(" Epsilon= ",math.e)
```
**OUTPUT**
PI= 3.141592653589793
Epsilon = 2. 718281828459045

Some of the most popular mathematical functions are defined in the math module. These include trigonometric functions, representation functions, logarithmic functions, angle conversion functions, etc. In addition, two mathematical constants – PI and Epsilon are also defined in this module. Let us print the two values. Remember that before using the math module, we must first import it by writing **import math**. Then, the specific function can be used by writing, **math.function_name**.

Functions like sin, cos, tan, etc. that need an angle accept the values in radians as an argument. In case you want to specify angle in degrees then the `math.degree()` function must be used. Table 6.1 lists some commonly used built-in function in the math module.

| Table 6.1 | Built-in functions in math module | |
|---|---|---|
| **Function** | **Description** | **Example** |
| `ceil(x)` | Returns the smallest integer greater than or equal to x. | `import math`<br>`print(math.ceil(1.2345))`<br>OUTPUT<br>2 |
| `fabs(x)` | Returns the absolute value of x | `import math`<br>`print(math.fabs(-5.6))`<br>OUTPUT<br>5.6 |
| `factorial(x)` | Returns the factorial of x | `import math`<br>`print(math.factorial(6))`<br>OUTPUT<br>720 |
| `floor(x)` | Returns the largest integer less than or equal to x | `import math`<br>`print(math.floor(-5.6))`<br>OUTPUT<br>-6 |
| `fmod(x, y)` | Returns the remainder when x is divided by y | `import math`<br>`print(math.fmod(-100,6))`<br>OUTPUT<br>-4.0 |
| `modf(x)` | Returns the fractional and integer parts of x | `import math`<br>`print(math.modf(-123.456))`<br>OUTPUT<br>(-0.45600000000000307, -123.0) |
| `trunc(x)` | Returns the truncated integer value of x | `import math`<br>`print(math.trunc(-123.456))`<br>OUTPUT<br>-123 |
| `exp(x)` | Returns e**x | `import math`<br>`print(math.exp(10))`<br>OUTPUT<br>22026.465794806718 |
| `log(x[, base])` | Returns the logarithm of x to the base (defaults to e) | `import math`<br>`print(math.log(100,10))`<br>OUTPUT<br>2.0 |
| `log2(x)` | Returns the base-2 logarithm of x | `import math`<br>`print(math.log2(1024))`<br>OUTPUT<br>10.0 |
| `log10(x)` | Returns the base-10 logarithm of x | `import math`<br>`print(math.log10(1000))`<br>OUTPUT<br>3.0 |
| `pow(x, y)` | Returns x raised to the power of y | `import math`<br>`print(math.pow(10,4))`<br>OUTPUT<br>10000.0 |

*(Continued)*

## Table 6.1  Continued

| Function | Description | Example |
|---|---|---|
| `sqrt(x)` | Returns the square root of x | `import math`<br>`print(math.sqrt(10000))`<br>OUTPUT<br>`100.0` |
| `cos(x)` | Returns the cosine of x | `import math`<br>`print(math.cos(90))`<br>OUTPUT<br>`-0.4480736161291701` |
| `hypot(x, y)` | Returns the Euclidean norm, sqrt(x*x + y*y) | `import math`<br>`print(math.hypot(6,8))`<br>OUTPUT<br>`10.0` |
| `sin(x)` | Returns the sine of x | `import math`<br>`print(math.sin(90))`<br>OUTPUT<br>`0.8939966636005579` |
| `tan(x)` | Returns the tangent of x | `import math`<br>`print(math.tan(90))`<br>OUTPUT<br>`-1.995200412208242` |
| `degrees(x)` | Converts angle x from radians to degrees | `import math`<br>`print(math.radians(90))`<br>OUTPUT<br>`1.5707963267948966` |
| `radians(x)` | Converts angle x from degrees to radians | `import math`<br>`print(math.degrees(1.5707963267948966))`<br>OUTPUT<br>`90.0` |
| `uniform (a,b)` | It returns a floating-point number x, such that a <= x < b | `>>>random.uniform (5,10)`<br>`5.52615217015` |
| `randrange([start,] stop [,step])` | It returns a random item from the given range | `>>>random.randrange(100,1000,3)`<br>`150` |

## 6.6 BUILT-IN FUNCTIONS

Built-in functions are the functions that are built into Python and can be accessed in programs. These functions are always available and for use, and the programmer does not have to import any module to use them. In Python, a small set of basic functions are available as built-in functions; the rest of the functions are available as a part of some other module. This was purposely done to keep the core language precise. Some of the frequently used built-in functions are given in Table 6.2.

Apart from these functions, we also have functions like `bool ( )`, `chr ( )`, `float ( )`, `int ( )`, `long ()`, `str ( )`, `type ( )`, `id ( )`, `tuple ( )`, etc. that we have already used until now.

| Table 6.2 | Built-in functions | |
|---|---|---|
| **Function** | **Purpose** | **Example** |
| `abs (x)` | Returns distance between x and zero, where x is a numeric expression. | `>>>abs(-90)`<br>`90` |
| `max()` | Returns the largest of its arguments | `>>> max(10,30,20)`<br>`30` |
| `min()` | Returns the smallest of its arguments | `>>> min(10,30,-20)`<br>`-20` |
| `divmod(x,y)` | Returns both quotient and remainder obtained when x is divided by y | `>>> divmod(S2, 7)`<br>`(7, 3)` |
| `len(x)` | Returns length or the number of items in a sequence (like string). | `>>> len("PYTHON")`<br>`6` |
| `round( x [, n])` | Returns float x rounded to n digits from the decimal point, where x and n are numeric expressions. If n is not provided then x is rounded with no digits after decimal. | `>>> round(12.3456, 2)`<br>`12.35` |

## 6.7   COMPOSITION

Composition is the art of combining simple function(s) to build more complicated ones, i.e., the result of one function is used as the input to another. For example, if there are two functions fn1 and fn2, such that

$$a= fn2\ (x)$$
$$b= fn1\ (a)$$

then call to the two functions can be combined as

$$b= fn1\ (fn2\ (x))$$

Similarly, we can have a statement composed of more than two functions. In such a case, the result of one function is passed as argument to the next and the result of the last function is the final result. For example, `math.exp (math.log (a+1))`.

Composition is used to package the code into modules so that they may be used in many different unrelated places. Also, composition makes the modules easy to maintain.

## 6.8   FUNCTION DECLARATION AND DEFINITION

Any function can be compared to a black box (that is used for an entity having unknown implementation) that takes in input, processes it and then spits out the result. However, we may also have a function that does not take any inputs at all, or that does not return anything at all. While using functions we use the terminology given below.

- A function *f* that uses another function *g* is known as the *calling function* and *g* is known as the *called function*.
- The inputs that the function takes are known as *arguments/ parameters*.
- When a called function returns some result back to the calling function, it is said to *return* that result.
- The calling function may or may not pass *parameters* to the called function. If the called function accepts *arguments*, the calling function will pass *parameters*, else it does not.
- *Function declaration* is a declaration statement that identifies a function with its name, a list of arguments that it accepts and the type of data it returns.
- *Function definition* consists of a function header that identifies the function, followed by the body of the function containing the executable code for that function

> Besides using built-in functions, users can also write their own functions. Such functions are called user-defined functions.

## 6.9 FUNCTION DEFINITION

There are two basic types of functions, built-in functions and user-defined ones. The built-in functions are available as a part of the Python language. For example, `dir()`, `len()` or `abs()`. The user-defined functions, on the other hand, are functions created by users in their programs using the `def` keyword.

As a Python programmer, you can write any number of functions in your program. However, to define a function, you must keep the following points in mind.

- Function blocks starts with the keyword **def.**
- The keyword is followed by the function name and parentheses (( )). The function name is used to uniquely identify the function.
- After the parentheses, a colon (:) is placed.
- Parameters or arguments that the function accepts are placed within parentheses. Through these parameters, values are passed to the function. They are optional. In case no values are to be passed, nothing is placed within the parentheses.
- The first statement of a function can be an optional statement – the documentation string of the function or *doc-string* describes what the function does. We will discuss this later in the book.
- The code block within the function is properly indented to form the block code.
- A function may have a **return[expression]** statement. That is, the return statement is optional. If it exits, it passes back an expression to the caller. A return statement with no arguments is the same as return None.
- You can assign the function name to a variable. Doing this will allow you to call the same function using the name of that variable.

> Function naming follows the same rules as writing identifiers in Python.

### Example 6.1   Program that subtracts one number from another using function.

```
def diff(x,y):          # function to subtract two numbers
    return x-y
a = 20
b = 10
operation = diff        # function name assigned to a variable
print(operation(a,b))   # function called using variable name
```

> The words before parentheses specify the function name, and the parentheses are function arguments.

**OUTPUT**
```
10
```

When a function is defined, space is allocated for that function in the memory. A function definition comprises of two parts:

> The indented statements form body of the function.

- Function header
- Function body

The syntax of a function definition can be given as:

```
def function_name(variable1, variable2,..)      ← Function Header
    documentation string
    statement block                              ← Function Body
    return [expression]
```

> The parameter list in the function definition as well as the function declaration must match with each other.

In the given code, the name of the function is func. It takes no arguments, and prints "Hello World" four times. The function is first defined before being called. The statements in the function are executed only when the function is called.

### Example 6.2 — To write a function that displays a string repeatedly.

```
def func():
    for i in range (4):
        print ("Hello world")
func()    # function call
```

**OUTPUT**
```
Hello world
Hello world
Hello world
Hello world
```

> Before calling a function, you must define it just as you assign variables before using them.

**Key points to remember**
- Function name and the number and type of arguments in the function call must be same as that given in the function definition.
- If, by mistake, the parameters passed to a function are more than that it is specified to accept, then an error would be returned.

### Example 6.3 — Program to demonstrate the mismatch between function parameters and arguments.

```
    def func(i, j):
        print("Hello World", i, j)
    func(5)
```

**OUTPUT**
```
TypeError: func() takes exactly 2 arguments (1 given)
```

> It is a logic error if the arguments in the function call are placed in a wrong order.

- If, by mistake, the parameters passed to a function are less than that the function is specified to accept, then an error would be returned.

### Example 6.4 — Program to demonstrate the mismatch between function parameters and arguments.

```
    def func(i):
        print("Hello World", i)
    func(5, 5)
```

**OUTPUT**
```
TypeError: func() takes exactly 1 argument (2 given)
```

> You can call a function from another function or directly from the Python prompt.

- Names of variables in function call and header of function definition may vary.

### Example 6.5 — Program to demonstrate mismatch of name of function parameters and arguments.

```
def func(i):         # function definition header accepts a
variable with name i
print("Hello World", i)
j = 10
func(j)    # Function is called using variable j
```

**OUTPUT**
```
Hello World 10
```

- If the data type of the argument passed does not match with that expected in function, then an error is generated.

### Example 6.6 — Program to demonstrate mismatch between data types of function parameters and arguments.

```
def func(i):
  print("Hello World" + i)
func(5)
```

**OUTPUT**
```
TypeError: cannot concatenate 'str' and 'int' objects
```

- Arguments may be passed in the form of expressions to the called function. In such a case, arguments are first evaluated and converted to the type of formal parameter and then the body of the function gets executed.

**Example 6.7** Program to demonstrate that the arguments may be passed in the form of expressions to the called function.

```
def func(i):
    print("Hello World", i)
func(5+2*3)
```

**OUTPUT**
```
Hello World 11
```

- The parameter list must be separated with commas.
- If the function returns a value then it may be assigned to some variable in the calling program. For example,

```
variable_name = function_name(variable1, variable2, …);
```

**Example 6.8** Program to add two integers using functions.

```
def total(a, b):    #function accepting parameters
      result = a+b
      print("Sum of", a, "and", b, "=", result)
a = int(input("Enter the first number :"))
b = int(input("Enter the second number :"))
total(a,b) #function call with two arguments
```

**OUTPUT**
```
Enter the first number : 10
Enter the second number : 20
Sum of 10 and 20 = 30
```

Let us now try a program using function. In the total() we have declared a variable result just like any other variable. Variables declared within a function are called local variables. We will read more about it in the next section.

## 6.10 VARIABLE SCOPE AND LIFETIME

In Python, you cannot just access any variable from any part of your program. Some of the variables may not even exist for the entire duration of the program. The part of the program in which you can access a variable and the parts of the program in which a variable exists depend on how the variable has been declared. Therefore, it is essential to understand these two things:

*Scope of the variable:* Part of the program in which a variable is accessible is called its *scope*.
*Lifetime of the variable:* Duration for which the variable exists is called its *lifetime*.

### 6.10.1 Local and Global Variables

Global variables are those variables which are defined in the main body of the program file. They are visible throughout the program file. As a good programming habit, you must try to avoid the use of global variables because they may get altered by mistake and then result in erroneous output. But this does not mean that you should not use them at all. As a golden rule, use only those variables or objects that are meant to be used globally, like functions and classes, which are put in the global section of the program (i.e., above any other function or line of code).

> Trying to access local variable outside the function produces an error.

Correspondingly, a variable which is defined within a function is *local* to that function. A local variable can be accessed from the point of its definition until the end of the function in which it is defined. It exists as long as the function is executing. Function parameters behave like local variables in the function. Moreover, whenever we use the

> Variables can only be used after the point of their declaration.

assignment operator (=) inside a function, a new local variable is created (provided a variable with the same name is not defined in the local scope).

> **Example 6.9** **Program to understand the difference between local and global variables.**
>
> ```
> num1 = 10      # global variable
> print("Global variable num1 =", num1)
> def func(num2):     # num 2 is function parameter
>     print("In Function - Local Variable num2 =",num2)
>     num3 = 30    #num3 is a local variable
>    print("In Function - Local Variable num3 =",num3)
> func(20)       #20 is passed as an argument to the function
> print("num1 again =", num1) #global variable is being accessed
> #Error- local variable can't be used outside the function
> in which it is defined
>
> print("num3 outside function =", num 3)
> ```
> **OUTPUT**
> ```
> Global Variable num1 = 10
> In Function - Local Variable num2 = 20
> In Function - Local Variable num3 = 30
> num1 again = 10
> num3 outside function =
> Traceback (most recent call last):
>   File "C:\Python27\Try.py", line 12, in <module>
>     print ("num3 outside function =", num 3)
> NameError: name 'num3' is not defined
> ```

Table 6.3 lists the differences between global and local variables.

**Table 6.3** Comparison between global and local variables

| Global Variables | Local Variables |
|---|---|
| 1. They are defined in the main body of the program file. | 1. They are defined within a function and are local to that function. |
| 2. They can be accessed throughout the program file. | 2. They can be accessed from the point of its definition until the end of the block in which it is defined. |
| 3. Global variables are accessible to all functions in the program. | 3. They are not related in any way to other variables with the same names used outside the function. |

### 6.10.2 Resolution of Names

As discussed in the previous section, *scope* defines the visibility of a name within a block. If a local variable is defined in a block, its scope is that particular block. If it is defined in a function, then its scope is all blocks within that function.

When a variable name is used in a code block, it is resolved using the nearest enclosing scope. If no variable of that name is found, then a **NameError** is raised. In the code given above, str is a global string because it has been defined before calling the function.

You cannot define a local variable with the same name as that of a global variable. If you want to do that, you must use the global statement. The code given below illustrates this concept.

> Try to avoid the use of global variables and global statement.

> **Example 6.10**
>
> **Program that demonstrates using a variable defined in global namespace.**
> ```
> def func():
>     print(str)
> str = "Hello World!!!"
> func()
> ```
> **OUTPUT**
> ```
> Hello World!!!
> ```

## Example 6.11
**Program that demonstrates using a local variable with the same name as that of global variable.**

```
def f():
    print(str) #global
    str = "Hello World!" #local
    print(str)
str = "Welcome to Python Programming!"
f()
```

**OUTPUT**
```
UnboundLocalError: local variable 'str' referenced before assignment
```

```
def f():
    global str
    print(str)
    str = "Hello World!"
    print(str)
str = "Welcome to Python Programming!"
f()
```

**OUTPUT**
```
Welcome to Python Programming!
Hello World!
```

## 6.11 THE return STATEMENT

In all our functions written above, nowhere have we used the return statement. But you will be surprised to know that every function has an implicit return statement as the last instruction in the function body. This implicit return statement returns nothing to its caller, so it is said to return NONE where NONE means nothing. But you can change this default behaviour by explicitly using the return statement to return some value back to the caller. The syntax of return statement is,

> A function may or may not return a value. A return statement with no arguments is the same as return None.

$$\text{return [expression]}$$

The expression is written in brackets because it is optional. If the expression is present, it is evaluated and the resultant value is returned to the calling function. However, if no expression is specified then the function will return **None**.

The return statement is used for two things.

- Return a value to the caller
- To end and exit a function and go back to its caller

It should be noted that in the output None is returned from the function. The return value may or may not be assigned to another variable in the caller.

## Example 6.12
**Program to write a function without a return statement and print its return value. As mentioned earlier, such a function should return None.**

```
def display(str):
  print(str)
#assigning return value to another variable
x = display("Hello World")
print(x)
#print return value without assigning it to another variable
print (display("Hello Again"))
```

**OUTPUT**
```
Hello World
None
Hello Again
None
```

## Example 6.13
**To write another function, which returns an integer to the caller.**

```
def cube(x):
  return (x*x*x)
num = 10
result = cube(num)
print('Cube of ', num, ' = ', result)
```

**OUTPUT**
```
Cube of 10 = 1000
```

## Key points to remember
- The return statement must appear within the function.
- Once you return a value from a function, it immediately exits that function. Therefore, any code written after the return statement is never executed. The program given below illustrates this concept.

### Example 6.14 — Program to demonstrate flow of control after the return statement.

```
def display():
   print("In Function")
   print("About to execute return statement")
   return
   print("This line will never be displayed")
display()
print("Back to the caller")
```

**OUTPUT**
```
In Function
About to execute return statement
Back to the caller
```

## 6.12 THE random MODULE IN PYTHON

The random module in Python generates numbers randomly and it has some very useful functions. In this section, we will study few functions defined in the random module.

> The return statement cannot be used outside of a function definition.

**random():** The `random()` function returns the next random floating-point number in the range [0.0, 1.0). Look at the code given below that generates a random floating-point number. Note that you may get another number as the system just generates any value every time you run this code.

```
import random
print(random.random())
```

**OUTPUT**
```
0.3793508665239418
```

**randint(a,b):** The `randint()` function is used to generate a random integer number in the range specified by the arguments a and b. The random integer generated is such that it is less than or equal to b and greater than or equal to a.
```
import random

print(random.randint(1,100))
```
**OUTPUT**
```
15
```

**random.randrange(start, stop [, step]):** The `randrange()` function is used to generate a random integer number within a given range. The range is specified using the `start` and `stop` arguments. The `step` argument is optional, and its default value is 1.
```
import random
print(random.randrange(70,100,10))
```
**OUTPUT**
```
90
```

**random.choice(seq):** Use the `random.choice()` method to pick a random element from the sequence. Here, the sequence can be a list or string. This method returns a single item from the sequence.

```
import random
print(random.choice("HELLO WORLD"))
```

**OUTPUT**
```
L
```

**random.sample(population, *k*):** The `random.sample()` function is used to pick multiple random elements from a population. The function returns a list of *k* unique elements chosen from the population. The population can be a list, set or any sequence in Python.

```
import random
print(random.sample("PYTHONPROGRAMMING",3))
```

**OUTPUT**
```
['M', 'N', 'O']
```

**random.choices(population, weights=None, *, cum_weights=None, k=1):** The `random.choices()` function is used to choose more than one element from the sequence randomly with replacement.
```
import random

print(random.choices("PYTHONPROGRAMMINGISFUN",k=5))
```

**OUTPUT**
```
['I', 'I', 'M', 'R', 'T']
```

**random.shuffle(x[, random]):** The `random.shuffle()` function is used to shuffle or randomize a list or any other sequence in Python.

```
import random
list = [1,2,3,4,5,6,7,8,9,10]
random.shuffle(list)
print(list)
```

**OUTPUT**
```
[8, 10, 2, 6, 3, 5, 1, 9, 4, 7]
```

```
import statistics
list = [1,2,3,4,9,5,6,8,8,9,8,9,7,6,5,4,3,2,1]
mean = statistics.mean(list)
print("MEAN = ",mean)
med = statistics.median(list)
print("MEDIAN = ",med)
mode = statistics.mode(list)
print("MODE = ",mode)
sd = statistics.stdev(list)
print("STANDARD DEVIATION = ",sd)
sd = statistics.variance(list)
print("VARIENCE = ",var)
Output
MEAN = 5.2105263157894735
MEDIAN = 5
MODE = 9
STANDARD DEVIATION = 2.7402138474623765
VARIENCE = 7.508771929824561
```

**random.uniform(start, end):** The `random.uniform()` is used to generate a floating-point number within a given range. The range is specified using the `start` and `end` arguments.

```
import random
print(random.uniform(70.0, 89.9))
```

**OUTPUT**
```
75.98148226789161
```

**The Statistics Module:** Since Python is extensively used for data analysis, it has a statistics package that has functions for calculating the mean, median, mode, standard deviation, and variance of data.

## PROGRAMMER'S ZONE

1. **Write a program that prints the absolute value and cube of a number.**
   ```
   import math
   a = -100
   print("a = ", a)
   a = abs(a)
   print("abs(a) = ", a)
   print("Cube of ",a, " = ", math.pow(a,3))
   ```

   **OUTPUT**
   ```
   a = -100
   abs(a) = 100
   Cube of 100 = 1000000.0
   ```

2. **Write a program to generate 10 random numbers between 1 and 100.**
   ```
   import random
   for i in range(10):
       value = random.randint(1,100)
       print(value)
   ```

   *imports all objects from a module.

   **OUTPUT**
   ```
   66 68 14 7 76 8 70 43 60 70
   ```

3. **Write a program to display the date and time using the Time module.**
   ```
   import time
   localtime = time.asctime( time.localtime(time.time()) )
   print("Local current time :", localtime)
   ```

   **OUTPUT**
   ```
   Local current time : Mon Dec 16 21:34:27 2019
   ```

4. **Write a program that prints the calendar of a particular month.**
   ```
   import calendar
   print(calendar.month(2017, 1))
   ```

   **OUTPUT**
   ```
   October 2020
   Mo Tu We Th Fr Sa Su
              1  2  3  4
    5  6  7  8  9 10 11
   12 13 14 15 16 17 18
   19 20 21 22 23 24 25
   26 27 28 29 30 31
   ```

5. **Write a program that uses the getpass module to prompt the user for a password, without echoing what they type to the console.**

```
import getpass
password = getpass.getpass(prompt='Enter the password : ')
if password == 'cu2moro':
 print('Welcome to the world of Python Programming. ')
else:
 print('Incorrect password... Sorry, you cannot read our book.')
```

**OUTPUT**
```
Enter the password : cu2moro
Welcome to the world of Python Programming.
```

## Key Terms

**Function:** A block of organized and reusable program code that performs a single, specific, and well-defined task.

**Called function:** A function that is called or invoked to use its functionality is known as the called function.

**Arguments/parameters:** A function may take some inputs for processing. These inputs are known as arguments/parameters.

**Module:** A file with a .py extension that has definitions of all functions and variables that you would like to use even in other programs.

**Package:** A hierarchical file directory structure that has modules and other packages within it.

**Composition:** Art of combining simple function(s) to build more complicated ones, i.e., the result of one function is used as the input to another.

**Function declaration:** A declaration statement that identifies a function with its name, a list of arguments that it accepts and the type of data it returns.

**User-defined function:** Besides using built-in functions, users can also write their own functions. Such functions are called user defined functions.

**Scope of the variable:** Part of the program in which a variable is accessible is called its scope.

**Lifetime of the variable:** Duration for which the variable exists is called its lifetime.

**Global variables:** Variables defined in the main body of the program file that are visible throughout the program file.

**Local variable:** Variable that can be accessed from the point of its definition until the end of the function in which it is defined.

## Chapter Highlights

- When a function is called, the program control is passed to the first statement in the function.
- Once the execution of the program is complete, the control passes to the next statement after the function call.
- Understanding, coding and testing multiple separate functions are far easier than doing the same for one huge function.
- Large programs usually follow the DRY principle, that is, Don't Repeat Yourself principle. Once a function is written it can be called multiple times, wherever its functionality is required.
- A bad repetitive code abides by the WET principle, i.e., Write Everything Twice, or We Enjoy Typing.
- A function f that uses another function g, is known as the calling function and g is known as the called function.
- When a called function returns some result back to the calling function, it is said to return that result.
- To use the functions or variables defined in a module, you must first import that particular module (or .py file).
- Once a module is located, it is loaded in memory. A compiled version of the module with file extension .pyc is generated. The next time when the module is imported, this .pyc file is loaded, rather than the .py file, to save the time of recompiling.

- Built-in functions are the function(s) that are built into Python and can be accessed in programs. These functions are always available and for use, and the programmer does not have to import any module to use them.
- Function definition consists of a function header that identifies the function, followed by the body of the function containing the executable code for that function
- The documentation string of the function or docstring describes what the function does.
- A function may have a return[expression] statement. That is, the return statement is optional. If it exits, it passes back an expression to the caller. A return statement with no arguments is the same as return None.

### Review Questions

1. Define function.
2. What happens when a function is called?
3. Differentiate between the called and the calling function.
4. Why should we use function in our programs?
5. Can a function call another function? Justify your answer with the help of an example.
6. Explain the syntax of function call statement.
7. What is a module? How can you use it?
8. Explain the utility of the `reload()` function.
9. Why do we use the as keyword while importing a module?
10. Differentiate between import and form..import statements.
11. What are command line arguments? How are they used in Python?
12. What do you understand by the term arguments? How do we pass them to a function?
13. Arguments may be passed in the form of expressions to the called function. Justify this statement with the help of an example.
14. What are modules? How do you use them in your programs?
15. Why do we use `dir()` function? What will happen if no name is specified in the `dir()` function?
16. What is a package? How is it different from a module?
17. What are built-in functions? Give some examples.
18. What do you understand by the term composition?
19. With the help of an example explain how a function can be defined in Python?
20. Explain the significance of return statement.
21. Differentiate between local and global variables.
22. Write the mathematical expressions corresponding to the following expressions in Python.
    a. `math.sqrt(a*a + b*b + c*c)`
    b. `5 + y*math.exp(3*y) - 7*y`
    c. `a + b /math.pow(x+y),3)`
    d. `1 + (math.cos(x) / math.tan(x))`
    e. `math.fabs(math.exp(3) - 2*x)`

### Programming Exercises

1. Write a program that prints the time taken to execute a program in Python.
2. Write a function that returns the absolute value of a number.
3. Write a program that plays a game IN–OUT. Generate a random number, if that number is divisible by 5 or 10, then print IN. If that number is divisible by both, print OUT and exit the program.

4. Write a program that prompts user to enter a number. Continuously generate a random number until the number generated by the system does not match with that of the user.
5. Write a function that accepts three integers, and returns True if they are sorted, otherwise it returns False.
6. Write a function `is_prime()` that returns a 1 if the argument passed to it is a prime a number and a 0 otherwise.
7. Write a menu-driven program to add, subtract, multiply, and divide two integers using functions.
8. Write a program using function that calculates the hypotenuse of a right-angled triangle.
9. Write a function that accepts a number *n* as input and returns the average of numbers from 1 to *n*.
10. Write a program using function to calculate *x* to the power of *y*, where *y* can be either negative or positive.
11. Write a program using function to calculate compound interest given the principal, rate of interest, and number of years
12. Write a function that accepts three integers and returns True if any of the integers is 0; otherwise it returns False.
13. Write a function that accepts two positive numbers *n* and *m* where *m<=n*, and returns numbers between 1 and *n* that are divisible by *m*.
14. Write a function that displays "Hello name", for any given name passed to it.
15. Write a program to print the prime factors of a number.
    Write a program that prompts user to enter 10 numbers. Find the smallest and the second smallest number entered by the user

## Fill in the Blanks

1. Once the execution of the program is complete, the control passes to the _____ statement after the function call.
2. The function _____ statement invokes the function.
3. In range(0, 100, 5) name of the function is _____ and it has _____ arguments.
4. _____ error is caused by importing an unknown module.
5. The _____ is used to uniquely identify the function.
6. After the called function is executed, the control is returned to the _____.
7. You can find the name of a module by using the _____ attribute of the module.
8. _____ is a built-in function that lists the identifiers defined in a module.
9. Every package in Python is a directory, which must have a special file called _____.
10. Packages have an attribute _____, which is initialized with a list having the name of the directory holding the __init__.py file.
11. To import the sqrt and cos function from the math module, write _____.
12. Trying to import a module that is not available results in _____.
13. Python's preinstalled modules forms the _____.
14. The _____ command is used to force the reloading of a given module.
15. When a function is called, the interpreter checks the _____ and _____ of parameters that are passed in the function call.
16. To use the functions or variables defined in a module, you must first _____ that particular module.
17. The import * statement imports all names except _____ .
18. We can find the name of a module by using the _____ attribute of the module.

19. _____ describes what the function does.
20. _____ *of the variable* specifies the part of the program in which a variable is accessible.
21. The _____ function returns the next random floating-point number in the range [0.0, 1.0).
22. The _____ function is used to pick multiple random elements from a population.
23. The _____ module has functions for calculating the mean, median, mode, standard deviation, and variance of data.

## State True or False

1. When a function is called, the program control is passed to the last statement in the function.
2. Every function can be written more or less independently of the others.
3. When a function call is encountered, the control jumps to the calling function.
4. A function can call only one function.
5. Code reuse is one of the most prominent reasons to use functions.
6. Large programs usually follow the WET principle.
7. We can have a function that does not take any inputs at all.
8. The calling function may or may not pass *parameters* to the called function.
9. The return statement is optional.
10. Every function takes a fixed number of arguments.
11. Arguments may be passed in the form of expressions to the called function.
12. A function cannot be used on the left side of an assignment statement.
13. It is mandatory to place all import statements at the beginning of a module.
14. With the "import *moduleName*" statement, any item from the imported module must be prefixed with the module name.
15. All Python Standard Library modules must be imported before any programmer-defined modules.
16. If a particular module is imported more than once in a Python program, the interpreter will load the module only once.
17. A function can be called from anywhere within a program.
18. A statement can call more than one function.
19. Function calls may contain arguments that are function calls.
20. The **argc** variable in the sys module keeps a track of command line arguments passed to the .py script.
21. All import statements must be written at the top of the program code.
22. Duration for which the variable exists is called its *lifetime*.
23. We should use more of global variables than local variables.
24. You cannot define a local variable with the same name as that of global variable.
25. A function must return a value.

## Multiple Choice Questions

1. DRY principle makes the code _____ .
   a. reusable      b. loop forever      c. bad and repetitive      d. complex.
2. A function can call _____ number of other functions.
   a. 0      b. 1      c. *n* – 1      d. *n*

3. Which of the following is not correct about a function?
   a. It is pre-written   b. It is pre-tested   c. It slows down development   d. it simplifies coding
4. What is the output of this code?
   ```
   import random as r
   print(random.randomint(1, 10))
   ```
   a. An error occurs   b. 1   c. 10   d. any random value
5. How would you refer to the sqrt function if it was imported like this?
   ```
   from math import sqrt as square_root
   ```
   a. math.square_root   b. math.sqrt   c. sqrt   d. square_root
6. If the number of arguments in a function definition and function call does not match then which type of error is returned?
   a. NameError   b. ImortError   c. TypeError   d. NumberError
7. If no variable of the given input name is found, then a _____ is raised.
   a. NameError   b. ImortError   c. TypeError   d. NumberError
8. Modules are files saved with _____ extension.
   a. .py   b. mod   c. mdl   d. imp
9. The import * statement imports all names in the module except those beginning with _____.
   a. %   b. $   c. _   d. !
10. How would you refer to the randint function if it were imported by writing
    ```
    from random import randint as r_int?
    ```
    a. random.rnd_int   b. r_int   c. randint.r_int   d. randint
11. Identify the correct way of calling a function named display() that prints Hello on screen.
    a. print(display)   b. displayHello   c. result = display()   d. displayHello()
12. Which function returns the smallest integer greater than or equal to x?
    a. ceil()   b. fabs()   c. factorial()   d. floor()
13. Which function is used to generate a random integer number in the range specified by the arguments a and b?
    a. random()   b. randint()   c. randrange()   d. choice()
14. Which function is used to pick a random element from a sequence?
    a. random()   b. randint()   c. randrange()   d. choice()

## Give the Output

1. ```
   from random import randint as r
   for i in range(10):
       value = r(1,100)
       print(value)
   ```
2. ```
   import math
   print(math.fmod(-12345,9))
   ```
3. ```
   num = 10
   def show():
       var = 20
       print("In Function var is - ",
           num)
   show()
   print("Outside function, var is - ",
       num)
   ```
4. ```
   def f():
       s = "Hello World!"
       print(s)
   s = "Welcome to Python Programming"
   f()
   print(s)
   ```
5. ```
   def f():
       global var
       print(var)
       var = 10
       print(var)
   var = 100
   f()
   ```
   ```

6. ```
   def display (str):
       print(str+"!")
   display ("Hello World")
   ```

7. ```
   def sqr(x):
       print(x*x)
   sqr(10)
   ```

8. ```
   def mul_twice(x,y):
       print(x*y)
       print(x*y)
   mul_twice(5, 10)
   ```

9. ```
   def func():
       global x
       print("x =", x)
       x = 100
       print('x is now = ', x)
   x = 10
   func()
   print('x =', x)
   ```

10. ```
    def func1():
        var = 3
        func2(var)
    def func2(var):
        print(var)
    func1()
    ```

11. ```
    def func(x):
        print 'x = ', x
        x = 100
        print('In Function, x after
           modification = ', x)
    x = 50
    func(x)
    print('Outside Function, x = ', x)
    ```

12. ```
    def display( str ):
        print(str)
        return;
    display("Hello World !!")
    display("Welcome to Python
        Programming")
    ```

13. ```
    def sum( num1, num2 ):
        total = num1 + num2
        print("Inside function, Total
        = ", total)
        return total;
    total = sum( 10, 20 )
    print("Outside the function, Total =
        ", total)
    ```

14. ```
    def min(x,y):
        if x<y:
            return x
        else:
            return y
    print(min(4, 7))
    ```

15. ```
    def add(x, y):
        sum = x + y
        return sum
        print("This won't be printed")
    print(add(10,20))
    ```

16. ```
    def func():
        """Do nothing.
        Nothing doing.
        """
        pass
    print(func.__doc__)
    ```

17. ```
    def C_to_F(c):
            return c * 9/5 + 32
    print C_to_F(37)
    def display(name, deptt, sal):
        print("Name: ", name)
        print("Department: ", deptt)
        print("Salary: ", sal)
    display(sal = 100000, name="Tavisha",
        deptt = "IT")
    display(deptt = "HR", name="Dev", sal
        = 50000)
    ```

18. ```
    def display(mesg):
        return mesg + "!"
    print_str = display
    str = print_str("Hello")
    print(str)
    ```

19. ```
    from random import randint as r
    for i in range(10):
        value = r(1,100)
        print(value)
    ```

20. ```
    def is_even(x):
        if x==0:
            return True
        else:
            return is_odd(x-1)
    def is_odd(x):
        return not is_even(x)
    print(is_even(22))
    ```
    ```

21. ```
    def display(x):
        for i in range(x):
            print(i)
        return
    display(5)
    ```

## Find the Error

1. ```
   import math as m
   print(math.sqrt(25))
   ```

2. ```
   def func():
       print("Hello World")
   ```

3. ```
   var1 = "Good"
   def show():
       var2 = "Morning"
       print(var1)
       print(var2)
   show()
   print(var1)
   print(var2)
   ```

4. ```
   def f():
       print var
       var = 10
       print(var)
   var = 100
   f()
   ```

5. ```
   def f():
       var = 100
       print(var)
   f()
   print(var)
   ```

6. ```
   def func(var):
       var+=1
       var *= 2
       print(var)
   func(9)
   print(var)
   ```

7. ```
   def func1():
       var = 3
       func2()
   def func2():
       print(var)
   func1()
   ```

8. ```
   def display(x,y):
       print (x+y)
   display(10)
   ```

9. ```
   def func(a, b):
       print(a)
       print(b)
   func(b=10, 20)
   ```

10. ```
    def func1():
        print("func1()")
    func1()
    func2()
    def func2():
        print("func2()")
    ```

11. ```
    def sum_to(x):
        return x+sum_to(x-1)
    print(sum_to(5))
    ```

## Answers

### Fill in the Blanks

1. next
2. call
3. range, 3
4. ImportError
5. function name
6. calling program
7. __name__
8. dir()
9. __init__.py
10. __path__
11. from math import sqrt, cos
12. ImportError
13. Standard Library
14. reload()
15. number, type
16. import
17. those beginning with ___
18. __name__
19. docstring
20. *scope*
21. random()
22. randomsample()
23. statistics

## State True or False

| | | | | |
|---|---|---|---|---|
| 1. False | 6. False | 11. True | 16. True | 21. False |
| 2. True | 7. True | 12. False | 17. True | 22. False |
| 3. True | 8. True | 13. False | 18. True | 23. False |
| 4. False | 9. True | 14. True | 19. True | 24. True |
| 5. True | 10. False | 15. True | 20. False | 25. False |

## Multiple Choice Questions

| | | | | |
|---|---|---|---|---|
| 1. a | 4. a | 7. a | 10. c | 13. b |
| 2. d | 5. a | 8. a | 11. c | 14. d |
| 3. c | 6. c | 9. c | 12. a | |

## Give the Output

1. 47 8 22 86 14 31 81 24 54 49
2. –6.0
3. In Function var is – 10
   Outside function, var is – 10
4. Hello World!
   Welcome to Python Programming
5. 100     10
6. Hello World!
7. 100
8. 50 50
9. x = 10
   x is now = 100
   x = 100
10. 3
11. x = 50
    In Function, x after modification = 100
    Outside Function, x = 50
12. Hello World !!
    Welcome to Python Programming
13. Inside function, Total = 30
    Outside the function, Total = 30
14. 4
15. This won't be printed
    30
16. Do nothing.
    Nothing doing.
17. 98.6
    Name: Tavisha
    Department: IT
    Salary: 100000
    Name: Dev
    Department: HR
    Salary: 50000
18. Hello!
19. 78  88  85  65  94  15  73  91  51  97
20. True
21. 0

## Find the Error

1. NameError: name 'math' is not defined
2. No output as function is not called
3. NameError: name 'var2' is not defined
4. brackets in print function missing
5. NameError: name 'var' is not defined
6. NameError: name 'var' is not defined
7. NameError: name 'var' is not defined
8. TypeError: display() missing 1 required positional argument: 'y'
9. Keyword argument should be present as the last parameter in the function call statement
10. NameError: name 'func2' is not defined
11. Base condition is missing. RecursionError: maximum recursion depth exceeded

# Strings

7

**Chapter Objectives**

The chapter discusses strings in detail to help the users understand key concepts such as:
- String indexing, traversal, comparing, appending, concatenation and multiplication
- Slicing a string
- Determining its length
- Formatting strings using formatting operators and format() function
- Built-in string methods, functions and operators

The Python string data type is a sequence made up of one or more individual characters, where a character could be a letter, digit, whitespace, or any other symbol enclosed within single, double or even triple quotes. Python has a built-in string class named "str" that has many useful features. We can create a variable of string type in many ways. For example,

```
lang = "Python"    gender = 'F'    choice = lang    message = str("How are you")
```

We have already seen that escape sequences works with each type of string literals. A multiple-line text within quotes must have a backslash \ at the end of each line to escape the new line.

## 7.1 STRING INDEXING

Individual characters in a string are accessed using the subscript ([ ]) operator. The expression in brackets is called an **index**. The index specifies the character to be accessed from the given set of characters in the string.

The index of the first character is 0 and that of the last character is $n-1$ where $n$ is the number of characters in the string. *If you try to exceed the bounds (below 0 or above $n-1$), then an error is raised.*

## 7.2 FINDING THE NUMBER OF CHARACTERS IN A STRING

Python determines the length of a string by counting the number of characters in it. For example, len("abcd") is 4 since there are four characters. Though this calculation is simple, some points must be considered while counting.

  a. An escape sequence is counted as a single character.
  b. In a multi-line string created with triple quotes, the **EOL** (End-Of-Line) character at the end of the line is also counted. Usually, the EOL is the carriage return character when the Enter key is pressed.
  c. In a multi-line string, backslash character at the end of the line is not counted.

| >>len("\n")<br>1 | >>>len("HELLO\tWORLD")<br>13 | >>>len("Neeru\'s Pen")<br>11 | >>>len("Neeru's Pen")<br>11 |
|---|---|---|---|
| >>>str1 = '''A<br>B<br>C<br>D''' | >>>len(str1)<br>7 | >>>str2 = '''A\<br>B\<br>C\<br>D''' | |

## 7.3 TRAVERSING A STRING

A string is a sequence type (sequence of characters). It can be traversed in two ways: first, by accessing each character in the string and second, by accessing the element at each index. The `len()` function returns the length of the string, i.e., the number of characters in the string. We can then use this function for loop in which the loop control variable varies from 0 to $n-1$, where $n$ is the number of characters in the string.

Whichever method you use, always remember that if you try to access a character *with index less than 0 and/or greater than n-1 then an IndexError:* string index out of range error will be generated.

### Example 7.1

```
# traversing string
lang = "PYTHON"
for i in lang:
    print(i,end = ' ') # print each character
```

**OUTPUT**
P Y T H O N

```
# traversing string using index
lang = "PYTHON"
for i in range(len(lang)):
    print(lang[i],end = ' ')
```

**OUTPUT**
P Y T H O N

In the first code, the `for` loop executes for every character in str. The loop starts with the first character and automatically ends when the last character is accessed. In the second code, the string is traversed using the index of each character (rather than the character itself). We can also iterate through the string using the `while` loop.

### Example 7.2

```
# traversing string using while loop
lang = "PYTHON"
index = 0
l = len(lang)
while index < l:
  ch = lang[index]
  print(ch,end = '')
  index +=1
```

**OUTPUT**
PYTHON

```
# access string out of index
lang = "PYTHON"
l = len(lang)
print(lang[l+1]) # not a part of string
```

**OUTPUT**
```
Traceback (most recent call last):
  File "C:\Users\Python37\try.py", line 3, in
<module>
    print(lang[l+1])
IndexError: string index out of range
```

In the above program, the `while` loop traverses the string and displays each character. The loop condition is index < len(lang); so the moment index becomes equal to the length of the string, the condition evaluates to false, and the body of the loop is not executed. As we said earlier, the index of the last character is len(message) – 1.

### Key points to remember

- Even the whitespace characters, exclamation mark and any other symbols (like ?, <,>,*, @, #, $, %, etc.) that form a part of the string would be assigned their own index number.
- Index can either be an integer or an expression that evaluates to an integer.
- A character cannot be used for string indexing.

### Example 7.3

```
# indexing string in different ways
msg = "PYTHON PROGRAMMING IS FUN"
i = 2
print(msg[i]) #index is an integer
print(msg[i*3+2]) #index is an expression that evaluates to an integer
print(msg['N']) #character as an index
```

**OUTPUT**
```
T
R
Traceback (most recent call last):
  File "C:\Users\Python37\try.py", line 5, in <module>
    print(msg['N']) #character as an index
TypeError: string indices must be integers
```

## 7.4 CONCATENATING, APPENDING AND MULTIPLYING STRINGS

The word **concatenate** means to join together. Python allows you to concatenate two strings using the + operator as shown below.

### Example 7.4

```
# String Concatenation
str1 = "Python"
str2 = "Programming"
str3 = str1 + str2 # string concatenation
print("The concatenated string is:", str3)
```

**OUTPUT**
```
The concatenated string is:
PythonProgramming
```

```
# Appending and concatenating strings
str1 = "Good morning,"
name = Input("\n Enter your name :")
str1 += name   #appending strings
str2 = str1+". Welcome to Python Programming."
print(str2)
```

**OUTPUT**
```
Enter your name : Priya
Good morning, Priya. Welcome to Python Programming.
```

**Append** means to add something at the end. In Python, one string can be added at the end of another string using the += operator.

We can **multiply** a string using the * operator. When a string is multiplied with an integer number *n*, then the string is repeated *n* number of times. The order of string and integer is not important. Therefore, `5*"HI"` is same as `"HI"*5`.

However, remember that you cannot multiply two strings. Also, you cannot multiply a string with a floating-point number.

### Example 7.5

```
# multiplying string
str = "I WILL DO IT "
print(str*3) #multiplying string
```

**OUTPUT**
```
I WILL DO IT I WILL DO IT I WILL DO IT
```

```
# multiplying string
str = "PYTHON" * '3'
print(str)
```

**OUTPUT**
```
Traceback (most recent call last):
  File "C:\Users\Python37\try.py", line 2, in <module>
    str = "PYTHON" * '3'
TypeError: can't multiply sequence by non-int of type 'str'
```

```
# multiplying string
str = "HELLO" * 3.0
print(str)
```

**OUTPUT**
```
Traceback (most recent call last):
  File "C:\Users\Python37\try.py", line 2, in <module>
    str = "HELLO" * 3.0
TypeError: can't multiply sequence by non-int of type 'float'
```

## 7.5 THE str() FUNCTION

The str() function is used to convert values of any other type into string type. This helps the programmer to concatenate a string with any other data, which is otherwise not allowed.

### Example 7.6

```
# concatenating string and a number
roll_no = 9
name = "Aditi"
print(name + " is roll number" + roll_no)
```

**OUTPUT**
```
Traceback (most recent call last):
  File "C:\Users\
TypeError: can only concatenate
str(not"int") to str
```

```
# concatenating string and a number
roll_no = 9
name = "Aditi"
print(name + " is roll number" + str(roll_no))
```

**OUTPUT**
```
Aditi is roll number 9
```

## 7.6 STRINGS ARE IMMUTABLE

Python strings are immutable. This means that once a string is created, it cannot be changed. If you try to modify an existing string variable, a new string is created.

Every object in Python is stored in memory. You can find out whether two variables are referring to the same object or not by using the id(). The id() returns the memory address of the given object. Since both str1 and str2 point to the same memory location, they both actually point to the same object.

*In Python, two objects that have the same value have the same id.* The moment the value of one object is changed, a new object is created with a different id.

From the output, it is clear that when values of str1 and str2 were same, their IDs were same as they were pointing to the same object. When we changed the value of str2 and later of str3, the ids of the object changed.

Now can you guess the output of the following code?

```
str = "PYTHON"
str[3] = 'A'
print(str)
```

The code will result in an error – "TypeError: 'str' object does not support item assignment" simply because the strings are immutable. It does now allow any changes. If you want to make any kind of changes you must create a new string as shown below.

*Always remember that we cannot delete or remove characters from a string. But can delete the entire string using the keyword del.*

### Example 7.7

```
# Checking object's ID
str1 = "Python"
str2 = "Python"
str3 = "Programming"
# ID of str1 and str2 will be same
print("ID OF STR1 = ",id(str1))
print("ID OF STR2 = ",id(str2))
print("ID OF STR3 = ",id(str3))
# changing the value of str2
str2 = "Programming"
# ID of str2 and str3 will be same
print("\n\n ID OF STR1 = ",id(str1))
print("ID OF STR2 = ",id(str2))
print("ID OF STR3 = ",id(str3))
# changing the value of str3
str2 = "Programming is fun"
# All IDs will be different
print("\n\n ID OF STR1 = ",id(str1))
print("ID OF STR2 = ",id(str2))
print("ID OF STR3 = ",id(str3))
```

**OUTPUT**
```
ID OF STR1 = 3091055531600
ID OF STR2 = 3091055531600
ID OF STR3 = 3091069698480

ID OF STR1 = 3091055531600
ID OF STR2 = 3091069698480
ID OF STR3 = 3091069698480

ID OF STR1 = 3091055531600
ID OF STR2 = 3091070019384
ID OF STR3 = 3091069698480
```

## 7.7 STRING FORMATTING OPERATOR

This string formatting operator (%) takes a format string on the left (that has %d, %s, etc.) and the corresponding values in a tuple (will be discussed in a subsequent chapter) on the right. The format operator, % allows users to construct strings, replacing parts of the strings with the data stored in variables. The syntax for the string formatting operation is:

> A tuple is made of values separated by commas inside parentheses.

"<FORMAT>" % (<VALUES>)

The statement begins with a *format* string consisting of a sequence of characters and *conversion specifications*. Conversion specifications start with a % operator and can appear anywhere within the string. Following the format string is a % sign and then a set of values, one per conversion specification, separated by commas and enclosed in parentheses. If there is a single value, then parentheses are optional.

In the output we can see that %s has been replaced by a string and %d has been replaced by an integer value. You can either supply these values directly or by using variables. Table 7.1 lists other string formatting characters.

*Note that the number and type of values in the tuple should match the number and type of format sequences or conversion specifications in the string, otherwise an error is returned.*

### Example 7.8

```
# Formatting strings
roll_no = 23
name = "Aarish"
print("ROLL NO. =%d Name =%s"%(roll_no, name))
print("ROLL NO. =%d Name =%s"%(39, "Anika"))
```

**OUTPUT**
ROLL NO. = 23 Name = Aarish
ROLL NO. = 39 Name = Anika

### Example 7.9

```
# number of arguments don't match
>>>'%d %f %s'%(15, 92.75)
Traceback (most recent call last):
  File "<pyshell#0>", line 1, in <module>
    '%d %f %s'%(15, 92.75)
TypeError: not enough arguments for format string
```

```
# type of argument don't match
>>>'%d%f%s'%(92, "Myra", "Sood")
Traceback (most recent call last):
  File "<pyshell#1>", line 1, in <module>
    '%d% f% s'%(92, "Myra", "Sood")
TypeError: must be real number, not str
```

**Table 7.1** Formatting symbols

| Format Symbol | Purpose |
| --- | --- |
| %c | Character |
| %d or %i | Signed decimal integer |
| %s | String |
| %u | Unsigned decimal integer |
| %o | Octal integer |
| %x or %X | Hexadecimal integer (x for lower case characters a-f and X for upper case characters A-F) |
| %e or %E | Exponential notation |
| %f | Floating-point number |
| %g or %G | Short numbers in floating-point or exponential notation |

### Example 7.10

```
# String Formatting for printing the power of a number
i = 1
print("%-4s%-5s%-6s%-8s%-13s"%('i', 'i**2', 'i**3', 'i**4', 'i**5',))
while(i<=5):
    print("%-4d%-5d%-6d%-8d%-13d"%)(i, i**2, i**3, i**4, i**5)
    i+=1
```

OUTPUT

```
i    i**2 i**3  i**4    i**5
1    1    1     1       1
2    4    8     16      32
3    9    27    81      243
4    16   64    256     1024
5    25   125   625     3125
```

In Example 7.10, we have set the width of each column independently using the string formatting feature of Python. The - after each % in the conversion string indicates left justification. The numerical values specify the minimum length. Therefore, %-15d means it is a left justified number that is at least 15 characters wide.

## 7.8 THE format() FUNCTION

The format() function is also used for formatting strings. Format strings have curly braces {} as placeholders or replacement fields which get replaced. We can even use positional arguments or keyword arguments to specify the order of fields that have to be replaced. Consider the code given below and carefully observe the sequence of fields in the output. Then, compare the sequence as given in the arguments of format() function.

### Example 7.11

```
# format() function with strings
str1 = "{}, {} {}".format('Python','is','Easy')
print("\n The default sequence of arguments is : " + str1)
str2 = "{1}, {0} {2}".format('Python','is','Easy')
print("\n The positional sequence of arguments (1, 0 and 2) is : " + str2)
str3 = "{c}, {b} Very {a}".format(a='Python',b='Is',c='Easy')
print("\n The keyword sequence of arguments is : " + str3)
```

OUTPUT

```
The default sequence of arguments is : Python, is Easy
The positional sequence of arguments (1, 0 and 2) is : Is Python Easy?
The keyword sequence of arguments is : Easy, Is Very Python
```

## 7.9 BUILT-IN STRING METHODS AND FUNCTIONS

Strings are an example of Python **objects**. An object is an entity that contains both data (the actual string itself) as well as functions to manipulate that data. These functions are available to any **instance** (variable) of the object.

Python supports many built-in methods to manipulate strings. A method is just like a function. The only difference between a function and a method is that method is invoked or called on an object. For example, if the variable str is a string, then you can call the upper() method as str.upper() to convert all the characters of str in upper case. Table 7.2 discusses some of the most commonly used string methods.

### Table 7.2  Commonly used string functions and methods

| Function | Usage | Example |
|---|---|---|
| `capitalize()` | This function is used to capitalize the first letter of the string. | `str = "python"`<br>`print(str.capitalize())`<br>**OUTPUT**<br>`Python` |
| `center(width, fillchar)` | Returns a string with the original string centered to a total of width columns and filled with fillchar in columns that do not have characters | `str = "python"`<br>`print(str.center(15, '*'))`<br>**OUTPUT**<br>`*****python****` |
| `count(str, beg, end)` | Counts the number of times `str` occurs in a string. You can specify beg and end as 0 to len of string to search the entire length of the string, or with any other value to just search a part of the string. | `str = "se"`<br>`message = "He sells sea shells on the sea shore"`<br>`print(message.count(str,0,len(message)))`<br>**OUTPUT**<br>`3` |
| `endswith(suffix, beg, end)` | Checks if string ends with suffix; returns True if so and False, otherwise. You can either set beg = 0 and end to length of the message to search the entire string or use any other value to search a part of it. | `message = "He sells sea shells on the sea shore"`<br>`print(message.endswith("ore", 0,len(message)))`<br>**OUTPUT**<br>`True` |
| `startswith(prefix, beg, end)` | Checks if string starts with prefix; returns True if so and False otherwise. You can either set beg = 0 and end to length of the message to search entire string or use any other value to search a part of it. | `message = "He sells sea shells on the sea shore"`<br>`print(message.startswith("sea", 0,len(message)))`<br>**OUTPUT**<br>`False` |
| `find(str, beg, end)` | Checks if `str` is present in string. If found, it returns the position at which `str` occurs in string; otherwise, it returns -1. You can either set beg = 0 and end to the length of the message to search the entire string or use any other value to search a part of it. | `message = "He sells sea shells on the sea shore"`<br>`print(message.find("sea",0,len(message)))`<br>**OUTPUT**<br>`9` |
| `index(str, beg, end)` | Same as find but raises an exception if `str` is not found. | `message = "He sells sea shells on the sea shore"`<br>`print(message.index("in", 0, len(message)))`<br>**ValueError**: substring not found |
| `rfind(str, beg, end)` | Same as find but starts searching from the end. So it will return index of the last occurrence of `str` in the main string. | `message = "He sells sea shells on the sea shore"`<br>`print(message.rfind("sea", 0, len(message)))`<br>**OUTPUT**<br>`27` |

*(Continued)*

## Table 7.2 Continued

| Function | Usage | Example |
|---|---|---|
| `rindex(str, beg, end)` | Same as `rindex` but starts searching from the end and raises an exception if `str` is not found | `message = "He sells sea shells on the sea shore"`<br>`print(message.rindex("gg", 0, len(message)))`<br>**OUTPUT**<br>`ValueError: substring not found` |
| `isalnum()` | Returns True if string has at least 1 character and every character is either a number or an alphabet and False otherwise. | `message = "JamesBond007"`<br>`print(message.isalnum())`<br>**OUTPUT**<br>`True` |
| `isalpha()` | Returns True if string has at least 1 character and every character is an alphabet and False otherwise. | `message = "JamesBond007"`<br>`print(message.isalpha())`<br>**OUTPUT**<br>`False` |
| `isdigit()` | Returns True if string contains only digits and False otherwise. | `message = "108"`<br>`print(message.isdigit())`<br>**OUTPUT**<br>`True` |
| `islower()` | Returns True if string has at least 1 character and every character is a lowercase alphabet and False otherwise. | `message = "Python"`<br>`print(message.islower())`<br>**OUTPUT**<br>`False` |
| `isspace()` | Returns True if string contains only whitespace characters and False otherwise. | `message = " "`<br>`print(message.isspace())`<br>**OUTPUT**<br>`True` |
| `isupper()` | Returns True if string has at least 1 character and every character is an uppercase alphabet and False otherwise. | `message = "PYTHON"`<br>`print(message.isupper())`<br>**OUTPUT**<br>`True` |
| `len(string)` | Returns the length of the string. | `str = "PYTHON"`<br>`print(len(str))`<br>**OUTPUT**<br>`6` |
| `ljust(width[, fillchar])` | Returns a string left-justified to a total of width columns. Columns without characters are padded with the character specified in the `fillchar` argument | `str = "PYTHON"`<br>`print(str.ljust(10, '*'))`<br>**OUTPUT**<br>`PYTHON****`<br>`23351823` |
| `rjust(width[, fillchar])` | Returns a string right-justified to a total of width columns. Columns without characters are padded with the character specified in the `fillchar` argument | `str = "PYTHON"`<br>`print(str.rjust(10, '&'))` **OUTPUT**<br>`&&&&PYTHON` |
| `zfill (width)` | Returns a string left-padded with zeros to a total of width characters. It is used with numbers and also retains its sign (+ or -). | `str = "5678"`<br>`print(str.zfill(10))`<br>**OUTPUT**<br>`0000005678` |

*(Continued)*

**Table 7.2  Continued**

| Function | Usage | Example |
|---|---|---|
| `lower()` | Converts all characters in the string into lowercase. | `str = "PYTHON"`<br>`print(str.lower())`<br>**OUTPUT**<br>`python` |
| `upper()` | Converts all characters in the string into uppercase. | `str = "python"`<br>`print(str.upper())`<br>**OUTPUT**<br>`PYTHON` |
| `lstrip()` | Removes all leading whitespace in the string. | `str = " PYTHON"`<br>`print(str.lstrip())`<br>**OUTPUT**<br>`PYTHON` |
| `rstrip()` | Removes all trailing whitespace in the string. | `str = "PYTHON    "`<br>`print(str.lstrip())`<br>**OUTPUT**<br>`PYTHON` |
| `strip()` | Removes all leading and trailing whitespace in the string. The `strip()` function, when used with a string argument, will strip (from both ends) any combination of the specified characters in the string | `str = "    PYTHON    "`<br>`print(str.strip())`<br>`str = "abcPYabcTHONabc"`<br>`print(str.strip("abc"))`<br>**OUTPUT**<br>`PYTHON`<br>`PYabcTHON` |
| `max(str)` | Returns the highest alphabetical character (having highest ASCII value) from the string str. | `str = "PyThoN pRoGrAmMiNg"`<br>`print(max(str))`<br>**OUTPUT**<br>`y` |
| `min(str)` | Returns the lowest alphabetical character (lowest ASCII value) from the string str. | `str = "PyThoNpRoGrAmMiNg"`<br>`print(min(str))`<br>**OUTPUT**<br>`A` |
| `replace(old, new [, max])` | Replaces all or max (if given) occurrences of old in string with new | `str = "She sells sea shells on the sea shore"`<br>`print(str.replace («se», «SE»))`<br>**OUTPUT**<br>`She SElls SEa shells on the SEa shore` |
| `title()` | Returns string in title case | `str = "she sells sea shells on the sea shore"`<br>`print(str.title())`<br>**OUTPUT**<br>`She Sells Sea Shells On The Sea Shore` |
| `swapcase()` | Toggles the case of every character (upper case character becomes lower case and vice-versa) | `str = "PyThoNpRoGrAmMiNg"`<br>`print(str.swapcase())` **OUTPUT**<br>`pYtHOnPrOgRaMmInG` |

*(Continued)*

### Table 7.2  Continued

| Function | Usage | Example |
|---|---|---|
| `split(delim)` | Returns a list of substrings separated by the specified delimiter. If no delimiter is specified, then by default, it splits strings at all whitespace characters | `str = "She, sells, sea shells, on the, sea shore"`<br>`print(str.split(','))`<br>**OUTPUT**<br>`['She', ' sells', ' sea shells', ' on the', ' sea shore']` |
| `join(list)` | It is the opposite of split. The function joins a list of strings using the delimiter with which the function is invoked. | `str = ['Power','of','the','Universe','HE-MAN']`<br>`print('#'.join(str))`<br>**OUTPUT**<br>`Power#of#the#Universe#HE-MAN` |
| `str.splitlines()` | Returns a list of the lines in the string. This method uses the newline characters like \r, \n to split lines. | `print('Python is \n\n a very \r simple language\r\n'.splitlines())`<br>**OUTPUT**<br>`['Python is ', '', ' a very ', ' simple language']` |

## 7.10 COMPARING STRINGS

In Python, strings can be compared using relational operators like >, <, <=, <=, ==, !=. The comparison is done lexicographically, i.e., using ASCII value of the characters. The ASCII values of A–Z are 65-90, ASCII codes for a–z are 97–122 and for 0–9 the code is 48–57. This means that bread is greater than Bread because the ASCII value of 'b' is 98 and 'B' is 66.

```
>>> "PYTHON"==        >>>"PYTHON"         >>> "SMILE"<        >>>"GIVE"!= "EXPECT"
"python"              >= "python"         "laughter"          True
False                 False               True
```

Did you notice that String values are ordered using lexicographical (dictionary) ordering? For this, the comparison is done internally.

## 7.11 ord() AND chr() FUNCTIONS

```
ch = 'P'              ch = 'y'            print(ch r(79))     print(chr(117))
print(ord(ch))        print(ord(ch))      OUTPUT              OUTPUT
OUTPUT                OUTPUT              O                   u
80                    121
```

`ord()` function returns the ASCII code of the character and `chr()` function returns a character represented by an ASCII number.

## 7.12 in AND not in OPERATORS

`in` and `not in` operators can be used with strings to determine whether a character or a string is present in another string. Therefore, the `in` and `not in` operators are also known as membership operators.

## Example 7.12

```
# using in operator
str1 = "Python programming is fun"
str2 ="is"
if str2 in str1:
  print("Found")
else:
  print("Not Found")
```
**OUTPUT**
Found

```
# using not in operator
str1 = "Arav is a very naughty boy"
str2 = "good"
if str2 not in str1:
  print("Arav is not a good boy.")
else:
  print("Arav is a very good boy.")
```
**OUTPUT**
Arav is not a good boy.

You can also use the `in` and `not in` operators to check whether a character is present in a word. Also remember that a string is a substring of itself.

```
>>> 'y' in "PYTHON"          >>> 'N' in "PYTHON"          >>> 'PYTHON' in 'PYTHON'          >>> 'V' in 'V'
False                         True                         True                              True
```

## PROGRAMMER'S ZONE

1. Write a program that takes the username of an email address as input. Validate the information using isX function. The username must have both alphabets and digits.

   ```
   username = input("\n Enter the user name : ")
   if username.isalpha() == True:
       print("The user name must have at least one digit.")
   elif username.isdigit() == True:
       print("The user name must have at least one alphabet.")
   elif username.isalnum() == True:
       print("Correct username... You may proceed")
   ```

   **OUTPUT**
   Enter the user name : abc123
   Correct username... You may proceed

2. Write a program that encrypts a message by adding a key value to every character. (Caesar Cipher)
   **Hint:** *Say, if key = 3, then add 3 to every character*
   ```
   message = "PythonProgramming"
   index = 0
   while index < len(message):
       letter = message[index]
       print(chr(ord(letter) + 3),end=" ")
       index += 1
   ```

   > Python does not have any separate data type for characters. They are represented as a single character string.

   **OUTPUT**
   S | w k r q S u r j u d p p l q j

3. Write a program that uses `split()` to split a multiline string.
   ```
   info = '''Dear Students,
   This to inform you that,
   the department is organizing a Hackathon
   on 31st of this month.
   ```

Interested students may give their names to the undersigned.
   Best Wishes,
   Reema Thareja'''
   print(info.split('\n'))
```

**OUTPUT**

['Dear Students,', 'This to inform you that, ', 'the department is organizing a Hackathon', 'on 31st of this month. ', 'Interested students may give their names to the undersigned. ', 'Best Wishes,', 'Reema Thareja']

4. **Write a program to generate an abecedarian series.**

   **Hint:** *Abecedarian refers to a series or list in which the elements appear in alphabetical order*
   ```
   str1 = "ABCDEFGH"
   str2 = "at"
   for letter in str1:
       print((letter + str2), end=" ")
   ```

   > The empty parentheses means that this method takes no argument.

   **OUTPUT**

   Aat   Bat   Cat   Dat   Eat   Fat   Gat   Hat

5. **Write a program that accepts a string from the user and re-displays the same string after removing the vowels from it.**
   ```
   str = input("\n Enter a string : ")
   new_str = ""
   for i in str:
       if i not in "aeiouAEIOU":
           new_str += i
   print("The string without vowels is : ", new_str)
   ```

   **OUTPUT**

   Enter a string : Python Programming
   The string without vowels is : Pythn Prgrmmng

6. **Write a program that finds whether a given character is present in a string or not. In case the character is present, it prints the index at which it is present. Do not use built-in find functions to search the character.**
   ```
   str = input("Enter a string : ")
   ch = input("Enter the character to be searched : ")
   index = 0
   found = 0
   while(index < len(str)):
       if str[index] == ch:
           found = 1
           print(ch, "found in string at index : ", index)
           break
       index += 1
   if(found == 0):
       print (ch, " is not present in the string")
   ```

   > Calling a method is also known as method invocation.

   **OUTPUT**

   Enter a string : Python Programming
   Enter the character to be searched : a
   a found in string at index : 12
   ```

7. **Write a program that emulates the r_find function.**
    ```
    str = input("Enter a string : ")
    ch = input("Enter the character to be searched : ")
    index = len(str)-1
    found = 0
    while(index >= 0):
       if str[index] == ch:
          found = 1
          print(ch, "found in string at index : ", index)
          break
       index -= 1
    if(found == 0):
       print (ch, " is not present in the string")
    ```

    > The start and end parameters in find() and rfind() are optional.

    **OUTPUT**
    ```
    Enter the character to be searched : a
    a found in string at index :12
    ```

8. **Write a program that counts the occurrences of a character in a string. Do not use built-in count function.**
    ```
    str = input("\n Enter a string : ")
    ch = input("\n Enter the character to be searched : ")
    count = 0
    for i in str:
       if i == ch:
          count += 1
    print("In ", str, ch, " occurs ", count, " times")
    ```

    **OUTPUT**
    ```
    Enter a string : Python Programming
    Enter the character to be searched : n
    In Python Programming n occurs 2 times
    ```

9. **Modify the above program so that it starts counting from the specified location.**
    ```
    str = input("\n Enter a string : ")
    ch = input("\n Enter the character to be searched : ")
    loc = int(input("\n From which position do you want to start counting : "))
    count = 0
    index = loc
    while index < len(str):
        if str[index] == ch:
           count += 1
        index += 1
    print("In the string:, ch, " occurs ", count, " times from position", loc, " to end")
    ```

    > Python uses negative numbers to access the characters at the end of the string. Negative index numbers count back from the end of the string.

    **OUTPUT**
    ```
    Enter a string : she sells sea shells on the sea shore
    Enter the character to be searched : s
    From which position do you want to start counting : 5
    In the string soccurs6times from position 5to end
    ```

10. **Write a program to reverse a string.**
    ```
    str = input("\n Enter a string : ")
    new_str = ''
    i = len(str)-1
    while i>=0:
        new_str += str[i]
        i -= 1
    print("\n The reversed string is : ", new_str)
    ```
    **OUTPUT**
    ```
    Enter a string : PYTHON
    The reversed string is :NOHTYP
    ```

11. **Write a program to parse an email id to print from which email server it was sent and when.**
    ```
    info = 'From shreya.kumar@gmail.com Sun Apr 19 20:29:16 2020'
    start = info.find('@') + 1      # Extract characters after @ symbol
    end = info.find(".com") + 4     # Extract till m, find returns index of .
    mailserver = info[start:end]    # Extract characters
    start = end                     # Ignore whitespace
    end = len(info) # Extract till last character
    date_time = info[start:end]
    print("The email has been sent through " , mailserver,
    end = ' ')
    print("on " + date_time)
    ```

    > When using negative index numbers, start with the lower number first as it occurs earlier in the string.

    **OUTPUT**
    ```
    The email has been sent throughgmail.com onSun Apr 19 20:29:16 2020
    ```

12. **Write a program to convert every alternate character in a string to uppercase.**
    ```
    str = "helloworldofpython"
    length = len(str)
    new_str = ""
    for i in range(length):
        if(i%2 != 0):
            new_str += str[i].upper()
        else:
            new_str += str[i]
    print(new_str)
    ```
    **OUTPUT**
    ```
    hElLoWoRlDoFpYtHoN
    ```

## Key Terms

**Traversing a string:** Accessing each character in the string, one at a time.

**Dot notation:** Use of the dot operator (.) to access functions inside a module.

**Index:** A variable or value used to access a member of an ordered set.

**Slice:** A part of a string obtained by specifying a range of indices.

**Whitespace:** Characters that move the cursor without printing visible characters.

**Method:** A function that is called on an object using dot notation.

**Sequence:** An ordered set of values in which each value is identified by an integer index.

**Empty string:** A string that has no characters and has a length = 0.

**Format operator:** % operator that takes a format string and a tuple to generate a string that includes values of the tuple formatted as specified by the format string.

**Format sequence:** Sequence of characters in a format string, like %d, which specifies how a value should be formatted.

**Format string:** String used with the % or format operator that contains format sequences.

**Invocation:** A statement that calls a method.

**Immutable:** The property of a sequence whose items cannot be assigned.

## Chapter Highlights

- The Python string data type is a sequence made up of one or more individual characters, where a character could be a letter, digit, whitespace, or any other symbol.
- The `in` operator checks if one character or string is contained in another string.
- The whitespace characters, exclamation mark and any other symbol (like ?, <,>,*, @, #, $, %, etc) that forms a part of the string would be assigned its own index number.
- Concatenate means to join together and append means to add something at the end.
- A raw string literal which is prefixed by an 'r' passes all the characters as it.
- Python strings are immutable, which means that once the strings are created they cannot be changed.
- The number and type of values in the tuple should match the number and type of format sequences or conversion specifications in the string; otherwise an error is returned.
- Strings are examples of Python objects.
- `in` and `not in` operators can be used with strings to determine whether a string is present in another string. Therefore, the `in` and `not in` operators are also known as membership operators.
- The string module consists of a number of useful constants, classes and functions. These functions are used to manipulate strings.

## Review Questions

1. With the help of an example, explain how we can create string variables in Python.
2. With the help of an example, explain how we can concatenate a string and a floating-point data.
3. Python strings are immutable. Comment on this statement.
4. Write a short note on format operator.
5. What will happen when the `strip()` is used with a string argument?
6. Explain the use of `format()` with the help of an example.
7. What is slice operation? Explain with an example.
8. With the help of an example, explain the significance of membership operators.
9. Differentiate between the following.
   a. a method and a function
   b. `find()` and `index()`
   c. `find()` and `rfind()`
   d. `captalize()` and `upper()`

10. Name the function to do the following operations:
    a. Returns a string with the original string centered to a total of width columns
    b. Checks if string ends with suffix; returns True if so and False otherwise
    c. Returns True if string has at least 1 character and every character is either a number or an alphabet and False otherwise
    d. Returns True if string has at least 1 character and every character is a lower case alphabet and False otherwise
    e. Removes all trailing whitespace in string
    f. Returns the highest alphabetical character (having highest ASCII value) from the string str.
    g. Toggles the case of every character
    h. Returns a list of substrings separated by the specified delimiter.
    i. The function joins a list of strings using the delimiter with which the function is invoked.
11. Returns a list of the lines in the string.
12. If str = 'Welcome to the world of Python Programming', answer the following:
    a. Write an instruction to print the tenth character of the string.
    b. Write an instruction that prints the index of the first occurrence of the letter 'o' in the string.

## Programming Exercises

1. Modify the find_ch function so that it starts finding the character from the specified position in the string.
2. Write a program to calculate the length of a string.
3. Write a program to count the number of vowels and consonants present in a user-inputted string.
4. Write a program to count the number of lower case and uppercase characters present in a user-inputted string.
5. Write a program to count the number of digits, spaces and alphabets present in a user-inputted string.
6. Write a Python program to get a string made of the first 2 and the last 2 chars from a given a string. If the string length is less than 2, return instead the empty string.
7. Write a Python program to get a string from a given string where all occurrences of its first char have been changed to '$', except the first char itself.
8. Write a Python program to get a single string from two given strings, separated by a space and swap the first two characters of each string.
9. Program to copy a string.
10. Write a Python program to add 'ing' at the end of a given string (length should be at least 3). If the given string is already ends with 'ing' then add 'ly' instead. If the string length of the given string is less than 3, leave it unchanged.
11. Write a program to find the first appearance of the substring 'not' and 'poor' from a given string, if 'bad' follows the 'poor', replace the whole 'not'...'poor' substring with 'good'. Return the resulting string.
12. Write a function that takes a list of words and returns the length of the longest one.
13. Write a program to remove the *n*th index character from a non-empty string.
14. Write a program to change a given string to a new string where the first and last chars have been exchanged.
15. Write a program to remove the characters which have odd index values of a given string.
16. Write a program to count the occurrences of each word in a given sentence.
17. Write a program that accepts a comma-separated sequence of words as input and prints the unique words in sorted form (alphanumerically).
18. Write a function to insert a string in the middle of a string.

19. Write a function to get a string made of 4 copies of the last two characters of a specified string (length must be at least 2).
20. Write a function to get a string made of its first three characters of a specified string. If the length of the string is less than 3 then return the original string.
21. Write a function to get the first half of a specified string of even length.
22. Write a function to reverses a string if its length is a multiple of 4.
23. Write a function to convert a given string to all uppercase if it contains at least 2 uppercase characters in the first 4 characters.
24. Write a program to sort a string lexicographically.
25. Write a program to remove newline characters from text.
26. Write a program to check whether a string starts with specified characters.
27. Write a program to remove existing indentation from all of the lines in a given text.
28. Write a program to add a prefix text to all of the lines in a string.
29. Write a program to set the indentation of the first line.
30. Write a program to print floating numbers up to 2 decimal places.
31. Write a program to print floating numbers up to 2 decimal places with sign.
32. Write a program to print floating numbers with no decimal places.
33. Write a program to print integers with zeros on the left of specified width.
34. Write a program to print integers with '*' on the right of specified width.
35. Write a program to display a number with comma separator.
36. Write a program to format a number with percentage.
37. Write a program to display a number in left-, right- and centre-aligned format of width 10.
38. Write a program to reverse words in a string.
39. Write a program to strip a set of characters from a string.
40. Write a program to create a mirror of the given string. For example, "abc" = "abccba".
41. Write a program that removes all the occurrences of a specified character from a given string.
42. Write a program to check whether a string is palindrome or not.
43. Write a program to remove all the occurrences of a given word from the string.
44. Write a program to concatenate two strings in a third string. Do not use + operator.
45. Write a program to append a string to another string. Do not use += operator
46. Write a program to swap two strings.
47. Write a program to insert a string in another string.
48. Write a program to delete a string from another string.
49. Write a program to replace a string with another string. Do not use the `replace()`.
50. Write a program that removes leading and trailing spaces from a string.
51. Write a program to read a name and then display it in abbreviated form, for example, Janak Raj Thareja should be displayed as JRT.

52. Write a program to read a name and then display it in abbreviated form, for example, Janak Raj Thareja should be displayed as J.R. Thareja.

53. Write a program to count the number of characters, words, and lines in the given text.

54. Write a program to count the number of digits, upper case characters, lower case characters, and special characters in a given string.

55. Write a program to extract the first *n* characters of a string.

56. Write a program to copy n characters of a string from the *m*th position in another string. Do not use the slice operation.

57. Write a program to delete the last character of a string.

58. Write a program to delete the first character of a string.

59. Write a program to encrypt a string using substitution cipher.

60. Write a program that encrypts a string using multiplicative cipher. Generate the key randomly.

61. Write the command to print "hello world" as "Hello world".

62. Write the command to print "hello world" as "Hello World".

63. Write the command to print "hElLo WoRlD" as "HeLlO wOrLd".

64. Write the command to print "hello world" as "Hello Friends".

65. Write a program that prompts the user to enter a 10-digit mobile number. Display the number by putting a '-' after area code and next three digits. (like 123-456-7890).

66. Write a program that prompts the user to enter five words. If the length of any word is less than 8 or if the word does not contain any digit then prompt the user to enter that word again.

## Fill in the Blanks

1. String is a sequence made up of one or more _____.
2. A multiple-line text within quotes must have a _____ at the end of each line.
3. Individual characters in a string are accessed using the _____ operator.
4. _____ error is generated when index out of bounds is accessed.
5. _____ means to join together.
6. The _____ function is used to convert values of any other type into string type.
7. The _____ returns the memory address of that object.
8. Conversion specifications start with a ___ operator.
9. A method is invoked or called on an _____.
10. _____ function checks if a string ends with suffix.
11. _____ function toggles the case of every character.
12. The _____ returns a list of the lines in the string.
13. Omitting both ends in the slice operation means selecting the _____.
14. If we access the string from the first character then we use a _____ based index but when doing it backward the index starts with ____.
15. _____ function returns the ASCII code of the character.

16. _____ and _____ operators are known as membership operators.
17. _____ function is used to know the details of a particular item.
18. _____ function displays the methods in a module.

## State True or False

1. Character in a string could be a letter, digit, whitespace, or any other symbol.
2. Python treats strings as contiguous series of characters delimited by single or double quotes but not triple quotes.
3. Python has a built-in string class as well as a string module that has many methods.
4. Index can either be an integer or an expression that evaluates to a floating point number.
5. In a string, all whitespace characters are also assigned an index value.
6. Raw strings do not process escape sequences.
7. 'r' is used as a prefix for Unicode strings.
8. We cannot delete or remove characters from a string.
9. The % operator takes a format string on the right and the corresponding values in a tuple on the left.
10. Conversion specifications start with a % operator and can appear anywhere within the string.
11. The number and type of values in the tuple should match the number and type of format sequences or conversion specifications in the string.
12. The - after each % in the conversion string indicates right justification.
13. You can access a string using negative indexes.
14. `odr()` function returns character represented by a ASCII number.
15. A string is a substring of itself.
16. Strings are compared based on ASCII values of their characters.

## Multiple Choice Questions

1. The index of the first character in the string is _____.
   a. 0           b. 1           c. n-1          d. n
2. The index of the last character in the string is _____.
   a. 0           b. 1           c. n-1          d. n
3. Which error is generated when the index is not an integer?
   a. IndexError  b. NameError   c. TypeError    d. BoundError
4. Which of the following word best means to add something at the end?
   a. Concatenate b. Append      c. Join         d. Add
5. In Python a string is appended to another string by using which operator?
   a. +           b. *           c. []           d. +=
6. Which operator is used to repeat a string n number of times?
   a. +           b. *           c. []           d. +=
7. The `print` statement prints one or more literals or values followed by a/an _____.
   a. Newline     b. Tab         c. Whitespace   d. Exclamation

8. Which error is generated when a character in a string variable is modified?
   a. IndexError
   b. NameError
   c. TypeError
   d. BoundError

9. You can delete the entire string by using which keyword?
   a. del
   b. erase
   c. remove
   d. delete

10. Which operator takes a format string on the left and the corresponding values in a tuple on the right?
    a. +
    b. *
    c. []
    d. %

11. Which character is used for hexadecimal integers in the format string?
    a. u
    b. x
    c. d
    d. s

12. When using find(), if str is not present in the string then what is returned?
    a. 0
    b. -1
    c. n-1
    d. ValueError

13. If "    Cool    " becomes "COOL", which two functions must have been applied?
    a. strip() and upper()
    b. strip() and lower()
    c. strip() and capitalize()
    d. lstrip() and rstrip()

14. In the split(), if no delimiter is specified then by default it splits strings on which characters?
    a. Whitespace
    b. comma
    c. newline
    d. colon

15. The splitlines(), splits lines in strings on which characters?
    a. Whitespace
    b. comma
    c. newline
    d. colon

16. By default, the value of stride is ____.
    a. 0
    b. -1
    c. 1
    d. n-1

17. To print the original string in reverse order, you can set the stride as ____.
    a. 0
    b. -1
    c. 1
    d. n-1

18. Identify the correct result from the following.
    a. ord('10') = 50
    b. chr(72) = 'H'
    c. chr(55) = 9
    d. ord('z') = 123

19. Which of these patterns would not match the string "Good Morning" when used with match()?
    a. Good
    b. Morning
    c. Go
    d. Good Morn

## Give the Output

1. ```
   s = "Welcome"
   print s[1:3]
   ```

2. ```
   s = "Welcome"
   print s[ : 6]
   ```

3. ```
   s = "Welcome"
   print s[4 : ]
   ```

4. ```
   s = "Welcome"
   print s[1:-1]
   ```

5. ```
   str = "Welcome"
   print "come" in str
   ```

6. ```
   str = "Welcome"
   print "come" not in str
   ```

7. ```
   "free" == "freedom"
   ```

8. ```
   print("12" + "34")
   ```

9. `"man" != "men"`

10. `>>> 3*"PYTHON"`

11. ```
    str = "Welcome to Python"
    print(str.isalnum())
    ```

12. `"Hello".isalpha()`

13. `"14-10-2106".isdigit()`

14. `print "hello".islower()`

15. `"\t".isspace()`

16. ```
    str = "Hello"
    print str.startswith("he")
    ```

17. ```
    str = "Hello, welcome to the world of Python"
    print str.find("o")
    ```

18. ```
    str = "Hello, welcome to the world of Python"
    print str.find("if")
    ```

19. ```
    str = "Hello, welcome to the world of Python"
    print str.rfind("of")
    ```

20. ```
    str = "Hello, welcome to the world of Python"
    print str.count("o")
    ```

21. `"us" not in "success"`

22. `"mi" in "ours"`

23. ```
    for i in 'Python':
        print 2 * i,
    ```

24. `string.find("abcdabcdabcd", "cd", 3)`

25. `string.find("abcdabcdabcdabcdabcd", "cd", 7, 13)`

26. ```
    a = 10
    b = 20
    print "3**4 = %d and %d * %d = %f" % (3**4, a, b, a * b)
    ```

27. ```
    print "%d %f %s" % (7, 15, 28)
    print "%-.2f" % 369
    print "%-10.2f%-10.2f" % (91, 23.456)
    print "%5.2f %5.2f $%5.2f" % (9, 1.2, 55.78)
    ```

28. ```
    str1 = 'Welcome!'
    str2 = 'to Python'
    str3 = str1[:2] + str2[len(str2) - 2:]
    print str3
    ```

29. `print("She sells sea shells on the sea shore.".find("sea", 3, -6))`

30. `len("She sells sea shells on the sea shore.")`

31. ```
    str = "Welcome to the world of Python"
    print(str[:10].find("t"))
    ```

32. ```
    str = "Welcome to the world of Python"
    start = 3
    end = 10
    print(str[start:end])
    ```

33. ```
    str = "Hello"
    print str.startswith('h')
    print str.lower().startswith('h')
    ```

34. ```
    'In %d years I have saved %g %s.' % (3, 4.5, 'lakh rupees')
    ```

35. ```
    ', '.join(['Sun', 'Stars', 'Planets'])
    ```

36. ```
    ' '.join(['Welcome', 'to', 'the', 'world', 'of', 'Python!'])
    ```

37. ```
    'Hello'.join(['Welcome', 'to', 'the', 'world', 'of', 'Python!'])
    ```

38. ```
    "Good morning students".split()
    ```

39. ```
    'WelcomeHellotoHellotheHelloworldHelloofHelloPython!'.split('Hello')
    ```

40. ```
    >>> s = 'abcdefghijkl'
    >>> print(s[-100:-5],s[-100:5])
    ```

41. ```
    s1 = "HELLO"
    s2 = s1 + s1[-1]
    print(s2)
    print(s1[:-1])
    print(s1[-1:])
    ```

42. ```
    str = "xyz"
    while(len(str)<=4):
        if(str[-1] == 'z'):
            str = str[0:3]+'c'
        elif 'a' in str:
            str = str[0] + 'bb'
        elif 'x' not in str:
            str = '1'+str[1:]+'z'
        else:
            str = str+'*'
    print(str)
    ```

43. ```
    str = "helloworldofpython"
    print(str[10],str[11:30])
    ```

44. ```
    str1 = '''PYTHON
    PRO'''
    str2 = '''PYTHON\
    PRO'''
    print(len(str1)>len(str2))
    ```

45. ```
    str1= 'PYTHON'; str1[-4]
    ```
    ```

# Strings

## Find the Error

1. ```
   str = "Hello world"
   str[6] = 'W'
   print(str)
   ```

2. ```
   "%s %s %s %s" % ('Welcome', 'to', 'Python')
   ```

3. ```
   "%s %s %s" % ('East', 'West', 'North', 'South')
   ```

4. ```
   "%d %f %f" % (10, 20, 'Hello')
   ```

5. ```
   str = 'abcdefgh'
   str[5] = 'a'
   print(str)
   str = 'Python'
   print(str)
   ```

6. ```
   str = "Hello World"
   del str[2]
   print(str)
   ```

7. ```
   print("Hello World" + 10)
   ```

8. ```
   print("Hello" * "World")
   ```

## Answers

### Fill in the Blanks

1. characters
2. backslash (\)
3. subscript ([ ])
4. IndexError
5. concatenate
6. str()
7. id()
8. %
9. object
10. endswith()
11. swapcase()
12. splitlines()
13. entire string
14. zero, −1
15. ord()
16. in and not in
17. type()
18. dir()

### State True or False

1. True
2. False
3. True
4. False
5. True
6. True
7. False
8. True
9. False
10. True
11. True
12. False
13. True
14. False
15. True
16. True

### Multiple Choice Questions

1. a
2. c
3. c
4. b
5. d
6. b
7. a
8. c
9. a
10. d
11. b
12. b
13. a
14. a
15. c
16. c
17. b
18. b
19. b

### Give the Output

1. el
2. Welcom
3. ome
4. elcom
5. True
6. False
7. False
8. 1234
9. True
10. 'PYTHONPYTHONPYTHON'
11. False
12. True
13. False
14. True
15. True
16. False
17. 4
18. −1
19. 28
20. 6

21. True
22. False
23. PP yy tt hh oo nn
24. 6
25. 10
26. 3**4 = 81 and 10 * 20 = 200.000000
27. 7  15.000000  28
    369.00
    91.00        23.46
    9.001.20 $55.78
28. Weon
29. 10
30. 38
31. 8
32. come to
33. False
    True

34. 'In 3 years I have saved 4.5 lakh rupees.'
35. 'Sun, Stars, Planets'
36. 'Welcome to the world of Python!'
37. 'WelcomeHellotoHellotheHelloworldHelloofHelloPython!'
38. ['Good', 'morning', 'students']
39. ['Welcome', 'to', 'the', 'world', 'of', 'Python!']
40. abcdefg abcde
41. HELLOO
    HELL
    O
42. xvzc*
43. o fpython
44. True
45. 'T'

## Find the Error

1. TypeError: 'str' object does not support item assignment
2. TypeError: not enough arguments for format string
3. TypeError: not all arguments converted during string formatting
4. TypeError: float argument required, not str
5. TypeError: 'str' object does not support item assignment
6. TypeError: 'str' object doesn't support item deletion
7. TypeError: can only concatenate str (not "int") to str
8. TypeError: can't multiply sequence by non-int of type 'str'

# Lists

8

## Chapter Objectives

This chapter introduces list as an important and very powerful data structure in Python. The reader will get to learn the following things in this chapter:

- Creating lists
- Accessing and updating its values
- Relational operations
- Nested lists
- The eval() function
- Creating deep copies and shallow copies of a given list
- Difference between list cloning and list aliasing
- List operations and methods

List is a versatile data type available in Python, in which elements are written as a list of comma-separated values (items) between square brackets. Lists in Python are mutable as we can change the value of their elements. This is in striking contrast with strings, which are immutable.

The key feature of list is that it can have elements that belong to different data types. The syntax of defining a list can be given as, **List_variable = [val1, val2, …]**

```
list_A = [1,2,3,4,5]                list_B = ['A', 1, 'C', 2, 'E']
print(list_A)                       print(list_B)
[1, 2, 3, 4, 5]                     ['A', 1, 'C', 2, 'E']
list_C = ["HELLO","WORLD")          list_D = [1, 'a ', 'HELLO')
print(list_ C)                      print( list_ D)
['HELLO', 'WORLD']                  [1, 'a ', 'HELLO']
```

We can even create an empty list by writing **list_variable = []**. An empty list is equivalent to False when used with logical operators.

```
>>> list = []
>>> list == True
    False
```

## 8.1 ACCESSING VALUES IN LISTS

Like strings, lists can also be sliced and concatenated. To access values in a list, square brackets are used to slice along with the index or indices to get the value stored at that index. As discussed earlier, the syntax for the slice operation is, **seq = List[start:stop:step]**

For example,
seq = List[::2]  *# gets every other element, starting with index 0*
seq = List[10::3]  *# gets every third element, starting with index 10*
seq = List[-3]  *# gets the third element from the end*
seq = List_A[-3] *# 3rd element from the end*
seq = List[3:] *# get all elements starting from the third index at the beginning*

```
num_list = [2,4,6,8,10,12,14,16,18,20]
print("num_list is:", num_list)
print("First element in the list is",
num_list[0])
print("num_list[2:5] = ", num_list[4:7])
print("num_list[::2] = ", num_list[::3])
print("num_list[1::3] = ", num_list[1::2])
```

**OUTPUT**
```
num_list is : [2, 4, 6, 8, 10, 12,
14, 16, 18, 20]
First element in the list is 2
num_list[2:5] = [10, 12, 14]
num_list[::2] = [2, 8, 14, 20]
num_list[1::3] = [4, 8, 12, 16, 20]
```

If the start and end values of the slice operation are beyond the size of the list, then all the elements within the specified range are returned. For example, consider the example given in which the start and end values are out of range of the size of the list.

Note that the valid index range of the list is 0–4. The values –9 and 9 are beyond the size of the list, so the entire list is returned. But in the second case, when start = –3 and end = 9, –3 lies in the valid range which is the third element from the end, hence the result.

```
I = [1,2,3,4,5]        I = [1, 2,3,4,5]
print(l[-9:9])         print(I[-3:9])
OUTPUT                 OUTPUT
[1, 2, 3, 4, 5]        [3, 4, 5]
```

## 8.2 THE eval() FUNCTION

```
>>> eval("10      >>> eval("20      >>> eval("30 - 5    >>> eval(" 'HELLO'
== 10")          <= 10")            * 4 + 20")           * 3")
True             False              30                   'HELLOHELLOHELLO'
```

The eval() function is used to evaluate and return the result of an expression as a string.

We can use the eval() function to read value(s) of any type. However, its use is discouraged as we may get unforeseen problems as a result of using this function.

## 8.3 UPDATING VALUES IN LISTS

### Example 8.1

**Let us write a program that uses the eval () function to accept a list of numbers and print the sum of the elements.**
```
list= eval(input("Enter values : "))
print (list)
sum(list)
print("SUM = " , sum(list))
```

**OUTPUT**
```
Enter values : [1,2,3,4,5,6,7,8,9,10]
[1 , 2 , 3 , 4 , 5 , 6 , 7 , 8 , 9 , 10]
SUM = 55
```

Once created, one or more elements of a list can be easily updated by giving the slice on the left-hand side of the assignment operator. You can also append new values in the list and remove existing value(s) from the list using the append() method and del statement respectively.

### Example 8.2

**Using the eval () function to accept input of different types.**
```
a = eval(input("Enter an integer : "))
print (type (a))
b = eval(input("Enter a float : "))
print (type (b))
c = eval(input( "Enter a tuple : "))
print (type (c))
d = eval(input("Enter a list : "))
print (type (d))
```

**OUTPUT**
```
Enter an integer : 1
<class 'int'>
Enter a float : 2.3
<class 'float'>
Enter a tuple : (4,5, 6)
<class 'tuple ' >
Enter a list : [7, 8, 9]
<class 'list'>
```

### Example 8.3

```
num_list = [2,4,6,8,10,12,14,16,18,20]
print("List is : ", num_list)
num_list[5] = 100
print("List after udpation is : ", num_list)
num_list.append(200)
print("List after appending a value is ", num_list)
del num_list[3]
print("List after deleting a value is ", num_list)
```

**OUTPUT**

```
List is :  [2, 4, 6, 8, 10, 12, 14, 16, 18, 20]
List after udpation is :  [2, 4, 6, 8, 10, 100, 14, 16, 18, 20]
List after appending a value is [2, 4, 6, 8, 10, 100, 14, 16, 18, 20, 200]
List after deleting a value is [2, 4, 6, 10, 100, 14, 16, 18, 20, 200]
```

If you know exactly which element(s) to delete, use the del statement; otherwise, use the remove() method to delete the unknown elements.

### Example 8.4

```
num_list = [2,4,6,8,10,12,14,16,18,20]
del num_list[3:6] #deletes numbers at index 3,4,5
print(num_list)
del num_list[:] #deletes all the numbers from the list
print(num_list) # an empty list is printed
```

**OUTPUT**

```
[2, 4, 6, 14, 16, 18, 20]
[]
```

```
del(num_list)
print(num_list)  # the list no longer exists
```

**OUTPUT**

```
Traceback (most recent call last):
  File "C:\Users\Reema\Python\Python37\try.py",
line 5, in <module>
    print(num_list) #the list no loger exists
NameError: name 'num_list' is not defined
```

Note that when we write del num_list, the entire variable is deleted. If you make any attempt to use this variable after the del statement, then an error will be generated.

## 8.4 RELATIONAL OPERATIONS ON LISTS

We can compare two list objects using relational operators like ==, >, <, >=, <=, !=, etc. Python compares elements of a list in lexicographical order. Each element of the list is compared with the corresponding element in the other list. However, to use operators like >=, <=, >, < the two values must be of compatible type; otherwise an error will be generated.

### Example 8.5

```
l1 = [1,2,3]
l2 = [1,2,3]
l3 = [1,[2,3]]
print(l1==l2)
print(l1==l3)
```

**OUTPUT**

```
True
False
```

```
l1 = [1,2,3]
l2 = [1,3,3]
print(l1>=l2)
print(l1<=l2)
```

**OUTPUT**

```
False
True
```

```
l1 = [1,2,3,4]
l2 = [1,3,3]
print(l1>=l2)
```

**OUTPUT**

```
True
```

```
l1 = [1,2,3,4]
l2 = ['a','b','c']
l3 = [1.0,2.0,3.0)
print(l1>=l3)
print(l2>=l3)
```

**OUTPUT**
```
True
Traceback (most recent call last):
  File "C:\Python37\try.py",line 5, in <module>
print(l2>=l3) Type Error: '>=' not supported between instances of 'str' and 'float'
```

## 8.5  NESTED LISTS

Nested list means a list within another list. We have already said that a list has elements of different data types. So besides other elements, a list can also have another list as its element. For example, `list1 = [1,2,'a',[5.0,6,"ABCD"], "BYE"]`. Here, `list1` is a list that has another list at index 3.

To *insert items from another list* at a particular location, we can use the slice operation. This would create a nested list, i.e., a list within another list.

Remember that you can specify an element in the nested list by using a set of indices. For example, assuming that the inner list starts at index 3 in the main list, to print the second element of the nested (or the inner) list, we will write `print list[3][1]`. The first index specifies the starting location of the nested list in the main list and the second index specifies the index of the element within the nested list. The code given below clarifies this concept.

### Example 8.6

```
# Creating a Nested List
list1 = [1,2,'a',[5.0,6,"ABCD"I,"BYE"]
i=0
while i<(le n(list1)):
  print{"List1[",i,"] = ",list1[i])
  i+=1
```

**OUTPUT**
```
List1[0] = 1
List1[1] = 2
List1[2] = a
List1[3] = [5.0, 6, 'ABCD']
List1[4 ] = BYE
```

```
#Inserting a list within another list-
creating a nested list
num_list = [2,4,12,14]
print("Original List : ", num_list)
num_list[2] = [6,8,10]
print("After inserting another list, the updated list is : ", num_list)
print("Second element of nested list is : ",num_list[2][1])
```

**OUTPUT**
```
Original List : [2, 4, 12, 14]
After inserting another list, the updated list is : [2, 4, [6, 8, 10], 14]
Second element of nested list is : 8
```

## 8.6  LIST ALIASING AND CLONING

When one list is assigned to another list using the assignment operator (=), then a new copy of the list is not made. Instead, assignment operation makes the two variables point to the same list in memory. This is also known as *aliasing*.

**Cloning lists:** If you want to modify a list and also keep a copy of the original list, then you should create a separate copy of the list (not just the reference). This process is called *cloning.* **The slice operation is used to clone a list.**

### Example 8.7

```
list1 = [1,2,3,4,5,6,7,8,9,10]
print("List1 = " , list1)
list2 = list1 #list aliasing
print("List2 = " , list2)
list3 = list1[2:5] #list cloning
print("List3 = ", list3)
```

OUTPUT
```
List1 = [1, 2, 3, 4, 5, 6, 7, 8, 9, 10]
List2 = [1, 2, 3, 4, 5, 6, 7, 8, 9, 10]
List3 = [3, 4, 5]
```

## 8.7 DELETING ELEMENTS

We can delete one or more elements from the list by using the **del** statement. The syntax to remove a single element from the list is **del list_variable[index]**. And to remove more than one element from the list, we use the syntax, **del[start:stop]**. Finally, to remove the entire list, we need to write **del list_variable**.

### Example 8.8

```
I =[1,2,3,4,5,6,7,8,9,10)
print(I)
#deleting third element
del I[2]
print(I)
#deleting fourth, fifth, sixth and seventh elements from the list
delI[2:6]
print(I)
#deleting the entire list
print("Deleting List ........ ")
del I
print(I)
```

OUTPUT
```
[1, 2, 3, 4, 5, 6, 7, 8, 9, 10)
[1, 2, 4, 5, 6, 7, 8, 9, 10)
[1, 2, 8, 9, 10)
Deleting List ....... .
Traceback (most recent call last): File "C:\Python37\try.py", line 12, in <module> print(I)
NameError: name 'I' is not defined
```

## 8.8 DEEP COPIES AND SHALLOW COPIES IN PYTHON

When copying lists or any other object in Python, we can make a deep copy of the original object or a shallow copy. *A deep copy makes a new and separate copy* of an *entire* object or list with its own unique memory address. Therefore, any changes made in the new copy of the object/list will not be reflected in the original one.

A deep copy creates a new list or object by recursively copying the elements from the original object to the new one. So, both the objects are completely independent of each other. This is similar to the concept of passing by value in languages like C++, Java and C#.

A shallow copy also makes a separate new object or list. However, in this case, instead of copying the elements to the new object, *it simply copies the references to their memory addresses*. Hence, changes made in the original object, would also be reflected in the copied object, and vice versa. Therefore, both the copies are dependent on each other. This is similar to the concept of passing by reference in programming languages like C++, C#, and Java.

Talking in terms of lists, **the `assignment` operator is used to create a shallow copy of the list and the `list()` creates a deep copy** as illustrated below.

### Example 8.9

```
#Creating a shallow copy of a list
l1 = [1,2,3,4,5]
l2 = l1
print("L1 = ", l1)
print("l2 = ", l2)
l1[2] = 10
print("Ll = ", l1)
print("L2 = ", l2)
OUTPUT
L1 = [1, 2, 3, 4, 5]
L2 = [1, 2, 3, 4, 5]
L1 = [1, 2, 10, 4, 5]
L2 = [1, 2, 10, 4, 5]
```

```
# Creating a deep copy of a list
l1 = [1,2,3,4,5]
l2 = list(l1)
print("L1 = ", l1)
print("L2 = ", l2)
l1[2] = 10
print("L1 = ", l1)
print("L2 = ", l2)
OUTPUT
L1 = [1, 2, 3, 4, 5]
L2 = [1, 2, 3, 4, 5]
L1 = [1, 2, 10, 4, 5]
L2 = [1, 2, 3, 4, 5]
```

## 8.9 BASIC LIST OPERATIONS

Lists behave in a similar way as strings when operators like + (concatenation) and * (repetition) are used. Common operations on lists are discussed in Table 8.1.

**Table 8.1** Operations on lists

| Operation | Description | Example | Output |
|---|---|---|---|
| `len` | Returns length of list | `len([1,2,3,4,5,6,7,8,9,10])` | 10 |
| `concatenation` | Joins two lists | `[1,2,3,4,5] + [6,7,8,9,10]` | [1, 2, 3, 4, 5, 6, 7, 8, 9, 10] |
| `repetition` | Repeat elements in the list | `"Love", "Python"*2` | ['Love', 'Python', 'Love', 'Python'] |
| `in` | Checks if the value is present in the list | `'a' in ['a','e','i','o','u']` | True |
| `not in` | Checks if the value is not present in the list | `9 not in [0,2,4,6,8]` | True |
| `max` | Returns maximum value in the list | `>>> num_list = [1,0,3,7,4,2,4,9]`<br>`>>> print(max(num_list))` | 9 |
| `min` | Returns minimum value in the list | `>>> num_list = [1,0,3,7,4,2,4,9]`<br>`>>> print(min(num_list))` | 0 |
| `sum` | Adds the values in the list that has numbers | `num_list = [1,2,3,4,5,6,7,8,9,10]`<br>`print("SUM = ", sum(num_list))` | SUM = 55 |
| `all` | Return True if all elements of the list are true (or if the list is empty) | `>>> num_list = [8,9,0,10]`<br>`>>> print(all(num_list))` | False |

*(Continued)*

### Table 8.1 Continued

| Operation | Description | Example | Output |
|---|---|---|---|
| any | Return True if any element of the list is true. If the list is empty, returns False | `>>> num_list = [,0,1,2,4,9]`<br>`>>> print(any(num_list))` | True |
| List | Convert tuple, string or to a list | `>>> list1 = list("PYTHON")`<br>`>>> print(list1)` | ['P', 'Y', 'T', 'H', 'O', 'N'] |
| Sorted | Return a new sorted list. The original list is not sorted. | `>>> list1 = [1,0,3,7,4,2,9]`<br>`>>> list2 = sorted(list1)`<br>`>>> print(list2)` | [0,1,2,3,4,7,9] |

## 8.10 LIST METHODS

Python has various methods to help programmers work efficiently with lists. Some of these methods are summarized in Table 8.2.

### Table 8.2 List methods

| Method | Description | Syntax | Example | Output |
|---|---|---|---|---|
| append() | Appends an element to the list. In insert(), if the index is 0, then element is inserted as the first element and if we write, list.insert(len(list), obj), then it inserts obj as the last element in the list. That is, if index = len(list), then insert() method behaves exactly the same as append() method. | list.append(obj) | num_list = [1,2,3,4]<br>num_list.append(5)<br>print(num_list) | [1,2,3,4,5] |
| count() | Counts the number of times an element appears in the list | list.count(obj) | num_list = [1,2,3,4,3,2,4,6]<br>print( num_list.count(4)) | 1 |
| index() | Returns the lowest index of obj in the list. Gives a ValueError if obj is not present in the list | list.index(obj) | num_list = [1,2,3,4,3,2,4,6]<br>print(num_list.index(3)) | 2 |
| insert() | Inserts obj at the specified index in the list. | list.insert(index, obj) | num_list = [1,2,3,4,5]<br>num_list.insert(3, 0)<br>print(num_list) | [1,2,3,0,4,5] |

(*Continued*)

| Table 8.2 | Continued | | | |
|---|---|---|---|---|
| Method | Description | Syntax | Example | Output |
| **pop()** | Removes the element at the specified index from the list. Index is an optional parameter. If no index is specified then it removes the last object (or element) from the list. | `list.pop([index])` | `num_list = [1,2,3,4,5]`<br>`print(num_list.pop())`<br>`print(num_list)` | 5<br>[1, 2, 3, 4] |
| **remove()** | Removes or deletes obj from the list. ValueError is generated if obj is not present in the list. If multiple copies of obj exist in the list, then the first value is deleted. | `list.remove(obj)` | `num_list = [0,1,2,3,4,5]`<br>`num_list.remove(0)`<br>`print(num_list)` | [1, 2, 3,4,5] |
| **reverse()** | Reverses the elements in the list. | `list.reverse()` | `num_list = [1,2,3,4]`<br>`num_list.reverse()`<br>`print num_list` | [4,3,2,1] |
| **sort()** | Sorts the elements in the list | `list.sort()` | `num_list = [3,5,0,4,1]`<br>`num_list.sort()`<br>`print(num_list)` | [0,1,3,4,5] |
| **extend()** | Adds the elements in a list to the end of another list. Using + or += on a list is similar to using `extend()`. | `list1.extend(list2)` | `num_list1 = [1,2,3]`<br>`num_list2 = [4,5,6]`<br>`num_list1.extend(num_list2)`<br>`print(num_list1)` | [1, 2, 3, 4, 5, 6] |

You may be confused between a method and a function. Observe the above two tables. Clearly, a **function** is a piece of code that is directly called by a name. It may or may not accept parameters and may or may not return data. All data that is to be used by a function is explicitly passed (or made global). Example, `len(list1)`.

However, a **method** is a piece of code that is called by name of the object followed by a dot operator and name of the method. Example, `list1.sort()`.

### Key points to remember
- The `sort()` method uses ASCII values to sort the values in the list. Since lower case characters' ASCII value starts from 97 and upper case character's starts from 65, upper case characters appear before lower case characters when sorting is done.
- Items in a list can be deleted by assigning an empty list to a slice of elements as shown in the codes below.
- The `range()` function can be used to print index as shown in the code given below.

### Example 8.10

```
list1 = ['1', 'a', "Abc",
'2', '8', "def"]
list1.sort()
print(list1)
```
**OUTPUT**
```
['1', '2 ', 'Abc', 'B',
'a', 'def']
```

```
list= ['P',' r','o','g','r','
a','m','m','i','n','g']
list[3:6] = []
print(list)
```
**OUTPUT**
```
('P', 'r', 'o', 'm', 'm',
'i', 'n', 'g']
```

```
list = [ 'B','Y','E']
for i in range(len(list)):
    print("index: ", i)
```
**OUTPUT**
```
index : 0
index : 1
index : 2
```

- If you give an index out of range of the legal indices, then an **IndexError** will be generated. For a list, the legal indices include index from 0 to length of the list − 1. Consider the example, given below.

### Example 8.11

```
list = [1,'a',3.4,"PYTHON"]
print(len(list))
# error because length is 4 and we are accessing an index out of range
print(list[4])
```

**OUTPUT**

```
4
Traceback (most recent call last):
  File "C:\Python37\try.py", line 4, in <module>
    print(list[4])
IndexError: list index out of range
```

- The + operator can also be used to join two lists. However, if you try to join a number or string or any other data with a list using the + operator, **TypeError** will be generated.

### Example 8.12

```
l1 = [1,2,3,4,5]
l2 = l1 + 6
print(l2)
```

**OUTPUT**

```
Traceback (most recent call last):
  File "C:\Python37\try.py", line 2, in <module>
    l2 = l1 + 6
TypeError: can only concatenate list (not "int") to list
```

```
#Correct Way
l1 = [1,2,3,4,5]
l2 = l1 + [6]
print(l2)
```

**OUTPUT**

```
[1, 2, 3, 4, 5, 6]
```

- Like strings, lists can also be repeated using the * operator.
- While the append() method adds a single element to a list, the extend() method is used to add multiple elements from one list to another list.

### Example 8.13

```
# Repeating a list
l1 = ['B','Y','E']
l2 = l1 * 3
print(l2)
```

**OUTPUT**

```
('B','Y','E','B','Y','E','B','Y','E']
```

```
#Difference between append() and extend()
l1 = [1,2,3,4,5]
l1.append(6)
l1.extend([7,8])
print(l1)
```

**OUTPUT**

```
[1, 2, 3, 4, 5, 6, 7, 8]
```

In the insert() method, if we specify a negative index that is not in the set of valid indices, the element is added at the beginning of the list (Example 8.14).

If the pop() method is called on an empty list, then an IndexError will be generated (Example 8.15).

### Example 8.14

```
l1 = [1,2,3,4,5]
l1.insert(-10,123)
print(l1)
```

**OUTPUT**

```
[123, 1, 2, 3, 4, 5]
```

### Example 8.15

```
l1 = []
l1.pop()
```

**OUTPUT**

```
Traceback (most recent call last):
File "C:\ Python37\try.py", line 2, in <module>    l1.pop()
IndexError: pop from empty list
```

# PROGRAMMER'S ZONE

1. Write a program that creates a list of numbers from 1-20 that are either divisible by 2 or divisible by 4 without using the filter function.

   ```
   div_2_4 = []
   for i in range(2, 22):
       if(i%2 == 0 or i%4 == 0):
           div_2_4.append(i)
   print(div_2_4)
   ```

   > The sort() method uses ASCII values to sort the values in the list.

   **OUTPUT**
   ```
   [2, 4, 6, 8, 10, 12, 14, 16, 18, 20]
   ```

2. Write a program that defines a list of countries that are a member of BRICS. Check whether a country is a member of BRICS or not.

   ```
   country = ["Brazil", "India", "China", "Russia", "Sri Lanka"]
   is_member = input("Enter the name of country : ")
   if is_member in country:
       print(is_member, "has also joined BRICS")
   else:
       print(is_member, " is not a member of BRICS")
   ```

   > An error is generated if you try to delete an element from the list or insert an element that is not present in the list.

   **OUTPUT**
   ```
   Enter the name of country : Pakistan
   Pakistan is not a member of BRICS
   ```

3. Write a program to create a list of numbers in the range 1 to 10. Then delete all the even numbers from the list and print the final list.

   ```
   num_list = []
   for i in range(1, 11):
       num_list.append(i)
   print("Original List : ", num_list)
   for index, i in enumerate(num_list):
       if(i%2==0):
           del num_list[index]
   print("List after deleting even numbers : ",num_list)
   ```

   **OUTPUT**
   ```
   Original List :  [1, 2, 3, 4, 5, 6, 7, 8, 9, 10]
   List after deleting even numbers :  [1, 3, 5, 7, 9]
   ```

4. Write a program to print the index at which a particular value exists. If the value exists at multiple locations in the list, then print all the indices. Also count the number of times that value is repeated in the list.

   ```
   num_list = [1,2,3,4,5,6,5,4,3,2,1]
   num = int(input("Enter the value to be searched : "))
   i=0
   count = 0
   while i<len(num_list):
       if num == num_list[i]:
           print(num, " found at location", i)
           count += 1
       i += 1
   print(num, " appears ", count, " times in the list")
   ```

   > It is safer to avoid aliasing when you are working with mutable objects.

**OUTPUT**
```
Enter the value to be searched : 4
4 found at location 3
4 found at location 7
4 appears 2 times in the list
list_words = []
```

> When using slice operation, an IndexError is generated in the index if the index is outside the list.

5. Write a program that creates a list of words by combining the words in two individual lists.
```
list_words = []
for x in ["Hello ", "World "]:
    for y in ["Python", "Programming"]:
        word = x + y
        list_words.append(word)
print("List combining the words in two individual lists is : ", list_words)
```

**OUTPUT**
```
List combining the words in two individual lists is : ['Hello Python', 'Hello Programming', 'World Python', 'World Programming']
```

6. Write a program that forms a list of the first character of every word in another list.
```
list1 = ["Hello", "Welcome", "To", "The", "World", "Of", "Python"]
letters = []
for word in list1:
    letters.append(word[0])
print(letters)
```

**OUTPUT**
```
['H', 'W', 'T', 'T', 'W', 'O', 'P']
```

7. Write a program to remove all duplicates from a list.
```
num_list = [1,2,3,4,5,6,7,6,5,4]
print("Original List : ", num_list)
i=0
while i<len(num_list):
    num = num_list[i]
    for j in range(i+1, len(num_list)):
        val = num_list[j]
        if val == num:
            num_list.pop(j)
    i = i + 1
print("List after removing duplicates : ",num_list)
```

> The index must be an integer. If you specify a non-integer number as the index, then TypeError will be generated.

**OUTPUT**
```
Original List : [1, 2, 3, 4, 5, 6, 7, 6, 5, 4]
List after removing duplicates : [1, 2, 3, 4, 5, 6, 7]
```

8. Write a program that counts the number of times each word is repeated in a list.
```
words =["abc","def","ghi","lmn","lmn","def","pqr","rst","abc","lmn","def","xyz"]
length = len(words)
dups = []
uniq = []
```

```
    i = 0
    for word in words:
        count = words.count(word)
        print(word,count, end = ' ')
        words.remove(word)
```

**OUTPUT**
```
abc 2    ghi 1    lmn 3    pqr 1    abc 1    def 3
```

9. Write a program to create a list of numbers in the specified range in particular steps. Reverse the list and print its values.

```
num_list = []
m = int(input("Enter the starting of the range : "))
n = int(input("Enter the ending of the range : "))
o = int(input("Enter the steps in the range : "))
for i in range(m,n, o):
    num_list.append(i)
print("Original List :", num_list)
num_list.reverse()
print("Reversed List : ", num_list)
```

**OUTPUT**
```
Enter the starting of the range : 2
Enter the ending of the range : 30
Enter the steps in the range : 3
Original List : [2, 5, 8, 11, 14, 17, 20, 23, 26, 29]
Reversed List : [29, 26, 23, 20, 17, 14, 11, 8, 5, 2]
```

> append() and insert() methods are list methods. They cannot be called on other values such as string or integers.

10. Write a program that passes a list to a function that scales each element in the list by a factor of 10. Print the list values at different stages to show that changes made to one list is automatically reflected in the other list.

```
def change(list1):
    for i in range(len(list1)):
        list1[i] = list1[i] * 10
    print("After change in function, List is : ", list1)
num_list = [1,2,3,4,5,6]
print("Original List is : ", num_list)
change(num_list)
print("List after change is : ", num_list)
```

**OUTPUT**
```
Original List is : [1, 2, 3, 4, 5, 6]
After change in function, List is : [10, 20, 30, 40, 50, 60]
List after change is : [10, 20, 30, 40, 50, 60]
```

11. Write a program to create a series of Fibonnacci numbers.

```
fib = [0,1]
sum = 0
a = 0
b = 1
for i in range(1,11):
```

```
            sum = a + b
            fib.append(sum)
            a = b
            b = sum
     print(fib)
```
**OUTPUT**
```
[0, 1, 1, 2, 3, 5, 8, 13, 21, 34, 55, 89]
```

12. **Write a program to add two matrices (using nested lists).**
```
     X = [[2,5,4],
         [1 ,3,9],
         [7 ,6, 2]]
     Y = [[1,8,5],
         [7,3,6],
         [4,0,9]]
     result = [[0,0,0],
              [0,0,0],
              [0,0,0]]
     for i in range(len(X)):
        for j in range(len(X[0])):
           result[i][j] = X[i][j] + Y[i][j]
     for r in result:
       print(r)
```
**OUTPUT**
```
[3, 13, 9]
[8, 6, 15]
[11, 6, 11]
```

13. **Program to find median of a list of numbers.**
```
     List = []
     n = int(input("Enter the number of elements to be inserted in the list : "))
     for i in range(n):
        print("Enter number ", i + 1, " : ")
        num = int(input())
        List.append(num)
     print("Sorted List is......")
     List = sorted(List)
     print(List)
     i = len(List) - 1
     if n%2 != 0:
        print("MEDIAN = ", List[i//2])
     else:
        print("MEDIAN = ", (List[i//2] + List[i+1//2])/2)
```
**OUTPUT**
```
Enter the number of elements to be inserted in the list : 6
Enter number 1 : 2
Enter number 2 : 9
Enter number 3 : 1
Enter number 4 : 7
```

```
Enter number 5 : 4
Enter number 6 : 8
Sorted List is......
[1, 2, 4, 7, 8, 9]
MEDIAN = 6.5
```

14. **Program to generate the Fibonacci sequence and store it in a list. Then find the sum of the even-valued terms.**

    ```
    a = 0
    b = 1
    n = int(input("Enter the number of terms : "))
    i=2
    List = [a,b]
    while i<n:
        s = a + b
        List.append(s)
        a = b
        b = s
        i += 1
    print(List)
    i=0
    sum = 0
    while i<n:
        sum += List[i]
        i += 2
    print("SUM = ", sum)
    ```

    > An alias is a second name for a piece of data. In Python, aliasing happens whenever one variable's value is assigned to another variable using the assignment operator[=].

    **OUTPUT**
    ```
    Enter the number of terms : 10
    [0, 1, 1, 2, 3, 5, 8, 13, 21, 34]
    SUM = 33
    ```

15. **Write a program that prompts the user to enter a list. Re-write the elements in another list in such a way that all even numbers are copied at the beginning and all odd numbers are copied at the end of the new list.**

    ```
    list = eval(input("ENter the list elements : "))
    length = len(list)
    new_list = []
    beg = 0
    end = length -1
    for i in list:
        if(i%2==0):
            new_list.insert(beg, i)
            beg +=1
        else:
            new_list.insert(end, i)
            end -= 1
    print(new_list)
    ```

    **OUTPUT**
    ```
    [2, 4, 6, 8, 10, 12, 1, 11, 3, 5, 9, 7]
    ```

16. **Write a program that prints the largest and the second largest value in a list of numbers.**
    ```
    list = eval(input("ENter the list elements : "))
    length = len(list)
    largest = sec_largest = list[0]
    for i in range(1,length-1):
        if(list[i]>largest):
            sec_largest = largest
            largest = list[i]
    print("LARGEST = ", largest,»SECOND LARGEST = ",sec_largest)
    ```
    **OUTPUT**
    ```
    ENter the list elements : [9,4,0,2,11,7,6,5]
    LARGEST = 11 SECOND LARGEST = 9
    ```

17. **Write a program that splits a string when a vowel is found. Also find the maximum length of the substring.**
    ```
    str = "HelloWorldPythonProgrammingisfun"
    l= []
    j=0
    k=0
    length = len(str)
    for i in range(length):
        if str[i] not in 'aeiou':
            j+=1
        else:
            l.append(str[k:j])      # appending consonant sub string
            k = j+1                 # starting index of next consonant substring
            j = i +1                # starting index of next consonant substring
    print(l)
    length = len(l)                 # finding len of list
    maxlen = 0
    for i in range(length):
        lenx = len(l[i])            # length of an element in list
        if(lenx>maxlen):
            maxlen = lenx
            maxsub = l[i]
    print(maxlen,maxsub)
    ```
    **OUTPUT**
    ```
    ['H', 'll', 'W', 'rldPyth', 'nPr', 'gr', 'mm', 'ng', 'sf']
    7 rldPyth
    ```

## Key Terms

**Immutable data:** Data which cannot be modified. Assigning values to elements or slices of immutable data results in a runtime error.

**Mutable data value:** Data which can be modified.

**List:** A mutable data structure that can have elements that belong to different data types.

**Nested list:** Nested list means a list within another list.

**List aliasing:** When one list is assigned to another list using the assignment operator (=), then a new copy of the list is not made. Instead, assignment makes the two variables point to the one list in memory. This is also known as aliasing.

**List cloning:** The process of creating a separate copy of the list (not just the reference) is known as list cloning. The slice operation is used to clone a list.

## Chapter Highlights

- List is a versatile data type available in Python, in which elements are written as a list of comma-separated values (items) between square brackets.
- Like strings, lists can also be sliced and concatenated.
- Once created, one or more elements of a list can be easily updated by giving the slice on the left-hand side of the assignment operator.
- We can append new values in the list and remove existing value(s) from the list using the `append()` method and `del` statement respectively.
- To insert items from another list at a particular location, we can use the `slice` operation. This would create a nested list, that is, a list within another list.
- Lists behave in a similar way as strings when operators like + (concatenation) and * (repetition) are used.

## Review Questions

1. What is a list?
2. How can we define a list in Python?
3. With the help of an example demonstrate how lists can be sliced to access its values?
4. Explain the syntax of the slice operation.
5. What is the role of `del` statement in list variables?
6. Differentiate between shallow copy and deep copy of an object in Python.
7. Differentiate between the use of `del` statement and `remove()` function.
8. What is a nested list? How can we make one in Python?
9. Differentiate between list cloning and list aliasing.
10. Differentiate between `pop()` and `remove()` methods of list objects.
11. Explain the purpose of the following functions:
    a. `sorted()`  b. `list()`  c. `any()`  d. `sum()`  e. `min()`
12. Name the function or the operator that can be used for the following tasks:
    a. Return length of list
    b. Repeat elements in the list
    c. Join two lists
    d. Check if the value is present in the list
    e. Return maximum value in the list.
13. Name the methods that can be used in the following situations:
    a. Append an element to the list
    b. Count the number of times an element appears in the list
    c. Return the lowest index of obj in the list.
14. Explain the purpose of the following methods in Python:
    a. `insert()`  b. `reverse()`  c. `extend()`

15. Given a list, l = [1,2,3,4,5], write instructions for the following tasks,
    a. Set the third element to 100
    b. Insert 200 at the second index
    c. Append 300 to the list
    d. Remove the fourth element from the list
    e. Sort the list
    f. Reverse the list.

16. Given a list L = [1,2,3,4,[5,6,7,8],9,10], write expressions that will print the values:
    a. [5,6,7,8]     b. [6,7]     c. [2,3,4]     d. [1,3,[5,6,7,8], 10]

## Programming Exercises

1. Write a program that creates a list of numbers in the series $2^n-1$. Display only the even indexed values in this list.

2. Write a program that prints the elements along with their indices from the start and end of the list.

3. Write a program that reads two lists. Make another list of all those elements in the first list that are also present in the second list.

4. Write a program that creates a list ['a','bb','ccc','dddd',....]

5. Write a program that forms a list of numbers in the series
   a. 2/9, −5/13, 8/17, …     b. $x, -x^2/2!, x^3/3!, -x^4/4!, x^5/5!,....$

6. Make a list of five random numbers. Write instructions to sum the elements and find the mean of the elements.

7. Write a program that adds the corresponding elements of two lists.

8. Make a list of the first ten letters of the alphabet, then using the slice operation do the following operations
   a. Print the first three letters from the list
   b. Print any three letters from the middle
   c. Print the letters from any particular index to the end of the list.

9. Write a program that prints the maximum value of the second half of the list.

10. Write a program that finds the sum of all the numbers using a `while` loop.

11. Write a program that finds the sum of all even numbers in a list.

12. Write a program that reverses a list using a loop.

13. Write a program to find whether a particular element is present in the list using a loop.

14. Write a program that prompts the user to enter an alphabet. Print all the words in the list that starts with that alphabet.

15. Write a program that prompts a number from user and adds it in a list. If the value entered by user is greater than 100, then add "EXCESS" in the list

16. Write a program that counts the number of times a value appears in the list. Use a loop to do the same.

17. Write a program to insert a value in a list at the specified location using while loop.

18. Write a program that creates a list of numbers from 1–50 that is either divisible by 3 or divisible by 6.

19. Write a program to create a list of numbers in the range 1 to 20. Then delete all the numbers from the list that are divisible by 3.

20. Write a program to randomly select an item from a list.

21. Write a program to print the string "HELLOWORLD" as
```
H       E
 L     L
  O   W
   O R
    LD
```

## Fill in the Blanks

1. _____ defines a particular way of storing and organizing data in a computer.
2. When using slice operation, _____ is generated if the index is outside the list.
3. [10,20] < [20,10] will return _____.
4. insert(), remove() and sort() returns _____.
5. The sort() method uses _____ values to sort the values in the list.
6. _____ is used to print both index as well as an item in the list.
7. Fill in the blanks to create a list and print its second element.
   ```
   List = ___10, 20, 30, 40]
   print(list[___])
   ```
8. Fill in the blanks to create a list, reassign its third element and print the list.
   ```
   List = [1,2,3,4,5__
   List[__] = 30
   print(___)
   ```
9. Fill in the blanks to print "Hello" if the list contains 'H':
   ```
   Letters = ['W', 'G', 'H']
   __ 'H' __ Letters:
   print("_____")
   ```
10. Fill in the blanks to add 'G' to the end of the list and print the list's length.
    ```
    Letters.____('G')
    print(__ ___)
    ```
11. Fill in the blanks to print the letters in the list.
    ```
    Letters = ['H', 'E', 'L', 'L','O']
    ___ i __Letters__
    print(i)
    ```
12. Fill in the blanks to print the first two elements of the list:
    ```
    List = [1,2,3,4,5,6]
    print(list[0_])
    ```
13. The range of index values for a list of 10 elements will be _____.

## State True or False

1. The index value starts from zero.
2. List is an immutable data structure.
3. Once created, one or more elements of a list can be easily updated.

4. It is possible to edit, add and delete elements from a list.
5. Slice operation can be used to insert items from another list or sequence at a particular location.
6. The slice operation is used to clone a list.
7. We cannot insert a list into another list.
8. When a list is assigned to another using the assignment operator, then a new copy of list is made.
9. Items in a list can be deleted by assigning an empty list to a slice of elements.
10. If you specify a non-integer number as the index, then IndexError will be generated.
11. Python sorts the original list with the help of sorted() function.

## Multiple Choice Questions

1. If List = [1,2,3,4,5], then List[5] will result in _____.
   a. 4        b. 3        c. 2        d. Error

2. If List = [1,2,3,4,5] and we write List[3] = List[1], then what will be List[3]?
   a. 1        b. 3        c. 2        d. 4

3. type(x) will print _____.
   a. <class 'list'>            b. <class 'tuple'>
   c. <class 'int'>             d. Error

4. If List = [1,2,3,4,5,6,7,8,9,10], then print List[8:4:-1] will give _____.
   a. [2,3,4,5]   b. [9,8,7,6]   c. [6,7,8,9]   d. [5,4,3,2]

5. If List = min([sum([10,20]),max(abs(-30),4)]), then List = _____
   a. 10       b. 20       c. 30       d. 4

6. Which slice operation will reverse the list?
   a. Lists[-1::]   b. numbers[::-1]   c. numbers[:-1:]   d. List[9:8:1]

7. If List = (12,8,7,5), then print(max(min(List[:2]),abs(-6))) will print _____.
   a. 12       b. 8        c. 7        d. 5

8. Which operator is used for list aliasing?
   a. =        b. +        c. *        d. &

9. Which operation is used for list cloning?
   a. assignment   b. slice   c. comparison   d. repetition

## Give the Output

1. ```
   colors = ['red', 'blue', 'green']
   print(colors[2])
   print(len(colors))
   ```

2. ```
   list = ['abc', 'def', 'ghi', 'jkl']
   print(list[1:-1])
   list[0:2] = 'xyz'
   print(list)
   ```

3. ```
   list = ['abc', 'def', 'ghi', 'jkl', [1,2,3,4,5]]
   print(list[4][2])
   ```
   ```

4. ```
   list = ['p','r','o','g','r','a','m','m','i','n','g']
   print(list[2:5])
   print(list[:-5])
   print(list[5:])
   print(list[:])
   ```

5. ```
   even = [2,4,6]
   print(even + [10, 12, 14])
   print(even*2)
   even.insert(1,0)
   print(even)
   del even[2]
   print(even)
   ```

6. ```
   list = ['p','r','o','g','r','a','m']
   list.remove('p')
   print(list)
   print(list.pop(1))
   print(list)
   print(list.pop())
   print(list)
   ```

7. ```
   list = [9,4,3,8,0,2,3,6]
   print(list.index(3))
   print(list.count(8))
   list.sort()
   print(list)
   list.reverse()
   print(list)
   print(0 in list)
   ```

8. ```
   list = [(1, 2), [3, 4], '56', 78, 9.0]
   print(list[0], type(list[0]))
   print(list[2:3], type(list[0:1]))
   print(list[2], type(list[2]))
   ```

9. ```
   list =[ [1,2]*3 ] *4
   print(list)
   ```

10. ```
    list = [10, 20, 30, 40, 50, 60, 70, 80, 90]
    print(list[-4:-1])
    print(list[-1:-4])
    print(list[-5:])
    print(list[-6:-2:2])
    print(list[::-1])
    ```

11. ```
    list = [[10, 20, [30, 40, [50, 60]]]]
    print(list[0])
    print(list[0][2])
    print(list[0][2][2])
    print(list[0][0])
    print(list[0][2][1])
    print(list[0][2][2][0])
    ```

12. ```
    List = [100, 90, 80, 70, 60, 50]
    List[2] = List[1] - 20
    if 30 in List:
        print(List[3])
    else:
        print(List[4])
    ```

13. ```
    List = list(range(2, 20, 3))
    print(List[5])
    ```

14. ```
    def add_two(x):
        return x+2
    List = [10,20,30,40,50]
    result = list(map(add_two,List))
    print(result)
    ```

15. ```
    str = "abcdefghijklmno"
    for i in range(0, len(str), 2):
        print(str[i], end = ' ')
    ```

16. ```
    >>> eval("10 ** 2")
    ```

17. ```
    eval("'hello' + 'py'")
    ```

18. ```
    l1 = [1,2,3]
    l2 = ['a','b','c']
    l3 = [1.2,3.4,5.6]
    l4 = l1 + l2 + l3
    print(l4)
    ```

19. ```
    print([1,2,8,9] < [1,2,8,9,10])
    ```

20. ```
    l = [1,2,3,4,5,6,7,8,9,10]
    print(l[-1])
    print(l[l[0]])
    print(l[l[-8]])
    print(l[l[l[0]+1]]+2)
    ```

21. ```
    msg = ["PYTHON","is","a",["simple","iterpreted","OOP"],"language"]
    print(msg[2:4])
    print(msg[2:4][1][2])
    print(msg[2:4][1][2][1])
    print("im" in msg[2:4][1][2][1])
    print(msg[2:4][1][1][3:])
    print(msg[1]+msg[4])
    ```

22. ```
    >>> [1,2,3] +[1,2,3] == [1,2,3]*2
    ```

23. ```
    l = [1,2,3]
    l * 3 == [1,1,1]
    ```

24. ```
    msg = ["PYTHON","is","a",["simple","interpreted","OOP"],"language"]
    print(msg[::2])
    print('n' in msg[4])
    print(msg[2] in msg[4])
    ```
    ```

25. ```
    l = [1,2,3]
    print((l + [4,5,6])[3])
    ```

26. ```
    [1,2] == [1,2]
    ```

27. ```
    [1,2] is [1,2]
    ```

28. ```
    L = [1,2,3,4,5,6,7,8,9,10,11,12,13,14]
    print(L[::-1])
    print(L[-1:-2:-3])
    ```

29. ```
    for i in [1,2,3]:
        for j in [4,5,6]:
            print(i,j, end = "   ")
    ```

30. ```
    count = 0
    for i in range(5):
        for j in range(10):
            count = count + 1
    print(count)
    ```

31. ```
    list = [55, 66, 77, 88, 99]
    print("random.choice to select a random element from a list - ", random.choice(list))
    ```

32. ```
    import random
    city_list = ['New York', 'Los Angeles', 'Chicago', 'Houston', 'Philadelphia']
    print("Select random element from list - ", random.choice(city_list))
    ```

## Find the Error

1. ```
   list = ['abc', 'def', 'ghi', 'jkl']
   print list[2.0]
   ```

2. ```
   even = [2,4,6]
   del even
   print(even)
   ```

3. ```
   list = [(1, 2), [3, 4], '56', 78, 9.0]
   list.remove('abc')
   ```

4. ```
   msg = "Hello"
   msg.append("World")
   print(msg)
   ```

5. ```
   [1,2,3] + 2
   ```

6. ```
   L = [1,2,3,4]
   L.remove(7)
   ```

7. ```
   [1,2,3] * 3.0
   ```
   ```

# Answers

## Fill in the Blanks
1. Data structure
2. IndexError
3. True
4. None
5. ASCII
6. enumerate() function
7. [, 1
8. ], 2, List
9. if, in, Hello
10. append, len, (, Letters,)
11. for, in, :
12. :2
13. 0–10

## State True or False
1. True
2. False
3. True
4. True
5. True
6. False
7. False
8. False
9. True
10. False
11. True

## Multiple Choice Questions
1. b
2. c
3. d
4. b
5. c
6. b
7. b
8. a
9. b

## Give the Output
1. green, 3
2. ['def', 'ghi']
   ['xyz', 'ghi', 'jkl']
3. 3
4. ['o', 'g', 'r']
   ['p', 'r', 'o', 'g', 'r', 'a']
   ['a', 'm', 'm', 'i', 'n', 'g']
   ['p', 'r', 'o', 'g', 'r', 'a', 'm', 'm', 'i', 'n', 'g']
5. [2, 4, 6, 10, 12, 14]
   [2, 4, 6, 2, 4, 6]
   [2, 0, 4, 6]
   [2, 0, 6]
6. ['r', 'o', 'g', 'r', 'a', 'm']
   o
   ['r', 'g', 'r', 'a', 'm']
   m
   ['r', 'g', 'r', 'a']
7. 2
   1
   [0, 2, 3, 3, 4, 6, 8, 9]
   [9, 8, 6, 4, 3, 3, 2, 0]
   True
8. ((1, 2), <type 'tuple'>)
   (['56'], <type 'list'>)
   ('56', <type 'str'>)
9. [[1, 2, 1, 2, 1, 2], [1, 2, 1, 2, 1, 2], [1, 2, 1, 2, 1, 2],
   [1, 2, 1, 2, 1, 2]]
10. [60, 70, 80]
    []
    [50, 60, 70, 80, 90]
    [40, 60]
    [90, 80, 70, 60, 50, 40, 30, 20, 10]
11. [10, 20, [30, 40, [50, 60]]]
    [30, 40, [50, 60]]
    [50, 60]
    10
    40
    50
12. 60
13. 17
14. [12, 22, 32, 42, 52]
15. a c e g i k m o
16. 100
17. 'hellopy'
18. [1, 2, 3, 'a', 'b', 'c', 1.2, 3.4, 5.6]
19. True
20. 10    2    4    6
21. ['a', ['simple', 'iterpreted', 'OOP']]
    OOP    O    False    rpreted    islanguage
22. True
23. False
24. ['PYTHON', 'a', 'language']
    True
    True
25. ['PYTHON', 'a', 'language']    True    True
26. True
27. False
28. [14, 13, 12, 11, 10, 9, 8, 7, 6, 5, 4, 3, 2, 1]
    [14]
29. 14    15    16    24    25    26    34    35    36
30. 50
31. random.choice to select a random element from a list - 55
32. Select random element from list - Chicago

## Find the Error

1. TypeError: list indices must be integers, not float
2. NameError: name 'even' is not defined
3. ValueError: list.remove(x): x not in list
4. AttributeError: 'str' object has no attribute 'append'
5. TypeError: can only concatenate list (not "int") to list
6. ValueError: list.remove(x): x not in list
7. TypeError: can't multiply sequence by non-int of type 'float'

# Tuple

9

## Chapter Objectives

The chapter analyzes another important data structure in Python – that is, tuple. The chapter explains where and how tuples can be used to manipulate data. The topics discussed in this chapter include:

- Creating and accessing values of a tuple
- Updating and deleting values
- Indexing, assigning, joining and unpacking tuple objects
- Using tuples to return multiple values from a function
- The count() and zip() methods
- Comparing tuples and lists
- Nested tuples

In the last chapter, we studied lists. In this chapter we will look into another data type in Python – the tuple. A tuple is very similar to lists but differs in two things.

- First, a tuple is an immutable object. This means that while you can change the value of one or more elements in a list, you cannot change the values in a tuple.
- Second, tuples use parentheses to define its elements whereas lists use square brackets.

## 9.1 CREATING A TUPLE

Creating a tuple is very simple and almost similar to creating a list. You need to just put the different comma-separated values within a parenthesis.

| #Creates an empty tuple<br>Tup1 = ()<br>print(Tup1)<br>OUTPUT<br>() | #Creates tuple with a single element<br>Tup1 = (5,)<br>print(Tup1)<br>OUTPUT<br>5 | #Tuple of integers<br>Tup1 = (1,2,3,4,5)<br>print(Tup1)<br>OUTPUT<br>(1, 2, 3, 4, 5) |
|---|---|---|
| #Creates a tuple of<br>#mixed values<br>Tup5 = (1,"abc",2.3,'d')<br>print(Tup5)<br>OUTPUT<br>(1, 'abc', 2.3, 'd') | #A tuple of characters<br>Tup1 = ('a','b','c','d')<br>print(Tup1)<br>OUTPUT<br>('a', 'b', 'c', 'd') | # Creates a tuple of strings<br>Tup1 = ("abc",''def'',''ghi'')<br>print(Tup1)<br>OUTPUT<br>('abc', 'def', 'ghi') |
| #Tuple of floating-point<br>#numbers<br>Tup1 = (1.2,2.3,3.4,4.5)<br>print(Tup1)<br>OUTPUT<br>(1.2, 2.3, 3.4, 4.5) | | |

## Key points to remember

- Any set of comma-separated values written without an identifying symbol like brackets or parentheses, etc., is treated as a tuple by default.
- If you want to create a tuple with a single element, you must add a comma after the element. In the absence of a comma, Python treats the element as an ordinary data type.
- We can use the `eval()` function to input a tuple. But while specifying the input elements, enclose them within parentheses as shown in the code.

```
print('A', "bed", 5, 6.7)
OUTPUT
A bcd 5 6.7
```

```
# comma after first element
Tup = (15,)
print type(Tup)
OUTPUT
<type 'tuple'>
```

```
a,b,c = 10, 20,30
print(a,b,c)
OUTPUT
10 20 30
```

```
#comma missing
Tup = (10)
print type(Tup)
OUTPUT
<type 'int'>
```

```
#eval() Function to read Tuple
Tup = eval(input("Enter values of the tuple :"))
print(Tup)
print(type(Tup))
OUTPUT
Enter values of the tuple: (1,2,'a','bcd',7.8)
(1, 2, 'a', 'bcd', 7.8)
<class 'tuple'>
```

- We can also use the `tuple()` function to create a tuple with the specified sequence.

```
#Using the tuple() Function
tup = tuple("abc")
print(tup)
tup = tuple ([1, 2,3))
print(tup)
OUTPUT
('a' , ' b ', 'c ")
(1, 2 , 3)
```

## 9.2 UTILITY OF TUPLES

In real-world applications, tuples are extremely useful for representing *records* or structures as we call in other programming languages. These structures store related information about a subject together. The information belongs to different data types. For example, a tuple that stores information about a student will have roll_no, name, course, total_marks, avg, etc. If you carefully observe these individual elements, you will see that they belong to different data types. For example, roll_no can be an integer or an alphanumeric value, name and course will be a string, total_marks and avg can be floating-point numbers.

Some built-in functions return a tuple. For example, the **divmod()** function returns two values – quotient as well as the remainder after performing the divide operation.

### Example 9.1

**Program to illustrates divmod() function**
```
quo, rem = divmod(157,4)
print("Quotient = ",quo)
print("Remainder = ",rem)
```
**OUTPUT**
```
Quotient= 39
Remainder= 1
```

## Example 9.2

```
Tup1 = (1,20,3,40,5,60,7,80,9,100,11,120)
print("Tup[4:8] = ", Tup1[4:8])
print("Tup[:5] = ", Tup1[:5])
print("Tup[3:] = ", Tup1[3:])
print("Tup[:] = ", Tup1[:])
print("Tup[:-4] =", Tup1[:-4])
print("Tup[-1:5] =", Tup1[-1:5])
print("Tup[::-2] =", Tup1[::-2])
```

**OUTPUT**
```
Tup[4:8] = (5, 60, 7, 80)
Tup[:5] = (1, 20, 3, 40, 5)
Tup[3:] = (40, 5, 60, 7, 80, 9, 100, 11, 120)
Tup[:] = (1, 20, 3, 40, 5, 60, 7, 80, 9, 100, 11, 120)
Tup[:-4] = (1, 20, 3, 40, 5, 60, 7, 80)
Tup[-1:5] = ()
Tup[::-2] = (120, 100, 80, 60, 40, 20)
```

## 9.3 ACCESSING VALUES IN A TUPLE

Again, like other sequences (like strings and lists), indices in a tuple start at 0. Slice operation, concatenation and other operations possible with other sequences can also be applied on tuples.

In the slice operation, we can also use negative indices, strides and even expressions.

When accessing a tuple, if the index is out of the range of legal indices of the tuple, then Python raises an IndexError.

The start and stop parameters of the slice operation specify the boundaries of elements to be accessed. All elements falling within the boundary are returned.

### Example 9.3

```
#Slice operation on a tuple
tup = (1,'a',2,'bcd',3.4,5,'e',6.7,'efg')
print(tup[3])
print(tup[10 - 4 *2 + 5])
print(tup[-5])
print(tup[3:6])
print(tup[2:7:2])
print(tup[-10:10])
```

**OUTPUT**
```
bcd
6.7
3.4
('bcd', 3.4, 5)
(2, 3.4, 'e')
(1, 'a', 2, 'bcd', 3.4, 5, 'e', 6.7, 'efg')
```

## 9.4 UPDATING TUPLE

We have already said that *tuple is immutable*. So, you cannot change the value(s) in the tuple. You can only extract values from a tuple to form another tuple.

### Example 9.4

```
#Updating tuple
tup = (1,'a ',2,'bcd',3.4,5,'e')
tup[3] = 'Not Possible'
print(tup)
```

**OUTPUT**
```
Traceback (most recent call last):
  File "C:\Python37\try.py",line 2, in <module>
    tup(3] = 'Not Possible'
TypeError: 'tuple' object does not support item assignment
```

### Example 9.5

```
tup = (1,2,3)
print(tup[10])
```

**OUTPUT**

```
Traceback (most recent call last):
  File "C:\Python37\try.py",line 2, in <module>
print(tup[10])
```
**IndexError: tuple index out of range**

```
tup = (1,2,3)
print(tup[ -10: 10])
```

**OUTPUT**

(1, 2, 3)

## 9.5 DELETING ELEMENTS IN TUPLE

Since tuple is an immutable data structure, you cannot delete value(s) from it. Of course, you can create a new tuple that has all elements in your tuple except the ones you do not want (those you wanted to be deleted). However, the entire tuple can be deleted by using the `del` statement.

### Example 9.6

```
Tup1 = (1,2,3,4,5)
Tup2 = (6,7,8,9,10)
Tup3 = Tup1 + Tup2
print(Tup3)
```
**OUTPUT**

(1, 2, 3, 4, 5, 6, 7, 8, 9, 10)

```
Tup1 = (1,2,3,4,5)
del Tup1[3] #delete an element
print(Tup1)
```

**OUTPUT**

```
Traceback (most recent call last):
  File "C:\Users\Python37\try.py", line 2, in <module>
    del Tup1[3]
Type Error: 'tuple' object doesn't support item deletion
```

```
Tup1 = (1,2,3,4,5)
#delete tuple
de1Tup1
print(Tup1)
```

**OUTPUT**

```
Traceback (most recent call last):
  File "C:\Users\Python37\try.py", line 4, in <module>
    print(Tup1)
NameError: name 'Tup1' is not defined
```

## 9.6 JOINING TUPLES

Like lists, two or more tuples can be joined using the + operator. The + operator requires that both the operands must be of tuple types. Numbers or any other type values cannot be added to a tuple. To add a single element to a tuple, we must use comma after the value.

### Example 9.7

```
#Joining Tuples
tup1 = (1,2,3)
tup2 = (4,5,6)
tup3 = tup1 + tup2
print(tup3)
```

**OUTPUT**

(1, 2, 3, 4, 5, 6)

```
#Joining tuples with a
#non-number value
tup1 = (1,2,3)
tup2 = tup1 + 'a'
print(tup2)
```

**OUTPUT**

```
Traceback (most recent call last):
  File "C:\Python37\try.py", line 2, in <module>
    tup2 = tup1 +'a'
```
**TypeError: can only concatenate tuple (not "str") to tuple**

```
#Joining single
#value to a tuple
tup1 = (1,2,3)
tup2 = tup1 + (4,)
print(tup2)
```

**OUTPUT**

(1, 2, 3, 4)

## 9.7 UNPACKING TUPLES

Creating a tuple from a set of values is called packing. Correspondingly, creating individual values from a tuple is known as unpacking. The syntax of unpacking can be given as,

```
var1, var2, var3, ...., varn = tuple_variable
```

While unpacking a tuple, remember that the number of elements in the tuple must match with the number of variables on the left side of the assignment operator.

Tuple packing and unpacking are very useful to change the values in a tuple. We know that tuples are immutable objects in Python, so their values cannot be changed. In case we need to change values, there are three ways – unpacking and packing the tuple is just one of them.

### Example 9.8

```
# Unpacking tuple
tup = (1,'a',2.0,'bcd',3)
(a,b,c,d,e) = tup
print("a = ",a, end = '')
print("b = ",b, end = '')
print("c = ",c, end = '')
print("d = ",d, end = '')
print("e = ",e, end = '')
```

**OUTPUT**
```
a = 1 b = a c = 2.0 d = bcd e = 3
```

```
# Packing tuple
a=1; b='a'; c=2.0; d='bcd'
tup = (a,b,c,d)
print("tup = " ,tup)
```

**OUTPUT**
```
tup = (1, 'a', 2.0, 'bcd')
```

The first way is to create a new tuple with modified values.

The second way is to first unpack the tuples into variables. Modify the value of the variables and then pack those variables to form a tuple.

The third way is to convert a tuple into a list using the `list()` function. Modify the list values and then use the `tuple()` function to convert the list into a tuple.

## 9.8 BASIC TUPLE OPERATIONS

Like strings and lists, you can also perform operations such as concatenation, repetition, etc. on tuples. The only difference is that a new tuple should be created when a change is required in an existing tuple. Table 9.1 summarizes some operations on tuples.

**Table 9.1** Operations on tuples

| Operation | Expression | Output |
|---|---|---|
| Length | `len((1,2,3,4,5,6))` | 6 |
| Concatenation | `(1,2,3) + (4,5,6)` | (1, 2, 3, 4, 5, 6) |
| Repetition | `('Python..')*3` | Python.. Python.. Python..' |
| Membership | `5 in (1,2,3,4,5,6,7,8,9)` | True |
| Iteration | `for i in (1,2,3,4,5,6,7,8,9,10):`<br>`    print(i,end=' ')` | 1,2,3,4,5,6,7,8,9,10 |
| Comparison (Use >, <, ==) | `Tup1 = (1,2,3,4,5)`<br>`Tup2 = (1,2,3,4,5)`<br>`print(Tup1>Tup2)` | False |

*(Continued)*

### Table 9.1  Continued

| Operation | Expression | Output |
|---|---|---|
| Maximum | max(1,9,3,6,4,0) | 9 |
| Minimum | min(1,9,3,6,4,0) | 0 |
| Convert to Tuple (converts a sequence into a tuple) | tuple("PYTHON")<br>tuple([1,2,3,4,5]) | ('P', 'Y', 'T', 'H', 'O', 'N')<br>(1, 2, 3, 4, 5) |

While using the **max()** and **min()** functions, remember that the values in the tuple must be of the same type. If the values are not of the same type, then **TypeError** will be returned.

### Example 9.9

```
# Finding largest and smallest
value
tup = (23,75,12,90,82)
print("Largest Value= ",max(tup))
print("Smallest Value = ",min(tup))
```

**OUTPUT**
```
Largest Value = 90
Smallest Value = 12
```

```
#Finding largest and smallest value in a tuple
tup = (23,'a',12.56,90,'bcd')
print("Largest Value= ",max(tup))
print("Smallest Value = ",min(tup))
```

**OUTPUT**
```
Traceback (most recent call last):
  File "C:\Python37\try.py", line 3, in <module>
    print("largest Value = ",max(tup))
TypeError: '>'not supported between instances
of 'str' and 'int'
```

## 9.9  TUPLE ASSIGNMENT

Tuple assignment is a very powerful feature in Python. It allows a tuple of variables on the left side of the assignment operator to be assigned values from a tuple given on the right side of the assignment operator. Each value is assigned to its respective variable.

In case an expression is specified on the right side of the assignment operator, that expression is first evaluated and then assignment is done. This feature makes tuple assignment quite versatile. The codes given below show the different ways of tuple assignment.

### Example 9.10

```
#An unnamed tuple of values assigned to values of
#another unnamed tuple
(val1, val2, val3) = (10,20,30)
print(val1, val2, val3)
Tup1 = (10, 20, 30)
(val1, val2, val3) = Tup1 #tuple assigned to
another tuple
print(val1, val2, val3)
```

**OUTPUT**
```
10 20 30
10 20 30
```

```
#Expressions are evaluated
before assignment
(val1, val2, val3, val4)= (1+2,
4/3 - 5 , 6%7, 8 ** 2)
print(val1, val2, val3, val4)
```

**OUTPUT**
```
3 -3.666666666666667 6 64
```

Note that *when assigning values to a tuple, you must make sure that the number of values on both the sides of the assignment operator must be same.* Otherwise, an error will be generated as shown in Example 9.11.

### Example 9.11

```
(val1, val2, val3, val4)= (1+2, 6%7, 8 ** 2)
print(val1, val2, val3, val4)
Traceback (most recent call last):
  File "C:\Users\Python37\try.py", line 1, in <module>
    (vall, val2, val3, val4)= (1+2, 6%7, 8 ** 2)
ValueError: not enough values to unpack (expected 4, got 3)
```

## 9.10 ACCESSING USING INDEX

Like other sequences, we can access an individual element of a tuple by using its index. Correspondingly, we can also get the index of an element by specifying the element in the index method. The index() method is used to get the index of an element in the tuple. If the element being searched is not present in the list, then error is generated. The syntax of index() is given as, **list.index(obj)** where, obj is the object whose index has to looked.

### Example 9.12

```
Tup = (11, 67, 642,'AB',          Tup = (11, 67, 642,'AB', "Good Morning", 4.5)
"Good Morning", 4.5)              print(Tup.index(5.4))
print(Tup.index('AB'))            Traceback (most recent call last):
                                    File "C:\Users\Python37\try.py", line 2, in <module>
OUTPUT                                print(Tup.index(5.4))
3                                 ValueError: tuple.index(x): x not in tuple
```

## 9.11 TUPLES FOR RETURNING MULTIPLE VALUES

We have learnt that a function can return only a single value. But at times, we need to return more than one value from a function. In such situations, it is preferable to group together multiple values and return them together.

### Example 9.13

```
#Program to return the highest as well as the lowest score
def max_min_score(vals):
  x = max(vals)
  y = min(vals)
  return (x,y)
score = (99, 98, 90, 97, 89, 86, 93, 82}
(max_ score, min_score) = max_min_score(score)
print(" Highest Score = ", max_ score)
print(" Lowest Score = ", min_score)
```

**OUTPUT**
```
Highest Score = 99
Lowest Score = 82
```

## 9.12 NESTED TUPLES

In Python, users can easily define a tuple inside another tuple. Such a tuple is called a nested tuple. Consider the nested table in the code given in Example 9.14 that stores and prints the details of employees.

## Example 9.14

```
#Nested Tuple
Emps = (("Arav", "Back Office", 35000), ("Chaitanya", "Technical Assistant",
50000), ("Dhruvika", "Programmer", 100000))
for i in Emps:
  print(i)
```

**OUTPUT**
```
('Arav', 'Back Office', 35000)
('Chaitanya', 'Technical Assistant', 50000)
('Dhruvika', 'Programmer', 100000)
```

You can even specify a list within a tuple. The code given below prints the name of the topper and her marks in 4 subjects. These marks are specified as a list in the tuple Topper.

## Example 9.15

```
# List within a nested tuple
Toppers = (("Janvi",[94, 95, 96, 97]),("Khushi",[99, 95, 90, 93]), ("Myra",[91,
95, 93, 94]))
print("SecondTopper is:", Toppers[1])
```

**OUTPUT**
```
Second Topper is: ('Khushi', [99, 95, 90, 93])
```

## 9.13 THE count() METHOD

The count() method returns the number of elements with a specific value in a tuple.

## Example 9.16

```
#count() method on tuple
tup = (10,7,8,10,9, 7,3,8,5,8,1,8)
print(tup.count(8))
tup = ("abc","def","abc","efg")
print(tup.count("abc"))
```

**OUTPUT**
```
4
2
```

## 9.14 THE zip() FUNCTION

Zip is a built-in function that takes two or more sequences and "zips" them into a list of tuples. The tuple thus formed has one element from each sequence. The code given below illustrates this concept.

## Example 9.17

```
#Count number of y using count()
tup = "xyyyyzyyyzxzzedbgsyyy"
print(" Number of y = ", tup.count('y'))
```

**OUTPUT**
```
Number of y = 10
```

```
# zip() method
Tup = (2,4,6,8,10)
List1 = ('A','E','I','O','U']
print(list((zip(Tup, List1))))
```

**OUTPUT**
```
[(2, 'A'), (4, 'E'), (6, 'I'), (8, 'O'),
(10, 'U')]
```

From the output, we see that the **result of `zip()` function is a list of tuples** where each tuple contains a character from the list and an integer from the tuple. The example, we had seen had an equal number of values in the list and tuple but **if the two sequences have different lengths then the result have the length of the shorter one** as illustrated in the code given below. We can even print the elements in a tuple using the for statement as shown below.

### Example 9.18

```
#zip() method with unequal parameters
Tup = (2,4,6)
list1 = ['A','E','I','O','U']
print(list((zip(Tup, List1))))
```

**OUTPUT**
[(2, 'A'), (4, 'E'), (6, 'I')]

```
#printing tuple with for loop
Tup = (2,4,6)
list1 = ['A','E','I','O','U']
Tup = list((zip(Tup, List1)))
for i, char in Tup:
    print(i, char)
```

**OUTPUT**
2 A
4 E
6 I

### Key points to remember
- Tuples can be converted into lists, and vice-versa using the built-in `tuple()` function that takes a list and returns a tuple with the same elements. Similarly, the `list()` function takes a tuple and returns a list.
- You cannot divide or subtract tuples. If you try to do so you will get a TypeError with "unsupported operand type."
- Since tuples are immutable, they do not support methods like `sort` and `reverse`, as these methods modify the existing sequence.

### Example 9.19

```
# list from tuple and
vice versa
Tup = {2,4,6}
List1 = list(Tup)
print("LIST = ", List1)
List1 = List1 +
[8,10,12]
Tup1 = tuple(List1)
print("TUPLE = ", Tup1)
```

**OUTPUT**
LIST = [2, 4, 6]
TUPLE= (2, 4, 6, 8, 10, 12)

```
#subtracting two tuples
Tup1 = (2,4,6)
Tup2 = (1,3,5)
Tup3 = Tup1 - Tup2
print(Tup3)
```

**OUTPUT**
Traceback (most recent call last):
  File " C:\Users\Python37\try.py", line 3, in <module>
    Tup3 = Tup1 - Tup2
TypeError: unsupported operand type(s) for -: 'tuple' and 'tuple'

```
# reverse method on tuple
Tup1 = (2,1,4,8,6)
Tup1.reverse()
print(Tup1)
```

**OUTPUT**
Traceback (most recent call last):
  File "C:\Users\try.py", line 2, in <module>
    Tup1.reverse()
AttributeError: 'tuple' object has no attribute 'reverse'

- However, Python has a built-in function `sorted()`, which takes any sequence as a parameter and returns a new list with the same elements but in a different order. For example, the code given below illustrates this concept.
- You can use string formatting feature to print values in the Tuple. This is shown in the code given below.

### Example 9.20

```
#Program to sort a tuple of values
Tup = {5,1,0,2,8,3,9}
print(sorted(Tup))
```

**OUTPUT**
[0, 1, 2, 3, 5, 8, 9]

```
#Program to illustrate string formatting
with tuple
Tup ={"Mira", 12, 94.534}
print("%s studying in class %d scored %.2f aggregate" %{Tup[0], Tup[1], Tup[2]})
```

**OUTPUT**
Mira studying in class 12 scored 94.53 aggregate

## 9.15 ADVANTAGES OF TUPLE OVER LIST

Although tuples are similar to lists, there are some advantages of implementing a tuple over a list. Some of these advantages are listed below.

- Since tuple are immutable, iterating through tuple is faster than iterating over a list. This means that tuple performs better than a list.
- Tuples can be used as key for a dictionary but lists cannot be used as keys. We will learn about dictionaries in the next chapter.
- Tuples are best suited for storing data that is write-protected (you can read the data but cannot write to it).
- Tuples can be used in place of lists where the number of values is known and small.
- If you are passing a tuple as an argument to a function, then the potential for unexpected behavior due to aliasing gets reduced.
- Multiple values from a function can be returned using a tuple.

## PROGRAMMER'S ZONE

1. Write a program to swap two values using tuple assignment.
   ```
   val1 = 5
   val2 = 7
   print("val1 = ",val1, " val2 = ",val2)
   (val1,val2) = (val2,val1)
   print("val1 = ",val1, " val2 = ",val2)
   ```

   > If a negative value is used for the step, the slice is done backwards.

   **OUTPUT**
   ```
   val1 = 5 val2 = 7
   val1 = 7 val2 = 5
   ```

2. Write a program using a function that returns the area and perimeter of a rectangle whose length and breadth are passed as argument.
   ```
   def cal_a_p(l,b):
       return (l*b, 2*(l+b))
   l = float(input("Enter the length of the rectangle : "))
   b = float(input("Enter the breadth of the rectangle : "))
   (area, perimeter) = cal_a_p(l,b)
   print("Area of the rectangle = ", area)
   print("Perimeter of the rectangle = ", perimeter)
   ```

   > Tuples are faster than lists, but they cannot be changed.

   **OUTPUT**
   ```
   Enter the length of the rectangle : 7
   Enter the breadth of the rectangle : 5
   Area of the rectangle =  35.0
   Perimeter of the rectangle =  24.0
   ```

   > You cannot add elements to a tuple. Methods like append or extend do not work with tuple.

3. Write a program that has a nested list to store toppers' details. Edit and reprint the details.
   ```
   Toppers = (("Mayank", "BCA",94.0), ("Chainika", "BTech", 90.0), ("Dhruv", "BSc", 89))
   for i in Toppers:
       print(i)
   choice = input("Do you want to edit the details : ")
   ```

   > Slicing can be done on tuples.

```
        if choice == 'y':
            name = input("Enter the name of the students whose details are to be edited
: ")
            new_name = input("Enter the correct name : ")
            new_course = input("Enter the correct course : ")
            new_aggr = input("Enter the correct aggregate : ")
            i = 0
            new_Toppers = ()
            while i<len(Toppers):
                if Toppers[i][0] == name:
                    new_Toppers += (new_name, new_course, new_aggr)
                else:
                    new_Toppers += Toppers[i]
                i+=1
    for i in new_Toppers:
        print(i,end = ' ')
```

> If the index specified in the Tuple slice is too big, then an IndexError exception is raised.

**OUTPUT**
```
('Mayank', 'BCA', 94.0)
('Chainika', 'BTech', 90.0)
('Dhruv', 'BSc', 89)
Do you want to edit the details : y
Enter the name of the students whose details are to be edited : chainika
Enter the correct name : Priyanshu
Enter the correct course : BTech
Enter the correct aggregate : 95
Mayank BCA 94.0 Chainika BTech 90.0 Dhruv BSc 89
```

4. **Write a program that scans an email address and forms a tuple of user name and domain.**
   ```
   addr = 'learn_python@gmail.com'
   user_name, domain_name = addr.split('@')
   print("User Name : ", user_name)
   print("Domain Name : ", domain_name)
   ```

> You can't delete elements from a tuple. Methods like remove or pop do not work with tuple.

   **OUTPUT**
   ```
   User Name : learn_python
   Domain Name : gmail.com
   ```

5. **Write a program that has numbers (both positive as well as negative). Make a new tuple that has only odd values from this list.**
   ```
   Tup = (-12,11,22,-19,13,44,-18,15,26)
   newTup = ()
   for i in Tup:
       if i%2 == 0:
           newTup += (i,)
   print(newTup)
   ```

> Unlike lists, tuples do not support remove(), pop(), append(), sort(), reverse(), and insert() methods.

   **OUTPUT**
   ```
   (-12, 22, 44, -18, 26)
   ```

6. **Write a program that has two sequences. The first program stores some questions and the second stores the corresponding answers. Use the zip() function to form a valid question-answer series.**

```
Ques = ["National Bird", "Prime Minister", " number of bones"]
Ans = ["Peacock", "Narendra Modi", 206]
for q,a in zip(Ques, Ans):
    print("Our", q, " is : ", end =" ")
    print( a)
```

> Reassigning a value in a tuple causes a TypeError.

**OUTPUT**
```
Our National Bird is : Peacock
Our Prime Minister is : Narendra Modi
Our number of bones is : 206
```

### Key Terms

**Tuple:** An immutable data structure that stores related items together.

**Packing a tuple:** Creating a tuple from a set of values is called packing.

**Unpacking a tuple:** Creating individual values from a tuple is known as unpacking.

**Nested tuple:** Tuple inside another tuple.

### Chapter Highlights

- A tuple is an immutable object. This means that while you can change the value of one or more elements in a list, you cannot change the values in a tuple.
- Tuples use parentheses to define their elements whereas lists use square brackets.
- Any set of comma-separated values written without an identifying symbol like brackets or parentheses, etc., is treated as a tuple by default.
- We can use the `eval()` function to input a tuple.
- The `tuple()` function is used to create a tuple with the specified sequence.
- When accessing a tuple, if the index is out of the range of legal indices of the tuple, then Python raises an IndexError.
- Since tuple is an immutable data structure, you cannot delete value(s) from it.
- Two or more tuples can be joined using the + operator. The + operator requires that both the operands must be of tuple types.
- Zip is a built-in function that takes two or more sequences and "zips" them into a list of tuples.
- Python has a built-in function `sorted()`, which takes any sequence as a parameter and returns a new list with the same elements but in a different order.

### Review Questions

1. With the help of an example, explain the significance of + and * operators when used with tuples.
2. Can we change the value of one or more elements in a tuple? Justify your answer.
3. How is a tuple different from a list?

4. Can we add or delete values from a tuple?
5. What are nested tuples?
6. Explain different ways of defining a tuple?
7. How will you join two tuples?
8. With the help of an example differentiate between packing and unpacking a tuple.
9. Why do we use the `index()` function?
10. Demonstrate the use of membership operators on a tuple.
11. Explain the use of `zip()` function.
12. Differentiate between `sort()` and `sorted()`.
13. List some advantages of using tuple over lists.

## Programming Exercises

1. Write a program that creates a list ['a', 'b', 'c'], then create a tuple from that list. Now, do the opposite. That is, create the tuple ('a', 'b', 'c'), and then create a list from it.
2. Create a tuple that has just one element, which in turn may have three elements 'a', 'b', and 'c'. Print the length of this tuple.
3. Write a program that has a predefined list. Create a copy of this list in such a way that only those values that are in valid_tuple are added in the new list.
4. Create a nested tuple that has marks of at least 5 students obtained in three subjects. Now, perform the following operations on it.
    a. Display the marks of the fourth student.
    b. Display the marks obtained by the second student in the first subject.
    c. Display the total marks obtained by each student.
    d. Find the average (or mean) marks obtained by each student.
    e. Using the average marks obtained by each student, calculate the average marks obtained by all the students (finding the mean of means).
    f. For each student display the maximum and minimum marks obtained.
5. Write a program that concatenates the first tuple at the end of the second tuple.
6. Write a program that creates the following tuples.
    i. Squares of first 10 natural numbers
    ii. Cube of first 10 odd numbers
    iii. First 10 multiples of 7
    iv. −5, −3, −1, 1, 3
7. Write a program that creates a tuple of at least 10 pair of values. Count the number of pairs having both values odd.
8. Write a program that has two tuples. Check if the first tuple is a super-set of the second tuple.

## Fill in the Blanks

1. _____ use parentheses to define its elements.
2. _____ function takes two or more sequences and "zips" them into a list of tuples.

3. To add a single element in the set, use the _____ method and to add multiple elements in the set, use the _____ method.
4. The _____ function to create a tuple with the specified sequence.
5. The entire tuple can be deleted by using the _____ statement.
6. If tup = ("abc", "def", "ghi", "jkl"), tup[–1] will print _____.
7. print(len((((('a',1,'bcd',3.0),'e',4.5),'fgh',(99,1.0)))) will give output ____.
8. We can access an individual element of a tuple by using its _____.
9. _____ are used to return more than one value from a function.
10. The _____ method returns the number of elements with a specific value in a tuple.

## State True or False

1. You cannot perform operations like concatenation, repetition, etc., on tuples.
2. It is possible to specify a list within a tuple.
3. If a sequence is specified without parenthesis, it is to be treated as a list by default.
4. Lists are faster than tuples.
5. A tuple can be sliced.
6. Once created, one or more elements of a tuple can be easily updated.
7. It is possible to edit, add and delete elements in a tuple.
8. Tuples can store information that belongs to different data types.
9. Numbers or any other type values cannot be added to a tuple.
10. `max()` and `min()` functions can be used on a tuple iff the values in it are of different data types.
11. In the `zip()` function, if the two sequences have different lengths, then the result has the length of the longer one.
12. Tuples cannot be divided or subtracted.

## Multiple Choice Questions

1. If tup = ("abc", "def", "ghi", "jkl"), then tup("def") will return _____.
   a. 1  b. 2  c. 0  d. Error
2. print((0, 10, 20) < (0, 30, 40)) will print _____.
   a. True  b. False  c. Equal  d. Error
3. Which data structure allows you to return multiple values from a function?
   a. List  b. Tuple  c. Dictionary  d. Set
4. Which of the following will not create a tuple?
   a. T = ()  b. t = (10)  c. t = ([1,2],)  d. t = ((1,2),3)
5. Which of the following functions can be used to input a tuple?
   a. `input()`  b. `eval()`  c. `tuple()`  d. `raw_input()`
6. Which function returns a tuple of two values?
   a. `divmod()`  b. `input()`  c. `eval()`  d. `tuple()`

7. Indices in a tuple start at _____.
   a. -1         b. 0         c. 1         d. 10

8. Which error is returned when index is out of the range of legal indices of the tuple?
   a. ValueError    b. TypeError    c. IndexError    e. SliceError

9. Which error is returned when we try to modify the value of an element in a tuple?
   a. ValueError    b. TypeError    c. IndexError    e. NameError

10. The result of zip() function is a list of _____.
    a. tuples       b. lists        c. values        d. strings

11. Which error is returned if we divide two tuples?
    a. ValueError   b. TypeError    c. IndexError    e. NameError

12. Identify the function or method which is not supported on tuples?
    a. `sorted()`   b. `reverse()`  c. `count()`     d. `index()`

13. Identify the function or method which is supported on tuples?
    a. `append()`   b. `extend()`   c. `sort()`      d. `list()`

## Give the Output

1. ```
   tup1 = (1,2,3)
   tup2 = (1.0,2.0,3.0)
   print(tup1 == tup2)
   ```

2. ```
   Tup = ("abc", "def")
   (key, value) = Tup
   print(key, value)
   ```

3. ```
   Tup = (1,2,3)
   Add_Tup = Tup + Tup
   print(Add_Tup)
   Mul_Tup = Tup * 3
   print(Mul_Tup)
   ```

4. ```
   msg = "HelloWorld"
   pairs = []
   for i in range(1, len(msg), 2):
       first = msg[i - 1]
       second = msg[i]
       pairs.append((first, second))
   for item in pairs:
       print(item)
   ```

5. ```
   Tup  = (1, 'abc')
   List = [1, 'abc']
   print(Tup == List)
   print(Tup == tuple(List))
   print(list(Tup) == List)
   print((1, 2) + (3, 4))
   ```
   ```

6.  ```
    list = ['Good', 'Morning']
    y, x = list
    print(x, y)
    ```

7.  ```
    A = ('Chinu', 30, 'Female')
    B = ('Varun', 32, 'Male')
    for i in [A, B]:
        print('%s is a %d year old %s' %i)
    ```

8.  ```
    Tup = ('Good',)
    for i in range(4):
        Tup = (Tup,)
        print(Tup)
    ```

9.  ```
    Tup1='a','bcd',12.34
    Tup2=Tup1,(5,6,7,8)
    print(Tup2)
    ```

10. ```
    Tup = (1, 2, [3, 4])
    Tup[2][0] = 5
    print(Tup)
    ```

11. ```
    Tup = ("Good Morning")
    print(Tup.index('M'), end = ' ')
    print(Tup.index('n', 5))
    print(Tup.index('r',4,8))
    ```

12. ```
    t = (1,2,3,'a')
    l = list(t)
    l
    ```

13. ```
    tup = (1,2,3,4,5,6,7,8,9)
    print(tup[3:5]*3)
    ```

14. ```
    tup = (10,7,8,9,6,3,4,5,0,1,2)
    print(tup[0])
    print(tup[tup[3]])
    print(tup[-4])
    print(tup[tup[-2]])
    print(tup[tup[tup[7]]-4])
    print(tup[10*2-15+3])
    ```

15. ```
    t = (1,2,3)
    a,b,c = (x,y,z) = t
    print(a,b,c)
    print(x,y,z)
    ```

16. ```
    t =('a')
    print(type(t))
    t =('a',)
    print(type(t))
    ```
    ```

17. ```
    t = (1,2,3)
    tup = ('GO',) + t
    print(tup)
    ```

18. ```
    t1 = (1,2,3)
    t2 = (4,5)
    print(t1 + t2)
    ```

19. ```
    t1 = (1,2,3)
    t2 = t1 * (3)
    print(t2)
    ```

20. ```
    t1 = (1,2,3)
    t2 = ('1','2')
    print(t1 + t2)
    ```

21. ```
    t = (78,98,80,76,53,54,78,98,87,74)
    print(t[3:])
    print(t[:6])
    print(t[-4:])
    print(t[-4:4])
    print(t[:])
    ```

22. ```
    t =("Python","Programming","is","fun")
    (a,b,c,d) = t
    print(t[0][0] + t[1][1]+t[1])
    ```

23. ```
    t1 = 'a','b'
    t2 = ("a","b")
    print(t1==t2)
    ```

24. ```
    t = ('a',('b',('c',('d',))))
    print(len(t))
    print(t[1][0])
    print('c' in t)
    ```

25. ```
    t = (1,2,(3,4),5,(6,(7,8),9))
    print(len(t))
    print(t[3]+10)
    print(t[t[1]])
    print(t[t[1]][1]*10)
    ```

26. ```
    t = ((1,2),)*7
    print(t)
    print(len(t[3:8]))
    ```

27. ```
    tup = ("abc","def")
    x,y = tup
    print x, y
    ```
    ```

## Find the Error

1. ```
   tup = ("abc", "def", "ghi", "jkl")
   tup.append("mno")
   ```

2. ```
   Tup1 = (9,8,7,6,5)
   Tup2 = (1,2,3,4,5)
   print(Tup1 - Tup2)
   ```

3. ```
   tup.remove("abc")
   ```

4. ```
   Tup = ('abc', 'def', 'ghi','jkl')
   Tup[2] = 'xyz'
   ```

5. ```
   x, y = 10, 20, 30
   ```

6. ```
   x = {1, 2, 3, 4, 5}
   x.add([6,7,8])
   print(x)
   ```

7. ```
   tup1 = (1,2,3)
   tup2 = tup1 + (2)
   print(tup2)
   ```

8. ```
   tup = (23,12.56,90,[34,56])
   print("Largest Value = ",max(tup))
   ```

9. ```
   (a,b,c,d) = (10,20,30)
   ```

10. ```
    t = (1,2,3,4,5)
    print(t[10])
    ```

11. ```
    t1 = (1,2,3)
    t2 = (1,2)
    print(t2-t1)
    ```

12. ```
    t1 = (1,2,3)
    t2 =  t1 *(4,)
    print(t2)
    ```

13. ```
    t = (1,)*3
    t[0] = 2
    print(t)
    ```

14. ```
    Tup = (1,2,3,4.0,"abc")
    print(min(Tup))
    ```

15. ```
    students = ("Bhavya", "Era", "Falguni","Huma")
    index = students.index("Falguni")
    print("Falguni is present at location : ", index)
    index = students.index("Isha")
    print("Isha is present at location : ", index)
    ```
    ```

# Answers

## Fill in the Blanks
1. Tuples
2. `zip()`
3. `add()`, `update()`
4. `tuple()`
5. `del`
6. `jkl`
7. 3
8. index
9. Tuples
10. `count()`

## State True or False
1. False
2. True
3. False
4. False
5. True
6. False
7. False
8. True
9. True
10. False
11. True
12. True

## Multiple Choice Questions
1. a
2. a
3. b
4. b
5. b
6. a
7. b
8. c
9. b
10. a
11. b
12. b
13. d

## Give the Output
1. True
2. abc def
3. (1, 2, 3, 1, 2, 3)
   (1, 2, 3, 1, 2, 3, 1, 2, 3)
4. ('H', 'e')
   ('l', 'l')
   ('o', 'W')
   ('o', 'r')
   ('l', 'd')
5. False
   True
   True
   (1, 2, 3, 4)
6. Morning Good
7. Chinu is a 30 year old Female
   Varun is a 32 year old Male
8. (('Good',),)
   ((('Good',),),)
   (((('Good',),),),)
   ((((('Good',),),),),)
9. (('a', 'bcd', 12.34), (5, 6, 7, 8))
10. (1, 2, [5, 4])
11. 5, 8, 7
12. [1, 2, 3, 'a']
13. (4, 5, 4, 5, 4, 5)
14. 10   1   5   7   2   0
15. 1 2 3
    1 2 3
16. <class 'str'>     <class 'tuple'>
17. ('GO', 1, 2, 3)
18. (1, 2, 3, 4, 5
19. (1, 2, 3, 1, 2, 3, 1, 2, 3)
20. (1, 2, 3, '1', '2')
21. (76, 53, 54, 78, 98, 87, 74)
    (78, 98, 80, 76, 53, 54)
    (78, 98, 87, 74)
    ()
    (78, 98, 80, 76, 53, 54, 78, 98, 87, 74)
    ['programming', 'is']
    False
    ('but', 'fun')
    False
22. PrProgramming
23. True
24. 2    b    False
25. 5    15    (3, 4)    40
26. ((1, 2), (1, 2), (1, 2), (1, 2), (1, 2), (1, 2), (1, 2))    4
27. abc def

## Find the Error
1. `AttributeError: 'tuple' object has no attribute 'append'`
2. `TypeError: unsupported operand type(s) for -: 'tuple' and 'tuple'`
3. `NameError: name 'tup' is not defined`
4. `TypeError: 'tuple' object does not support item assignment`
5. `ValueError: too many values to unpack (expected 2)`
6. `TypeError: unhashable type: 'list'`

7. TypeError: can only concatenate tuple (not "int") to tuple
8. TypeError: '>' not supported between instances of 'list' and 'int'
9. ValueError: not enough values to unpack (expected 4, got 3)
10. IndexError: tuple index out of range
11. TypeError: unsupported operand type(s) for -: 'tuple' and 'tuple'
12. TypeError: can't multiply sequence by non-int of type 'tuple'
13. TypeError: 'tuple' object does not support item assignment
14. ValueError:
15. Falguni is present at location : 2
    Traceback (most recent call last):
      File "C:\Users\Reema\AppData\Local\Programs\Python\Python38-32\try1.py",
        line 4, in <module>
      index = students.index("Isha")
    ValueError: tuple.index(x): x not in tuple

# 10 Dictionaries

## Chapter Objectives

This chapter introduces dictionary data structure for mapping identifiers to their respective values. To this end, we shall discuss the following topics:

- Creating dictionaries
- Accessing and traversing values
- Adding, deleting and modifying items
- `pop()` and `copy()` method
- Nested dictionaries
- Built-in functions and methods
- Comparison of list with dictionary

Dictionary is a data structure in which we store values as a **pair of key and value.** Each key is separated from its value by a colon (:) and consecutive items are separated by commas. The entire set of items in a dictionary is enclosed in curly braces ({}). The syntax for defining a dictionary is

```
dictionary_name = {key_1: value_1, key_2: value_2, key_3: value_3}
```

If there are many keys and values in dictionaries, then we can also write just one key-value pair on a line to make the code easier to read and understand. This is shown below.

```
dictionary_name = {key_1: value_1,
                   key_2: value_2,
                   key_3: value_3,
                   }
```

While keys in the ***dictionary must be unique and be of any immutable data type (like strings, numbers, or tuples), there is no stringent requirement for uniqueness and type of values.*** That is, value of a key can be of any type. Remember that dictionaries are not sequences, rather they are **mappings**. Mappings are collections of objects in which the objects are stored by key instead of by relative position.

Dictionary is like an associative array (also known as a hash) in which any key of the dictionary can be associated or mapped to a value.

> Using a mutable object as a dictionary key causes a TypeError.

## 10.1 CREATING A DICTIONARY

The syntax to create an empty dictionary can be given as **dictionary_variable** = [], and the syntax to create a dictionary with key-value pair is: `dictionary_variable = {key1 : val1, key2 : val2, …}`. In this syntax, we can specify key-value pairs separated by a colon in curly brackets as shown below.

```
#To create an empty dictionary
Dict = {}
print Dict
OUTPUT
{}
```

```
#Create a dictionary with key-value pairs
Dict = {'EMP NO' : '123', 'Name' : 'Aaditya',
'Department': 'SALES'}
print(Dict)
OUTPUT
{'EMP NO': '123', 'Name': 'Aaditya',
'Department': 'SALES'}
```

## 10.1.1 Creating a Dictionary using `dict()` Method

To create a dictionary with one or more key-value pairs, you can also use the `dict()` function. The `dict()` creates a dictionary directly from a sequence of key-value pairs. For example, the line of code given below creates a dictionary using a list of key-value pairs.

### Example 10.1

```
#Creating a dictionary using diet() function
Dict = dict([('EMP _NO', '123'),('Name', Aaditya'),('Department', 'SALES')])
print(Dict)
```

**OUTPUT**

```
{'EMP NO': '123', 'Name': 'Aaditya', 'Department': 'SALES'}
```

We can enclose the keys and values in a separate tuple and then use them as argument in the `zip()` function. The output of the `zip()` function can then be passed as an argument to the `dict()` function so that the dictionary can be created using the two tuples.

Note that in the program, the `zip()` function clubs the first value from the heads tuple with the first value in the vals tuple, then the second value from both the tuples are clubbed, and finally the third value is clubbed.

### Example 10.2

```
#Creating dictionary using keys and values that
#are stored as tuples
heads = ('Roll No','Name','Marks')
vals = ('101','Mishti',99)
Student = dict(zip(heads,vals))
print(Student)
```

**OUTPUT**

```
{'Roll No': '101', 'Name': 'Mishti', 'Marks': 99}
```

## 10.2 ACCESSING VALUES IN A DICTIONARY

To access values in a dictionary, square brackets are used along with the key. Note that if you try to access an item with a key that is not specified in the dictionary, a KeyError is generated.

### Example 10.3

```
#Accessing dictionary values
Diet= {'EMP NO' : '123', 'Name' :
'Aaditya', 'Department' : 'SALES'}
print("Dict[EMP NO) = ", Dict['EMP_NO'])
print("Dict[Name) = ", Dict['Name'])
print("Dict[Department] =",
Dict['Department'])
```

**OUTPUT**

```
Dict[EMP_NO) = 123
Dict[Name] = Aaditya
Dict[Department] = SALES
```

```
# Accessing key which is not present in
dictionary
Dict= {'EMP NO' : '123', 'Name' :
'Aaditya'}
print("Dict[EMP_NO] =", Dict['EMP_NO'])
print("Dict[Name] = ", Dict['Name'])
print("Dict[Department] =",
Dict['Department'])
```

**OUTPUT**

```
Dict[EMP NO)= 123
Dict[ Name]= Aaditya
Traceback (most recent call last):
  File "C:\Users\Python37\try.py",
line 4, in <module>
    print("Dict[Department] =",
Dict['Department'])
KeyError: 'Department'
```

## 10.3 ADDING AN ITEM IN A DICTIONARY

To add a new entry or a key-value pair in a dictionary just specify the key-value pair as you had done for the existing pairs. The syntax to add an item in a dictionary is **dictionary_variable[key] = val**.

## 10.4 MODIFYING AN ITEM IN A DICTIONARY

### Example 10.4

```
# adding and modifying values in a dictionary
Dict= {'EMP _NO' : '123', 'Name' : 'Aaditya'}
print("Original dictionary", Dict)
Dict['Department']= 'Sales' #new key-value pair added
Dict['Name']= 'Aadi' #existing value modified
print("Updated Dictionary",Dict)
```

**OUTPUT**
```
Original dictionary {'EMP_NO': '123', 'Name': 'Aaditya'}
Updated Dictionary {'EMP_NO': '123', 'Name': 'Aadi', 'Department': 'Sales'}
```

To modify an entry, just overwrite the existing value with the new value.

## 10.5 DELETING ITEMS

One or more items in a dictionary can be deleted using the **del** keyword. To delete or remove all the items in just one statement, use the `clear()` function. Note that the `clear()` method does not delete the dictionary, it just deletes all the elements inside the dictionary. To remove an entire dictionary from the memory, we can again use the `del` statement **as del Dict_name**. The syntax to use the `del` statement can be given as, **del dictionary_variable[key]**.

```
#deleting entries and the entire dictionary
Dict= {'EMP _NO': '123', 'Name': 'Aaditya','Department': 'Sales'}
print("Original Dictionary", Dict)
del Dict['EMP _ NO'] #a particular key-value pair deleted
print("After deleteing EMP _NO", Dict)
Dict.clear() #all entries deleted
print("After deleteing all entries ", Dict)
del Dict #delete dictionary
print("Printing Dictionary after deleting it", Dict)
```
**OUTPUT**
```
Original Dictionary {'EMP NO': '123', 'Name': 'Aaditya', 'Department': 'Sales'}
After deleteing EMP _NO {'Name': 'Aaditya', 'Department': 'Sales'}
After deleteing all entries {}
Traceback (most recent call last):
  File "C:\Users\Python37\try.py", line 8, in <module>
    print("Printing Dictionary after deleting it", Dict)
NameError: name 'Dict' is not defined
```

### 10.5.1 The `pop()` Method

The `pop()` method can be used to delete a particular key from the dictionary. The syntax of the `pop()` method is, **dict.pop(key [, default])**.

The `pop()` method removes an item from the dictionary and returns its value. *If the specified key is not present in the dictionary, then the default value is returned.* Since default value is optional, if you do not specify the default value and the key is also not present in the dictionary, then a KeyError is generated.

Another method, **popitem()**, randomly pops and returns an item from the dictionary. The use of these methods is illustrated in the program given below.

```
#Program to randomly pop an element from a dictionary
Dict= {'EMP _NO' : '123', 'Name': 'Aaditya','Department': 'Sales'}
print("Original Dictionary", Dict)
print("Name is : ", Dict.pop('Name')) #returns Name
print("Dictionary after popping Name is : ", Dict)
print("Salary is : " , Dict.pop('Salary', -1}} #returns default value
print("Randomly popping any item : ",Dict.popitem())
print("Dictionary after random popping is:", Dict)
print("Designation is:", Dict.pop('Designation')) #generates error
print("Dictionary after popping Designation is : ", Dict)
OUTPUT
Original Dictionary {'EMP _ NO': '123', 'Name': 'Aaditya', 'Department': 'Sales'}
Name is : Aaditya
Dictionary after popping Name is : {'EMP _ NO': '123', 'Department': 'Sales'}
Salary is : -1
Randomly popping any item : ('Department', 'Sales')
Dictionary after random popping is : {'EMP _NO': '123'}
Traceback (most recent call last):
  File "C:\Users\Python37\try.py", line 9, in <module>
    print("Designation is :", Dict.pop('Designation')) #generates error
KeyError: 'Designation'
```

## Key points to remember

- Keys must have unique values. ***Keys should not be duplicated in a dictionary***. If you try to add a duplicate key then the last assignment is retained.

### Example 10.5

```
#Dictionary with duplicate keys
Dict = {'EMP_NO' : '123', 'Name' : 'Aaditya','Department' : 'Sales',
'EMP_NO' : '456'}
print(Dict)
```

**OUTPUT**

```
{'EMP_NO': '456, 'Name ': 'Aaditya', 'Department': 'Sales'}
```

- In a dictionary, ***keys should be strictly of a type that is immutable***. This means that a key can be of strings, number or tuple type but it cannot be a list which is mutable. In case you try to make your key a mutable type, then a **TypeError** will be generated.
- The keys() method of dictionary returns a list of all the keys used in the dictionary, in an arbitrary order. Use the sorted() function to sort the keys.

### Example 10.6

```
# Program to use tuple as keys
Dict = {(1,2),([3,4])}
print{Dict)
```

**OUTPUT**

```
Traceback (most recent call last):
  File "C:\Users\Python37\try.py",
line 5, in <module>
    Dict = {{1,2),([3,4))}
TypeError: unhashable type: 'list'
```

```
# Dictionary with sorted keys
Dict= {'EMP_NO' : '123', 'Name' :
'Aaditya','Department': 'Sales','EMP_NO':
'456'}
print(sorted{Dict.keys()))
```

**OUTPUT**

```
['Department', 'EMP_NO', 'Name']
```

### Example 10.7

```
# Program to check single key in a dictionary
Dict = {'EMP_NO' : '123', 'Name' : 'Aaditya', 'Department' : 'Sales',
'EMP_NO' : '456'}
if 'Department' in Dict
  print(Dict['Department'])
```

**OUTPUT**
```
Sales
```

- The **in keyword** can be used to check whether a single key is in the dictionary.

The key-value pairs can be specified as a list or as a tuple. To create a dictionary out of this list or tuple, it must be passed as an argument to the `dict()` function.

### Example 10.8

```
# Dictionary using a tuple of lists having key-value pairs
Student = dict((['RoiiNp', '101 '),('Name', 'Krish'],['Marks ',90]))
print( Student)
```

**OUTPUT**
```
{'Roll Np': '101', 'Name ': 'Krish', 'Marks': 90}
```

In the given program, we have used a tuple having a list of keys and values as its elements. In the same way, we could have also used nested tuples.

## 10.6 TRAVERSING A DICTIONARY

Looping over a Dictionary can be done to access only values, only keys or both using the `for` loop. We can use the `items()` method that returns a list of tuples (key-value pair). The `keys()` method returns a list of keys in the dictionary. The `values()` method returns a list of values in dictionary.

### Example 10.9

```
#Program to access items in a dictionary
Dict: = {'EMP _ NO' : '123', 'Name' : ' Aaditya'.'Department' : 'Sales',
'EMP_NO' : '456'}
print:("KEYS : " ,end = ' ')
for key in Dict:
  print:(key, end ='') #accessing only keys
print("\nVALUES : ", end = ' ')
for val in Dict:.values():
  print(val, end = ' ') # accessing only values
print("\nDICTIONARY : ", end = ' ')
for key, val in Dict.items():
  print:(key, val, "\t", end = ' ') # accessing keys and values
```

**OUTPUT**
```
KEYS : EMP_NO Name Department
VALUES : 456 Aaditya Sales
DICTIONARY : EMP_NO 456    Name Aaditya    Department Sales
```

## 10.7 NESTED DICTIONARIES

Like any other sequence, we can also have nested dictionary in Python. A nested dictionary has a dictionary defined inside another dictionary.

### Example 10.10

```
#Program to illustrate nested dictionary
Employees= {'Aman' : {'EMP _NO':90, 'Sal':89, 'Desig': 'Analyst'},
    'Sadhvi' : {'EMP NO':91, 'Sal':87, 'Desig': 'Programmer'},
    'Kiyan' : {'EMP NO':92, 'Sal':92, 'Desig': 'Testing Professional'}}
for key, val in Employees.items():
  print(key, val}
```

**OUTPUT**
```
Aman {'EMP _NO': 90, 'Sal': 89, 'Desig': 'Analyst'}
Sadhvi {'EMP NO': 91, 'Sal': 87, 'Desig': 'Programmer'}
Kiyan {'EMP _ NO': 92, 'Sal': 92, 'Desig': 'Testing Professional'}
```

## 10.8 THE copy() METHOD

The `copy()` method of dictionary returns a shallow copy of the dictionary, i.e., the dictionary returned will not have a duplicate copy of the original dictionary but will have the same reference. This means that both the copies of dictionaries will point to the same object (or address) in the computer's memory.

### Example 10.11

```
# Program using copy() method
Emp = {'EMP _ NO' :90, 'Sal ' :89, 'Desig': 'Analyst'}
print("Original Emp : " ,Emp)
Emp_ Copy = Emp.copy()
print("Copied Emp : " , Emp_ Copy)
Emp_Copy('Sal' ] = 99
print("Emp after modification : ", Emp)
print("Copy of Emp after modification : " , Emp_Copy)
```

**OUTPUT**
```
Original Emp : {'EMP _ NO': 90, 'Sal' : 89, 'Des ig': 'Analyst'}
Copied Emp : { 'EMP _ NO' : 90, 'Sal': 89, 'Desig': 'Analyst'}
Emp after modification : {'EMP _ NO': 90, 'Sal ' : 89, 'Desig': 'Analyst'}
Copy of Emp after modification : {'EMP _ NO' : 90, 'Sal' : 99,
Desig': 'Analyst' }
```

## 10.9 BUILT-IN DICTIONARY FUNCTIONS AND METHODS

Table 10.1 discusses some methods and functions that can be used on dictionaries in Python.

**Table 10.1** Methods and functions of dictionaries

| Operation | Description | Example | Output |
|---|---|---|---|
| `len(Dict)` | Returns the length of dictionary. That is, the number of items (key-value pairs) | `Emp = {'EMP_NO':90, 'Sal':89, 'Desig': 'Analyst'}`<br>`print(len(Emp))` | 3 |

*(Continued)*

| Table 10.1 | Continued | | |
|---|---|---|---|
| Operation | Description | Example | Output |
| `str(Dict)` | Returns a string representation of the dictionary | `Emp = {'EMP_NO':90, 'Sal':89, 'Desig': 'Analyst'}`<br>`print(str(Emp))` | {'EMP_NO': 90, 'Sal': 89, 'Desig': 'Analyst'} |
| `Dict.get(key)` | Returns the value for the key passed as argument. If the key is not present in the dictionary, it will return the default value. If no default value is specified, then it will return None | `Emp = {'EMP_NO':90, 'Sal':89, 'Desig': 'Analyst'}`<br>`print(Emp.get('Desig'))` | Analyst |
| `Dict.setdefault(key, value)` | Sets a default value for a key that is not present in the dictionary | `Emp = {'EMP_NO':90, 'Desig': 'Analyst'}`<br>`Emp.setdefault('Sal',0)`<br>`print("Emp gets a salary = ", Emp.get('Sal'))` | Emp gets a salary = 0 |
| `Dict1.update(Dict2)` | Adds the key-value pairs of Dict2 to the key-value pairs of Dict1 | `Emp1 = {'EMP_NO':90, 'Desig': 'Analyst'}`<br>`Emp2 = {'Name' : 'Krish', 'Sal' : 89}`<br>`Emp1.update(Emp2)`<br>`print(Emp1)` | {'EMP_NO': 90, 'Desig': 'Analyst', 'Name': 'Krish', 'Sal': 89} |
| `in and not in` | Checks whether a given key is present in the dictionary or not. | `Emp = {'EMP_NO':90, 'Sal':89, 'Desig': 'Analyst'}`<br>`print('Name' in Emp)`<br>`print('Name' not in Emp)` | False<br>True |

## 10.10 DIFFERENCE BETWEEN A LIST AND A DICTIONARY

Given below are the main differences between a list and a dictionary.

- First, a list is an ordered set of items. But a dictionary is a data structure that is used for matching one item (key) with another (value).
- Second, in lists, you can use indexing to access a particular item. But the index should be a number. In dictionaries, you can use any type (immutable) of value as an index. For example, when we write `Dict['Name']`, where `Name` acts as an index but it is not a number but a string.
- Third, lists are used to look up a value whereas a dictionary is used to take one value and lookup another value. For this reason, dictionary is also known as a *lookup table*.
  In fact, the main advantage of a dictionary is that you don't need to search for a value one by one in the entire set of values; you can find a value instantly.
- Fourth, the key-value pair may not be displayed in the order in which it was specified while defining the dictionary. This is because Python uses complex algorithms (called hashing) to provide fast access to the items stored in the dictionary. This also makes the dictionary preferable to use over a list of tuples.

## PROGRAMER'S ZONE

1. **Write a program that has a dictionary of metropolitan cities and their codes. Add another city in the pre-defined dictionary; print all the items in the dictionary and try to print the code for a state that does not exist. Set a default value prior to printing.**

   ```
   Codes = {'Delhi' : '011', 'Mumbai' : '022', 'Chennai' : '044'}
   Codes['Kolkatta'] = '033'    # add another state
   Codes.setdefault('','Sorry, no idea')
   print("Code for Kolkata is : ", Codes['Kolkata'])
   print("-" * 5, "CODES", "-" * 5)
   for i in Codes.items():
       print(i)
   print("Code for Mumbai : ", Codes.get('Mumbai'))
   ```

   **OUTPUT**
   ```
   (Code for Kolkata is : 033
   ----- CODES -----
   ('Delhi', '011')
   ('Mumbai', '022')
   ('Chennai', '044')
   ('Kolkata', '033')
   ('', 'Sorry, no idea')
   Code for Mumbai : 022
   ```

   > Dictionary keys are case sensitive. Two keys with same name but in different case are not the same in Python.

2. **Write a program that has two dictionaries. The first dictionary has subject names and codes. The second dictionary has subject codes and their average marks. Print the average marks of all the subjects.**

   ```
   subjects = {'Computer Science' : 'CS', 'Political Science' : 'Pol', 'Philosophy' : 'Phil', 'Commerce' : 'Com'}
   avg_marks = {'CS' : 96, 'Pol' : 78, 'Phil' : 84, 'Com' : 95}
   for i in subjects:
       print("Average Marks in ", i, "(", subjects[i], ") = ", avg_marks[subjects[i]])
   ```

   **OUTPUT**
   ```
   Average Marks in Commerce ( Com ) = 95
   Average Marks in Philosophy ( Phil ) = 84
   Average Marks in Computer Science ( CS ) 5 = 96
   Average Marks in Political Science ( Pol ) = 78
   ```

3. **Write a program that creates a dictionary of squares and cubes of numbers entered by the user.**

   ```
   print("Enter -1 to exit....")
   Squares = {}
   while True:
       r = int(input("Enter number : "))
       if r == -1:
           break
       else:
           Dict = {r:[r*r , r*r*r]}
           Squares.update(Dict)
   print(Squares)
   ```

   > In Python "None" is a special value like null or nil, which means no value.

**OUTPUT**
```
Enter -1 to exit....
Enter number : 3
Enter number : 5
Enter number : 2
Enter number : 7
Enter number : -1
{3: [9, 27], 5: [25, 125], 2: [4, 8], 7: [49, 343]}
```

4. Write a program that has a set of words in the English language and their corresponding words in Hindi. Define another dictionary that has a list of words in Hindi and their corresponding words in Hindi. Take all words from the English language and display their meanings in both the languages.

```
E_H = {'Friend' : 'Mitr', 'Teacher' : 'Shikshak', 'Book' : 'Pustak', 'Queen' :
'Rani'}
H_U = {'Mitr' : 'Dost', 'Shikshak' : 'Adhyapak', 'Pustak' : 'Kitab', 'Rani' :
'Begum'}
for i in E_H:
    print(i, "in Hindi means", E_H[i], "and in Urdu means", H_U[E_H[i]])
```

**OUTPUT**
```
Book in Hindi means Pustak and in Urdu means Kitab
Teacher in Hindi means Shikshak and in Urdu means Adhyapak
Friend in Hindi means Mitr and in Urdu means Dost
Queen in Hindi means Rani and in Urdu means Begum
```

5. Write a program that calculates fib(n) using a dictionary.

```
Dict = {0: 0, 1: 1}
def fib(n):
    if n not in Dict:
        val = fib(n-1) + fib(n-2)
        Dict[n] = val
    return Dict[n]
n = int(input("Enter the value of n : "))
print("Fib(", n, ") = ", fib(n))
```

> A KeyError occurs on an invalid access of a key, like when a key that is used is not present in dictionary.

**OUTPUT**
```
Enter the value of n : 10
Fib( 10 ) = 55
```

6. Write a program that prompts the user to enter a message. Now count and print the number of occurrences of each character.

```
def count(message):
    letter_counts = {}
    for letter in message:
        letter_counts[letter] = letter_counts.get(letter, 0) + 1
    print(letter_counts)
message = input("Enter a message : ")
count(message)
```

**OUTPUT**
```
Enter a message : Python Programming is Fun
{'P': 2, 'y': 1, 't': 1, 'h': 1, 'o': 2, 'n': 3, ' ': 3, 'r': 2, 'g': 2, 'a': 1, 'm': 2, 'i': 2, 's': 1, 'F': 1, 'u': 1}
```

7. **Write a program to store a sparse matrix as a dictionary.**
```
matrix = [[0,1,0,0,2],
          [0,0,3,0,],
          [4,0,0,5,0]]
Dict = {}
print ("Sparse Matrix")
for i in range(len(matrix)):
    print("\n")
    for j in range(len(matrix[i])):
        print(matrix[i][j], end = ' ')
        if matrix[i][j]!=0:
            Dict[(i,j)] = matrix[i][j]
print("\n Sparse Matrix can be efficiently represented as Dictionary : ")
print(Dict)
```

**OUTPUT**
```
Sparse Matrix
0 1 0 0 2
0 0 3 0
4 0 0 5 0
 Sparse Matrix can be efficiently represented as Dictionary :
{(0, 1): 1, (0, 4): 2, (1, 2): 3, (2, 0): 4, (2, 3): 5}
```

> Collision means two or more keys pointing to the same location.

8. **Write a program that inverts a dictionary. That is, it makes key of one dictionary the value of another and vice-versa.**
```
Emp = {'EMP_NO':90, 'Sal':89, 'Desig': 'Analyst'}
inverted = {}
for key, val in Emp.items():
    inverted[val] = key
print("Original Dictionary : ", Emp)
print("Inverted Dictionary : ", inverted)
```

**OUTPUT**
```
Original Dictionary : {'EMP_NO': 90, 'Sal': 89, 'Desig': 'Analyst'}
Inverted Dictionary : {90: 'EMP_NO', 89: 'Sal', 'Analyst': 'Desig'}
```

9. **Write a program that has a dictionary of names of students and a list of their marks in 4 subjects. Create another dictionary from this dictionary that has name of the students and their total marks.**
```
Marks = {'Amish' : [87,90,91, 85], 'Anand' : [85,90,91,89], 'Siya' : [80,79, 81,75]}
Tot_Marks = Marks.copy()
for key, val in Marks.items():
    tot = sum(val)
    Tot_Marks[key] = tot
print(Tot_Marks)
```

**OUTPUT**
```
{'Amish': 353, 'Anand': 355, 'Siya': 315}
```

10. **Find the employee getting the highest salary.**
    ```
    Emp = {'Amish': 35, 'Anand': 55, 'Siya': 65}
    max = 0
    New_Emp = ''
    for key, val in Emp.items():
        if val>max:
            max = val
            New_Emp = key
    print("Employee with maximum salary is : ", New_Emp, "with salary = ", max)
    ```
    **OUTPUT**
    ```
    Employee with maximum salary is : Siya with salary = 65
    ```

11. **Write a program that prompts the user to enter a filename. Open the file and print the frequency of each word in it.**
    ```
    text = input('Enter the message: ')
    counts = dict()
    for line in text:
        words = line.split()
        for word in words:
            if word not in counts:
                counts[word] = 1
            else:
                counts[word] += 1
    print(counts)
    ```

    > Trying to index a key that isn't part of the dictionary returns a KeyError.

    **OUTPUT**
    ```
    Enter the file name: File1.txt
    {'a': 1, 'and': 1, '#': 1, 'language': 1, 'Python': 1, 'of': 1, 'is': 1,
    'Welcome': 1, 'Programming': 1, 'to': 1, 'interesting': 1, 'very': 1, 'world':
    1, 'the': 1, 'Reading': 1, 'Hello': 1, 'simple': 1, 'Happy': 1}
    ```

12. **Write a program to count the number of characters in the string and store them in a dictionary data structure.**
    ```
    str = "Python is a wonderful programming language"
    len = len(str)
    Dict = {str:len}
    print(Dict)
    ```
    **OUTPUT**
    ```
    {'Python is a wonderful programming language': 42}
    ```

13. **Write a program combine_lists that combines these lists into a dictionary.**
    ```
    keys = ['EName', 'Degignation', 'Salary']
    values = ["Om", 'Vice President', 1000000]
    details = zip(keys, values)
    Dict = dict(details)
    print(Dict)
    ```

    > In the get() method, if we specify the key as argument which does not even exist in dictionary, then NameError will be returned.

    **OUTPUT**
    ```
    {'EName': 'Om', 'Degignation': 'Vice President', 'Salary': 1000000}
    ```

14. **Write a program that finds whether a particular value is present in the dictionary or not. Do not use `values()` method.**

    ```
    Dict = {"Amna":4,"Brij":2,"Chaitanya":5,"Divyanka":3}
    v = int(input("Enter the value to be searched : "))
    flag = 0
    for i in Dict:
        if(Dict[i] == v):
            print(i)
            flag = 1
    if(flag == 0):
        print("Value not present")
    ```

    **OUTPUT**
    ```
    Enter the value to be searched : 5
    Chaitanya
    ```

15. **Write a program that has a dictionary of states and their codes. Add another state in the pre-defined dictionary; print all the items in the dictionary and try to print the code for a state that does not exist. Set a default value prior to printing.**

    ```
    states = {'Delhi' : '011', 'Mumbai' : '022', 'Chennai' : '044', 'Rajasthan' : 'RJ'}
    states['Tamil Nadu'] = 'TN'      # add another state
    states.setdefault('Karnataka','Sorry, no idea')
    print("Code for Rajasthan is : ", states['Rajasthan'])
    print("-" * 5, "CODES", "-" * 5)
    for i in states.items():
        print(i)
    print("Code for Karnataka : ", states.get('Karnataka'))
    ```

## Key Terms

**Dictionary:** A collection of key-value pairs that map the keys to values. While keys can be of any immutable type, there is no such restriction on its associated value which can be of any type.

**Key:** Data that is *mapped to* a value in a dictionary. Keys are unique data items that are used to look up values in a dictionary.

**Key-value pair:** A pair of items in a dictionary. Key is used to lookup for a value stored in the dictionary.

**Hash function:** A function used to compute the location for a key.

**Lookup:** A dictionary operation that takes a key and finds the corresponding value.

**Nested dictionary:** A dictionary inside another dictionary.

**Mappings:** A collection of objects where objects are stored by key instead of by relative position.

## Chapter Highlights

- While keys in the dictionary must be unique and be of any immutable data type (like strings, numbers or tuples), there is no stringent requirement for uniqueness and type of values.
- Dictionaries are not sequences, rather they are mappings.
- To create a dictionary with one or more key-value pairs, the `dict()` function is used.

- To access values in a dictionary, square brackets are used along with the key to obtain its value.
- If an item with a key that is not specified in the dictionary is accessed, a KeyError is generated.
- One or more items in a dictionary can be deleted using the `del` keyword.
- The `clear()` method does not delete the dictionary, it just deletes all the elements inside the dictionary.
- The `pop()` method removes an item from the dictionary and returns its value. If the specified key is not present in the dictionary, then the default value is returned.
- Keys must have unique values. Keys should not be duplicated in a dictionary.
- The `keys()` method of dictionary returns a list of all the keys used in the dictionary in an arbitrary order. Use the `sorted()` function to sort the keys.
- The key-value pairs can be specified as a list or as a tuple.
- The `copy()` method of dictionary returns a shallow copy of the dictionary, i.e., the dictionary returned will not be a duplicate copy of the original dictionary but will have the same reference.

## Review Questions

1. What is a dictionary?
2. How is a dictionary different from a list?
3. Discuss at least two ways in which you can create a dictionary.
4. Can lists be used as keys? Justify your answer.
5. How is the `zip()` function used to create a dictionary?
6. How will you add key-value pairs in a dictionary?
7. How will you modify key-value pairs in a dictionary?
8. Differentiate between the `del` statement and `clear()` method.
9. When will we use the `pop()` method?
10. List some restrictions which you will keep in mind when creating a dictionary.
11. Draw a comparison between a list and a dictionary.

## Programming Exercises

1. Create a dictionary of products purchased and their MRPs. Calculate the bill and display to the customer.
2. Find `fib(n)` using dictionaries.
3. Write a program that prompts the user to enter a string and returns in alphabetical order, a letter and its frequency of occurrence in the string. (Ignore Case)
4. Write a program to implement sparse matrix using a dictionary.
5. Write a program that has a dictionary of your friends' names (as keys) and their birthdays. Print the items in the dictionary in a sorted order. Prompt the user to enter a name and check if it is present in the dictionary. If the name does not exist, then ask the user to enter DOB. Add the details in the dictionary.
6. Write a program that displays a menu and its price. Take the order from the customer. Check if the ordered product is in the menu. In case it is not there, the customer should be asked to reorder and if it is present then product should be added in the bill.
7. Write a program that prints the maximum and minimum value in a dictionary.

8. Write a program to get a dictionary from an object's fields.
9. Write a program to remove duplicates from a dictionary.
10. Write a program to check if a dictionary has some key-value pairs stored in it.
11. Using dictionary comprehension, create a dictionary of numbers and their squares in the range (10).
12. Write a program that displays information about an employee. Use nested dictionary to do the task.
13. Write a program that prints keys with same values in the dictionary.
14. Write a program that prints keys with different values in the dictionary.
15. Write a program that accepts two dictionaries. Print all the keys that are present in both the dictionaries.
16. Create a dictionary which has name of the student as key and his total marks as value. Now, perform the following operations on this dictionary.
    a. Display the marks obtained by a particular student.
    b. Display the names of all the students who scored 90 and above.
    c. Display all key-value pairs sorted by keys.
    d. Display all key-value pairs sorted by marks.
    e. Create a list of all students.
    f. Create another list having marks obtained by the students.
17. Create a dictionary storing names of months as keys and the number of days as values.
18. Create a dictionary using nested tuple.

## Fill in the Blanks

1. Fill in the blanks to print "Hi", if the key 90 is present in the dictionary named "Dict".
   if ___ ___ ___
   print("Hi")

2. Fill in the blanks to create a list, dictionary, and tuple.
   List=__"abc", "def"__
   Dict=__1:"abc", 2:"def"__
   Tup=__"abc","def"__

3. _____ is a collection of objects that stores objects by key instead of by relative position.

4. The _____ function can be used to create a dictionary with one or more key-value pairs.

5. One or more items in a dictionary can be deleted using the _____ keyword.

6. The _____ method of dictionary returns a list of all the keys used in the dictionary in an arbitrary order.

7. The _____ method of dictionary returns a shallow copy of the dictionary.

8. The _____ function returns a string representation of the dictionary.

9. The _____ function returns the value for the key passed as argument.

10. Dictionary is also known as a _____ table.

## State True or False

1. Keys in the dictionary must be of any mutable data type.
2. Tuples can be used as key for a dictionary but lists cannot be used as keys.

3. Values in a dictionary must be unique.
4. Slicing and concatenation operations are not possible on dictionaries.
5. Dictionary keys are case insensitive.
6. Dictionaries are sequences.
7. To remove an entire dictionary from the memory, we can use the `clear()` method.
8. `pop()` method randomly pops and returns an item from the dictionary.
9. Keys of a dictionary can be sorted using the `sorted()`.
10. The key-value pairs can be specified as a list or as a tuple.

## Multiple Choice Questions

1. If Dict = {1:2, 3:4, 4:11, 5:6, 7:8}, then print(Dict[Dict[3]]) will print _____ .
   a. 2　　　　　b. 8　　　　　c. 11　　　　　d. 6

2. Which data structure does not allow duplicate values?
   a. List　　　　b. Tuple　　　c. Dictionary　　d. Set

3. Which data structure does not support indexing?
   a. List　　　　b. Tuple　　　c. Dictionary　　d. Set

4. Using a mutable object as dictionary will result in which error?
   a. TypeError　　b. KeyError　　c. NameError　　d. IndexError

5. Which error is returned if an item with a key, which is not specified in the dictionary, is accessed?
   a. TypeError　　b. KeyError　　c. NameError　　d. IndexError

6. _____ method can be used to delete a particular key from the dictionary.
   a. `clear()`　　b. `del`　　　c. `pop()`　　　d. `delete()`

7. Which error will the `pop()` method generate if the default value is not specified and the key is also not present in the dictionary?
   a. TypeError　　b. KeyError　　c. NameError　　d. IndexError

8. A _____ cannot be used as a key in the dictionary.
   a. strings　　　b. number　　　c. tuple　　　d. list

9. Which error will be generated if the key of the dictionary is a list?
   a. TypeError　　b. KeyError　　c. NameError　　d. IndexError

## Give the Output

1. ```
   Dict = {"India":"New Delhi", "Nepal":"Kathmandu", "USA":"Washington DC"}
   del Dict["Nepal"]
   for key,val in Dict.items():
       print(key,val)
   ```

2. ```
   Dict = {"India":"New Delhi", "Nepal":"Kathmandu", "USA":"Washington DC"}
   print(Dict.get("Russia"))
   print(Dict.get("Pakistan", "No Idea"))
   ```

3. ```
   Studs = {'Mitanshi', 'Harshita', 'Pritika'}
   Toppers = {}.fromkeys(Studs, 0)
   ```
   ```

```
   print(Toppers)
   Toppers['Mitanshi'] = 97
   Toppers['Harshita'] = 92
   Toppers['Pritika'] = 89
   Toppers.setdefault('Nisha', -1)
   print(Toppers)
```

4. ```
   Toppers = {}
   Toppers['Mitanshi'] = 97
   Toppers['Harshita'] = 92
   Toppers['Pritika'] = 89
   print('Harshita got ' + str(Toppers.get('Harshita')) + ' marks.')
   ```

5. ```
   rec = {'Name': {'First': 'Chaitanya', 'Last': 'Raj'},
                  'Marks': [80, 76, 84],
                  'Course': 'BTech'}
   print(rec['Name'])
   print(rec['Name']['Last'])
   print(rec['Marks'])
   rec['Marks'].append(72)
   print(rec)
   ```

6. ```
   Dict = {"Amna":4,"Brij":2,"Chaitanya":5,"Divyanka":3}
   s = 0
   for v in Dict.values():
       s = s + v
   print(s)
   ```

7. ```
   Dict = {"Amna":4,"Brij":2,"Chaitanya":5,"Divyanka":3}
   n = ''
   for i in Dict:
       if n < i:
           n = i
   print(n)
   ```

8. ```
   Dict = {"Amna":4,"Brij":2,"Chaitanya":5,"Divyanka":3}
   n = 'Chaitanya'
   v = 10
   if n in Dict:
       Dict[n] = v
   print(Dict)
   ```

9. ```
   Dict = {'a':1, 'b':2, ('c','d'):3}
   print(Dict)
   ```

10. ```
    Dict = {'a':1, 'b':2, 'c':3,'d':4}
    v = Dict['c']
    if v in Dict:
        print("FOUND")
    ```
    ```

```
    else:
        print("NOT FOUND")
```

11. ```
    Dict = {'a':1, 'b':2, 'c':3,'d':4}
    k = ''
    for i in Dict:
      if i > k:
          k = i
          v = Dict[i]
    print(k,v)
    List = list(Dict.items())
    List.sort()
    print(List)
    ```

12. ```
    Dict = {'a':1, 'b':2, 'c':3,'d':4, 'e':[5,6,7,8]}
    print(Dict)
    ```

13. ```
    Dict = {10:"TEN","HUNDRED":100,(1,2):("ONE","TWO")}
    print(Dict)
    ```

14. ```
    List = [10,10,10,20,30,30,20,40,40,40]
    counts= {}
    L= []
    for i in List:
        if i not in L:
            L.append(i)
            counts[i] = 1
        else:
            counts[i] += counts[i]
    print(counts)
    ```

15. ```
    List = [10,10,10,20,30,30,20,40,40,40]
    counts = {}
    for i in List:
        if i in counts:
            counts[i] += 1
        else:
            counts[i] = 1
    print(counts)
    ```

16. ```
    Dict = {}
    Dict[1] = 1
    Dict['1'] = 2
    Dict[1] += 1
    sum = 0
    for i in Dict:
        sum += Dict[i]
    print(sum)
    ```

## Find the Error

1. ```
   Dict = {"India":"New Delhi", "Nepal":"Kathmandu"}
   print(Dict["USA"])
   ```

2. ```
   Dict = {}
   print(Dict[0])
   ```

3. ```
   Dict = {'a':1, 'b':2, ['c','d']:[3,4]}
   print(Dict)
   ```

4. ```
   msg = "How are you doing?"
   counts = {}
   for c in msg:
       counts[c] = counts[c] + 1
   print(counts)
   ```

5. ```
   Dict = {}
   Dict[(1,2,3)] = 10
   Dict[[3,2,1]] = 20
   print(DIct)
   ```

6. ```
   Dict = {'a':1,'b':2,'c':3,'d':4}
   print(Dict['a','b'])
   ```

## Answers

### Fill in the Blanks
1. 90, in, Dict
2. [], {}, ()
3. Mappings
4. dict()
5. del
6. keys()
7. copy()
8. str()
9. get()
10. lookup

### State True or False
1. False
2. True
3. False
4. True
5. False
6. False
7. False
8. False
9. True
10. True

### Multiple Choice Questions
1. c
2. b
3. d
4. a
5. b
6. c
7. b
8. d
9. a

### Give the Output
1. India New Delhi
2. None
   No Idea
3. {'Pritika': 0, 'Harshita': 0, 'Mitanshi': 0}
   {'Pritika': 89, 'Harshita': 92, 'Nisha': −1, 'Mitanshi': 97}
4. Harshita got 92 marks.

5. {'Last': 'Raj', 'First': 'Chaitanya'}
   Raj
   [80, 76, 84]
   {'Course': 'BTech', 'Name': {'Last': 'Raj', 'First': 'Chaitanya'}, 'Marks': [80, 76, 84, 72]}
6. 14
7. Divyanka
8. {'Amna': 4, 'Brij': 2, 'Chaitanya': 10, 'Divyanka': 3}
9. {'a': 1, 'b': 2, ('c', 'd'): 3}
10. NOT FOUND
11. d 4
    [('a', 1), ('b', 2), ('c', 3), ('d', 4)]
12. {'a': 1, 'b': 2, 'c': 3, 'd': 4, 'e': [5, 6, 7, 8]}
13. {10: 'TEN', 'HUNDRED': 100, (1, 2): ('ONE', 'TWO')}
14. {10: 4, 20: 2, 30: 2, 40: 4}
15. {10: 3, 20: 2, 30: 2, 40: 3}
16. 4

## Find the Error
1. KeyError: 'USA'
2. KeyError
3. TypeError: unhashable type: 'list'
4. KeyError: 'H'
5. TypeError: unhashable type: 'list'
6. KeyError: ('a', 'b')

# Data Handling using NumPy

## 11

### Chapter Objectives

Data is a collection of facts that is processed to obtained information. This data can be anything including numbers, words, measurements, observations, etc. In this chapter our focus will therefore be on understanding the importance of data and learn how this data can be structured and analyzed to derive useful information in Python using the NumPy module. The topics covered in the chapter include:

- Importance and type of data
- Steps in data processing
- Descriptive statistics
- Creating NumPy Arrays, Sub-arrays and subsets of array objects
- Converting 2D arrays into 1 D arrays
- Reshaping, resizing, splitting, joining, sorting and normalizing arrays
- Working with unknown dimensions
- Performing mathematical operations on NumPy arrays
- Inserting and deleting values from NumPy arrays
- Saving arrays to CSV
- Handling missing data.

## 11.1 DATA AND ITS PURPOSE

Data can exist in different forms – numbers or text on paper or in a computer. Irrespective of the industry, collection and analysis of data have changed the way we do things today. For example, data is analyzed to study symptoms and appropriate treatment for a disease; increase the revenue of a company; generate targeted ads, etc.

Data helps companies to make better decisions. These days, every business generates lot of data. Any business with a website, presence on social media, or involvement in any kind of electronic payments is collecting data about customers, user demographics, and more. Businesses can harness this data to make decisions about:

- finding new customers
- increasing customer retention
- improving customer service
- better managing marketing efforts
- tracking social media interaction
- predicting sales trends.

Thus, data helps business leaders make smarter decisions about where to take their companies.

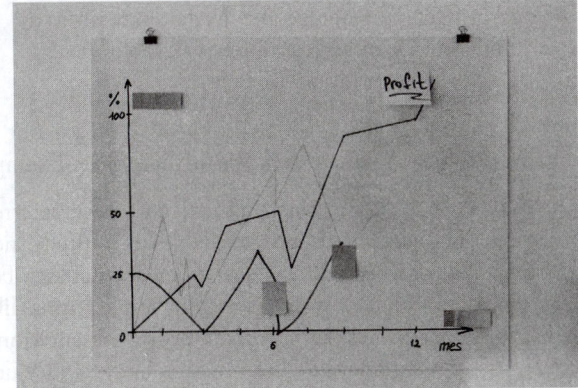

**Figure 11.1** Data for analyzing market trends and making strategic decisions

### 11.1.1 Importance of Data

- Data helps companies solve problems. For example, companies can analyze their data to find out if there is a drop in sales or observe the effectiveness of their marketing campaign. Anomalies in sales figures can be easily tracked and reviewed by analysing data from business processes. Data helps business managers to know if their products or services are performing well. It also helps them to identify which of their products or services are performing below par and what steps are need to improve them.

- Data helps companies to monitor business performance and improve business processes. This will help companies to efficiently utilize time and money.
- Data enables companies to understand their consumers and strategically develop their theories. It also facilitates business groups to get better **return on investments**
- Thus, data improves the quality of life of not only business employees but also of customers and the entire business ecosystem.
- Companies also use data to know how they should design their next product. For this, they collect and extract keywords to learn exactly what features or solutions the customers are looking for.
- Business organizations get information about current trends in the industry by monitoring the relative change in keyword frequencies. This can then be used to predict trends in customer behaviour.

**Figure 11.2** Data for preparing budgets, setting goals and monitoring performance

## 11.2 STRUCTURED, SEMI-STRUCTURED AND UNSTRUCTURED DATA

Massive amount of data available today can be categorized into three groups – Structured data, Semi-structured data, and Unstructured data.

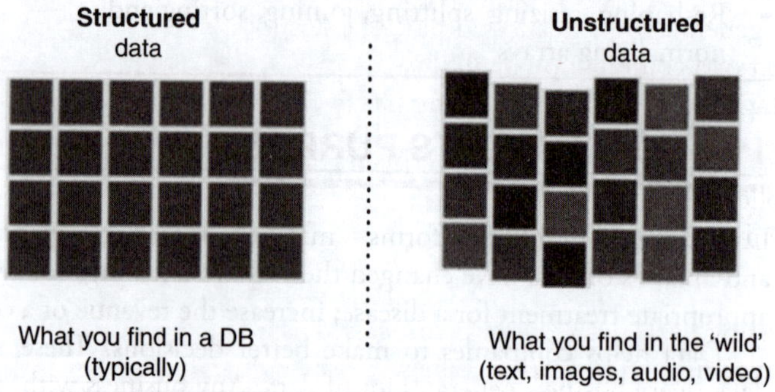

**Structured data:** Structured data, also referred to as quantitative data, is that data which can be used for effective analysis. It is stored in a database and has well-defined structure and format. However, the downside of structured data is that it lacks flexibility in data storage and analysis techniques. The format of the data is fixed and storage and retrieval are limited to a pre-defined format. Example: SQL tables.

**Semi-structured data:** Semi-structured data is not stored in a database. So, analysing such data is not easy. However, after processing this data, it can be stored in a database to make it convenient for further usage. Example: XML data.

**Unstructured data:** Unstructured data, also referred to as qualitative data, is not available in a predefined format. This data cannot be stored in a database. For example, data stored in Word Processing applications (like MS Word), PDF files, social media posts, presentations, chats, IoT sensor data, satellite imagery, audio and video files, text messages and locations are all important sources of unstructured data. Though this type of data is flexible to be stored in different formats, it is difficult to analyze. Special expertise and tools are required for data storage and retrieval for analysis.

The graph shown in Fig. 11.4 illustrates that over the past few decades, applications have generated more unstructured data than structured data and this trend is likely to continue in the years to come. Table 11.1 summarizes the difference between structured and unstructured data.

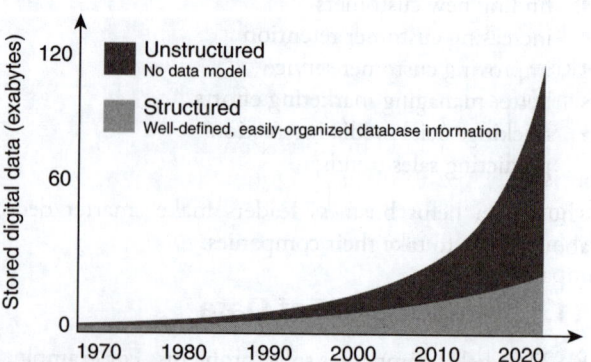

**Figure 11.3** Structured vs. unstructured data

**Figure 11.4** Constant increase in unstructured data
Source: https://www.researchgate.net/figure/The-growth-of-structured-versus-unstructured-data-over-the-past-decade-41_fig1_335927263

## Table 11.1  Comparison between structured and unstructured data

| Properties | Structured Data | Unstructured Data |
|---|---|---|
| Characteristics | Predefined format | Raw/native format |
| Ease of searching | Easy and straight-forward | Difficult |
| Data types | Defined data types | Many varied data types |
| Storage | Relational databases | Cannot be stored in relational databases |
| Flexibility | Not flexible; schema-dependent | Flexible; not schema-dependent |
| Availability | Approx. 20% of data | Approx. 80% of data |
| Examples | Excel, Google Sheets, SQL, customer data, phone records, transaction history | Text data, social media comments, phone calls transcriptions, various logs files, images, audio, video |

## 11.3  DATA PROCESSING

Data processing means the process of converting raw data to meaningful information. This information may help to resolve a problem or improve an existing scenario. Data processing follows a cycle where inputs are fed to a computer to generate some quality output. The output is usually expressed in appropriate forms like diagrams, reports, graphics, text or a combination of all this.

**Stages of the Data Processing Cycle can be explained as given below.**

*Step 1: Data Collection:* This stage is very crucial to the success of data processing activities as the quality of data collected will have an immense effect on the output. The data collection process must be well-defined and accurate. Only an effective collection process can ensure that subsequent decisions based on the findings are valid.

*Step 2: Data Preparation:* This involves manipulation of data into a format suitable for further analysis and processing. Raw data cannot be processed as it is. For better accuracy, it has to be first prepared. The collected data may have missing or incorrect values. All these discrepancies must be removed during data preparation stage.

*Step 3: Data Input:* Data input is the activity in which verified data is coded or converted into machine-readable form so that it can be processed using a computer software. Data can be entered using a keyboard, scanner, or from an existing source data source. Data input is a time-consuming process that needs to be done accurately in the specified format. If there is even a single error during input, then the result will be adversely affected, Garbage-In–Garbage-Out.

*Step 4: Data Processing* is done by applying different techniques for technical manipulations using suitable algorithm (like Machine Learning and Artificial Intelligence) to generate an output or interpretation of the data. Time taken for processing data depends on complexity of the data.

*Step 5: Output* and interpretation is the stage where processed information is displayed to the user. Output can be presented in various formats like graphical reports, audio, video, or in textual format. This output conveys meaningful information that will guide future decisions taken by the company.

*Step 6: Storage* is the last stage in the data processing cycle, where data is preserved for future use.

Thus, we see that the Data Processing Cycle includes a series of steps that are performed to extract useful information from raw data. Every step must be carried out in the specified order. Partial output from one stage is passed as an input for the next stage. Failure in any one stage will not give the expected output.

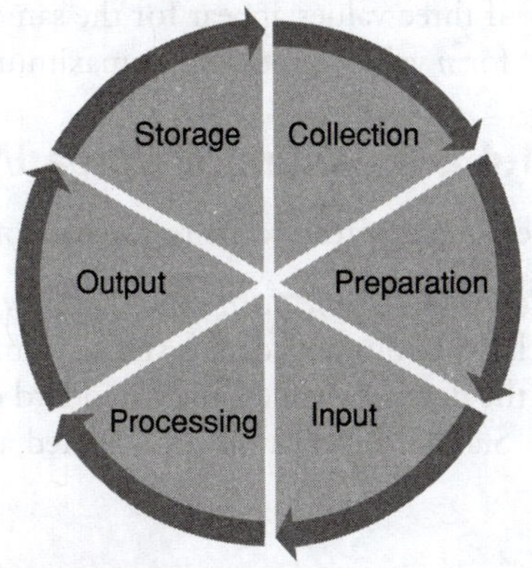

**Figure 11.5**  Data processing cycle

All the above-mentioned activities are cyclic in nature as the output and storage stages may result in repeating the data collection stage leading to another cycle of data processing.

## 11.4 DESCRIPTIVE STATISTICS

Descriptive statistics are evaluated to summarize and organize data for better understandability. As the name suggests, descriptive statistics describe data but they do not make inferences from the sample to the whole population. There are two types of descriptive statistics – Measures of central tendency and Measures of variability (spread).

### 11.4.1 Measure of Central Tendency

Central tendency indicates that there is one number that best summarizes the entire set of measurements. This number is "central" to the set.

*Mean/Average:* Mean or Average is a central tendency of the data. So, in other words, it is a number around which a whole data is spread out. It is that single number which can estimate the value of whole data set. Mean is calculated by dividing the sum of all elements by the number of elements.

$$\overline{X} = \frac{1+2+3+4+5+6+7+8+9+10}{10} = 5.5$$

*Median:* Median is the value which divides the data in to two equal parts. Number of elements on right side of it is same as number of elements on left side of the median. Median is obtained after arranging data either in ascending or descending order.

To make it simple, median is the middle term, if number of elements is odd. In case of even number of elements, median is the average of middle two terms.

Median of 11 + 23 + 35 + 49 + 50 + 77 + 18 + 96 + 10 = 50 (odd number of elements)
Median of 11 + 23 + 35 + 49 + 50 + 62 + 77 + 18 + 96 + 10 = (50 + 62 )/2 = 112/ 2 = 56
(even number of elements)

***When values are in arithmetic progression (difference between the consecutive terms is constant),*** *median is always equal to mean*. For example, in data set 1, 3, 5, 7, 9, 11, 13, both mean and median are same.

*Mode:* Mode is the term appearing most frequently in a data set. This means that the mode has highest frequency of occurrence in the data set.

Mode of 11, 23, 39, 35, 41, 50, 41, 23, 39, 77, 23 = 23 because it is occurring thrice in the data.

### Key points to remember
- In some data sets, there can be no mode at all as all values appears same number of times.
- If two values appear for the same maximum number of times then the data set is said to be **bimodal**.
- If three values appear for the same maximum number of times then the data set is said to be **trimodal**. Similarly, for *n* values appearing at maximum fequency, the data set is said to be **multimodal**.

### 11.4.2 Measure of Spread/Dispersion

Measure of spread refers to the idea of variability within your data.

*Standard deviation:* Standard deviation measures the average distance between each value and the mean. This gives a clarity about how data is spread out from mean. A low standard deviation indicates that values are closer to the mean of the data set, while a high standard deviation means that the data values are spread out over a wider range of values.

Standard Deviation is calculated as,

$$S.D. = \sqrt{\frac{1}{n}\sum_{i=0}^{n}(x-\mu)^2}$$

where $\mu$ is the mean of a population.
For example, consider the data set given below.
12, 7, 8, 11, 5, 4, 10, 9, 6, 9, 4, 9, 2, 5, 4, 9, 3, 7, 4, 12

Mean of the values $= \dfrac{\text{Sum of all values}}{\text{Number of values}} = 7$

For each number, subtract the Mean and square the result
This is the part of the formula that says: $(x_i - \mu)^2$
$x_1 = 12$, $x_2 = 7$, $x_3 = 8$, etc.
For each value, subtract the mean and square the result, as shown below.
$(12 - 7)^2 = (5)^2 = 25$
$(7 - 7)^2 = (0)^2 = 0$
$(8 - 7)^2 = (1)^2 = 1$
$(11 - 7)^2 = (4)^2 = 16$
$(5 - 7)^2 = (-2)^2 = 4$
$(4 - 7)^2 = (-3)^2 = 9$
$(10 - 7)^2 = (3)^2 = 9$
$(9 - 7)^2 = (2)^2 = 4$
$(6 - 7)^2 = (-1)^2 = 1$
$(9 - 7)^2 = (2)^2 = 4$
... etc ...

Now, find the mean of these squared differences. For this, add up all the values then divide by number of values. In our data set, the mean of squared differences = 178

Finally, divide this mean by number of values and find its squared root. So,
Mean of squared differences $= (1/20) \times 178 = 8.9$
Standard Deviation, $\sigma = \sqrt{8.9} = 2.983$

**Variance:** Variance is calculated as the square of average distance between each quantity and mean. This means that variance is the square of standard deviation.

$$\text{Variance} = (S.D.)^2$$

**Range:** Range is calculated as the difference between lowest and highest value. For example,

Range of 11, 23, 39, 35, 41, 50, 41, 23, 39, 77, 23 $= 77 - 11 = 60$

## 11.5 THE NUMPY MODULE

NumPy, which stands for "Numeric Python" or "Numerical Python", is the most important library for scientific computing in Python. It has a large variety of functions that can be used to solve problems in Science and Engineering.

NumPy is one of the important packages used for data science, mainly because this library provides the array data structure. Arrays are superior to Python lists as they are more compact, convenient, efficient and provide faster access in reading and writing items.

Another important tool of NumPy is high-performance multidimensional arrays which are a powerful data structure for efficient computation of arrays and matrices. To work with these arrays, NumPy provides a large number of high-level mathematical functions.

## 11.6 INTRODUCTION TO ARRAYS

Before we study about NumPy module in detail, we need to realize the need of an array. Consider a situation in which there are 20 students in a class. We have been asked to write a program that reads and prints the marks of all these 20 students. In this program we will need 20 integer variables with different names, as shown in Fig. 11.6.

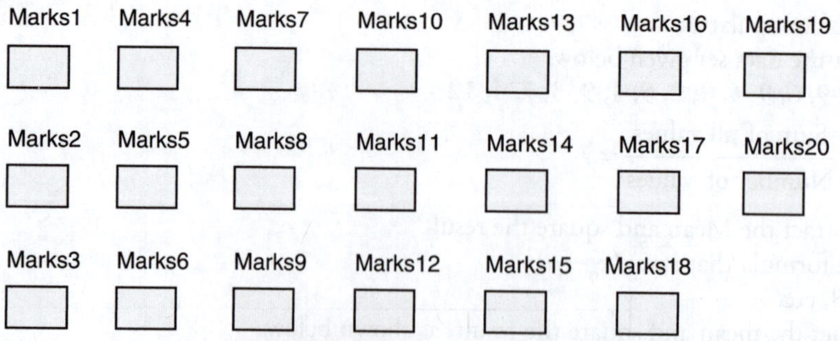

## 230 Informatics Practices for CBSE Class XI

[Figure showing 20 boxes labeled Marks1 through Marks20 arranged in 3 rows]

**Figure 11.6** Twenty variables

As per the figure, Marks1 will store marks obtained by the first student, Marks2 will store marks obtained by second student, and so on. Now, to read values for these twenty variables, we must have twenty read statements. Similarly, to print the value of these variables, we need 20 write statements. If it is just a matter of 20 variables, then it might be acceptable for the user to follow this approach. But, imagine if it will be possible to follow this approach to read and print marks of the students

- in the entire course (say 100 students)
- in the entire college (say 500 students)
- in the entire university (say 10000 students).

The answer is no, definitely not. To process large amount of data, we need a data structure known as **array**.

*An array is a collection of similar data elements. These data elements have the same data type. The elements of the array are stored in consecutive memory locations and are referenced by an index (also known as the subscript). The subscript indicates an ordinal number of the element counting from the beginning of the array.*

The array index starts from zero. Consider an array of 10 elements named marks that contains 10 elements in all. The first element will be stored at 0th index and accessed as marks[0], second element at 1st index to be accessed as marks[1], and so on. Note that 0, 1, 2, 3, etc., written within square brackets are subscripts/index. An array can thus be thought of a group of elements placed in consecutive memory locations as shown in Fig. 11.7.

> The array holds and represents any regular data in a structured way.

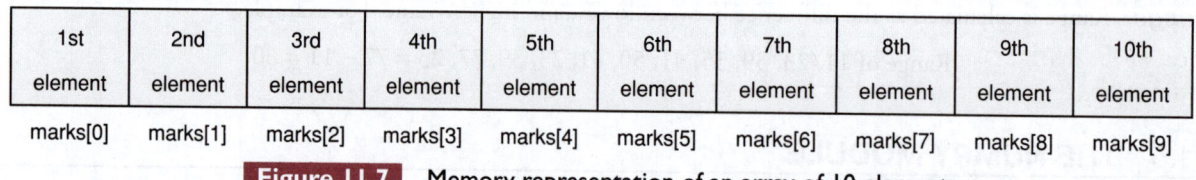

**Figure 11.7** Memory representation of an array of 10 elements

Thus, it is clear that an array holds and represents any regular data in a structured way. It contains information about the raw data, how to locate an element and interpret it. Storing the related data items in a single array enables the programmers to develop concise and efficient programs.

### 11.6.1 Matrices or Two-dimensional Arrays

Continuing with our problem of storing marks, imagine that we have to store marks obtained by 20 students in 5 different subjects. The problem has added one more dimension – marks in different subjects. Initially, we had one set of marks for different students. Now both parameters are different – five sets of marks for 20 sets of students.

We have read that one-dimensional array is organized linearly in only one direction. But at times, we need to store data in the form of matrices or tables. In such situations, the concept of single dimension arrays is extended to incorporate two-dimensional data structures. A two-dimensional array is specified using two subscripts where one subscript denotes row and the other denotes column. You may think of a two-dimensional array as an array of a one-dimensional arrays.

As evident from the Fig. 11.8, a two-dimensional $m \times n$ array can store $m*n$ data elements, where $m$ is the number of rows and $n$ is the number of columns. Each element is accessed using two subscripts, $i$ and $j$ where $i <= m$ and $j <= n$, where $m$ is the number of rows and $n$ is the number of columns.

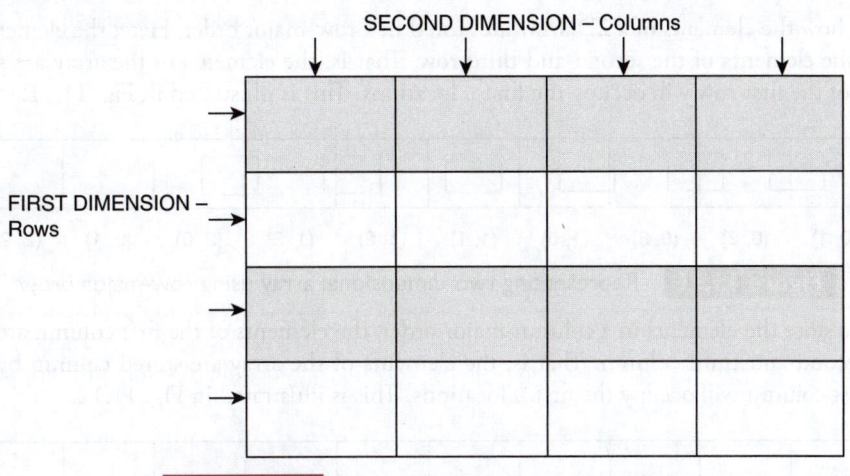

**Figure 11.8** Two-dimensional array or matrix

In a 2D array or a matrix named marks, first element is denoted by marks[0][0], the second element as marks[0][1], and so on. Here, marks[0][0] stores the marks obtained by the first student in the first subject, marks[1][0], stores the marks obtained by the second student in the first subject.

The pictorial form of a two-dimensional array is given in Fig 11.9.

| Rows/Columns | Col 0 | Col 1 | Col2 | Col 3 | Col 4 |
|---|---|---|---|---|---|
| Row 0 | Marks[0][0] | Marks[0][1] | Marks[0][2] | Marks[0][3] | Marks[0][4] |
| Row 1 | Marks[1][0] | Marks[1][1] | Marks[1][2] | Marks[1][3] | Marks[1][4] |
| Row 2 | Marks[2][0] | Marks[2][1] | Marks[2][2] | Marks[2][3] | Marks[2][4] |

**Figure 11.9** Two-dimensional array or matrix

Hence, we see that a 2D array is treated as a collection of 1D array. To understand this better, we can also represent the two-dimensional array as shown in Fig. 11.10.

| Marks[0] | Marks[0] | Marks[1] | Marks[2] | Marks[3] | Marks[4] |
|---|---|---|---|---|---|
| Marks[1] | Marks[0] | Marks[1] | Marks[2] | Marks[3] | Marks[4] |
| Marks[2] | Marks[0] | Marks[1] | Marks[2] | Marks[3] | Marks[4] |
| Marks[3] | Marks[0] | Marks[1] | Marks[2] | Marks[3] | Marks[4] |

**Figure 11.10** Understanding two-dimensional array

**Row-major and column-major way of representing matrices:** Although we have shown a rectangular picture of a two-dimensional array, in computer memory actually these elements are stored sequentially. There are two ways of storing a two- dimensional array in memory. The first way is row-major order and the second is column-major order.

Let us first see how the elements of a 2D array are stored in a row-major order. Here, the elements of the first row are stored before the elements of the second and third row. That is, the elements of the array are stored row by row where *n* elements of the first row will occupy the first *n* locations. This is illustrated in Fig. 11.11.

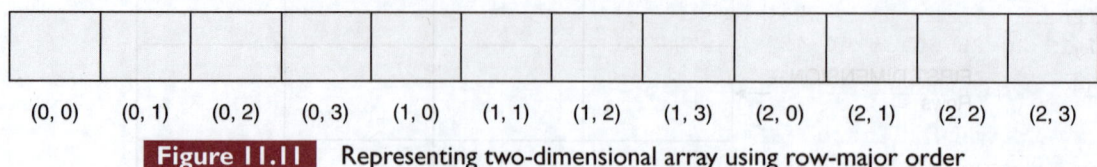

**Figure 11.11** Representing two-dimensional array using row-major order

However, when we store the elements in a column-major order, the elements of the first column are stored before the elements of the second and third column. That is, the elements of the array are stored column by column where *n* elements of the first column will occupy the first *n* locations. This is illustrated in Fig. 11.12.

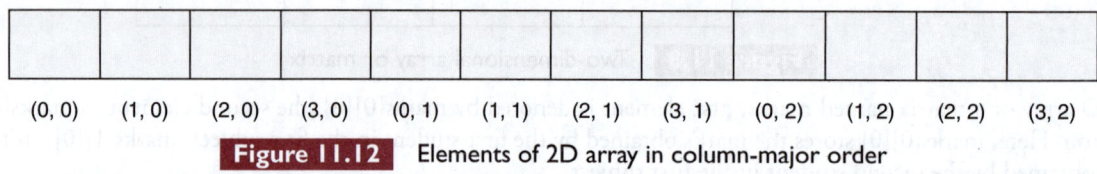

**Figure 11.12** Elements of 2D array in column-major order

## 11.7 THE NUMPY MODULE

NumPy module contains a rich collection of essential functions that support computations on multi-dimensional arrays. When using NumPy, you must remember the following points.

- To use this module, we must first import it by writing, import NumPy as np.
- NumPy is mainly used for creating homogeneous multi-dimensional arrays. Homogeneous means elements of same data type.
- In NumPy, dimensions are called axes.
- Number of axes is called the rank.

## 11.8 CREATING NUMPY ARRAYS

There are several ways to create an array in NumPy like np.array, np.zeros, no.ones, etc. Each of them provides some flexibility.

**np.array:** np.array is a function that allows users to create an array of elements supplied as an argument. NumPy array() functions take a list of elements as argument and returns a one-dimensional array.

```
import numpy as np
a = np.array([1,2,3])
b = np.array((5,6,7))
print(a)
print(b)
OUTPUT
[1 2 3]
[5 6 7]
```

Here, a is an array of a list of integers. b is an array of a tuple of integers. Likewise, we can have arrays of elements that belong to other data types *np.arange:* NumPy `arange()` function takes **start**, **end** of a range and the **interval** as arguments and returns a one-dimensional array with evenly spaced elements from the interval specified by the value of start and stop in the gap of step. The syntax is:

```
numpy.arange([start, ]stop, [step, ], dtype=None)
import numpy as np
a = np.arange(5,50,5)
print(a)
OUTPUT
[ 5 10 15 20 25 30 35 40 45]
```

Here, a is a one-dimensional array with elements from 5 to 50 in steps of 5.

*np.linspace:* NumPy `linspace()` functions takes **start**, **end** and the **number of elements** to be created as arguments and returns a one-dimensional array that has evenly spaced numbers over the specified interval. It is similar to `arrange()` function but it uses the number instead of the step as an interval. The syntax of `linespace()` function is,

```
numpy.linspace(start, stop, num, endpoint=True, retstep=False, dtype=None)
```

Here, num specifies the number of values to generate.

```
import numpy as np
a = np.linspace(1,2/3,4)
print(a)
OUTPUT
[1.         0.91666667 0.83333333 0.75      ]
```

*Create NumPy Array from List:* A Python list having elements enclosed between square brackets can be converted into a NumPy array by using the `array()` method of the NumPy module. This is shown in the codes given below.

*Create NumPy Array from Tuple:* The same `array()` method of the NumPy module can be used to create a NumPy array from a tuple. Recall that a tuple contains a number of elements enclosed in round brackets. The code given below demonstrates the creation of such an array.

### Example 11.1

```
#Creating NumPy Array From list
import numpy as np
L = [1,2,3,4,5,6,7,8,9,10]
arr = np.array(L)
print("NUMPY ARRAY CREATED FROM LIST IS : ",arr)
OUTPUT
NUMPY ARRAY CREATED FROM LIST IS :
[ 1  2  3  4  5  6  7  8  9 10]
```

```
#Creating NumPy Array From Tuple
import numpy as np
Tup = (1,2,3,4,5,6,7,8,9,10)
arr = np.array(Tup)
print("NUMPY ARRAY CREATED FROM TUPLE IS : ",arr)
OUTPUT
NUMPY ARRAY CREATED FROM TUPLE IS :
[ 1  2  3  4  5  6  7  8  9 10]
```

*Miscellaneous Functions:* NumPy also allows users to create "empty" arrays that are placeholders for values that can be filled up later. Apart from empty arrays, we can create arrays and initialize them with ones or zeros or create arrays that get filled up with evenly spaced values, constant or random values. All these functions are given in Table 11.2.

### Key points to remember
- Functions like `np.ones()`, `np.zeroes()`, `np.random.random()`, `np.empty()` and `np.full()` take the shape of the array to be created as an argument.
- We can specify the data type of the array to be created in the `np.ones()` and `np.zeroes()` function.
- The `np.full()` function has to specify the constant value that has to be inserted into the array.
- `np.linspace()` and `np.arrange()` functions are used to create arrays of evenly spaced values. While `np.linspace()` function specifies the step value, `np.arrange()` function, on the other hand, specifies the number of samples in the array.
- We can also create an identity matrix (matrix is another name of 2D array) using `np.eye()` and `np.identity()` functions. An identity matrix is a square matrix in which all elements in the principal diagonal are ones, and all other elements are zeros. When a matrix is multiplied with an identity matrix, the given matrix is left unchanged.

**Table 11.2** Functions for creating NumPy arrays

| Function | Description | Example | Remarks |
|---|---|---|---|
| `np.ones` | Creates a matrix of specified data type and shape (or size) filled with ones. | `import numpy as np`<br>`a = np.ones((4,5), dtype=np.int16)`<br>`print(a)`<br>**OUTPUT**<br>`[[1 1 1 1 1]`<br>`[1 1 1 1 1]`<br>`[1 1 1 1 1]`<br>`[1 1 1 1 1]]` | a is a two-dimensional array with 4 rows and 5 columns. All elements in this array are 1. |
| `np.zeros` | Creates a matrix of specified data type and shape (or size) filled with ones. | `import numpy as np`<br>`a = np.zeros((4,5), dtype=np.int16)`<br>`print(a)`<br>**OUTPUT**<br>`[[0 0 0 0 0]`<br>`[0 0 0 0 0]`<br>`[0 0 0 0 0]`<br>`[0 0 0 0 0]]` | a is a two-dimensional array with 4 rows and 5 columns. All elements in this array are 0. |
| `np.full` | Returns a new array with the specified size and type. It also fills the array with specified value. | `import numpy as np`<br>`a = np.full((3,2), 2.3)`<br>`print(a)`<br>**OUTPUT**<br>`[[2.3 2.3]`<br>`[2.3 2.3]`<br>`[2.3 2.3]]` | a is a two-dimensional array with 3 rows and 2 columns. All elements in this array have value 2.3. |
| `np.random.rand` | Creates an array of specified shape and fills it with random values. | `import numpy as np`<br>`a = np.random.rand(3,2)`<br>`print(a)`<br>**OUTPUT**<br>`[[0.46632055 0.19445536]`<br>`[0.93474084 0.70868838]`<br>`[0.18377336 0.55481711]]` | a is a two-dimensional array with 3 rows and 2 columns. to specify a 3D array, we could have given three values within the function. |
| `np.empty` | Returns a new array of given shape and type, filled with random values. | `import numpy as np`<br>`a = np.empty((3,2))`<br>`print(a)`<br>**OUTPUT**<br>`[[ 4.35009137e-313 0.00000000e+000]`<br>`[ 2.71827661e-311 4.46033568e-313]`<br>`[-1.68577438e-037 2.12510837e-311]]` | a is a two-dimenional array with 3 rows and 2 columns filled with random values. |

## 11.9 ARRAY ATTRIBUTES

Some of the important attributes of a NumPy array are:

- **Ndim:** displays the dimension of the array
- **Shape:** returns a tuple of integers indicating the size of the array
- **Size:** returns the total number of elements in the NumPy array
- **Dtype:** returns the type of elements in the array, i.e., int64, character
- **Itemsize:** returns the size in bytes of each item
- **Reshape:** Reshapes the NumPy array

  ```
  import numpy as np
  a = np.empty((5,3))
  print("The Array is : \n",a)
  print("Number of Dimensions in a : ",np.ndim(a))
  print("Shape of a : ",np.shape(a))
  ```
  **OUTPUT**
  ```
  The Array is :
   [[6.23042070e-307 3.56043053e-307 1.60219306e-306]
   [2.44763557e-307 1.69119330e-306 1.33514617e-307]
   [3.56043053e-307 1.37961641e-306 8.06613040e-308]
   [1.24610383e-306 1.69118108e-306 8.06632139e-308]
   [1.20160711e-306 1.69119330e-306 1.39234638e+188]]
  Number of Dimensions in a : 2
  Shape of a : (5, 3)
  ```

> The `head()` and `tail()` methods are used to view a small sample of a Series of the DataFrame object.

- `head(n)`: Returns the first *n* rows. If the value of *n* is not specified then by default, first 5 rows will be displayed.
- `tail(n)`: Returns the last *n* rows. If the value of *n* is not specified then by default, first 5 rows will be displayed.

### Example 11.2

```
import numpy as np

import pandas as pd

#Create a series with 10 random numbers

S = pd.Series(np.random.randn(10))

print("The original series is : " )

print(S)

print ("The first four rows of the data
series : ")

print(S.head(4))

print ("The last four rows of the data
series : ")

print(S.tail(4))
```

**OUTPUT**
```
The original series is :
0    0.867655
1    0.989083
2    0.460942
3    0.612183
4   -1.D84612
5    0.959498
6    0.110584
7   -0.881249
8    2.333609
9    1.372371
dtype: float64
The first four rows of the data series :
0    0.867655
1    0.989083
2    0.460942
3    0.612183
dtype: float64
The last four rows of the data series :
6    0.110584
7   -0.881249
8    2.333609
9    1.372371
dtype: float64
```

## 11.10 CONVERTING 2D NUMPY ARRAY INTO 1D ARRAY

There are three ways in which a 2D NumPy array can be converted into a 1D array – np.flatten(), np.ravel() and np.reshape(). These techniques are discussed below.

### 11.10.1 np.flatten()

The np.flatten() function returns a copy of an array collapsed into one dimension as shown in Fig. 11.13. The function takes a parameter order. The syntax of this function can be given as,

ndarray.flatten(order)

where order is an optional argument that can take values 'C','K','F'.
order = 'C' means that the array gets flattened in row-major order.
order = 'F' means that the array gets flattened in column-major order.
order = 'K' flattens the array in same order in which the elements occurred in the memory. By default, this parameter is set to 'C'

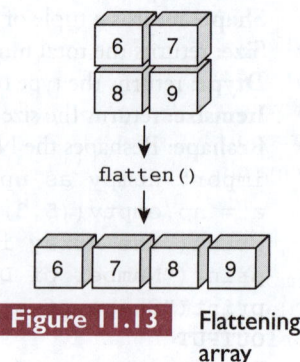

**Figure 11.13** Flattening array

### Example 11.3

```
import numpy as np
TwoD_arr = np.array([[1,2,3],
[4,5,6],[7,8,9]])
print("2D Array is : ", str(TwoD_arr))
OneD_arr = TwoD_arr.flatten()
print("1D Array is : ", OneD_arr)
```

OUTPUT
2D Array is : [[1 2 3]
 [4 5 6]
 [7 8 9]]
1D Array is : [1 2 3 4 5 6 7 8 9]

### 11.10.2 np.ravel()

numpy.ravel() is a method in the NumPy module which changes a 2D array or a multi-dimensional array into a contiguous flattened 1D array as shown in Fig. 11.14. The returned array has the same data type as the source array or input array. The function makes a copy only if needed. The returned array will have the same type as that of the input array. The syntax of np.ravel() function can be given as,

numpy.ravel(a, order)

where,
a is the input array that has to be converted into a contiguous flattened array.
order can take values 'C','K', or 'F'. 'C' specifies row-major. 'F' denotes column-major and 'K' flattens the array in the order in which the elements occur in the memory.

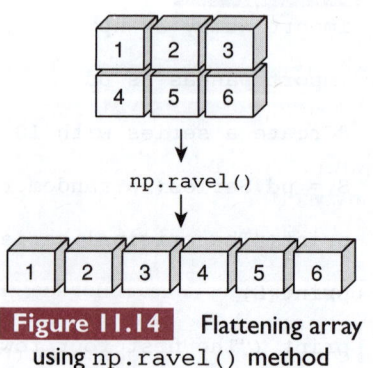

**Figure 11.14** Flattening array using np.ravel() method

In the code given below, we have used the ravel() method without any arguments and called the method using the two-dimensional array object.

### Example 11.4

```
import numpy as np
TwoD_arr = np.array([[1,2,3],[4,5,6],[7,8,9]])
print("TwoD Array is : ", str(TwoD_arr))
OneD_arr = TwoD_arr.ravel()
print("OneD Array is : ", OneD_arr)
```

OUTPUT
TwoD Array is : [[1 2 3]
 [4 5 6]
 [7 8 9]]
OneD Array is : [1 2 3 4 5 6 7 8 9]

## 11.10.3 np.reshape()

The `reshape()` method of the NumPy module is used to give a new shape to an array without changing its data. The syntax of this function can be given as,

numpy.reshape(a, newshape, order='C')

where,
a is the array to be reshaped.
newshape should be compatible with the original shape. If the array has integer values, then the result will be a 1D array of corresponding length. If one shape dimension is –1, then the value depends on the length of the array and remaining dimensions.

Order can take values 'C','F','K'.

The code given below reshapes a 2D array into a 1D array.

```
import numpy as np
TwoD_arr = np.array([[1,2,3],[4,5,6],[7,8,9]])
print("TwoD Array is : ", str(TwoD_arr))
OneD_arr = TwoD_arr.reshape([1,9])
print("OneD Array is : ", OneD_arr)
```
OUTPUT
```
TwoD Array is :  [[1 2 3]
 [4 5 6]
 [7 8 9]]
OneD Array is :  [[1 2 3 4 5 6 7 8 9]]
```

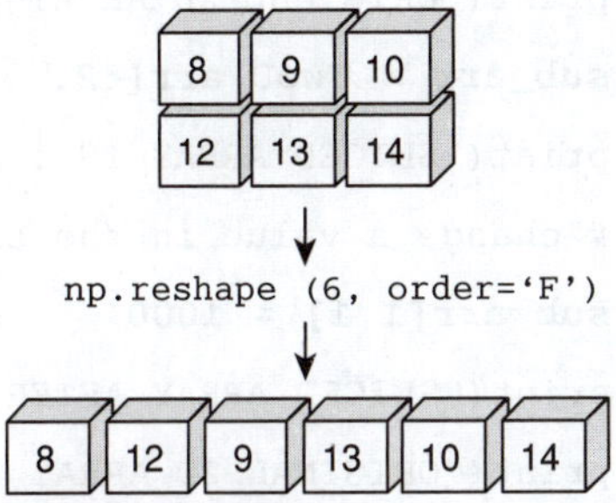

**Figure 11.15** Flattening array using `np.reshape()` method

Alternatively, we could have also passed –1 as value in the `reshape()` method to convert a 2D array into 1D array by writing,

OneD_arr = TwoD_arr.reshape(-1)

## 11.11 ARRAY SLICING: ACCESSING SUBARRAYS

Slicing an array is important when we have to analyze some array elements in other operations. These operations are very similar to how we performed on Python lists.

We use square brackets to access individual array elements. The same brackets can also be used to access subarrays with the *slice* notation, marked by the colon (:) character. Do you recall that the slicing syntax to access a slice of an array x is:

x[start:stop:step]

If any of these values is not specified, then default values are, start = 0, stop = size of dimension, step = 1. The step value can also be negative. In this case, the default values for start and stop are swapped. It helps in reversing the array. Let us see some examples to understand how slicing operation works.

Arr[3:6] will print elements from index 3 to 6. Index in an array starts from 0.
Arr[1::2] will print every second element from index items 1 to the end.
Arr[::-1] will print the array in the reverse order
Arr[4:] will print from index 4 to the end.

### Example 11.5

```
import numpy as np
Arr = np.array([0,1,2,3,4,5,6,7,8,9,10])
print("Arr[3:6] = ", Arr[3:6])
print("Arr[1::2] = ", Arr[1::2])
print("Arr[::-1] = ", Arr[::-1])
print("Arr[4:] = ", Arr[4:])
print("Arr[5::-2] = ", Arr[5::-2])
```

OUTPUT
```
Arr[3:6] =  [3 4 5]
Arr[1::2] =  [1 3 5 7 9]
Arr[::-1] =  [10 9 8 7 6 5 4 3 2 1 0]
Arr[4:] =  [ 4 5 6 7 8 9 10]
Arr[5::-2] =  [5 3 1]
```

## 11.11.1 Subarrays as No-copy Views

Note that when we create array slices, *views* from the array are returned rather than *copies* of the array data. This is, in fact, the main difference between a Python List and a NumPy Array. A list produces slices that are copies. The code given below clarifies this concept.

### Example 11.6

```python
import numpy as np
TwoD_arr = np.array([[1,2,3,4], [5,6,7,8],[9,4,5,1]])
print("ORIGINAL 2D ARRAY IS : \n",TwoD_arr)
sub_arr = TwoD_arr[:2, :2]
print("SLICED ARRAY IS : \n",sub_arr)
# change a value in the sliced array
sub_arr[1,1] = 1000
print("SLICED ARRAY AFTER MODIFICATION IS : \n",sub_arr)
print("ORIGINAL 2D ARRAY AFTER MODIFICATION IS : \n",TwoD_arr)
```

**OUTPUT**
```
ORIGINAL 2D ARRAY IS :
[[1 2 3 4]
 [5 6 7 8]
 [9 4 5 1]]
SLICED ARRAY IS :
[[1 2]
 [5 6]]
SLICED ARRAY AFTER MODIFICATION IS :
[[ 1 2]
 [ 5 1000]]
ORIGINAL 2D ARRAY AFTER MODIFICATION IS :
[[ 1 2 3 4)
 [ 51000 7 8)
 [ 9 4 5 1]]
```

Note that this feature of NumPy array is very important especially when we have to access large datasets. We can simply access and process pieces of these datasets without copying the entire dataset.

## 11.11.2 Creating Copies of Arrays

Though creating a view is a very important feature of NumPy array, at times we may need to create a copy of the data within an array or a subarray. In such a situation, we must use the `copy()` method.

### Example 11.7

```python
import numpy as np
TwoD_arr = np.array([[1,2,3,4], (5,6,7,8),(9,4,5,1]])
print("ORIGINAL 2D ARRAY IS : \n",TwoD_arr)
sub_arr = TwoD_arr[:2, :2].copy()
print ("SLICED ARRAY IS : \n",sub_arr)
# change a value in the sliced array
sub_arr[1,1] = 1000
print("SLICED ARRAY AFTER MODIFICATION IS : \n",sub_arr)
print("ORIGINAL2D ARRAY AFTER MODIFICATION IS: \n",TwoD_arr)
```

**OUTPUT**
```
ORIGINAL2D ARRAY IS :
[[1 2 3 4]
 [5 6 7 8]
 [9 4 5 1]]
SLICED ARRAY IS :
[[1 2]
 [5 6]]
SLICED ARRAY AFTER MODIFICATION IS :
[[ 1 2]
 [ 5 1000]]
ORIGINAL 2D ARRAY AFTER MODIFICATION IS :
[[1 2 3 4]
 [5 6 7 8]
 [9 4 5 1]]
```

## 11.12 RESHAPING OF ARRAYS

As discussed earlier, the shape of an array is the number of elements in each dimension. Reshaping an array means changing the shape of an array. This can be done by adding or removing dimensions or changing the number of elements in each dimension. In Python, any array can be reshaped using the `reshape()` method.

> Trying to convert a 1D array with 8 elements to a 2D array with 3 elements in each dimension will raise an error.

*Can we reshape into any shape?* Yes, we can reshape an array into any shape as long as number of elements in both the original as well as reshaped array is same. This means that we can reshape an 8 elements 1D array into a 2D array with 4 elements in 2 rows or 2 elements in 4 rows. But it cannot be reshaped into a 2D array with 3 elements in 3 rows as a 3 × 3 2D array will have 3 × 3 = 9 elements.

Let us now put the numbers 1 through 9 in a two-dimensional 3 × 3 array, we can write

```
import numpy as np
TwoD_arr = np.arange(1, 10).reshape((3, 3))
print("TWO DIMENSIONAL ARRAY IS : \n",TwoD_arr)
```

OUTPUT
```
TWO DIMENSIONAL ARRAY IS :
 [[1 2 3]
 [4 5 6]
 [7 8 9]]
```

In the above code, size of the initial array must match the size of the reshaped array. Usually, the `reshape()` method uses a no-copy view of the initial array, but this is not always the case (when dealing with non-contiguous memory buffers).

The `reshape()` method can also be used for converting a one-dimensional array into a two-dimensional row or column matrix as shown below.

```
import numpy as np
OneD_arr = np.array([1,2,3,4,5,6])
print(" ORIGINAL 1-D ARRAY: \n",OneD_arr)
arr - OneD_arr.reshape((2,3))
print("2-D ARRAY WITH 2 ROWS AND 3 COLUMNS : \n",arr)
arr = OneD_arr.reshape((3,2))
print("2-D ARRAY WITH 3 ROWS AND 2 COLUMNS : \n",arr)
```

OUTPUT
```
ORIGINAL 1-D ARRAY
[1 2 3 4 5 6]
2-D ARRAY WITH 2 ROWS AND 3 COLUMNS :
[[1 2 3]
 [4 5 6]]
2-D ARRAY WITH 3 ROWS AND 2 COLUMNS :
[[1 2]
 [3 4]
 [5 6]]
```

### 11.12.1 Unknown Dimension

NumPy also allows users to specify one "unknown" dimension while reshaping an array. This means that you do not have to specify an exact number for one of the dimensions in the reshape method. You can simply pass –1 as value for any one dimension and let NumPy calculate its correct value for you.

For example, in the code given below, we have specified –1 for number of rows. NumPy has, by itself, calculated the number of rows to be 3 so as to accommodate all 12 elements and thus, given the desired output.

### Example 11.8

```
import numpy as np
a= np.array([400,200,350,550,500, 800, 200, 700, 1000, 2000, 300,400])
arr = a.reshape(2,-1,2)
print("3D Array is :\n",arr)
```

OUTPUT
```
3D Array is :
[[[ 400  200]
  [ 350  550]
  [ 500  800]]
 [[ 200  700]
  [1000 2000]
  [ 300  400]]]
```

However, note that we cannot pass –1 for more than one dimension.

## 11.12.2 Reshaping vs. Resizing Arrays

When operating with arrays that do not have same dimensions, we can resize one of them. The `np.resize()` function returns a new array with specified shape (passed as argument to this function).

If we pass the original array along with the new dimensions and the new array is larger than the original one, the new array is filled with copies of the original array that are repeated as many times as is needed.

**Example 11.9**

```
# Resizing Array
import numpy as np
arr = np.array([[1,2,3],[4,5,6],[7,8,9]])
print("ORIGINAL ARRAY :\n",arr)
arr1 = np.resize(arr,(4,4))
print("RESIZED ARRAY :\n",arr1)
```

OUTPUT
ORIGINAL ARRAY :
[[1 2 3]
[4 5 6]
[7 8 9]]
RESIZED ARRAY :
[[1 2 3 4]
[5 6 7 8]
[9 1 2 3]
[4 5 6 7]]

Besides resizing, we can also reshape the array. Reshaping means giving a new shape to an array without changing its data. When an array is reshaped, the total size of the new array is unchanged. For example, a 4 × 3 array has 12 elements; while reshaping the total number of elements will still remain 12.

> NumPy allow users to ask for more information about the modules, functions or classes. For example, `lookfor()` function is used to do a keyword search on docstrings. Similarly, the `info()` function is used to get quick explanations and code examples of functions, classes, or modules. The instructions using these functions are given below.
> ```
> #Look up info on 'mean' with 'np.lookfor()'
> print(np.lookfor("mean"))
> #Get info on data types with 'np.info()'
> np.info(np.ndarray.dtype)
> ```

## 11.13 ARRAY CONCATENATION (JOINING) AND SPLITTING

We can combine multiple arrays into a single array and also split a single array into multiple arrays.

### 11.13.1 Joining Arrays

Two arrays can be joined or concatenated in NumPy using methods like `np.concatenate()`, `np.hstack()` and `np.vstack()`. In this section, we will discuss all of these methods.

**np.concatenate()** method takes a tuple or list of arrays to be concatenated as its first argument. We can concatenate two or more arrays together using this method.

However, remember that while concatenating two arrays, the number of dimensions needs to be the same. This means that only a 1D array can be concatenated to another 1D array.

```
# Concatenating two arrays
import numpy as np
arr1 = np.array([1,2,3,4])
arr2 = np.array([5,6,7])
arr3 = np.concatenate([arr1,arr2})
print("THE CONCATENATED ARRAY IS : ",arr3)
OUTPUT
THE CONCATENATED ARRAY IS : [1 2 3 4 5 6 7]
```

```
#Concatenating three 1D arrays
import numpy as np
arr1 = np.array([1,2,3,4]}
arr2 = np.array([5,6,7])
arr3 = np.array([8,9]}
arr4 = np.concatenate([arr1,arr2,arr3])
print{"THE CONCATENATED ARRAY IS : ",arr4)
OUTPUT
THE CONCATENATED ARRAY IS : [1 2 3 4 5 6 7 8 9]
```

| | |
|---|---|
| `#Concatenating two 2D arrays rowwise`<br>`import numpy as np`<br>`arr1 = np.array([[1,2,3],[4,5,6]])`<br>`arr2 = np.array([[7,8,9],[1,3,5]])`<br>**`arr3 = np.concatenate([arr11arr2])`**<br>`print("THE CONCATENATED ARRAY IS : \n",arr3)`<br>**OUTPUT**<br>`THE CONCATENATED ARRAY IS :`<br>`[[1 2 3]`<br>`[4 5 6]`<br>`[7 8 9]`<br>`[1 3 5]]` | `#Concatenating two 2D arrays columnwise`<br>`import numpy as np`<br>`arr1 = np.array([[1,2,3],[4,5,6]])`<br>`arr2 = np.array([[7,8,9],[1,3,5]])`<br>**`arr3 = np.concatenate([arr1,arr2], axis=1}`**<br>`print("THECONCATENATED ARRAY IS : \n",arr3)`<br>**OUTPUT**<br>`THE CONCATENATED ARRAY IS :`<br>`[[1 2 3 7 8 9]`<br>`[4 5 6 1 3 5]]` |

`np.vstack()` and `np.hstack()`: When the two arrays to be concatenated are of different dimensions, then it is better to use the `np.vstack()` method (vertical stack) or the `np.hstack()` method (horizontal stack). The use of these two dimensions is illustrated in the code given below. In fact, there is another method – `np.dstack()` that will stack arrays along the third axis.

### Example 11.10

| | |
|---|---|
| `#Concatenating using vstack()`<br>`import numpy as np`<br>`arr1 = np.array([1,2,3])`<br>`arr2 = np.array([[4,5,6],[7,8,9]])`<br>**`arr3 = np.vstack([arr1,arr2])`**<br>`print{"THE CONCATENATED ARRAY IS : \n ",arr3}`<br>**OUTPUT**<br>`THE CONCATENATED ARRAY IS :`<br>`[[1 2 3]`<br>`[4 5 6]`<br>`[7 8 9]]` | `#Concatenating using hstack()`<br>`import numpy as np`<br>`arr1 = np.array([[1,2],[3,4]])`<br>`arr2 = np.array{[[4,5,6),[7,8,9]])`<br>**`arr3 = np.hstack([arr1,arr2])`**<br>`print("THE CONCATENATED ARRAY IS : \n ",arr3)`<br>**OUTPUT**<br>`THE CONCATENATED ARRAY IS :`<br>`[[1 2 4 5 6]`<br>`[3 4 7 8 9]]` |

Note that while using the `np.hstack()` function, the number of dimensions is the same and that the number of rows in both arrays is the same. This means that when we stack arrays with shapes (2,3) and (2,4), the resultant array has a shape of (2,4). The two arrays must have the same number of rows. Similarly, the number of columns must match while using the `vstack()` method.

## 11.14 APPENDING ARRAYS

Two arrays can be appended in such a way that values from the second array is glued to the end of the first array. The NumPy `np.append()` function does the work of appending two arrays. The syntax of this function can be given as,

> `numpy.append(arr, values, axis=None)`

where,
**arr** is an array-like object or a NumPy array. The values are appended to a copy of this array.
**values** are array-like objects and they are appended to the end of the "arr" elements.
**axis** specifies the axis along which values are appended. If no value is specified, the arrays are flattened.

## Example 11.11

```
# Appending a 1-D array
import numpy as np
arr1 = np.array([1,2,3,4,5])
arr2 = np.array([6,7,8,9])
print("APPENDED ARRAY IS :\n")
arr3 = np.append(arr1,arr2)
print(arr3)
OUTPUT
APPENDED ARRAY IS:
[1 2 3 4 5 6 7 8 9]
```

```
# Appending 2-D array
import numpy as np
arr1 = np.array([[1,2,3],[4,5,6],(7,8,9)])
arr2 = np.array([[0,1,2],[3,4,5],[6,7,8]])
print("APPENDED ARRAY IS :\n")
arr3 = np.append(arr1,arr2,axis=1)
print(arr3)
OUTPUT
APPENDED ARRAY IS :
[[1 2 3 0 1 2]
 [4 5 6 3 4 5]
 [7 8 9 6 7 8]]
```

Note that when appending 2D arrays, we have appended as an extra column by specifying axis = 1. If axis = 0, then the array is appended as rows.

## 11.15 SPLITTING OF ARRAYS

The opposite of concatenation is splitting. An array can be split using np.split(), np.hsplit() or the np.vsplit() methods. For each of these, we can pass a list of indices giving the split points.

Create a two-dimensional 4 × 4 array using np.arrange() method. Split the array vertically as well horizontally into two halves.

## Example 11.12

```
# vsplit()
import numpy as np
arr = np.arange(16).reshape((4,4))
print("TWO DIMENSIONAL ARRAY IS :
\n", arr)
upper, lower = np.vsplit(arr,[2])
print("THE UPPER HALF OF THE ARRAY IS :
\n",upper)
print("THE LOWER HALF OF THE ARRAY IS :
\n",lower)
OUTPUT
TWO DIMENSIONAL ARRAY IS :
[[ 0  1  2  3)
 [ 4  5  6  7]
 [ 8  9 10 11]
 [12 13 14 15]]
```

```
# hsplit()
import numpy as np
arr = np.arange(16).reshape((4,4))
print("TWO DIMENSIONAL ARRAY IS : \n", arr)
left, right = np.hsplit(arr, [2])
print("THE LEFT HALF OF THE ARRAY IS :
\n",left)
print("THE RIGHT HALF OF THE ARRAY IS :
\n",right)
OUTPUT
TWO DIMENSIONAL ARRAY IS :
[[ 0  1  2  3]
 [ 4  5  6  7]
 [ 8  9 10 11]
 [12 13 14 15]]
THE LEFT HALF OF THE ARRAY IS :
[[ 0  1]
 [ 4  5]
 [ 8  9]
 [12 13]]
THE RIGHT HALF OF THE ARRAY IS :
[[ 2  3]
 [ 6  7]
 [10 11]
 [14 15]]
```

## 11.16 HOW NUMPY BROADCASTING WORKS

The concept of broadcasting is also applicable to NumPy arrays. This happens when arithmetic operations are performed on arrays of different shapes. For example, when an array that is larger in size is operated with an array of smaller size, the smaller array is repeated multiple times to perform an operation (such as a sum, multiplication, etc.) on the larger array. Here, we need to apply broadcasting mechanism.

However, there are some rules that we need to follow to use broadcasting with arrays. First, we must make sure that the broadcasting is successful and that the dimensions of the two arrays are compatible. Two dimensions are compatible when they are equal. Also, two dimensions are compatible when one of them is 1. If the dimensions of two arrays are not compatible, then ValueError will be returned.

### Example 11.13

```
import numpy as np
# Initialize 'x'
x = np.ones((4,3))
# Check shape of 'x'
print("Dimensions of x: ",x.shape)
# Initialize 'y'
y = np.random.random((4,3))
#Check shape of 'y'
print("Dimensons of y : ", y.shape)
#Add 'x' and 'y'
print(x + y)
OUTPUT
Dimensions of x : (4, 3)
Dimensions of y : (4, 3)
[[1.2388898  1.61297487 1.16992323]
 [1.33369933 1.12230165 1.10217694]
 [1.07697973 1.14186119 1.36611884]
 [1.00416233 1.5186616  1.3807092 ]]
```

```
import numpy as np
# Initialize 'x'
x = np.ones((4,3))
#Check shape of 'x'
print(" Dimensions of x: ",x.shape)
#Initialize 'y'
y = np.random.random((4,1))
# Check shape of 'y'
print("Dimensons of y : ",y.shape)
#Add 'x' and 'y'
print(x + y)
OUTPUT
Dimensions of x : (4, 3)
Dimensons of y : (4, 1)
[[1.51196632 1.51196632 1.51196632]
 [1.75200391 1.75200391 1.75200391]
 [1.96067045 1.96067045 1.96067045]
 [1.07990718 1.07990718 1.07990718]]
```

Note that when two arrays that have not same but compatible dimensions are operated, then the size of the resulting array is the maximum along each dimension of the input arrays. This means that if we subtract two arrays x and y with dimensions (4,3) and (1,3) respectively the resultant array will have dimensions (4,4).

Last, but not the least, the arrays can only be broadcast together if they are compatible in all dimensions. Consider the given example, which illustrates this concept.

Note that two arrays are compatible even when one of them is equal to 1. When one array has size 1 and the other array has a size greater than 1, then the first array behaves as if it were copied along that dimension. However, the shape of the resulting array will always be the maximum size along each dimension of the two arrays.

### Example 11.14

```
import numpy as np
# Initialize 'x'
x = np.ones((3,4))
# Initialize 'y'
y = np.arange(2,3,4)
# Subtract 'x' and 'y'
print(x - y)
OUTPUT
[[-1. -1. -1. -1.]
 [-1. -1. -1. -1.]
 [-1. -1. -1. -1.]]
```

```
import numpy as np
# Initialize 'x'
x = np.ones((3,4))
# Initialize 'y'
y = np.arange(2,1,4)
# Subtract 'x' and 'y'
print(x - y)
OUTPUT
ValueError
```

## 11.17 PERFORMING MATHEMATICAL OPERATIONS ON NUMPY ARRAYS

Like data of any other type, we can also perform mathematical operations like +, –,*, /or % to add, subtract, multiply, divide or calculate the remainder of two (or more) arrays. Besides these mathematical operators, NumPy also has functions like `np.add()`, `np.subtract()`, `np.multiply()`, `np.divide()` and `np.remainder()` to do the same task.

NumPy also has functions to calculate exponentiation – `np.exp()`, square root – `np.sqrt()`, natural logarithm – `np.log()`, sines or cosines with `np.sin()` and `np.cos()`. Other aggregate functions that work with arrays are given in Table 11.3.

For comparing two array elements, we have the ==, > and < operators. To check for equality between two arrays, we can also use `np.array.equal()` function. In addition to comparing, logical operations on arrays can be performed with `np.logical_or()`, `np.logical_not()` and `np.logical_and()` functions. Recall that AND returns 1 if both elements are same, OR returns 1 if either or both of them are same and NOT negates the input value to give the output.

Instead of specifying the normal integer index of the element to be accessed, we can specify Boolean indexing to select those values from the array that fulfil a certain condition. To formulate this condition, we can also use logical operators | (OR) and & (AND) as shown in the accompanying code.

| Table 11.3 | Aggregate functions |
|---|---|
| a.sum() | Array-wise sum |
| a.min() | Array-wise minimum value |
| b.max(axis=0) | Maximum value of an array row |
| b.cumsum(axis=1) | Cumulative sum of the elements |
| a.mean() | Mean |
| b.median() | Median |
| a.corrcoef() | Correlation coefficient |
| np.std(b) | Standard deviation |

### Example 11.15

```
import numpy as np
arr = np.array([1,2,3,4,5,6,7,8,9,10])
print(arr[arr>5])
print(arr[(arr>6) I (arr%2==0)])
OUTPUT
[ 6 7 8 9 10)
[ 2 4 6 7 8 9 10]
```

## 11.18 TRANSPOSING ARRAYS

Transposing an array means switching its dimensions. An array with 3 rows and 4 columns will now have 4 rows and 3 columns after being transposed.

There are two NumPy functions for transposing an array – `T()` and `np.transpose()`. Note that there will be no effect of `transpose()` function on a 1D array.

### Example 11.16

```
#Transposing a 1-D array
import numpy as np
arr = np.array([1,2,3,4])
print{"ORIGINAL ARRAY :\n",arr)
print("TRANSPOSED ARRAY IS :\n",arr.T)
OUTPUT
ORIGINAL ARRAY :
[1 2 3 4)
TRANSPOSED ARRAY IS :
[1 2 3 4)
```

```
#Transposing a 2-D array
import numpy as np
arr = np.array(
[[1,2,3,4],
 [5,6,7,8],
 [9,0,1,2],
 [3,4,5,6]])
print("ORIGINALARRAY :\n" ,arr)
print("TRANSPOSED ARRAY IS :\n",np.trans-
pose(arr))
OUTPUT
ORIGINAL ARRAY :
[[1 2 3 4]
 [5 6 7 8]
 [9 0 1 2]
 [3 4 5 6]]
TRANSPOSED ARRAY IS :
[[1 5 9 3]
 [2 6 0 4]
 [3 7 1 5]
 [4 8 2 6]]
```

## 11.19 INSERTING AND DELETING ARRAY ELEMENTS

We can also insert elements or delete elements from an existing array. In NumPy, the `insert()` method is used to insert an element or column. The difference between the `insert()` and the `append()` method is that when using the former, we can specify the index at which the element(s) are to be added. However, the `append()` method always adds a value to the end of the array.

The `insert()` function inserts values in the input array along the given axis and before the given index. If the axis is not mentioned, the input array is flattened. The syntax of the `insert()` function is,

> **numpy.insert(arr, obj, values, axis)**

where,
**arr** is the Input array
**obj** specifies the index before which insertion is to be made
**values** are the array of values to be inserted
**axis** denotes the axis along which values have to be inserted.

### Example 11.17

```
# Inserting Values in Array
import numpy as np
arr = np.array([1,2,3,4,5])
print("ORIGINAL ARRAY IS :\n",arr)
arr = np.insert(arr, 2, 10)
print("ARRAY AFTER INSERTING VALUE IS :\n",arr)
```
OUTPUT
```
ORIGINAL ARRAY IS :
[1 2 3 4 5)
ARRAY AFTER INSERTING VALUE IS:
[ 1 2 10 3 4 5)
```

### 11.19.1 Deleting Values from an Array

The NumPy `np.delete()` function is used to delete one or more elements from an array. It returns a new array with the specified subarray deleted from the input array. The syntax of `np.delete()` function can be given as,

> **numpy.delete(arr, obj, axis)**

where,
**arr** is the input array
**obj** can be a slice, an integer or array of integers, indicating the subarray to be deleted from the input array.
**axis** is the axis along which values have to be deleted from the given subarray. If axis not specified then arr is flattened.

### Example 11.18

```
import numpy as np
arr = np.arange(10)
print(" ORIGINAL ARRAY IS : ", arr)
print("Shape : ", arr.shape)
# deletion from 1D array
arr1 = np.delete(arr, 5)
print("Array after deleting 5 : ", arr1)
print("Shape : ", arr1.shape)
arr1 = np.delete(arr, [6,7))
print(" Array after deleting 6 and 7 is : " , arr1)
print(" Shape : ", arr.shape)
```

OUTPUT
```
ORIGINAL ARRAY 15: [0 1 2 3 4 5 6 7 8 9]
Shape : (10,)
Array after deleting 5 : [0 1 2 3 4 6 7 8 9]
Shape: (9,)
Array after deleting 6 and 7 is : [0 1 2 3 4 5 8 9]
Shape : (10,)
```

## 11.19.2 Check if NumPy Array is Empty

The `size()` method which returns the total number of elements in the array can be used to check if an array has values or if it is empty. This is illustrated in the code given below.

### Example 11.19

```
import numpy as np
arr = np.ones(10)
if(arr.size == 0):
    print("The given Array is empty")
else:
    print("The array = ", arr)
```

OUTPUT
The array = [1. 1. 1. 1. 1. 1. 1. 1. 1. 1.]

In the above code, since there were elements in the array, the array was printed. Otherwise, a message stating that the array is empty would have been displayed.

Note that the `size()` method is also used to find the length of the array. The code given below prints the length of the 2D array.

### Example 11.20

```
import numpy as np
arr = np.arange(12).reshape(3,4)
print("THE ARRAY IS: ", arr)
print("LENGTH OF THE ARRAY IS :", arr.size)
```

OUTPUT
THE ARRAY IS:  [[ 0  1  2  3]
 [ 4  5  6  7]
 [ 8  9 10 11]]
LENGTH OF THE ARRAY IS : 12

## 11.20 FIND THE INDEX OF A VALUE

The `where()` method of NumPy module is used to find the index of value in an array. The code given below demonstrates the use of this method.

Note that we have printed only `index[0]`. This is because the `where()` method will also return the `datatype`. `Index[0]` will just print the location of the value and not its data type.

### Example 11.21

```
import numpy as np
arr = np.arange(10)
print("THE ARRAY IS: ", arr)
index = np.where(arr==6)
print("THE INDEX OF VALUE 6 is: ", index[0])
```

OUTPUT
THE ARRAY IS:  [0 1 2 3 4 5 6 7 8 9]
THE INDEX OF VALUE 6 is: [6]

## 11.21 SAVING NUMPY ARRAY TO CSV FILE

To export a NumPy array to a CSV file, the `savetxt()` method of the NumPy module can be used as shown in the code given below.

### Example 11.22

```
import numpy as np
arr = np.arange(10)
np.savetxt("myArray.csv",arr)
print("SAVED TO THE FILE......")
```

OUTPUT
SAVED TO THE FILE......

Note that the above code will generate a CSV file in the location where your Python code file is stored. However, to create a file in a specific location, the complete path has to be specified in the `savetxt()` method.

## 11.22 SORTING A NUMPY ARRAY

A NumPy array can be sorted using the `sort()` method of the NumPy module. The syntax of the `sort()` function can be given as,

```
numpy.sort(array, axis=-1, kind='quicksort', order=None)
```

where,
array is the NumPy array that has to be sorted
axis is the axis along which the array will be sorted. The default value is –1, i.e., the last axis.
kind specifies the type of sorting algorithm to be used. Values can be 'mergesort', 'heapsort', 'stable' and 'quicksort'.
order can be a single-column name or list of column names along which sorting needs to be done.

The code given below demonstrates the application of the `sort()` method.

### Example 11.23

```
import numpy as np
arr = np.array([4,0,9,1,6,8,2,3,7,5])
print("ORIGINAL ARRAY IS : ", arr)
arr.sort()
print("SORTED ARRAY IS : ", arr)
```

OUTPUT
```
ORIGINAL ARRAY IS :  [4 0 9 1 6 8 2 3 7 5]
SORTED ARRAY IS :  [0 1 2 3 4 5 6 7 8 9]
```

## 11.23 NORMALIZE ARRAY

Normalizing an array is the process of bringing the array values to some defined range. For example, we can normalize an array so that its values vary from –1 to 1. The formula for normalization is as follows:

$$x = (x - xmin) / (xmax - xmin)$$

The code given below illustrates normalizing a NumPy array.

### Example 11.24

```
import numpy
arr = numpy.array([450,620,390,530,250,320,410])
arr_max = arr.max()
arr_min = arr.min()
arr = (arr - arr_min)/(arr_max - arr_min)
print("After normalization array is : ",arr)
```

OUTPUT
```
After normalization array is :
[0.54054054  1.          0.37837838
 0.75675676
 0.          0.18918919  0.43243243]
```

## 11.24 ARRAY SUBSETS

We can create one or more subsets of a NumPy array. These subsets will also be NumPy array objects. However, while doing this, make sure that the returned objects are copies.

Creating such subsets from an existing NumPy array is based on several criteria. For example, we can create a subset of an array that has only diagonal elements from the original array. Or, we can create a subset having a dimension omitted if there is only one element in that dimension. The subset can also be created based on Boolean conditions for each of the indices or based on an array of indices.

The NumPy module provides several methods that allow users to create arrays containing a subset of elements from an existing array of objects. These methods can create subsets depending on user specified criteria. Some of these methods are `compress()`, `diagonal()`, `squeeze()` and `take()`. All these methods are discussed in this section.

### 11.24.1 Subset an Array Based on a Boolean condition

The `compress()` method of the NumPy module can be used to specify a Boolean expression for each element in the array. The result of this Boolean expression will indicate the presence or absence of that element in the new array. Note that this Boolean expression for each element is specified as a flat 1D array.

### Example 11.25

```
import numpy as np
arr3D = np.arange(36).reshape(3,4,3)
print("3D ARRAY IS : \n", arr3D)
newarr = arr3D.compress([1,1,1])
print("FIRST THREE ELEMENTS OF 3D ARRAY : ",
newarr)
newarr = arr3D.compress([0,0,1,1,1])
print("THIRD FOURTH AND FIFTH ELEMENTS OF 3D
ARRAY : ", newarr)
```

OUTPUT
3D ARRAY IS :
[[[ 0  1  2]
  [ 3  4  5]
  [ 6  7  8]
  [ 9 10 11]]
 [[12 13 14]
  [15 16 17]
  [18 19 20]
  [21 22 23]]
 [[24 25 26]
  [27 28 29]
  [30 31 32]2
  [33 34 35]]]
FIRST THREE ELEMENTS OF 3D ARRAY
: [0 1 2]
THIRD FOURTH AND FIFTH ELEMENTS
OF 3D ARRAY : [2 3 4]

### 11.24.2 Remove a Redundant Dimension from an Array Object

Consider an array needs to be reduced of a dimension. This is possible only when there is one element in that dimension. To reduce dimension of an array, the `squeeze()` method of the NumPy module is used as shown in the code given below.

### Example 11.26

```
import numpy as np
arr2D = np.array([[1,2,3]])
print("2D ARRAY IS : ",arr2D)
squeezed_arr = arr2D.squeeze()
print("ARRAY AFTER REDUCING DIMESNION IS : ",squeezed_arr)
```

OUTPUT
2D ARRAY IS :    [[1 2 3]]
ARRAY AFTER REDUCING DIMESNION
IS :  [1 2 3]

### 11.24.3 Retrieve Diagonals from an Array

The `diagonal()` of the NumPy module is used to retrieve diagonals of multi-dimensional arrays and matrices.

### Example 11.27

```
import numpy as np
arr3D = np.arange(27).reshape(3,3,3)
print("3D ARRAY IS : \n", arr3D)
print("DIAGONAL ELEMENTS FOR AXIS1 = 1 AND
AXIS2 = 2 ARE : ")
print(arr3D.diagonal(axis1=1,axis2=2))
```

OUTPUT
3D ARRAY IS :
[[[ 0  1  2]
  [ 3  4  5]
  [ 6  7  8]]
 [[ 9 10 11]
  [12 13 14]
  [15 16 17]]
 [[18 19 20]
  [21 22 23]
  [24 25 26]]]
DIAGONAL ELEMENTS FOR AXIS1 = 1 AND
AXIS2 = 2 ARE :
[[ 0  4  8]
 [ 9 13 17]
 [18 22 26]]

## 11.24.4 Sub-setting NumPy Arrays Using Indexing

We have so far been using regular indexing to create subsets of a 2D array. The indexes before the comma refer to the rows while those after the comma refer to the columns. Note that in the code given below, the : is used for slicing. Here, it tells Python to include all rows.

### Example 11.28

```
import numpy as np
arr = np.arange(12).reshape(4,3)
print("TWO DIMENSIONAL ARRAY IS :\n", arr)
print("VALUES IN FIRST COLUMN ARE : ", arr[:,0])
```

OUTPUT
```
TWO DIMENSIONAL ARRAY IS :
 [[ 0  1  2]
  [ 3  4  5]
  [ 6  7  8]
  [ 9 10 11]]
VALUES IN FIRST COLUMN ARE :  [0 3 6 9]
```

## 11.24.5 Indexing using Index Arrays

NumPy also allows users to do indexing by using an array as an index. When we do this, a copy of the original array is returned. Apart from arrays, NumPy arrays can be indexed with any other sequence except tuples. Before we get into this, do not forget the index of the first element is 0 and that of the last element is –1.

### Example 11.29

```
import numpy as np
# Create a sequence of integers from 10 to 1 with a step of -2
arr = np.arange(20,1,-2)
print("ARRAY IS : ",arr)
#Creating an index array
arr_index = [4,-5,9,1,-7]
newarr = arr[arr_index]
print("ELEMENTS AT INDEX 4,-5,9,1 and -7 IN THE ARRAY ARE : ",newarr)
```

OUTPUT
```
ARRAY IS :    [20 18 16 14 12 10  8  6  4  2]
ELEMENTS AT INDEX 4,-5,9,1 and -7 IN THE ARRAY ARE :    [12 10  2 18 14]
```

We can also slice a NumPy array by specifying the values for start : stop : step. This will create a shallow copy or a view of the original array.

### Example 11.30

```
import numpy as np
# Create a sequence of integers from 10 to 1 with a step of -2
arr = np.arange(50,1,-3)
print("ARRAY IS : ",arr)
print("ARRAY FROM 10th ELEMENT ONWARDS : ",arr[10:])
print("ELEMENTS FROM 12th POSITION FROM THE END TILL 15th POSITION FROM THE BEGINNING : ",arr[-12:15:1])
```

OUTPUT
```
ARRAY IS :    [50 47 44 41 38 35 32 29 26 23 20 17 14 11  8  5  2]
ARRAY FROM 10th ELEMENT ONWARDS : [20 17 14 11  8  5  2]
ELEMENTS FROM 12th POSITION FROM THE END TILL 15th POSITION FROM THE BEGINNING :    [35 32 29 26 23 20 17 14 11  8]
```

We can also use Ellipsis along with basic slicing. Ellipsis (…) selects elements of the same length as obtained from the dimensions of the array. Therefore, indexing a 2D array by writing arr[…,1] is same as writing arr[::1].

## 11.24.6 Purely Integer Indexing in 2D Arrays

When integers are used for indexing a 2D array, each element of the first dimension is paired with the element of the second

### Example 11.31

```
import numpy as np
a = np.array([[1,2,3],[4,5,6],[7,8,9]])
print(a[[0 ,1 ,2 ],[2 ,1 ,0]])
```

OUTPUT
```
[3 5 7]
```

dimension. For example, in the code given below, the pairing goes as (0,2),(1,1),(2,0). This will select second element of the first 1D array, first element of the second 1D array and first element of the third 1D array respectively.

### 11.24.7 Boolean Indexing

We can specify indexing with Boolean expression as the index. Elements satisfying the Boolean expression are returned. Such an indexing is used for filtering the desired values.

**Example 11.32**

```
import numpy as np
arr = np.arange(2,50,2)
print(arr[arr<25])
```

OUTPUT
```
[ 2  4  6  8 10 12 14
 16 18 20 22 24]
```

## PROGRAMMER'S ZONE

1. **Write a Python program to insert elements in a row as well as in a column of a 2D array.**
   ```
   import numpy as np
   arr = np.arange(12).reshape(4,3)
   print("\n\n2D arr : \n", arr)
   print("Shape : ", arr.shape)
   arr = np.insert(arr, 1, 5, axis = 1)
   print("\nArray after insertion : \n", arr)
   print("Shape : ", arr.shape)
   arr = np.insert(arr, 2, 6, axis = 0)
   print("\nArray after insertion : \n", arr)
   print("Shape : ", arr.shape)
   ```

   **OUTPUT**
   ```
   2D arr :
    [[ 0  1  2]
    [ 3  4  5]
    [ 6  7  8]
    [ 9 10 11]]
   Shape :  (4, 3)
   Array after insertion :
    [[ 0  5  1  2]
    [ 3  5  4  5]
    [ 6  5  7  8]
    [ 9  5 10 11]]
   Shape :  (4, 4)
   Array after insertion :
    [[ 0  5  1  2]
    [ 3  5  4  5]
    [ 6  6  6  6]
    [ 6  5  7  8]
    [ 9  5 10 11]]
   Shape :  (5, 4)
   ```

2. **Write a Python program to insert elements in a row as well as in a column of a 2D array at multiple insertion points.**
   ```
   import numpy as np
   arr = np.arange(12).reshape(4,3)
   # 7 will be inserted just before 1 and 5 in the array
   ```

```
arr = np.insert(arr, (1,5),7)
print("\n Array after inserting at two points :\n", arr)
print("Shape : ", arr.shape)
arr = np.arange(12).reshape(4,3)
# 8 will be inserted before the first and second column in the array
arr = np.insert(arr, (1,2),8, axis = 1)
print("\nArray after inserting at at two points : \n", arr)
print("Shape : ", arr.shape)
```

**OUTPUT**
```
Array after inserting at two points :
[ 0  7  1  2  3  4  7  5  6  7  8  9 10 11]
Shape : (14,)
Array after inserting at at two points :
 [[ 0  8  1  8  2]
  [ 3  8  4  8  5]
  [ 6  8  7  8  8]
  [ 9  8 10  8 11]]
Shape : (4, 5)
```

3. **Write a Python program to delete a row as well as a column from a 2D array.**
```
import numpy as np
arr = np.arange(16).reshape(4,4)
print("ORIGINAL ARRAY IS : \n",arr)
print("Shape : ", arr.shape)
arr1 = np.delete(arr, 1, 0)
print("ARRAY AFTER DELETING FIRST ROW :\n",arr1)
print("Shape : ", arr1.shape)
arr1 = np.delete(arr, 2, axis = 1)
print("ARRAY AFTER DELETING SECOND COLUMN :\n",arr1)
print("Shape : ", arr1.shape)
```

**OUTPUT**
```
ORIGINAL ARRAY IS :
 [[ 0  1  2  3]
  [ 4  5  6  7]
  [ 8  9 10 11]
  [12 13 14 15]]
Shape : (4, 4)
ARRAY AFTER DELETING FIRST ROW :
 [[ 0  1  2  3]
  [ 8  9 10 11]
  [12 13 14 15]]
Shape : (3, 4)
ARRAY AFTER DELETING SECOND COLUMN :
 [[ 0  1  3]
  [ 4  5  7]
  [ 8  9 11]
  [12 13 15]]
Shape : (4, 3)
```

4. **Write a program that masks multiple elements in a 1D array using a mask array.**
   ```
   import numpy as np
   arr = np.arange(10)
   print("ORIGINAL ARRAY IS : ", arr)
   mask = np.ones(len(arr), dtype=bool)
   # Masking elements at locations 1,3 and 5 from the array
   mask[[1,3,5]] = False
   print("\nMask set as : ", mask)
   arr1 = arr[mask]
   print("\n ARRAY AFTER MASKING ELEMENTS : ", arr1)
   ```

   **OUTPUT**
   ```
   ORIGINAL ARRAY IS :  [0 1 2 3 4 5 6 7 8 9]
   Mask set as :   [ True False  True False  True False  True  True  True  True]
   ARRAY AFTER MASKING ELEMENTS :   [0 2 4 6 7 8 9]
   ```

5. **Write a program to create a 2D array and demonstrate deleting multiple rows and columns from it.**
   ```
   import numpy as np
   arr = np.arange(25).reshape(5,5)
   print("ORIGINAL ARRAY IS : \n",arr)
   print("Shape : ", arr.shape)
   arr1 = np.delete(arr,[2,3], axis= 0)
   print("ARRAY AFTER DELETING SECOND AND THIRD ROWS IS :\n", arr1)
   arr1 = np.delete(arr,[1,3], axis= 1)
   print("ARRAY AFTER DELETING SECOND AND FOURTH COLUMNS IS :\n", arr1)
   ```

   **OUTPUT**
   ```
   ORIGINAL ARRAY IS :
    [[ 0  1  2  3  4]
    [ 5  6  7  8  9]
    [10 11 12 13 14]
    [15 16 17 18 19]
    [20 21 22 23 24]]
   Shape :  (5, 5)
   ARRAY AFTER DELETING SECOND AND THIRD ROWS IS :
    [[ 0  1  2  3  4]
    [ 5  6  7  8  9]
    [20 21 22 23 24]]
   ARRAY AFTER DELETING SECOND AND FOURTH COLUMNS IS :
    [[ 0  2  4]
    [ 5  7  9]
    [10 12 14]
    [15 17 19]
    [20 22 24]]
   ```

   > The `tolist()` method coverts the array to a list.

6. **Write a program that converts a NumPy array into a list in Python.**
   ```
   import numpy as np
   arr = np.arange(10)
   print("LIST OBTAINED FROM ARRAY IS : ",arr.tolist())
   ```

   **OUTPUT**
   ```
   LIST OBTAINED FROM ARRAY IS :   [0, 1, 2, 3, 4, 5, 6, 7, 8, 9]
   ```

7. **Write a program to sort a NumPy array in descending order.**

   ```
   import numpy as np
   arr = np.array([4,0,9,1,6,8,2,3,7,5])
   print("ORIGINAL ARRAY IS : ", arr)
   # Get a sorted copy of numpy array (Descending Order)
   arr = np.sort(arr)[::-1]
   print("SORTED ARRAY IS : ", arr)
   ```

   **OUTPUT**
   ```
   ORIGINAL ARRAY IS :   [4 0 9 1 6 8 2 3 7 5]
   SORTED ARRAY IS :    [9 8 7 6 5 4 3 2 1 0]
   ```

8. **Write a program that sorts rows of a 2D NumPy array in descending order. Also sort its columns in ascending order.**

   ```
   import numpy as np
   arr = np.array([[4,8,1],[6,3,9],[5,0,2],[4,8,1]])
   print("ORIGINAL ARRAY IS : \n", arr)
   # Sort the contents of each column in ascending order
   arr = np.sort(arr,axis=0)
   print("ARRAY WITH EACH COLUMN SORTED IS : \n", arr)
   # Sort the contents of each row in descending order
   arr = np.sort(arr,axis=1)[::-1]
   print("ARRAY WITH EACH ROW SORTED IN DESCENDING IS : \n", arr)
   ```

   **OUTPUT**
   ```
   ORIGINAL ARRAY IS :
    [[4 8 1]
     [6 3 9]
     [5 0 2]
     [4 8 1]]
   ARRAY WITH EACH COLUMN SORTED IS :
    [[4 0 1]
     [4 3 1]
     [5 8 2]
     [6 8 9]]
   ARRAY WITH EACH ROW SORTED IN DESCENDING IS :
    [[6 8 9]
     [2 5 8]
     [1 3 4]
     [0 1 4]]
   ```

9. **Write a program that converts a 1D array into a 3D array.**

   ```
   import numpy as np
   a= np.array([400,200,350,550,500, 800, 200, 700, 1000, 2000, 300,400])
   arr = a.reshape(2,3,2)
   print("3D Array is :\n",arr)
   ```

   **OUTPUT**
   ```
   3D Array is :
    [[[ 400  200]
      [ 350  550]
      [ 500  800]]
   ```

```
[[ 200  700]
 [1000 2000]
 [ 300  400]]]
```

10. **Write a program that prints the diagonal as well as lower diagonal and upper diagonal elements of a 2D array.**

    ```
    import numpy as np
    arr = np.array([[5,2,8],[4,1,9],[2,7,6]])
    print("TWO DIMENSIONAL ARRAY IS :\n", arr)
    print("DIAGONAL WITH OFFSET 0 IS : ", arr.diagonal(0))
    print("DIAGONAL WITH OFFSET -1 (LOWER DIAGONAL) IS : ", arr.diagonal(-1))
    print("DIAGONAL WITH OFFSET 1 (UPPER DIAGONAL) IS : ", arr.diagonal(1))
    ```

    **OUTPUT**
    ```
    TWO DIMENSIONAL ARRAY IS :
     [[5 2 8]
     [4 1 9]
     [2 7 6]]
    DIAGONAL WITH OFFSET 0 IS :  [5 1 6]
    DIAGONAL WITH OFFSET -1 (LOWER DIAGONAL) IS :  [4 7]
    DIAGONAL WITH OFFSET 1 (UPPER DIAGONAL) IS :  [2 9]
    ```

11. **Write a program that prints the square of even numbers in the array.**

    ```
    import numpy as np
    arr = np.arange(10)
    print(arr[arr%2==0]**2)
    ```

    **OUTPUT**
    ```
    [ 0  4 16 36 64]
    ```

12. **Write a program that sums the rows of a 2D array and prints the rows whose sum is a multiple of 10.**

    ```
    import numpy as np
    arr = np.array([[7,3],[13,6],[16,14]])
    sumrow = arr.sum(-1)  # -1 indicates sum the elements of a row
    print(arr[sumrow%10==0])
    ```

    **OUTPUT**
    ```
    [[ 7  3]
     [16 14]]
    ```

## 11.25 COMPARISON OF DIFFERENT DATA STRUCTURES

Data structures like lists, NumPy arrays, and Pandas data frames can all be used to hold a sequence of data. Each of these data structures are built for a specific purpose. For example,

**Lists** are simple built-in data structures in Python, which can be easily used as a container to hold data of different data types like integer, float, and object.

A list is a simple and flexible way to deal with a small amount of data in Python. It can be created by writing values within a pair of square brackets []. Lists are mutable, so they are naturally suitable for dealing with a dynamic sequence of data.

**NumPy array** supports N-dimensional array objects to allow fast scientific computing. Python lists and NumPy arrays are similar to traditional arrays in other programming languages including C, C++, Java.

While Python list focuses on flexibility, numpy.ndarray offers performance benefits. They are specifically optimized for high scientific computation as they support built-in mathematical functions and array operations. NumPy.ndarray has always been a preferred choice for working with large amount of data or high-dimensional data.

Table 11.4 given below summarizes key differences between the two data structures.

**Table 11.4** Comparison between Python list and NumPy.ndarray

|  | Mutability | Mutability | Accessibility | Others |
|---|---|---|---|---|
| list | Mutable | Heterogeneous | Integer position | Python built-in data structure |
| numpy.ndarray | Immutable | Homogeneous | Integer position | High-performance array calculation |

However, despite these differences, we can at any time, transform an object from one type to another. Figure 11.16 given below illustrates built-in functions that help us to do so.

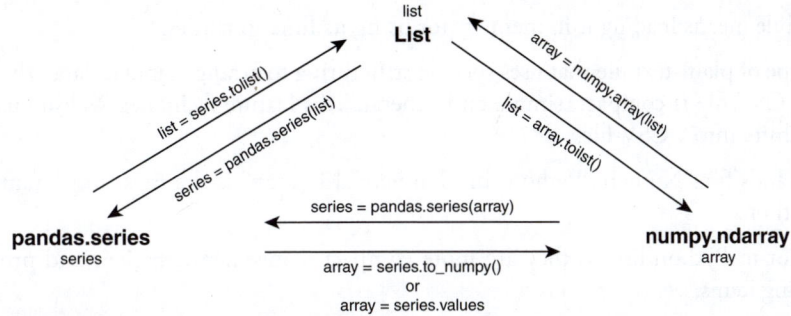

**Figure 11.16** Converting NumPy array to and from Pandas series and Python lists

## Key Terms

**Data:** A collection of facts that is processed to obtain information. This data can be anything including numbers, words, measurements, observations, etc.

**Data processing:** The process of converting raw data to meaningful information. This information may help to resolve a problem or improve an existing scenario.

**NumPy:** An open-source module of Python, which provides fast mathematical computation on arrays and matrices.

**Array:** A collection of similar data elements (of the same data type) that are stored in consecutive memory locations and are referenced by an index (also known as the subscript).

**Subscript:** An ordinal number indicating the position of the element counting from the beginning of the array.

**Two-dimensional array:** An array of one-dimensional arrays. Every element in a 2D array is specified using two subscripts where one subscript denotes the row and the other denotes the column.

**Multi-dimensional array:** An array of arrays.

**Axes:** In NumPy, dimensions of the array are called axes.

**Rank:** Number of axes in the a NumPy array is called the rank.

**Lists:** Simple built-in data structures in Python, which can be easily used as a container to hold data of different data types like integer, float, and object.

**Matrix:** A two-dimensional array specified using two subscripts where one subscript denotes the row and the other denotes the column.

**Identity matrix:** A square matrix of which all elements in the principal diagonal are ones, and all other elements are zeros.

**Reshaping an array:** Changing the shape of an array. This can be done by adding or removing dimensions or changing the number of elements in each dimension.

**Normalizing an array:** The process of bringing the array values to some defined range.

**Standard deviation:** A measure of the dispersion of data from its average.

## Chapter Highlights

- Structured data, also referred to as quantitative data, is that data which can be used for effective analysis. It is stored in a database and has well-defined structure and format.
- Unstructured data, also referred to as qualitative data, is not available in a pre-defined format.
- Descriptive statistics are evaluated to summarize and organize data for better understandability.
- In a row-major order, elements of the first row are stored before the elements of the second and third row. In a column-major order, the elements of the first column are stored before the elements of the second and third column.
- `np.arrange()` returns an array with evenly spaced elements from the interval specified by the value of start and stop in the gap of step.
- Importing a module means loading it in memory for using its functionalities.
- A CSV file is a type of plain-text file that uses specific structuring to arrange tabular data. The format used for data interchange by a CSV file is compact, simple and general. This feature facilitates Website users to export tabular data from the website into a CSV file.
- NumPy which stands for "Numeric Python" or "Numerical Python" is the most important library for scientific computing in Python.
- Arrays are superior to Python lists as they are more compact, convenient, efficient and provides faster access to reading and writing items.
- NumPy `arange()` function takes start, end of a range and the interval as arguments and returns a one-dimensional array with evenly spaced elements from the interval specified by the value of start and stop in the gap of step.
- NumPy `linspace()` functions takes start, end and the number of elements to be created as arguments and returns a one-dimensional array that has evenly spaced numbers over the specified interval.
- Subscript indicates an ordinal number of the element counting from the beginning of the array.
- When we create array slices, views from the array are returned rather than copies of the array data.
- When operating with arrays that do not have same dimensions, we can resize one of them. The `np.resize()` function returns a new array with specified shape.
- We can combine multiple arrays into a single array, and also split a single array into multiple arrays.
- When two arrays that have not same but compatible dimensions are operated, then the size of the resulting array is the maximum along each dimension of the input arrays.
- Instead of specifying the normal integer index of the element to be accessed, we can specify Boolean indexing to select those values from the array that fulfil a certain condition.
- Transposing an array means switching its dimensions. An array with 3 rows and 4 columns will now have 4 rows and 3 columns after being transposed.
- To export a NumPy array to a CSV file, the `savetxt()` method of the NumPy module can be used.
- We can create one or more subsets of a NumPy array. These subsets will also be NumPy array objects
- The `compress()` method of the NumPy module can be used to specify a Boolean expression for each element in the array. The result of this Boolean expression will indicate the presence or the absence of that element in the new array.
- If an array needs to be reduced of a dimension, then it should have only one element in that dimension. To reduce dimension of an array, the `squeeze()` method of the NumPy module is used
- NumPy also allows users to do indexing by using an array as an index. When we do this, a copy of the original array is returned.
- Ellipsis (…) selects elements of the same length as obtained from the dimensions of the array.

## Review Questions

1. Define data and state its importance.
2. Differentiate between structured and unstructured data.
3. What is data processing? Explain the set of activities involved to process data.
4. With the help of an example, explain the difference between bimodal, trimodal and multi-modal datasets.
5. Why do we calculate descriptive statistics? Explain with the help of relevant examples.
6. What is NumPy?
7. Which one will you prefer and why – a Python list or a NumPy array?
8. What is an array? How does it store data elements?
9. List different methods that can be used to create arrays in NumPy.
10. With the help of an example, explain the difference between `np.arange()` and `np.linspace()`.
11. Explain the different methods that convert a 2D array into a 1D array.
12. Why do we slice an array? How can it be done?
13. What happens when we supply a negative value for the step argument when slicing an array?
14. Which elements will be printed when the following slicing operations are performed?
    a. Arr[2:5]      b. Arr[3::3]      c. Arr[::-2]      d. Arr[2:]
15. Explain the significance of `copy()` method when slicing an array.
16. What do you understand by reshaping an array? Is there any restriction to be considered while doing so?
17. Is it possible to convert a 1D array into a 2D array using the `reshape()` method?
18. Differentiate between `reshape()` and `resize()` with the help of a relevant example.
19. Compare different methods of joining two or more arrays.
20. What do you mean by Boolean indexing?
21. Differentiate between `insert()` and `delete()` methods to add an element in an existing array.
22. What do you understand by normalizing an array? How is it done?
23. With the help of an example, explain the utility of `compress()` method.
24. How can we reduce a dimension of an array? Illustrate with an example.
25. What is covariance? Explain its significance.
26. Write instructions to:
    a. create an array of ones
    b. create an array of zeros
    c. create an array with random values
    d. create an empty array
    e. create a full array
    f. create an array of evenly-spaced values
    g. print the number of my_array's elements
    h. print the length of one array element in bytes
    i. print the total consumed bytes by my_array's elements
    j. select the element at row 1 column 2
    k. select items at index 0 and 1

l. select items at row 0 and 1, column 1
m. select items at row 1 of a 3D array
n. delete the value at index 1.

27. Identify the significance of the following instructions.
    a. `np.linspace(0,2,9)`
    b. `print(len(my_array))`
    c. `my_array.astype(float)`
    d. `print(my_array[1])`
    e. `print(my_3d_array[bigger_than_3])`
    f. `np.insert(arr, 1, 5)`
    g. `x_new = np.arange(5).reshape((-1, 1))`.

28. Compare different data structures in Python

29. What do you understand by a CSV file? With the help of an example, demonstrate how you will read and write data to such a file.

## Programming Exercises

1. Create a Python list that stores the temperature of 10 consecutive days measured in degree Celsius. Convert this list into a NumPy array.

2. Create a NumPy array containing multiples of 3 in the range 1 to 100.

3. Create a NumPy array containing 10 evenly spaced values from 100 to 105.

4. Create a 4 × 3 NumPy array filled with value 3.9.

5. Create a 5 × 5 NumPy array filled with random values.

6. Create a two-dimensional array and print its attributes.

7. Create an array of students enrolled in Arts, Dance and Music activities. Form a single array containing a list of all the students.

8. Create an array storing marks obtained by 5 students in 4 different subjects.
   a. Find the highest marks obtained in each subject.
   b. Print the minimum marks obtained by each student.
   c. Insert marks of one more student in this array.
   d. Insert marks of one more subject in this array.
   e. Delete a specific row from this array.
   f. Delete a user specified column from this array.

9. Create a 3D array and print elements at even column and odd-row index.

10. Write a program that prints the first column elements of a 2D array.

11. Write a program that creates an array from a tuple and vice-versa.

12. Create a program that converts a 1D array into 3D array and vice-versa.

13. Write a program that prints the cube of odd numbers in the array.

14. Write a program that sums the columns of a 2D array and prints the columns whose sum is divisible by 5.

15. Write a program that prints the sum of columns of a 3D array.

16. Convert a 1D array with 12 elements into a 2D array. The outermost dimension will have 4 arrays, each with 3 elements.
17. Create a 3D array with only one 2D array as its element. Reduce the dimension of this array and print the resultant array.

## Fill in the Blanks

1. SQL table is an example of _____ data.
2. _____ is a collection of facts that is processed to obtained information.
3. _____ is the process of converting raw data to meaningful information.
4. _____ are evaluated to summarize and organize data for better understandability.
5. _____ specifies the value appearing maximum time in data set.
6. _____ module provides fast mathematical computation on arrays and matrices.
7. The elements of the array are stored in consecutive memory locations and are referenced by an _____.
8. _____ is an array of one-dimensional arrays.
9. Every element in a _____ is specified using two subscripts.
10. In a _____ representation of a 2D array, element (1,0) is followed by element (1,1).
11. Before using a module, we must first _____ it.
12. _____ creates a matrix of specified data type and shape (or size) filled with ones.
13. _____ returns an array with evenly spaced elements from the interval specified by the value of start and stop in the gap of step.
14. _____ displays the dimension of the NumPy array.
15. _____ a module means loading it in memory for using its functionalities.
16. The _____ function is used to check whether all elements are True.
17. The _____ method is used to return value associated with a specified label.
18. If we compare NumPy objects of different lengths then objects can be _____.
19. The elements of the array are referenced by an _____.
20. Number of axes is called the _____.
21. _____ function takes start, end and the number of elements to be created as arguments and returns a one-dimensional array that has evenly spaced numbers over the specified interval.
22. _____ creates a matrix filled with ones.
23. _____ attribute returns a tuple of integers indicating the size of the array.
24. The _____ function displays first 5 rows of the data.
25. When we create array slices, _____ from the array are returned.
26. _____ method is used to create a copy of NumPy array data.
27. If the dimensions of two arrays are not compatible, then _____ will be returned.
28. The arrays can only be broadcast together if they are _____ in all dimensions.

29. _____ an array means switching its dimensions.
30. The _____ of the NumPy module is used to retrieve diagonals of multidimensional arrays.
31. NumPy arrays can be indexed with any other sequence except _____.
32. _____ selects elements of the same length as obtained from the dimensions of the array.
33. Mode = 'w' indicates that the file is being opened for _____ data.
34. Machine Learning and Artificial Intelligence algorithms are applied in _____ stage of data processing cycle.
35. _____ measures the average distance between each value and the mean.

## State True or False

1. Unstructured data is stored in a database and has well-defined structure and format.
2. Array indexes are written in round brackets.
3. Array elements are placed in consecutive memory locations.
4. Measure of Spread refers to the idea of variability within your data.
5. An $m \times n$ matrix has $m$ columns and $n$ rows.
6. In a row-major order, the elements of the first column are stored before the elements of the second and third columns.
7. NumPy is mainly used for creating heterogeneous multi-dimensional arrays.
8. Shape returns a tuple of integers indicating the size of the array.
9. Python list is more powerful than NumPy array.
10. A list is a collection of elements having the same data type.
11. The elements of the array are stored in consecutive memory locations.
12. Data elements of a 2D array are not stored consecutively in memory.
13. `np.empty()` returns a new array of given shape and type, filled with random values.
14. Default value of size = 0.
15. While slicing an array, the value of step cannot be negative.
16. A list produces slices that are views of data.
17. We can convert a 1D array into a 2D array using the `reshape()` method.
18. The `size()` method is also used to find the length of the array.
19. Array subsets are themselves NumPy array objects.
20. When arrays are used for indexing NumPy arrays, a view of the original array is returned.
21. A high standard deviation indicates that values are closer to the mean of the data set.
22. The NOT in operator returns True if the index is present and False otherwise.
23. The `isnull()` function returns False if a particular value is null and True otherwise.
24. During data collection, verified data is coded or converted into machine readable form.
25. Mode is the value which divides the data in to two equal parts.

## Multiple Choice Questions

1. XML is an example of _____ data.
   a. structured    b. unstructured    c. semi-structured    d. All of these.

2. Which of the following is not an example of unstructured data?
   a. XML tags    b. Data from sensors    c. Data from satellites images    d. PDF files

3. NumPy stands for _____.
   a. Number Python    b. Number Pandas    c. Numeric Python    d. Numeric Pandas

4. The array index starts from _____.
   a. 0    b. –1    c. 1    d. 10

5. An element in a multi-dimensional array is specified using ____ indices.
   a. 0    b. 1    c. n    d. 10

6. In NumPy, dimensions of the array are called _____.
   a. axes    b. rank    c. index    d. subscript

7. _____ is a function that allow users to create an array of elements supplied as an argument.
   a. `np.ones`    b. `np.zeroes`    c. `np.array`    d. `np.full`

8. _____ returns the total number of elements in the NumPy array.
   a. Shape    b. Size    c. Itemsize    d. Reshape

9. By default, `head()` function displays the first _____ rows.
   a. 2    b. 5    c. 6    d. 10

10. A 3 × 4 matrix will have how many elements?
    a. 3    b. 4    c. 7    d. 12

11. _____ denotes the second element in the first row.
    a. Arr[2][3]    b. arr[0][1]    c. arr[2][1]    d. arr[1][2]

12. NumPy arrays can be created from _____.
    a. Python lists    b. Python tuples    c. individual integers    d. All of these.

13. Which function takes **start**, **end** of a range and the **interval** as arguments to create an array?
    a. `np.array()`    b. `np.arange()`    c. `np.linspace()`    d. All of these.

14. Which function will be used to convert a tuple into a NumPy array?
    a. `np.array()`    b. `np.arange()`    c. `np.linspace()`    d. `np.flatten()`

15. Which function has to specify the constant value that has to be inserted into the array?
    a. `np.ones()`
    b. `np.random.random()`
    c. `np.full()`
    d. `np.arrange()`

16. Which function(s) is/are used to create arrays of evenly spaced values?
    a. `np.linespace()`    b. `np.arange()`    c. Both of these.    d. None of these.

17. _____ returns the size in bytes of each item.
    a. `size`    b. `itemsize`    c. `shape`    d. `ndim`

18. Which of the following function is not used to convert a 2D array into a 1D array?
    a. `np.arange()`    b. `np.ravel()`    c. `np.flatten()`    d. `np.reshape()`

19. When joining arrays, which function must have same dimensions?
    a. `np.concatenate()`
    b. `np.vstack()`
    c. `np.hstack()`
    d. All of these.

20. Which method of NumPy module is used to find the index of value in an array?
    a. where()      b. index()      c. at()      d. loc()

21. _____ is the last stage in the data processing cycle, where data is preserved for future use.
    a. Data Storage    b. Output     c. Data Processing    d. Data Collection

22. Identify the statistic which is not a measure of central tendency?
    a. Mean       b. Mode       c. Median       d. Variance

23. _____ is calculated as the square of average distance between each quantity and mean.
    a. Standard Deviation    b. Median    c. Variance    d. Range

## Give the Output

1. 
```
import numpy as np
a = np.arange(5, 14, 2)
print(a)
```

2. 
```
import numpy as np
a = np.linspace(5, 25, 4)
print(a)
```

3. 
```
x = np.arange(10)
x
x[:5]
x[5:]
x[4:7]
x[::2]
x[1::2]
```

4. 
```
x = np.array([1, 2, 3])
x.reshape((1, 3))
x[np.newaxis, :]
x.reshape((3, 1))
x[:, np.newaxis]
```

5. 
```
grid = np.array([[1, 2, 3],
                 [4, 5, 6]])
np.concatenate([grid, grid])
np.concatenate([grid, grid], axis=1)
```

6. 
```
x = np.array([1, 2, 3])
grid = np.array([[9, 8, 7],
                 [6, 5, 4]])
np.vstack([x, grid])
y = np.array([[99],
              [99]])
np.hstack([grid, y])
```

7. 
```
x = [1, 2, 3, 99, 99, 3, 2, 1]
x1, x2, x3 = np.split(x, [3, 5])
print(x1, x2, x3)
```

8. ```
   import numpy as np
   x = np.ones((4,3))
   print("Dimensions of x : ",x.shape)
   y = np.random.random((1,3))
   print("DImensons of y  : ", y.shape)
   print(x + y)
   ```

9. ```
   import numpy as np
   arr  = np.array(
   [[1,2,3,4],
      [5,6,7,8],
      [9,0,1,2],
      [3,4,5,6]])
   print("Elements at (1,0), (0,1), (1,2) and (0,0) \n")
   print(arr[[1, 0, 1, 0],[0, 1, 2, 0]])
   ```

10. ```
    import numpy
    a = numpy.array([1, 2, 3, 4, 5])
    b = numpy.array([10, 20, 30, 40, 50])
    newArray = numpy.append(a, b)
    print("The new array = ", newArray)
    ```

11. ```
    import numpy as np
    a = np.array([[1,2],[3,4],[5,6]])
    print( np.insert(a,3,[11,12]) )
    print( np.insert(a,1,[11],axis = 0) )
    print( np.insert(a,1,11,axis = 1))
    ```

12. ```
    import numpy as np
    arr = np.arange(6).reshape(2, 3)
    print("1D arr : \n", arr)
    print("Shape : ", arr.shape)
    a = np.insert(arr, (2, 4), 9)
    print("\nInsertion at two points : ", a)
    print("Shape : ", a.shape)
    ```

13. ```
    arr = np.arange(12).reshape(3, 4)
    print("\n\n2D arr : \n", arr)
    print("Shape : ", arr.shape)
    a = np.insert(arr, (0, 3), 66, axis = 1)
    print("\nInsertion at two points : \n", a)
    print("Shape : ", a.shape)
    ```

14. ```
    import numpy as np
    a = np.arange(12).reshape(3,4)
    print(a)
    print(np.delete(a,5) )
    print(np.delete(a,1,axis = 1))
    ```

15. ```
    a = np.array([1,2,3,4,5,6,7,8,9,10])
    print(np.delete(a, np.s_[::2]))
    ```

16. ```
    arr = np.arange(12).reshape(3, 4)
    print("arr : \n», arr)
    print("Shape : ", arr.shape)
    ```

17. ```
    import numpy
    a = numpy.array([1, 2, 3])
    newArray = numpy.delete(a, 1, axis = 0)
    print(newArray)
    ```

18. ```
    import numpy
    a = numpy.array([[1, 2, 3], [4, 5, 6], [10, 20, 30]])
    newArray = numpy.delete(a, 1, axis = 0)
    print(newArray)
    ```

19. ```
    import numpy as np
    arr = np.array([])
    if(arr.size == 0):
        print("The given Array is empty")
    else:
        print("The array = ", arr)
    ```

20. ```
    import numpy
    a = numpy.array([1, 2, 3, 4, 5, 6, 7, 8])
    print("A subset of array a = ", a[2:5])
    ```

21. ```
    import numpy as np
    arr = np.array([1, 2, 3, 4, 5, 6, 7, 8])
    newarr = arr.reshape(2, 2, -1)
    print(newarr)
    ```

22. ```
    import numpy as np
    arr = np.array([[1, 2, 3], [4, 5, 6]])
    newarr = arr.reshape(-1)
    print(newarr)
    ```

23. ```
    import numpy as np
    a = np.arange(10, 1, -2)
    newarr = a[np.array([3, 1, 2 ])]
    print("\n Elements at these indices are:\n",newarr)
    ```

24. ```
    import numpy as np
    x = np.array([1, 2, 3, 4, 5, 6, 7, 8, 9])
    arr = x[np.array([1, 3, -3])]
    print("\n Elements are : \n",arr)
    ```

25. ```
    import numpy as np
    a = np.arange(20)
    print("\n a[-8:17:1]  = ",a[-8:17:1])
    print("\n a[10:]  = ",a[10:])
    ```

26. ```
    import numpy as np
    b = np.array([[[1, 2, 3],[4, 5, 6]],
                  [[7, 8, 9],[10, 11, 12]]])
     print(b[...,1]) #Equivalent to b[: ,: ,1 ]
    ```
    ```

27. ```
    import numpy as np
    a = np.array([10, 40, 80, 50, 100])
    print(a[a>50])
    ```

## Fill in the Blanks to Complete the Code

1.  ```
    # Import `numpy` as `np`
    _____
    # Make the array `arr`
    arr = _____([[1,2,3,4], [5,6,7,8]], dtype=np.int64
    )
    # Print `arr`
    print(_____)
    ```

2.  ```
    # Initialize `x` with all ones
    x = np.ones((3,4))
    # Check shape of `x`
    print(_____)
    # Initialize `y` with random values
    y = np.random.random((3,4))
    # Check shape of `y`
    print(_____)
    # Add `x` and `y`
    Print(_____)
    ```

3.  ```
    # Add `x` and `y`
    _____(x,y)
    # Subtract `x` and `y`
    _____(x,y)
    # Multiply `x` and `y`
    _____(x,y)
    # Divide `x` and `y`
    _____(x,y)
    # Calculate the remainder of `x` and `y`
    _____(x,y)
    # `a` AND `b`
    _____(a, b)
    # `a` OR `b`
    _____(a, b)
    # `a` NOT `b`
    _____(a,b)
    ```

4.  ```
    # Append a 1D array to your `arr`
    new_arr = _____(arr, [7, 8, 9, 10])
    # Print `new_arr`
    _____(new_arr)
    ```

5.  ```
    # Append an extra column to your `arr`
    new_arr = _____(arr, [[7], [8]], axis=1)
    # Print `new_arr`
    _____(new_arr)
    ```

### Find the Error

1. ```
   import numpy as np
   x = np.ones((3,4))
   print(x.shape)
   y = np.arange(1,4)
   print(y.shape)
   x - y
   ```

2. ```
   import numpy as np
   arr = np.array([1, 2, 3, 4, 5, 6, 7, 8])
   newarr = arr.reshape(2, 2)
   print(newarr)
   ```

3. ```
   import numpy as np
   arr = np.array([1, 2, 3, 4, 5, 6, 7, 8])
   newarr = arr.reshape(3, 3)
   print(newarr)
   ```

4. ```
   import numpy as np
   a = np.array([1, 2, 3, 4, 5, 6, 7, 8])
   print("A subset of array a = ", a[-3:])
   print(np.hsplit(a, 2))
   print(np.vsplit(a, 2))
   ```

5. ```
   import numpy as np
   a = np.delete(a, 1, 0)
   print("Shape : ", a.shape)
   a = np.delete(a, 1, 1)
   print("Shape : ", a.shape)
   ```

6. ```
   import numpy as np
   z = [99, 99, 99]
   print(np.concatenate([z, 'y', 'z']))
   ```

### Answers

#### Fill in the Blanks

1. structured
2. Data
3. Data processing
4. Descriptive statistics
5. Mode
6. NumPy
7. index
8. Two-dimensional array
9. matrix/ 2D array
10. row
11. import
12. `np.ones`
13. `np.arrange()`
14. Ndim
15. Importing
16. `all()`
17. `get()`
18. broadcast
19. index
20. rank
21. NumPy `linspace()`
22. `np.ones()`
23. Shape
24. `head()`
25. views
26. `copy()`
27. ValueError
28. compatible
29. Transposing
30. `diagonal()`
31. tuples
32. Ellipsis (…)
33. writing
34. Data Processing
35. Standard deviation

#### State True or False

1. False
2. False
3. True
4. True
5. False
6. False
7. False
8. True
9. False
10. False
11. True
12. False
13. True
14. False
15. False
16. False
17. True
18. True
19. True
20. False
21. False
22. False
23. False
24. False
25. False

#### Multiple Choice Questions

1. c
2. a
3. c
4. a
5. c
6. a
7. c
8. b
9. b
10. d
11. b
12. d
13. a
14. a
15. c
16. c
17. b
18. a
19. a
20. a
21. a
22. d
23. c

## Give the Output

1. [ 5  7  9 11 13]
2. [ 5.         11.66666667 18.33333333 25.        ]
3. [0 1 2 3 4 5 6 7 8 9]
   [0 1 2 3 4]
   [5 6 7 8 9]
   [4 5 6]
   [0 2 4 6 8]
   [1 3 5 7 9]
4. [[1 2 3]]
   [[1 2 3]]
   [[1]
    [2]
    [3]]
   [[1]
    [2]
    [3]]
5. [[1 2 3]
    [4 5 6]
    [1 2 3]
    [4 5 6]]
   [[1 2 3 1 2 3]
    [4 5 6 4 5 6]]
6. [[1 2 3]
    [9 8 7]
    [6 5 4]]
   [[ 9  8  7 99]
    [ 6  5  4 99]]
7. [1 2 3] [99 99] [3 2 1]
8. Dimensions of x : (4, 3)
   DImensons of y : (1, 3)
   [[1.55316063 1.83239962 1.06017565]
    [1.55316063 1.83239962 1.06017565]
    [1.55316063 1.83239962 1.06017565]
    [1.55316063 1.83239962 1.06017565]]
9. Elements at (1,0), (0,1), (1,2) and (0,0)
   [5 2 7 1]
10. The new array = [ 1  2  3  4  5 10 20 30 40 50]
11. [ 1  2  3 11 12  4  5  6]
    [[ 1  2]
     [11 11]
     [ 3  4]
     [ 5  6]]
    [[ 1 11  2]
     [ 3 11  4]
     [ 5 11  6]]
12. 1D arr :
    [[0 1 2]
     [3 4 5]]
    Shape : (2, 3)
    Insertion at two points : [0 1 9 2 3 9 4 5]
    Shape : (8,)
13. 2D arr :
    [[ 0  1  2  3]
     [ 4  5  6  7]
     [ 8  9 10 11]]
    Shape : (3, 4)

    Insertion at two points :
    [[66  0  1  2 66  3]
     [66  4  5  6 66  7]
     [66  8  9 10 66 11]]
    Shape : (3, 6)
14. [[ 0  1  2  3]
     [ 4  5  6  7]
     [ 8  9 10 11]]
    [ 0  1  2  3  4  6  7  8  9 10 11]
    [[ 0  2  3]
     [ 4  6  7]
     [ 8 10 11]]
15. [ 2  4  6  8 10]
16. arr :
    [[ 0  1  2  3]
     [ 4  5  6  7]
     [ 8  9 10 11]]
    Shape : (3, 4)
17. [1 3]
18. [[ 1  2  3]
     [10 20 30]]
19. The given Array is empty
20. A subset of array a = [3 4 5]
21. [[[1 2]
     [3 4]]
    [[5 6]
     [7 8]]]
22. [1 2 3 4 5 6]
23. Elements at these indices are:
    [4 8 6]
24. Elements are : [2 4 7]
25. a[-8:17:1] = [12 13 14 15 16]
    a[10:] = [10 11 12 13 14 15 16 17 18 19]
26. [[ 2  5]
     [ 8 11]]
27. [ 80 100]

## Fill in the Blanks to Complete the Code

1. import numpy as np
   np.array
   print(arr)

2. import numpy as np
   print(x.shape)
   print(y.shape)
   print(x + y)

3. np.add
   np.subtract
   np.multiply
   np.divide
   np.remainder
   np.logical_and
   np.logical_or
   np.logical_not

4. np.append
   print
5. np.append
   print

## Find the Error

1. ValueError: operands could not be broadcast together with shapes (3,4) (3,)
2. ValueError: cannot reshape array of size 8 into shape (2,2)
3. ValueError: cannot reshape array of size 8 into shape (3,3)
4. ValueError: vsplit only works on arrays of 2 or more dimensions
5. NameError: name 'a' is not defined
6. ValueError: all the input arrays must have same number of dimensions, but the array at index 0 has 1 dimension(s) and the array at index 1 has 0 dimension(s)

# Data Management

## 12

### Chapter Objectives

In this chapter, we will read about storing data in databases for fast and efficient access and manipulation, with focus on the following:

- Problems with file management system
- Database approach – applications, pros and cons
- ACID property
- Relational databases
- Components of DBMS
- Relational databases
- Database keys
- Data integrity rules

## INTRODUCTION

When computers were first used for business applications, a related group of records were stored in a file. Each department had its own files that were specifically designed for applications or services provided by that particular department. For example, did you notice in that in your school, there are three departments – academics, accounts and library. Each of these departments maintain a student's file that has details of a student that are specific for their purpose.

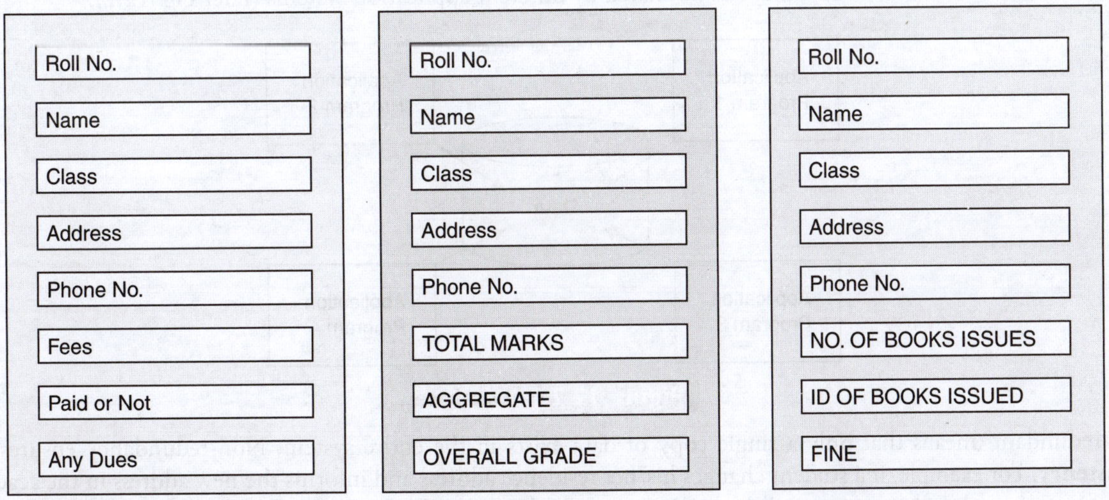

| Roll No. | Roll No. | Roll No. |
|---|---|---|
| Name | Name | Name |
| Class | Class | Class |
| Address | Address | Address |
| Phone No. | Phone No. | Phone No. |
| Fees | TOTAL MARKS | NO. OF BOOKS ISSUES |
| Paid or Not | AGGREGATE | ID OF BOOKS ISSUED |
| Any Dues | OVERALL GRADE | FINE |
| Student's details in the accounts department | Student's details in the academic department | Student's details in the library |

**Figure 12.1** Student's details as stored in File Management System

Although maintaining a separate student's file (computerized file) in each department seems a good and an easy way of storing details, this approach suffers from various drawbacks.

*Data redundancy:* Redundancy means repetition. From the Fig. 12.1, it is clear that if a particular data is required by two different applications, then it may be stored in two or more files. Here, name, class, roll number, address and phone number of a student is recorded in three different files.

***Lack of flexibility:*** When we store data in separate files, the user can generate only limited reports and execute a limited number of queries. Such systems cannot respond to un-anticipatory queries and any kind of investigative or trend analysis that has now become mandatory for any business to survive in the competitive world.

***Difficulty in accessing data:*** Storing data in separate files does not allow data to be retrieved in a convenient and efficient manner. For example, if there is a need to make a list of all the students who have not paid their fees and also have some library dues, then two files have to be accessed for the purpose. Making such a list will also be a time consuming and cumbersome task.

***Data isolation:*** Since data is scattered in different files in distinct departments and stored in different formats, retrieving data from different files is very difficult.

***Data integrity issues:*** Data stored in files must satisfy certain types of consistency constraints. For example, the student cannot be issued more than three books. It is very difficult for computer programmers to write applications or programs that can retrieve as well as store only the data that satisfies the specified constraints. For example, the moment a student is issued the fourth book, the program must disallow the task.

***Data atomicity issues:*** In case of a failure, data must be restored to the correct state that existed prior to the failure. It is difficult to accomplish this when separate files are used. For example, if a user is running a banking software to transfer Rs 10K from his account to another account and if the computer automatically shuts down because of some failure, then either the money should be deducted from his account and added to another or nothing should happen. Just imagine how difficult it would be if the amount was deducted from the account but not added in the other account. So, either the work should be done in entirety or not at all.

## 12.1 DATABASE

A database is a collection of related data organized in a way that allows users to easily access, update and maintain the data. It stores non-redundant data that can be shared by different application systems (refer Fig. 12.2).

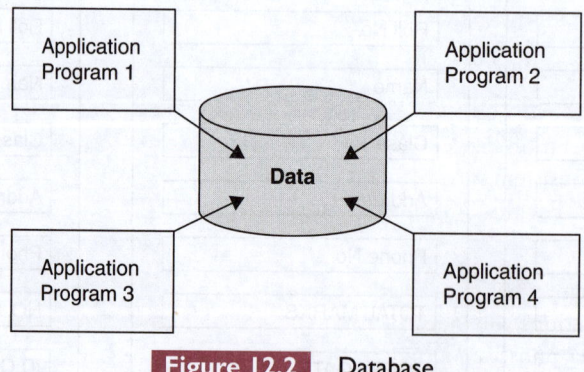

**Figure 12.2** Database

'Non-redundant' means that only a single copy of data exists in the entire system. Non-redundancy ensures **data consistency**. For example, if a student changes his/her residence address and informs the new address in the academic department then that department will have the updated value but others will have the incorrect old value. This is called inconsistent data which occurred due to redundancy of data (existence of same data at multiple locations). In databases, only a single copy of data exists that is shared by all the applications running in every department.

### 12.1.1 Advantages of a Database

The following are the advantages of using database to store data:

- It reduces data redundancy because databases are shared rather than being stored as independent files.
- It minimizes data inconsistencies.
- It maintains data integrity and quality.
- Information about the stored data including its meaning and interpretation can be saved in the data dictionary.

- Data stored is secured as a database, with appropriate security tools to control access.
- Ease of searching data by using keywords.
- Data can be shared among multiple branches of the same organization.
- Data can be used to analyze trends such as which product is most popular among customers.

### 12.1.2 Application of Database System

Database systems are widely used in almost all areas we can think of. They have been successfully implemented for the following applications:

- Databases are used for reserving air as well as train tickets.
- Airlines and railways use databases for displaying the route and schedule of trains and flights.
- In hospitals, databases are used to store details of patients, their medical history and other details.
- Financial institutions (like banks) use database for storing details of customers, their accounts, loans, and other transactions. They also use databases to record purchases on credit cards for generating monthly bills.
- Database is used in schools and colleges to store the information about students.
- Database is used in every organization to maintain records of all their employees, their salaries, perks, taxes, etc.
- In telecommunication departments, database is used to store information about telephone numbers. They also store record of calls for generating monthly bills, etc.
- Online shopping websites and other business activities use database to store details of products, customers, transactions and other payment details.
- The world wide web maintains enormous amount of textual and multimedia data in databases.
- Databases are used in online trading for storing information about sales and purchases of stocks and bonds.

## 12.2 ACID PROPERTY

Every operation that takes place in a database system must maintain ACID properties where ACID means **A**tomicity, **C**onsistency, **I**solation and **D**urability. ACID ensures accuracy, completeness and data integrity.

*Atomicity:* It states that an operation must either complete fully or must not be performed at all. There should not be any middle state, especially when updating the data. So, this rule says "All or Nothing".

*Consistency:* When any operation takes place, it should not have any adverse effect on the data stored in the database. If the database was in a consistent state before the execution of an operation, it must remain consistent even after the execution of the operation. For this, a database ensures that only valid data that satisfies all rules and constraints are written in the database.

*Isolation:* In a database system, when more than one transaction is executed at the same time, the property of isolation states that all the transactions will be carried out and executed as if it is the only transaction in the system. No transaction will affect any other transaction.

For example, if user A withdraws Rs 10,000 and user B withdraws Rs 15,000 from user C's account, which has a balance of Rs 50,000, then only one person will be allowed to draw from C's account and the other person will have to wait until the first operation is completed. After both operations, balance in C's account will be Rs 50,000 – Rs 10,000 – Rs 15,000.

However, if they both are allowed to withdraw at the same time then both operations will read balance as 50,000, draw their amount and will update accordingly, i.e., Rs 50,000 – Rs 10,000 or Rs 50,000 – Rs 15,000.

*Durability:* External factors like system crash or power failure should not affect the data once the database operation is completed on the server.

In the above example, user B may withdraw Rs 15,000 only after user A's transaction is completed and is updated in the database. If the system fails before A's transaction is logged in the database, then A cannot withdraw any money, and the amount in C's account is not affected.

Every database must guarantee all the above properties to ensure reliability, robustness and consistency. All of the major relational DBMSs support ACID principles. They all include features that ensure that data remains consistent throughout software and hardware crashes, as well as any failed transactions.

## 12.3 COMPONENTS OF A DATABASE SYSTEM

An effective database system comprises of four main components that are shown in Fig. 12.3.

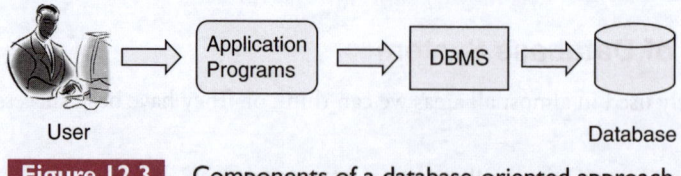

**Figure 12.3** Components of a database-oriented approach

*Data:* The most crucial component of a database is the data stored in it. This data can be accessed by users through application programs. A database stores two types of data – users' data and metadata. While user data contains data to supports users' applications, the metadata on the other hand, stores data about data. It describes the structure of the database and includes information regarding number of tables and table names, number of fields and field names, primary key fields, types of pre-defined queries, etc.

*Hardware:* Hardware consists of secondary storage devices on which data is stored. These include input and output devices for receiving/giving data to users, and processor and main memory for processing the data in a fast and efficient manner.

*Software:* Software consists of the Database Management System (DBMS) which acts as a bridge between the user and the database. The DBMS software interacts with the user's application programs and database to insert, update, delete and retrieve data. DBMS is responsible for maintaining the integrity and security of stored data and for recovering information in case of system failure. Some common examples of DBMS are MS ACCESS, SQL Server, Oracle, dBase and FoxPro.

*Users:* Users are the people who access the data from the database. They may vary from clerical staff to managers and executives. Based on the job profile, these users are either given full or partial access to the database data. Database users (refer Fig. 12.4) can be broadly classified into the following categories:

*Application Programmers:* An application programmer writes application programs to access, retrieve, update, delete or add new data to the database. These programs are written using a high-level language preferably SQL which is a 4GL.

*End-users:* End-users are those users who use the application programs developed by the application developers. They need not know about the database design, working, access mechanism and other technical details of the database. It is sufficient if they just use the underlying database to get their work done. End-users may be further categorized in two groups.

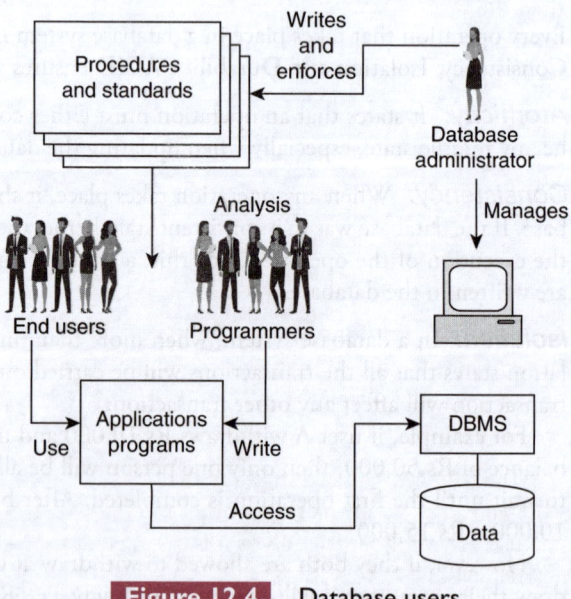

**Figure 12.4** Database users

*Sophisticated end-users* who write their own queries to access and process the data stored in the database.

*Unsophisticated end-users* who interact with the system through an already-written application program. They follow the instructions provided in the user interface to retrieve data from the database. For example, people working at railways reservation counters interact with the system through an already-written application program. Another example of unsophisticated users is bank customers who use ATMs to draw money or check their balance.

*Database Administrator (DBA):* DBAs makes strategic and policy decisions regarding the data. They provide technical support for implementing these decisions and are responsible for overall control of the system at the technical level. They monitors as well as perform all activities related to database design, implementation, maintenance and security. Besides administering the database, they also train employees in database management and use.

*System Analyst:* System analysts identify end-users' requirements, plan solutions and recommend hardware and software that best meet business goals. They conduct a technical and economic feasibility analysis of the identified requirements.

## 12.4 RELATIONAL DATABASES

Relational databases were developed by E F Codd in 1970. In a relational database, data and the relationship that exist between those data are represented using tables also known as **relations**. Therefore, a table is a collection of data records where each record contains the same fields but with a different value for the fields. The main features of relational data model are:

- A table consists of rows and columns.
- Each row stores a record.
- A record represents an entity.
- Each row is unique.
- Each column represents an attribute of that entity. It is also called field.
- Each field has a unique name.
- A common attribute (and not physical links) is used to maintain a relationship between two tables.
- The sequence of rows and columns is insignificant.

Look at Fig. 12.5. It shows the relational model and consists of two tables. The first table stores the roll number, name, address and phone number of the students. The second table stores the roll number, course and the year of admission. Note that these two tables have a common field – RNo. Now, if there is a query like in which course Fatima studies, then the first table will be searched to obtain the roll number of Fatima. This roll number will then be used to search for a particular record in the second table. In this way, we are joining two tables based on a common attribute. The result of this query would return – BCA.

| RNo | Name | Phone No | Address |
|---|---|---|---|
| 1 | Anant | 9838098789 | Bank Street |
| 2 | Chaitanya | 7838912345 | Park Avenue |
| 3 | Deep | 7981086413 | Jai Singh Road |
| 4 | Fatima | 9913534791 | Copernicus Marg |
| 5 | Harpreet | 9729980654 | Mall Road |

| RNo | Course | Year |
|---|---|---|
| 1 | BTech | 2020 |
| 2 | BTech | 2018 |
| 3 | BSc | 2019 |
| 4 | BCA | 2019 |
| 5 | BSc | 2020 |

**Figure 12.5** Relational model

### 12.4.1 Advantages of Relational Databases

- The data is organized in a way that makes it simple to understand and use.
- Data access is simpler than other models (like network and hierarchical).
- It is programmer friendly as it is easy to develop application programs for a relational database as compared to other databases.
- Provides flexible data organization.
- Future enhancements to the database like adding new table, row, field, etc. can be easily done.
- Relational model is close to the intuitive or logical model of real-life applications.

### 12.4.2 Disadvantages of Relational Databases

Not all types of data can be represented using relational data model. Some examples of such data include multimedia, temporal, spatial and unstructured data.

## 12.5 COMPONENTS OF DBMS

Database management system is a software that is used to manage an organization's data. **It enables users to create a database, define constraints, manipulate data, execute queries and generate reports**. Besides users, the database administrators use DBMS to administer, monitor, manage and take backup of the ever-growing database. For this reason, DBMS has the following components (refer Fig. 12.6).

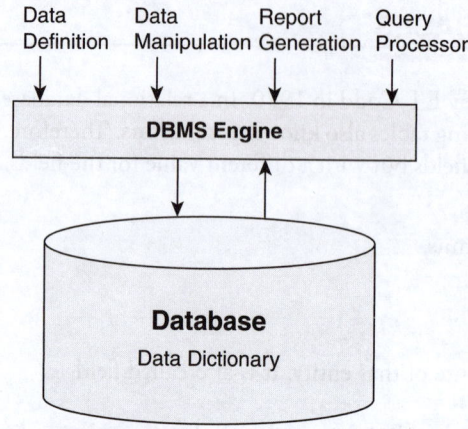

**Figure 12.6** Components of DBMS

*DBMS engine:* DBMS Engine is the core service for creating tables, storing, processing and securing database data. It provides controlled access and fast processing to meet the time constraints of the most complex applications. Database Engine can be used to create relational databases for online transaction processing or online analytical processing of data. This includes creating tables for storing data and database objects such as indexes, views, and stored procedures for viewing, managing, and securing data.

*Data dictionary:* In every database, a certain amount of space is reserved for data dictionary. The data dictionary stores information about the data stored in the database. It stores information about different tables, schemas, views, indexes, functions, procedures, user permissions, user statistics, database design information, database growth and performance statistics, etc.

*Query processor:* The query processor accepts user queries and transforms them into a series of instructions. For this, the query processor accesses the data dictionary to find the structure of relevant data and uses this information to restructure the query to optimally access the database. To hide all technical details from users, the query processor consists of three modules – DDL interpreter, DML compiler and a query evaluation engine

*Report writer:* A report generator is a program that creates a report in the prescribed format. It is an essential part of the DBMS that utilizes the output of query execution to display it in an easy-to-understand format. Although results of queries are self-describing, users can also get the results in the form of pie charts, bar charts, and other diagrams.

In most of the DBMS available today, frequently used reports are already created and stored so that users can use them as and when required. Users can also create a new report if none of the available reports satisfy their requirements. In such a case, the newly created report can be stored in the list of available reports so that it can be used in future.

### 12.5.1 Other Important Modules of DBMS

A database management system is a complex software system. In addition to the components listed above, DBMS also has other important modules for data definition and manipulation, data integrity, security, data recovery and concurrency control, and performance optimization. These modules can be explained as below:

*Data definition:* The data definition module of DBMS provides functions to define the structure of the data. These functions are written using the data definition language (DDL). DDL enables the data administrators to define and modify the structure of the table, data type of fields, and integrity constraints to be satisfied before storing the data in each field.

> Every time a DDL statement is issued, the data dictionary gets modified.

Only the database administrator can define the database and make changes to its definition as and when required. The DDL compiler component of DBMS processes these definitions and stores them in the data dictionary.

*Data manipulation:* After the structure of data is defined, the data may be manipulated by adding, deleting and modifying records. For this, the DBMS contains a data manipulation module that provides functions to perform these operations. These functions are written using the Data Manipulation Language (DML). The DML commands are compiled by query compiler, optimized by query optimizer and finally executed by query evaluation engine.

> The query optimizer refers the data dictionary to find information about the stored data.

**There are two types of data manipulation languages:**
The *non-procedural (also called high-level) DML* enables the users to easily and precisely specify complex database operations. The users just have to specify *what* data is required. They do not have to specify *how* the data will be retrieved. The most commonly used example of a non-procedural DML is the structured query language (or SQL).

The *procedural (also called low-level) DML* requires users to write a step-by-step procedure to specify *what* data is required and *how* that data has to be accessed. The most commonly used example of procedural DML is relational algebra which provides a set of operations like select, project, union, etc., to manipulate the data in the database.

> Query is the statement which is written to retrieve information. The part of the DML that retrieves the information is called a query language.

*Data security and integrity:* The data security and integrity module of DBMS provides functions to handle security and integrity of data stored in the database. Data integrity ensures correctness, completeness and consistency of data.

*Concurrency and data recovery:* The concurrency and data recovery module of the DBMS provides functions to allow multiple users to access the database simultaneously. It also provides functions to recover data in case of system failure.

*Performance optimization:* The performance optimization module provides a set of functions to optimize the performance of user queries. The module formulates and evaluates different execution plans of a given query and then selects the most efficient plan to be executed on the database.

> Some functions of the DBMS are supported by the operating system while others are built on top of it.

## 12.6 BASIC TERMINOLOGY OF RELATIONAL DATABASE SYSTEMS

In this section, we will learn about some terms that are frequently used when relational databases are used.

**Relation:** As discussed earlier, a relation is a table. In a table, data is arranged in rows and columns. Every relation exhibits some basic features like,

- In any given column of a table, all the items are of the same type. Correspondingly, items in different columns may not be of the same type.
- Every row must have a single value for each column.
- Every row must have a unique value. That is, no two rows should have same value for all the fields.
- The ordering of rows in a relationship is insignificant.
- Every column must have a unique name.
- The order of columns is insignificant.

**Tuple:** The rows of tables are known as Tuples.

**Attributes:** The columns or fields of a table are called Attributes of the table.

**Degree:** The number of attributes in a relation determines the degree of relation. A table that has five columns has a relation of degree 5.

**Cardinality:** The number of tuples or rows in a relation is known as cardinality of the relation.

## 12.7 DATABASE KEYS

Real-world applications may have tables containing millions of records or rows and thousands of fields or columns. Just imagine how difficult it would be to uniquely identify each record of such a huge table.

In your school, there are thousands of students and each student is uniquely identified by his/her admission number. In our country, there are billions of people and each person is uniquely identified by his/her Adhaar Number. In a hospital, every patient has a unique Patient_ID. In a company, every employee has a unique Employee_ID. Similarly, in a table – big or small, there must be some field or a combination of fields which should have only unique values. Such a field(s) is called a **database key** or simply, a **key**.

Just think and answer: Can we use name of the student as a key? No. This is because names are not unique. Two or more students in the school may have the same name. So key is a field or a combination of fields that forms a unique combination.

A table can have different types of keys like candidate key, primary key, super key or alternate key. Let us know the difference between each of them.

### 12.7.1 Candidate Key

Candidate keys are those attributes or columns of a table, which have the properties of uniqueness and irreducibility. Here, uniqueness means that a relation (or table) must not have two different rows with the same value for that column (or attribute or field). Irreducibility means that no proper subset of the candidate key has the uniqueness property. In simple words, no individual attribute of the candidate key should be unique.

For example, **Roll Number** field of a student table is a candidate key as every student has a unique roll number. But the combination of **Roll Number and Name** is not an example of appropriate candidate key as it does not satisfy the property of irreducibility which says that no subset of candidate key has uniqueness property. In our example, Roll Number has the uniqueness property.

However, if **Name and Class** combination of students are unique, then these two attributes can together form the candidate key. This is possible only when no two students in the same class have the same name.

#### Key points to remember
- Every relation has at least one candidate key.
- A candidate key should not have null value.
- There can be any number of candidate keys in a table.

*Composite Key:* When we create a key using more than one column then that key is known as composite key.

*Super Key:* A super key is a combination of two or more fields that satisfies the uniqueness property but not necessarily the irreducibility property. This means that a candidate key is a special case of a super key.

For example, if Roll Number of every student is unique then the set of attributes **(Roll Number, Name), or (Roll Number, Name, Class)** is a super key for the STUDENT table. This set of attributes is unique, but it does not satisfy the property of irreducibility because Roll Number, which is a subset of the composite key, is unique.

### 12.7.2 Primary Key

The primary key is an attribute or a set of attributes that uniquely identifies a specific record in the table. In case we have multiple candidate keys in a relation, any one of the candidate keys can be chosen as the primary_key. Since a candidate key cannot have null value, the primary key can also not contain any null value because we cannot uniquely identify multiple null values.

Every candidate key satisfies the properties of becoming the primary key. In our example, if we have two candidate keys, **Roll Number** and **(Name, Class),** then any one can be chosen as the primary key.

**Points to remember about Primary Key:** To qualify as a primary key for an entity, an attribute must have the following properties:

1. The value of a primary key must *not change or should not become null*. For example, the admission number of a student can neither become null nor can change throughout the time the student is in the school.

Data Management **277**

2. The primary key must have *minimum number of attributes* that are sufficient enough to ensure uniqueness of the record. This also means that a super key should not be made the primary key. That is, if a combination of Name and Class are chosen as the primary key then Name, Class and Phone Number should not be set as the primary key.
3. The record must have a valid value for the primary key field when it is being entered in the table. Without primary key's existence, the record cannot be entered in the table.

*Candidate keys, which are not chosen as the primary key, are known as Alternate Keys.*

## 12.7.3 Foreign Key

Foreign key is an attribute or a combination of attributes which defines the relationship between two tables. Basically, foreign key is a primary key in one table that appears as a field in another table. Refer Fig. 12.7 to understand the difference between these keys.

| STUDENT_ID | NAME | PHONE NUMBER | COURSE_ID |
|---|---|---|---|
| | | | |
| | | | |
| | | | |

Candidate Keys = STUDENT_ID and (NAME, PHONE NUMBER)
Primary Key = STUDENT_ID
Foreign Key = COURSE_ID
Alternate Key = (NAME, PHONE NUMBER)
Composite Key = (NAME, PHONE NUMBER)

**Figure 12.7** Keys in a database

For example, consider one table that has fields **Roll Number, Name, Class and Teacher ID** and another table that has fields **Teacher ID and Teacher Name** where Teacher ID is the primary key of Teacher's table. We see that the primary key, Teacher ID in Teacher's table is also a field in the Student's Table. Hence, *Teacher ID acts as a foreign key that connects the two tables.*

We can tell which teacher is teaching a student by seeing his/her Teacher ID and fetching the teacher's name from the Teacher's table using the Teacher ID field. Thus, we see that foreign keys are used to link together two or more different tables which have some form of relationship or link with each other.

### Uses of foreign key
1. A foreign key helps to maintain data integrity in the table (also known as referential integrity).
2. It is also used for navigating between different occurrences of an entity.

For the above two reasons, *foreign key values should always be matched by corresponding primary key values.* For example, in the above tables, if Teacher ID = 9 does not exist in Teacher's table and the user tries to enter Teacher ID as 9 in the Student's table, then it points to data incorrectness and violates data integrity.

So, we must first enter the Teacher Name and Teacher ID (= 9) in the Teacher's table and then use it in Student's table to maintain referential integrity. Look at Fig12.8, can you tell details of student with roll number S04? Can you tell his/her name, course fees, status, teacher and the course he/she is studying? Now do you realize the utility of foreign keys in real-world databases? Doesn't it keep our data better organized?

| Roll_No | Name | Course ID | Teacher ID | Fees | Status |
|---------|---------|-----------|------------|--------|----------|
| S01 | Mehek | C07 | T011 | 300000 | Paid |
| S02 | Chahal | C05 | T024 | 500000 | Not Paid |
| S03 | Tamanna | C03 | T007 | 100000 | Paid |
| S04 | Anushka | C01 | T036 | 400000 | Not Paid |
| S05 | Anika | C08 | T018 | 800000 | Paid |

| Teacher ID | Teacher Name | Course ID |
|------------|----------------|-----------|
| T003 | Jaya Sood | C03 |
| T007 | Mansi Jain | C01 |
| T011 | Shefali Garg | C08 |
| T015 | Divya Tripathi | C05 |
| T018 | Vaishnavi | C02 |
| T022 | Rahul | C10 |
| T024 | Manish Kumar | C07 |
| T029 | Knshna Aiyyar | C04 |
| T035 | Nagarajan | C06 |
| T036 | Sai Murthy | C09 |

| Course ID | Course Name |
|-----------|----------------------|
| C01 | IT |
| C02 | CS |
| C03 | Electronics |
| C04 | Electrical Engtneering |
| C05 | Chemtcal Engtneering |
| C06 | Management |
| C07 | Material Management |
| C09 | Mathemattcs |
| C10 | Operational Research |
| C11 | Statistics |

**Figure 12.8** Use of foreign keys to access information from multiple tables

**Artificial keys:** Sometimes the DBA has to create keys known as artificial keys in the table. This happens in two situations: when no attribute has all the primary key properties, or when the primary key is too large and complex to use.

For example, using the combination of **Name and Phone Number** fields as primary key is a little complicated. Therefore, if roll number of the student is not given, then the DBA may add a ROW_ID column as primary key of the table. In such a scenario, the ROW_ID field is known as the Artificial Key.

## 12.8 RELATIONAL DATA INTEGRITY RULES

To maintain data integrity, certain rules must be enforced on tables in the database. These rules are implemented as constraints or restrictions and include:

**Null or Unknown Value Constraint:** Null represents a value for an attribute that is currently unknown or is not applicable for the row. Null values are used to denote incomplete or exceptional data. It is wrong to treat a null value equivalent to zero or a text string filled with spaces as they represent the absence of a value.

**Entity Integrity rule:** This rule states that value of primary key of a row cannot be null. This is important as the primary key identifies a particular record and it must have a valid value.

**Referential Integrity:** Referential Integrity rule states that if a foreign key exists in a relation, then the foreign key value must match with the corresponding primary key value in the other table.

**Enterprise Constraints:** These are additional rules specified by the users or database administrators of a database. For example, while entering PHONE NUMBER in the Student's Table, a constraint can be added to check that the phone number must be of exactly 10 digits. When such a constraint is enforced on the table, it will not be possible to add a new student or update a record with a phone number that has less than or more than 10 digits.

## Key Terms

**Data atomicity:** Feature that allows data to be restored to the correct state that existed prior to the failure.

**Database:** A collection of related data organized in a way that allows users to easily access, update and maintain the data.

**Data dictionary or Metadata:** Repository that stores information about data stored data in the database.

**Database Management System (DBMS):** Software that interacts with users' application programs and database to insert, update, delete and retrieve data.

**Database Administrator (DBA):** The person responsible for making strategic and policy decisions regarding the data.

**Table:** A collection of data records where each record contains the same fields but with a different value for the fields.

**Report generator:** An essential part of the DBMS program that utilizes the output of query execution to create a report in the prescribed format.

**Data Definition Language:** Language that has modules and functions to define the structure of the data. This is useful for adding, deleting and modifying records.

**Query:** A DML statement that is written to retrieve information from the database.

**Tuple:** The rows of tables are known as Tuples.

**Attributes:** The columns or fields of a table are called attributes of the table.

**Degree:** The number of attributes in a relation determines the degree of relation. A table that has five columns have a relation of degree 5.

**Cardinality:** The number of tuples or rows in a relation is known as cardinality of the relation.

**Candidate key:** Candidate keys are those attributes or columns of a table, which have the properties of uniqueness and irreducibility.

**Composite key:** When we create keys using more than one column then that key is known as composite key.

**Primary key:** The primary key is an attribute or a set of attributes that uniquely identifies a specific record in the table.

**Alternate key:** Candidate keys, which are not chosen as the primary key, are known as Alternate Keys.

**Foreign key:** An attribute or a combination of attributes which defines relationship between two tables.

**Null or Unknown Value Constraint:** Null represents a value for an attribute that is currently unknown or is not applicable for the row.

**Entity Integrity Rule:** Integrity constraint which states that the value of primary key of a row cannot be null.

**Referential Integrity:** Referential Integrity rule states that if a foreign key exists in a relation, then the foreign key value must match with the corresponding primary key value in the other table.

## Chapter Highlights

- Files do not respond to un-anticipatory queries or any kind of investigative or trend analysis.
- Database stores non-redundant data that can be shared by different application systems.
- Non-redundancy of data means that only a single copy of data exists in the entire system. Non-redundancy ensures data consistency.
- The hardware consists of secondary storage devices on which data is stored; input and output devices for receiving/giving data to users; and processor and main memory for processing the data in a fast and efficient manner.
- DBMS is responsible for maintaining the integrity and security of stored data and for recovering information in case of system failure.
- An application programmer writes application programs to access, retrieve, update, delete or add new data to the database.

- System analysts identify end-users' requirements, plan solutions, recommend hardware and software and conduct a feasibility analysis of the identified requirements.
- In a relational database, data and the relationship that exist between the data are represented using tables, also known as relations.
- In a table, each column represents an attribute of an entity. A common attribute in two tables is used to maintain a relationship between them.
- RDBMS organizes data in a way that is simple to understand and use. It also provides flexible data organization.
- The DBMS engine is used to create tables, store, process and secure database data.
- The query processor accepts user queries and transforms them into a series of instructions.
- DML commands are compiled by query compiler, optimized by query optimizer and finally executed by query evaluation engine.
- In a table, big or small, there must be some field or a combination of fields which should have only unique values. Such a field(s) is called a database key or simply, a key.
- A super key is a combination of two or more fields that satisfies the uniqueness property but not necessarily the irreducibility property. This means that a candidate key is a special case of a super key.
- The primary key must have the minimum number of attributes that are sufficient enough to ensure uniqueness of the record.
- Sometimes DBA has to create artificial keys in the table. This happens in two situations: when no attribute has all the primary key properties, or when the primary key is too large and complex to use.

## Review Questions

1. List some disadvantages of using files for storing data.
2. Define database. List some advantages of using a database.
3. How is a file different from a database?
4. What do you mean by data consistency?
5. List at least five applications of databases.
6. What is metadata? What information does it give?
7. What is DBMS?
8. Categorize different database users.
9. What do you understand by the term 'relation'?
10. Give the advantages of using a RDBMS.
11. Write a short note on Query processor.
12. Why do we add artificial keys in a table?
13. Define the different types of constraints on table.
14. Differentiate between data definition and data manipulation.
15. Explain the types of DML.
16. With the help of an example, explain the concept of candidate keys, primary key, super key, alternate key and composite key.

17. What is ACID test?
18. Imagine that you have been assigned to design a database for storing student's name, class, section, activity of their interest (Cooking, Sports, Arts, Music, Dance or Dramatics) and date of joining the activity. Design the table(s). Specify the column(s) in the table(s). Demonstrate the design by inserting at least five records.

## Fill in the Blanks

1. Redundancy means _____.
2. _____ means data is restored to the correct state that existed prior to the failure.
3. Non-redundancy ensures _____.
4. In a _____, only a single copy of data exists that is shared by all the applications running in every department.
5. _____ is a repository that stores information about data stored data in the database.
6. _____ maintains enormous amount of textual and multimedia data in databases.
7. _____ is the software that interacts with user application programs and database to insert, update, delete and retrieve data.
8. _____ identify end-user requirements and plan solutions.
9. A _____ is a collection of data records where each record contains the same fields but with a different value for the fields.
10. In a table, each _____ represents an attribute of an entity.
11. _____ consists of three modules – DDL interpreter, DML compiler and a query evaluation engine.
12. _____ utilizes the output of query execution to create a report in the prescribed format.
13. Every time DDL is executed, _____ gets modified.
14. Data type of fields can be changed and integrity constraints can be added using _____ language.
15. SQL is an example of _____ DML.
16. A row of tables are known as _____.
17. The columns or fields of a table are called _____ of the table.
18. _____ means that a relation (or table) must not have two different rows with the same value for that column (or attribute or field).
19. _____ means that no proper subset of the candidate key has the uniqueness property.
20. When we create keys using more than one column, then that key is known as _____ key.
21. _____ values are used denote incomplete or exceptional data.
22. _____ constraint states that the value of primary key of a row cannot be null.
23. _____ requires that concurrent transactions execute separately from each other.
24. _____ requires the ability to recover from an unexpected system failure or power outage to the last known state.
25. _____ requires that when a transaction has been committed, the data must conform to the database schema.

## State True or False

1. Data can be retrieved conveniently and efficiently from files.
2. A DBMS is a collection of related data organized in a way that allows users to easily access, update and maintain the data.
3. Files store non-redundant data that can be shared by different application systems.
4. Non-redundancy means that only a single copy of data exists in the entire system.
5. A database administrator writes application programs to access, retrieve, update, delete or add new data to the database.
6. Unsophisticated end-users write their own queries to access and process the data stored in the database.
7. In a table, each row is unique.
8. Multimedia, temporal, spatial and unstructured data can be efficiently represented in relational databases.
9. Data Manipulation Language has modules and functions to define the structure of the data.
10. Only the database administrator can define the database and make changes to its definition as and when required.
11. Relational Algebra is an example of non-procedural DML.
12. The number of tuples or rows in a relation is known as cardinality of the relation.
13. No individual attribute of candidate key should be unique.
14. Every relation has only one candidate key.
15. A candidate key may have null value.
16. In case we have multiple candidate keys in a relation, any one of the candidate keys can be chosen as the primary key.
17. The primary key must have maximum number of attributes that are sufficient enough to ensure uniqueness of the record.
18. Files support data isolation.

## Multiple Choice Questions

1. Files lack flexibility. This means that files do not support _____.
   a. un-anticipatory queries
   b. investigative analysis
   c. trend analysis
   d. All of these.

2. Advantages of a database do not include _____.
   a. data inconsistency
   b. data consistency
   c. data integrity
   d. data atomicity

3. _____ is responsible for maintaining the integrity and security of stored data and for recovering information in case of system failure.
   a. Database
   b. DBMS
   c. Operating System
   d. MS Excel

4. Which of the following is not an example of DBMS?
   a. MS ACCESS
   b. SQL Server
   c. FoxPro
   d. None of these.

5. _____ need not know about the database design, working, access mechanism and other technical details of the database.
   a. Application Programmers
   b. DBA
   c. End-users
   d. System Analyst

6. A DBA does not _____.
   a. train users	b. administer database
   c. ensure database security	d. write queries to process data

7. _____ accepts users' queries and transforms them into a series of instructions.
   a. Query Processor	b. DBMS Engine	c. Data Dictionary	d. Report Writer

8. A DML cannot be used for _____.
   a. adding records	b. deleting records	c. adding integrity constraints	d. modifying records

9. Which module of the DBMS provides functions to allow multiple users to access the database simultaneously?
   a. Data Security and Integrity	b. Data Concurrency
   c. Performance Optimization	d. Query Processor

10. The number of attributes in a relation determines the _____ of relation.
    a. Degree	b. Cardinality	c. Order	d. Tuple

11. _____ key is a combination of two or more fields that satisfies the uniqueness property but not necessarily the irreducibility property.
    a. Candidate	b. Composite	c. Super	d. Primary

12. _____ key is an attribute or a combination of attributes which defines relationship between two tables.
    a. Candidate	b. Foreign	c. Super	d. Primary

13. Which Integrity rule states that if a foreign key exists in a relation, then the foreign key value must match with the corresponding primary key value in the other table?
    a. Entity	b. Referential	c. Enterprise	d. Null Value

14. _____ requires a transaction to execute completely or not at all.
    a. Atomicity	b. Consistency	c. Isolation	d. Durability

## Answers

### Fill in the Blanks
1. repetition
2. Data atomicity
3. data consistency
4. database
5. Data dictionary or metadata
6. World Wide Web
7. DBMS
8. System analysts
9. table
10. column
11. Query processor
12. Report generator
13. data dictionary
14. Data Definition
15. non-procedural
16. Tuples
17. attributes
18. Uniqueness
19. Irreducibility
20. composite
21. Null
22. Entity Integrity
23. Isolation
24. Durability
25. Consistency

### State True or False
1. False
2. False
3. False
4. True
5. False
6. False
7. True
8. False
9. False
10. True
11. False
12. True
13. True
14. False
15. True
16. True
17. False
18. False

## Multiple Choice Questions

1. d
2. a
3. b
4. d
5. c
6. d
7. a
8. c
9. b
10. a
11. c
12. b
13. b
14. a

# Structured Query Language (SQL) 13

## Chapter Objectives

We have already gone through the need and basic concepts of databases. Going a step further, in this chapter we will read about SQL, which is the most widely used database query language. Topics discussed here include:

- How MySQL works
- Data types and operators in SQL
- Performing simple calculations with SELECT statement
- SQL numeric and string functions
- Creating and removing databases
- Creating, deleting, altering and updating tables
- WHERE, WHERE IN, WHERE LIKE, SELECT DISTINCT, ORDER BY clauses
- Using the SQL MIN, MAX, COUNT, AVG, SUM functions
- Creating column aliases
- Handling NULL values
- Adding primary and foreign key constraints

## 13.1 MYSQL DATABASE

Before starting with SQL, we must first have a database. In this chapter, we have used the MySQL database. We have used MySQL because it is a fast, easy-to-use RDBMS that is widely used because of the following reasons:

- MySQL is an open-source software; so users do not have to pay to use it.
- It is a very powerful program that can handle a large subset of the functionality of the most expensive and powerful database packages.
- MySQL uses SQL data language.
- It can be used on a number of operating systems.
- MySQL can be integrated with many languages including PHP, PERL, C, C++, JAVA, etc.
- It performs well with even large data sets having up to 50 million rows or more in a table. The default file size limit for a table is 4GB. In fact, a database of even 8 million terabytes (TB) is not uncommon these days.
- MySQL can be customized as per user requirements.
- It satisfies ACID property.
- MySQL supports powerful techniques to ensure that only authorized users can access the database.

> MySQL is developed, marketed and supported by a Swedish company MySQL AB.

> The US tech company Sun Microsystems bought MySQL AB in 2008. Later, in 2010 Oracle acquired Sun Microsystems and MySQL has been practically owned by Oracle since then.

## 13.2 INTRODUCTION TO SQL

SQL, pronounced as S-Q-L or sometime See-Qwell, is a database query language. Many people think of it as a database but it is a language that helps users to access and manipulate data stored in a relational database. SQL queries (or statements) can be used to perform operations like retrieving, inserting, updating and deleting data. They can also be used to create tables or modify the structure of existing tables. However, to use SQL queries, you must first install a database, like Oracle, MySQL, MongoDB, PostGres SQL, SQL Server, DB2, etc.

### 13.2.1 How MySQL Works

MySQL works on client-server model. Computers that install and run RDBMS software are called clients. Whenever they need to access data, they connect to the RDBMS server. That is the "client-server" part.

Figure 13.1 explains the basic structure of the client-server structure. One or more devices (clients) connect to a server to access data stored in the database server. Every client can make a request from the graphical user interface (GUI) on their screens and the server responds with the desired output. The basic working of such a client-server model can be understood as,

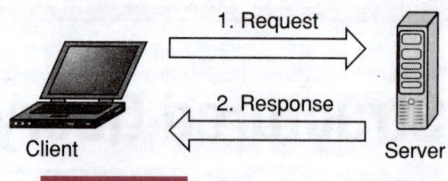

**Figure 13.1** Client-server model

1. MySQL creates a database for storing and manipulating data.
2. Clients request data using specific SQL statements that are executed on the MySQL.
3. The server application responds with the requested information that is then displayed on the client machine.

> MySQL is written in C and C++.

### 13.2.2 Uses of SQL

SQL allows users to create queries where a query is a request for data stored in one or more tables in the database. These queries are simple English-like statements. With the help of queries, users can **access, modify, insert and delete data** from table(s) stored in the database.

SQL can also be used to create metadata for describing the data. With SQL, users can **create and drop (delete) tables**.

Users can **create procedures** and functions and set permission on them to restrict their usage.

### 13.2.3 Types of SQL Queries

The two types of SQL queries that we will be reading about in this section are DDL and DML. While DDL or the Data Definition Language is used to create or modify database objects (like tables, views, indexes, users, etc), the DML or the Data Manipulation Language, on the other hand, is used to manipulate data (like inserting, updating, deleting data).

## 13.3 SQL DATA TYPES

Before we actually start creating tables and inserting records into it using DDL and DML, we must first know the permitted data types in SQL. Each column in a table must have a valid name and a data type.

While creating a table, the SQL developer must specify what type of data will be stored in each column. In this chapter, we have used MySQL version 8.0. Some important data types used in MySQL are given in Table 13.1.

**Table 13.1** Data types in SQL

| Data type | Description |
|---|---|
| **CHAR(SIZE)** | A fixed-length string that may have alphabets, digits, and special characters. The size parameter specifies maximum number of characters. Its value may vary from 0 to 255. By default, its size is 1. |
| **VARCHAR(SIZE)** | A variable-length string that may have alphabets, digits, and special characters. The size parameter specifies maximum number of characters. Its value may vary from 0 to 65535. |
| **BOOL** | Zero is considered as false, nonzero values are considered as true. |
| **INT( SIZE)** | It can be used to specify a signed or unsigned integer. A signed integer is in the range −2147483648 to 2147483647 and an unsigned integer is in the range 0 to 4294967295. The size parameter which can take any value from 0–255, specifies the maximum width for displaying the value. |
| **FLOAT(P)** | A floating-point number. MySQL uses the P value to determine whether to use FLOAT or DOUBLE for the resulting data type. If P is from 0 to 24, the data type becomes float and double when P varies from 25 to 53. |

Table 13.2 makes a comparison between char and varchar data types.

**Table 13.2** Difference between CHAR and VARCHAR

| CHAR data type | VARCHAR data type |
|---|---|
| It stands for Character. | It stands for a Variable Character. |
| Values are stored in fixed lengths and are padded with space characters to match the specified length. | Values are stored in variable length and are not padded with any characters |
| It can hold a maximum of 255 characters. | It can hold a maximum of 65,535 characters. |
| It uses static memory allocation. | It uses dynamic memory allocation. |
| Takes 1 byte per character for storage. | Takes 1 byte per character plus an additional 1 or 2 extra bytes for storing length information. |
| Used when the length of the variable is known. | Used only when the length of the variable is not known. |
| It only accepts characters. | It accepts both characters and numbers. |
| Performs faster than Varchar. | It is slower than Char |

## 13.3.1 Date and Time Types

The MySQL date and time datatypes are as follows:

*Date:* A date is stored in YYYY-MM-DD format, between 1000-01-01 and 9999-12-31. For example, September 30th, 2021 would be stored as 2021-09-30.

*Datetime:* A date and time combination in YYYY-MM-DD HH:MM:SS format, between 1000-01-01 00:00:00 and 9999-12-31 23:59:59. For example, 2:20 in the afternoon on September 30th, 2021 would be stored as 2021-09-30 14:20:00.

*Timestamp:* A timestamp between midnight, January 1st, 1970 and sometime in 2037. This looks like the previous DATETIME format, only without the hyphens between numbers; 2:20 in the afternoon on September 30th, 2021 would be stored as 20210930142000 ( YYYYMMDDHHMMSS ).

*Time:* Stores the time in a HH:MM:SS format.

*Year(m):* Stores a year in a 2-digit or a 4-digit format. If the length is a 2-digit number then it can specify any year from 1970 to 2069 (70 to 69). If the length is a 4-digit number, then YEAR can be from 1901 to 2155. The default length of year is 4.

## 13.4 OPERATORS IN SQL

An operator is a reserved word or a character in SQL statement that is extensively used in WHERE clause of the query to perform arithmetic (discussed in Table 13.3) or comparison (discussed in Table 13.4) operations. These operators are used to specify conditions in an SQL statement. Go through the arithmetic and logical operators given below and observe the result when a = 100 and b = 50.

### Table 13.3  Arithmetic operators in SQL

| Operator | Description | Example | Result |
|---|---|---|---|
| + | Adds values on either side of the operator | a + b | 150 |
| – | Subtracts right-side value from the left-side value | a – b | 100 |
| * | Multiplies values on either side of the operand | a * b | 5000 |
| / | Divides left-side value with the right-side value | a / b | 2 |
| % | Divides left-side value with the right-side value and returns the remainder | a % b | 0 |
| > | Returns True if the left value is greater than the right and False otherwise. | a > b | True |
| >= | Returns True if the left value is either equal to or greater than the right and False otherwise. | a >= b | True |
| < | Returns True if the left value is less than the right and False otherwise. | a < b | False |
| <= | Returns True if the left value is either equal to or less than the right value and False otherwise. | a <= b | False |
| = | Returns True if the two values on either side are equal and False otherwise. | a = b | False |
| != | Returns True if the two values on either side are not equal and False otherwise. | a != b | True |
| <> | | a <> b | True |
| !< | Returns True if the left value is not less than the right value and False otherwise. | a !< b | True |
| !> | Returns True if the left value is not greater than the right value and False otherwise. | a !> b | False |

### Table 13.4  Comparison operators in SQL

| Operator | Description |
|---|---|
| ALL | The ALL operator is used to compare a value to all values in another value set. |
| AND | The AND operator allows the existence of multiple conditions in an SQL statement's WHERE clause. |
| OR | The OR operator is used to combine multiple conditions in an SQL statement's WHERE clause. |
| ANY | Compares a value to any applicable values in the list as given in the condition. |
| BETWEEN | Searches for values that are within a set of values, provided the minimum value and the maximum value are specified. |
| IN | Checks for the presence of a value in the list of specified literal values. |
| LIKE | Searches for similar values using wildcard characters. |
| NOT | The NOT operator reverses the meaning of the logical operator with which it is used. Eg: NOT EXISTS, NOT BETWEEN, NOT IN, etc. This is a negate operator. |
| IS NULL | Checks if a given value is NULL. |
| UNIQUE | Ensures no duplicate values. |

## 13.5 PERFORMING SIMPLE CALCULATIONS WITH SELECT STATEMENT

We can even use the SQL SELECT statement to perform mathematical calculations. In this special type of SELECT statement, no table is specified in the FROM clause. Examples of such SELECT statements are given below.

```
mysql> select 10 + 9;
+--------+
| 10 + 9 |
+--------+
|     19 |
+--------+
1 row in set (0.00 sec)
mysql> select 11*10;
+-------+
| 11*10 |
+-------+
|   110 |
+-------+
1 row in set (0.00 sec)
mysql> select 360/60;
+--------+
| 360/60 |
+--------+
| 6.0000 |
+--------+
1 row in set (0.00 sec)
```

```
mysql> select 100 > 50;
+----------+
| 100 > 50 |
+----------+
|        1 |
+----------+
1 row in set (0.00 sec)
mysql> select 90%4;
+------+
| 90%4 |
+------+
|    2 |
+------+
1 row in set (0.00 sec)
```

## 13.6 SQL NUMERIC FUNCTIONS

Numeric Functions are used to perform operations on numbers and return numbers. Some commonly used numeric functions used in SQL are discussed below.

**ABS()** returns the absolute value of a number.
```
mysql> SELECT ABS(-98.7);
+------------+
| ABS(-98.7) |
+------------+
|       98.7 |
+------------+
1 row in set (0.01 sec)
```

**COS(), SIN(), TAN(), COT()** functions return the cosine, sine, tangent and cotangent of the given number respectively.
```
mysql> SELECT TAN(45);
+--------------------+
| TAN(45)            |
+--------------------+
| 1.6197751905438615 |
+--------------------+
1 row in set (0.00 sec)
```

**CEIL()** returns the smallest integer value that is greater than or equal to a number.
```
mysql> SELECT CEIL(21.345);
+--------------+
| CEIL(21.345) |
+--------------+
|           22 |
+--------------+
1 row in set (0.00 sec)
```

**DEGREES()** converts a radian value into degrees.
```
mysql> SELECT DEGREES(1.02);
+-------------------+
| DEGREES(1.02)     |
+-------------------+
| 58.44169510334397 |
+-------------------+
1 row in set (0.00 sec)
```

**DIV()** is used for integer division.
```
mysql> SELECT 100 DIV 20;
+------------+
| 100 DIV 20 |
+------------+
|          5 |
+------------+
1 row in set (0.00 sec)
```

**EXP()** returns *e* raised to the power of a number.
```
mysql> SELECT EXP(2);
+------------------+
| EXP(2)           |
+------------------+
| 7.38905609893065 |
+------------------+
1 row in set (0.00 sec)
```

**GREATEST()** returns the greatest value in the given list.
```
mysql> SELECT GREATEST(-10,210,20,-20,30,-30,100,-100);
+------------------------------------------+
| GREATEST(-10,210,20,-20,30,-30,100,-100) |
+------------------------------------------+
|                                      210 |
+------------------------------------------+
1 row in set (0.00 sec)
```

**LEAST()** returns the smallest value in the given list.
```
mysql> SELECT LEAST(-10,210,20,-20,30,-30,100,-100);
+---------------------------------------+
| LEAST(-10,210,20,-20,30,-30,100,-100) |
+---------------------------------------+
|                                  -100 |
+---------------------------------------+
1 row in set (0.00 sec)
```

**LN()**, **LOG10()**, **LOG2()** returns the natural logarithm, base-10 logarithm and base-2 logarithm of a number respectively.
```
mysql> SELECT LOG10(100);
+------------+
| LOG10(100) |
+------------+
|          2 |
+------------+
1 row in set (0.01 sec)
```

**MOD()** returns the remainder of *n* divided by *m*.
```
mysql> SELECT 103 MOD 5;
+-----------+
| 103 MOD 5 |
+-----------+
|         3 |
+-----------+
1 row in set (0.00 sec)
```

**FLOOR()** returns the largest integer value that is less than or equal to a number.
```
mysql> SELECT FLOOR(21.345);
+---------------+
| FLOOR(21.345) |
+---------------+
|            21 |
+---------------+
1 row in set (0.00 sec)
```

**PI()** returns the value of PI displayed with 6 decimal places.
```
mysql> SELECT PI();
+----------+
| PI()     |
+----------+
| 3.141593 |
+----------+
1 row in set (0.00 sec)
```

**POW()** returns *m* raised to the *n*th power.
```
mysql> SELECT POW(10,3);
+-----------+
| POW(10,3) |
+-----------+
|      1000 |
+-----------+
1 row in set (0.00 sec)
```

**RADIANS()** converts a value in degrees to radians.
```
mysql> SELECT RADIANS(360);
+-------------------+
| RADIANS(360)      |
+-------------------+
| 6.283185307179586 |
+-------------------+
1 row in set (0.00 sec)
```

**RAND()** returns a random number.
```
mysql> SELECT RAND();
+--------------------+
| RAND()             |
+--------------------+
| 0.8558367722256451 |
+--------------------+
1 row in set (0.00 sec)
```

**ROUND()** returns a number rounded to a certain number of decimal places.
```
mysql> SELECT ROUND(3.14156,2);
+------------------+
| ROUND(3.14156,2) |
+------------------+
|             3.14 |
+------------------+
1 row in set (0.00 sec)
```

**SQRT()** returns the square root of a number.
```
mysql> SELECT SQRT(144);
+-----------+
| SQRT(144) |
+-----------+
|        12 |
+-----------+
1 row in set (0.00 sec)
```

**TRUNCATE()** truncates the given number after a specified number of places right of the decimal point.
```
mysql> SELECT TRUNCATE(3.141567,3);
+----------------------+
| TRUNCATE(3.141567,3) |
+----------------------+
|                3.141 |
+----------------------+
1 row in set (0.00 sec)
```

## 13.7 STRING FUNCTIONS

The string functions in MySQL are used to manipulate textual data stored in tables. These functions can also be used along with update commands to change data values stored in tables. Some most frequently used string functions are discussed below.

**ASCII()** function is used to find the ASCII value of a character.
```
mysql> SELECT ASCII('R');
+------------+
| ASCII('R') |
+------------+
|         82 |
+------------+
1 row in set (0.02 sec)
```

**CHAR_LENGTH()** function is used to find the length of a string.
```
mysql> SELECT CHAR_LENGTH('GOOD MORNING');
+-----------------------------+
| CHAR_LENGTH('GOOD MORNING') |
+-----------------------------+
|                          12 |
+-----------------------------+
1 row in set (0.02 sec)
```

**CONCAT()** function is used to add two words or strings.
```
mysql> SELECT CONCAT('GOOD','--','MORNING');
+-------------------------------+
| CONCAT('GOOD','--','MORNING') |
+-------------------------------+
| GOOD--MORNING                 |
+-------------------------------+
1 row in set (0.05 sec)
```

**FIND_IN_SET()** function is used to find a symbol from a set of symbols.
```
mysql> SELECT FIND_IN_SET('I','M,O,R,N,I,N,G');
+---------------------------------+
| FIND_IN_SET('I','M,O,R,N,I,N,G') |
+---------------------------------+
|                               5 |
+---------------------------------+
1 row in set (0.00 sec)
```

**INSTR()** function is used to find the occurrence of an alphabet.
```
mysql> SELECT INSTR('GOOD MORNING','R');
+---------------------------+
| INSTR('GOOD MORNING','R') |
+---------------------------+
|                         8 |
+---------------------------+
1 row in set (0.02 sec)
```

**LCASE()** function is used to convert the given string into lower case. You can even use the LOWER() function to do the same work.
```
mysql> SELECT LCASE('GOOD MORNING');
+-----------------------+
| LCASE('GOOD MORNING') |
+-----------------------+
| good morning          |
+-----------------------+
1 row in set (0.05 sec)
```

**UCASE()** function is used to convert the given string into upper case. You can even use the UPPER() function to do the same work.
```
mysql> SELECT UPPER('good morning');
+-----------------------+
| UPPER('good morning') |
+-----------------------+
| GOOD MORNING          |
+-----------------------+
1 row in set (0.02 sec)
```

**LEFT()** function is used to SELECT a sub string from the left of given size or characters.
```
mysql> SELECT LEFT('GOOD MORNING',7);
+------------------------+
| LEFT('GOOD MORNING',7) |
+------------------------+
| GOOD MO                |
+------------------------+
1 row in set (0.01 sec)
```

**LPAD()** function makes a string of the specified size by adding the given symbol.
```
mysql> SELECT LPAD('GOOD MORNING',20,'*');
+-----------------------------+
| LPAD('GOOD MORNING',20,'*') |
+-----------------------------+
| ********GOOD MORNING        |
+-----------------------------+
1 row in set (0.01 sec)
```

**LTRIM()** function removes leading white spaces from the given string.
```
mysql> SELECT LTRIM('     GOOD MORNING');
+----------------------------+
| LTRIM('     GOOD MORNING') |
+----------------------------+
| GOOD MORNING               |
+----------------------------+
1 row in set (0.00 sec)
```

**MID()** function displays a sub-string of given length starting from the specified position. The SUBSTR() also performs the same task.
```
mysql> SELECT MID('GOOD MORNING WORLD',8,4);
+-------------------------------+
| MID('GOOD MORNING WORLD',8,4) |
+-------------------------------+
| RNIN                          |
+-------------------------------+
1 row in set (0.00 sec)
```

**REPEAT()** function re-writes the given string, the specified number of times.
```
mysql> SELECT REPEAT('BYE',2);
+-----------------+
| REPEAT('BYE',2) |
+-----------------+
| BYEBYE          |
+-----------------+
1 row in set (0.01 sec)
```

**REVERSE()** function reverses a string.
```
mysql> SELECT REVERSE('GOOD MORNING');
+-------------------------+
| REVERSE('GOOD MORNING') |
+-------------------------+
| GNINROM DOOG            |
+-------------------------+
1 row in set (0.00 sec)
```

**RIGHT()** function selects a sub-string of given size from the right side of the string.

```
mysql> SELECT RIGHT('GOOD MORNING',10);
+--------------------------+
| RIGHT('GOOD MORNING',10) |
+--------------------------+
| OD MORNING               |
+--------------------------+
1 row in set (0.00 sec)
```

**RPAD()** function makes the given string as long as the given size by adding the given symbol on the right.

```
mysql> SELECT RPAD('GOOD MORN-
ING',20,'*');
+-------------------------------+
| RPAD('GOOD MORNING',20,'*')   |
+-------------------------------+
| GOOD MORNING********          |
+-------------------------------+
1 row in set (0.01 sec)
```

**RTRIM()** function removes white spaces from the end of the given string.

```
mysql> SELECT RTRIM('GOOD MORNING    ');
+---------------------------+
| RTRIM('GOOD MORNING    ') |
+---------------------------+
| GOOD MORNING              |
+---------------------------+
1 row in set (0.00 sec)
```

**STRCMP()** function compares two strings. If both the strings are equal, it returns 0. If the first string is smaller than the second, –1 is returned. Otherwise, the function will return 1.

```
mysql> SELECT STRCMP('GOOD MORNING','GOOD EVENING');
+---------------------------------------+
| STRCMP('GOOD MORNING','GOOD EVENING') |
+---------------------------------------+
|                                     1 |
+---------------------------------------+
1 row in set (0.00 sec)
```

**TRIM()** function removes leading and trailing white spaces from the given string.

```
mysql> SELECT TRIM('    GOOD MORNING    ');
+------------------------------+
| TRIM('    GOOD MORNING    ') |
+------------------------------+
| GOOD MORNING                 |
+------------------------------+
1 row in set (0.01 sec)
```

## 13.8 CREATING DATABASE

As mentioned before, a database is a collection of related tables. So, before we create any table, we must first create a database. This can be done using the CREATE DATABASE statement. The syntax of using this statement can be given as,

**CREATE DATABASE database_name;**

where database_name is a unique name or identifier for the database.

**Example 13.1** Let us create a database named mydb.

```
mysql> create database myDB;
Query OK, 1 row affected (0.24 sec)
```

Once the database is created, we can use the **show databases;** statement to see a list of all the databases present in MySQL. Our newly created database must appear in this list.

```
mysql> show databases;
+--------------------+
| Database           |
+--------------------+
| information_schema |
| mydb               |
| mysql              |
| performance_schema |
| sys                |
+--------------------+
5 rows in set (0.33 sec)
```

Now, we need to select a particular database in which we would be working. Any table created will be added in the selected database. To select a particular database and start using it, we need the **use database** command as given below.

```
mysql> use mydb;
Database changed
```

## 13.9 REMOVING DATABASE

The DROP DATABASE statement is used to drop or remove an existing database. The syntax of this statement can be given as,

**DROP DATABASE databasename;**

However, before removing a database, always remember that when we delete a database, all the information stored in it is lost.

```
mysql> show databases;
+--------------------+
| Database           |
+--------------------+
| information_schema |
| mb                 |
| mydb               |
| mysql              |
| performance_schema |
| sys                |
+--------------------+
6 rows in set (0.00 sec)
```

```
mysql> drop database mb;
Query OK, 0 rows affected (0.11 sec)

mysql> show databases;
+--------------------+
| Database           |
+--------------------+
| information_schema |
| mydb               |
| mysql              |
| performance_schema |
| sys                |
+--------------------+
5 rows in set (0.00 sec)
```

## 13.10 CREATING TABLES

To create a table, we must specify the name of the table. We must also define its columns and each column's data type. In SQL, the **CREATE TABLE** statement is used to create a table. The basic syntax of this statement can be given as,

```
CREATE TABLE table_name(
    column1 datatype,
    column2 datatype,
    column3 datatype,
    .....
    columnN datatype,
                PRIMARY KEY(one or more columns )
);
```

In the above syntax,
**CREATE TABLE** is the keyword that specifies that you want to create a table in the database.
**table_name** is a unique name or identifier for the table. A round bracket is opened following the table_name. Within the opening and closing brackets, list of columns and their corresponding data types are specified.

> **Example 13.2**
> Let us create a Student table with columns – Roll_Number, Name, Phone_Number, Marks and Class. Remember that NOT NULL is a constraint that means value for a particular field cannot be NULL. In the Student table, we will explicitly specify that the Roll_Number, Name and Phone_Number cannot be NULL. We will also set Roll_Number as the primary key of the table.

```
mysql>  CREATE TABLE STUDENT (
    -> ROLL_NUMBER INT NOT NULL,
    -> NAME VARCHAR(20) NOT NULL,
    -> PHONE_NUMBER CHAR(10) NOT NULL,
    -> AGE INT,
    -> MARKS INT,
    -> CLASS CHAR(10),
    -> PRIMARY KEY (ROLL_NUMBER)
    -> );
Query OK, 0 rows affected, 1 warning (1.32 sec)
```

Once the table is created, we can use the DESC command to see the description of the newly created table.

```
mysql> DESC STUDENT;
+--------------+-------------+------+-----+---------+-------+
| Field        | Type        | Null | Key | Default | Extra |
+--------------+-------------+------+-----+---------+-------+
| ROLL_NUMBER  | int(11)     | NO   | PRI | NULL    |       |
| NAME         | varchar(20) | NO   |     | NULL    |       |
| PHONE_NUMBER | char(10)    | NO   |     | NULL    |       |
| AGE          | int(11)     | YES  |     | NULL    |       |
| MARKS        | int(11)     | YES  |     | NULL    |       |
| CLASS        | char(10)    | YES  |     | NULL    |       |
+--------------+-------------+------+-----+---------+-------+
6 rows in set (0.04 sec)
```

The above results verify that the student table is created in our database with the specified fields and constraints.

## 13.11 DELETING TABLE

A table can be deleted using the **DROP TABLE** statement. When a table is deleted, all its definition, data, indexes, views, triggers, constraints and permission specifications are removed from the database. the syntax of DROP TABLE statement can be given as,

**DROP TABLE table_name;**

> You should be very careful while using the DROP TABLE command as once it is executed, the table is completely deleted along with all the information in it.

### Example 13.3 — Let us delete our table STUDENT.

```
mysql> drop table student;
Query OK, 0 rows affected (0.56 sec)
```

Note that 0 rows are affected as we have not inserted any row till now. To verify whether our table was deleted or not, let us again use the DESC statement and observe the result.

```
mysql> desc student;
ERROR 1146 (42S02): Table 'mydb.student' doesn't exist
```

Note that the error indicates that the student table in mydb database no longer exists.

## 13.12 INSERTING VALUES IN TABLE

To insert values in a table, it must first be created using the CREATE TABLE command. In the last section, we had deleted the STUDENT table but for executing other SQL statements, we have re-created the table using CREATE TABLE command.

In a table, values can be inserted using the **INSERT INTO** statement. This statement is used to add new rows of data in a table that exists in the database.

There are two basic syntaxes of the INSERT INTO statement, which are shown below.

```
INSERT INTO TABLE_NAME VALUES (value1,value2,value3,...valueN);
```

### Example 13.4 — Let us insert at least five rows in our student table.

```
mysql> INSERT INTO STUDENT VALUES(1,'RAHUL','9876543210',18, 89,'12-D');
Query OK, 1 row affected (0.26 sec)
mysql> INSERT INTO STUDENT VALUES(2,'SARFARAZ','9823416790',17, 97,'11-A');
Query OK, 1 row affected (0.07 sec)
mysql> INSERT INTO STUDENT VALUES(3,'RIA','7825516230',16,67,'10-C');
Query OK, 1 row affected (0.04 sec)
mysql> INSERT INTO STUDENT VALUES(4,'PALAK','9999123456',9,75,'9-B');
Query OK, 1 row affected (0.18 sec)
mysql> INSERT INTO STUDENT VALUES(5,'KRISH','9807126534',14,90,'8-D');
Query OK, 1 row affected (0.12 sec)
```

## 13.13 RETRIEVING DATA FROM TABLE

The **SELECT** statement in SQL is used to fetch or retrieve data from one or more tables in the database. The results of the SELECT statement is in the form of a table. This resultant table is known as the result-set. The syntax of the SELECT statement can be given as,

```
SELECT column1, column2, columnN FROM table_name;
```

Here, column1, column2... are fields of the table from which data has to be fetched. To fetch all fields from the table, the syntax is

```
SELECT * FROM table_name;
```

**Example 13.5** Let us select the entire data from all fields in the student table. Also select only the Roll_Number and Marks fields from the student table.

```
mysql> SELECT * FROM STUDENT;
+-------------+----------+--------------+------+-------+-------+
| ROLL_NUMBER | NAME     | PHONE_NUMBER | AGE  | MARKS | CLASS |
+-------------+----------+--------------+------+-------+-------+
|           1 | RAHUL    | 9876543210   |   18 |    89 | 12-D  |
|           2 | SARFARAZ | 9823416790   |   17 |    97 | 11-A  |
|           3 | RIA      | 7825516230   |   16 |    67 | 10-C  |
|           4 | PALAK    | 9999123456   |    9 |    75 | 9-B   |
|           5 | KRISH    | 9807126534   |   14 |    90 | 8-D   |
+-------------+----------+--------------+------+-------+-------+
5 rows in set (0.00 sec)

mysql> SELECT ROLL_NUMBER, MARKS FROM STUDENT;
+-------------+-------+
| ROLL_NUMBER | MARKS |
+-------------+-------+
|           1 |    89 |
|           2 |    97 |
|           3 |    67 |
|           4 |    75 |
|           5 |    90 |
+-------------+-------+
5 rows in set (0.00 sec)
```

## 13.14 THE WHERE CLAUSE

The WHERE clause is used in the SELECT statement to specify a condition for retrieving data from one or more tables. We use the WHERE clause to filter the records in the table and fetch only those that meet the specified criteria.

In addition to the SELECT statement, the WHERE clause is also used with the UPDATE and DELETE statements. The basic syntax of the SELECT statement with the WHERE clause can be given as,

```
SELECT column1, column2, columnN
FROM table_name
WHERE [condition]
```

We can even use comparison and logical operators in the WHERE clause. Let us see a couple of queries to see how the SELECT statement with WHERE clause actually works.

**Example 13.6** Display the name and class of the students who scored less than 90 marks.

```
mysql> SELECT NAME, CLASS FROM STUDENT WHERE MARKS < 90;
+-------+-------+
| NAME  | CLASS |
+-------+-------+
| RAHUL | 12-D  |
| RIA   | 10-C  |
| PALAK | 9-B   |
+-------+-------+
3 rows in set (0.00 sec)
```

### Example 13.7 — Let us now select the phone number, marks and class of a student whose name is SARFARAZ.

```
mysql> SELECT PHONE_NUMBER, MARKS, CLASS FROM STUDENT WHERE NAME = 'SARFARAZ';
+--------------+-------+-------+
| PHONE_NUMBER | MARKS | CLASS |
+--------------+-------+-------+
| 9823416790   |    97 | 11-A  |
+--------------+-------+-------+
1 row in set (0.00 sec)
```

Observe that all the character and strings should be specified within single quotes (' ') but numeric values should be given without any quotes (as shown in the Example 13.6).

## 13.15 SQL AND AND OR OPERATORS

The SQL AND and OR operators are used for combining multiple conditions to specify a criterion for fetching data from a table. These two operators are called as the conjunctive operators.

As the name specifies, the AND operator allows the existence of multiple conditions in an SQL statement's WHERE clause. The basic syntax of using the AND operator can be given as,

```
SELECT column1, column2, columnN
FROM table_name
WHERE [condition1] AND [condition2]...AND [conditionN];
```

We can specify any number of conditions in the WHERE clause using the AND operator. For an action to be taken by the SQL statement, all conditions separated by the AND operator must be TRUE.

### Example 13.8 — Let us write a query to display the name and class of all the students having marks more than 90 and age >=15.

*Note that we have inserted an additional row in the table.*

```
mysql> SELECT NAME, CLASS FROM STUDENT WHERE MARKS < 90 AND AGE>=15;
+-------+-------+
| NAME  | CLASS |
+-------+-------+
| RAHUL | 12-D  |
| RIA   | 10-C  |
+-------+-------+
2 rows in set (0.00 sec)
```

The basic syntax of the OR operator with a WHERE clause can be given as,

```
SELECT column1, column2, columnN
FROM table_name
WHERE [condition1] OR [condition2]...OR [conditionN]
```

As per the syntax, *n* number of conditions can be tested using the OR operator. To execute the query, any one of the conditions separated by the OR operator must be TRUE.

### Example 13.9 — Display the name and class of students scoring more than 90 marks or having age = 18.

```
mysql> SELECT NAME, CLASS FROM STUDENT WHERE MARKS < 90 OR AGE = 18;
+-------+-------+
| NAME  | CLASS |
+-------+-------+
| RAHUL | 12-D  |
| RIA   | 10-C  |
| PALAK | 9-B   |
+-------+-------+
3 rows in set (0.00 sec)
```

| Example 13.10 | Display the name and class of students who have scored between 75 and 90 (boundaries inclusive). |

```
mysql> SELECT NAME, CLASS FROM STUDENT
    -> WHERE MARKS >=75 AND MARKS <=90;
+-------+-------+
| NAME  | CLASS |
+-------+-------+
| RAHUL | 12-D  |
| PALAK | 9-B   |
| KRISH | 8-D   |
+-------+-------+
3 rows in set (0.00 sec)
```

## 13.16 THE WHERE BETWEEN CLAUSE

The WHERE BETWEEN clause returns values that fall within a given range. This clause is a shorthand for >= AND <=. Note that WHERE BETWEEN operator is inclusive of starting and ending values. The syntax of this clause can be given as,

```
SELECT column-names
FROM table-name
WHERE column-name BETWEEN value1 AND value2
```

| Example 13.11 | Display the Name, Class and Marks of students who scored between 75 and 90 (boundaries inclusive) using the WHERE BETWEEN clause. |

```
mysql> SELECT NAME, CLASS, MARKS FROM STUDENT
    -> WHERE MARKS BETWEEN 75 AND 90;
+-------+-------+-------+
| NAME  | CLASS | MARKS |
+-------+-------+-------+
| RAHUL | 12-D  |   89  |
| PALAK | 9-B   |   75  |
| KRISH | 8-D   |   90  |
+-------+-------+-------+
3 rows in set (0.01 sec)
```

## 13.17 THE SQL WHERE IN CLAUSE

The WHERE IN clause returns values that match values in a list or a sub-query. This clause is a shorthand for multiple OR conditions. The general syntax of WHERE IN clause can be given as,

```
SELECT column-names
FROM table-name
WHERE column-name IN (values)
```

**Example 13.12** Display the details of all the students who have got marks 89, 67 or 90.

```
mysql> SELECT * FROM STUDENT
    -> WHERE MARKS IN (89, 67, 90);
+-------------+--------+--------------+------+-------+-------+
| ROLL_NUMBER | NAME   | PHONE_NUMBER | AGE  | MARKS | CLASS |
+-------------+--------+--------------+------+-------+-------+
|           1 | RAHUL  | 9876543210   |   18 |    89 | 12-D  |
|           3 | RIA    | 7825516230   |   16 |    67 | 10-C  |
|           5 | KRISH  | 9807126534   |   14 |    90 | 8-D   |
+-------------+--------+--------------+------+-------+-------+
3 rows in set (0.00 sec)
```

## 13.18 THE SQL SELECT DISTINCT STATEMENT

The SELECT DISTINCT statement is used to return only distinct (different) values. Thus, this clause eliminates duplicate entries while displaying data from the table. The syntax of DISTINCT clause, when used with the SELECT statement, can be given as,

```
SELECT DISTINCT column1, column2,.....columnN
FROM table_name
WHERE [condition]
```

table_name specifies name of the table(s) from which data has to be retrieved. We can specify more than one table name also.

The WHERE condition is optional. If present, it specifies the conditions that must be satisfied before retrieving data.

Note that the DISTINCT clause does not ignore NULL values. So, if a table has null values, DISCTINCT clause will include them as well in the result set.

> The SQL DISTINCT keyword is used in conjunction with the SELECT statement to eliminate all duplicate records and fetch only unique records.

**Example 13.13**

Consider the table given below.
```
mysql> SELECT * FROM ISSUE;
+--------+--------+-------------+-------+
| RollNO | Name   | Book_Issued | Class |
+--------+--------+-------------+-------+
|    121 | MAHEK  | LAB MANUAL  | XI-A  |
|    253 | NIYON  | PHYSICS     | IX-C  |
|    390 | GIRIJ  | SCIENCE     | X-B   |
|    404 | CHINUK | PHYSICS     | XII-B |
|    507 | fAIZAL | BIOLOGY     | X-D   |
|    611 | NASIMA | MATHS       | VI-A  |
|    729 | KIARA  | SCIENCE     | VII-C |
+--------+--------+-------------+-------+
7 rows in set (0.00 sec)
```

Let us select value for Book_Issued from the table without using the DISTINCT clause first.

```
mysql> SELECT Book_Issued FROM ISSUE;
+-------------+
| Book_Issued |
+-------------+
| LAB MANUAL  |
| PHYSICS     |
| SCIENCE     |
| PHYSICS     |
| BIOLOGY     |
| MATHS       |
| SCIENCE     |
+-------------+
7 rows in set (0.00 sec)
```

Now let us use the same query but with DISTINCT clause to appreciate the results.

```
mysql> SELECT DISTINCT Book_Issued FROM ISSUE;
+-------------+
| Book_Issued |
+-------------+
| LAB MANUAL  |
| PHYSICS     |
| SCIENCE     |
| BIOLOGY     |
| MATHS       |
+-------------+
5 rows in set (0.00 sec)
```

Did you notice that the first select statement selected all values including duplicates from the Book_Issued column? The SELECT statement with DISTINCT clause selected only non-duplicate values. To know how many distinct subjects books were issued, we can write

```
mysql> SELECT COUNT(DISTINCT Book_Issued) FROM ISSUE;
+-----------------------------+
| COUNT(DISTINCT Book_Issued) |
+-----------------------------+
|                           5 |
+-----------------------------+
1 row in set (0.00 sec)
```

## 13.19 ORDER BY CLAUSE

The ORDER BY statement in SQL is used to sort the retrieved data in either ascending or descending order. We can sort the values in the result-set by one or more columns using the ORDER BY clause.

By default, ORDER BY sorts the data in ascending order. To sort in descending order, we can use the keyword DESC. To specifically state ascending as the sorting order, the keyword ASC is used.

Syntax of all ways of using ORDER BY clause with the SELECT statement can be given as,

*Sort according to one column:* To sort in ascending or descending order we can use the keywords ASC or DESC respectively. The syntax for this can be given as,

```
SELECT expressions
FROM tables
[WHERE conditions]
ORDER BY expression [ ASC | DESC ]
```

where,
**Expressions** specifies the columns to be retrieved.
**Tables** is the table from which the records have to be retrieved. At least one table must be listed in the FROM clause.
**WHERE** condition is optional. If specified, the condition must be satisfied for the records to be selected.
**ASC** is optional as it is the default sorting order. ASC sorts the result-set in ascending order by *expression*.
**DESC** is optional. If present, it sorts the result-set in descending order by *expression*.

*Sort according to multiple columns:* To sort according to multiple columns, separate the names of columns by (,) operator. The syntax can be given as,
```
SELECT * FROM table_name ORDER BY column1 ASC|DESC , column2 ASC|DESC
```

**Example 13.14** **To sort records of Employee table in ascending order of their salaries, we can write**

```
mysql> SELECT EMPNO, SAL FROM EMPLOYEE ORDER BY SAL;
+-------+-------+
| EmpNo | SAL   |
+-------+-------+
|   456 |  NULL |
|   567 |  NULL |
|   678 |  NULL |
|   123 | 35000 |
|   234 | 50000 |
|   345 | 75000 |
+-------+-------+
6 rows in set (0.05 sec)
```

Correspondingly, to sort records based on ascending order of name and further on descending order of salary, if some employees have the same name, then we can write

```
mysql> SELECT * FROM EMPLOYEE ORDER BY NAME ASC, SAL DESC;
```

## 13.20 UPDATING THE TABLE

The SQL UPDATE statement is used to modify the existing data in a table. We can even use the WHERE clause with the UPDATE query to update only selected rows, so that not all the rows are affected. The basic syntax of the UPDATE query with a WHERE clause can be given as,

```
UPDATE table_name
SET column1 = value1, column2 = value2...., columnN = valueN
WHERE [condition];
```

Again, according to the syntax, any number of conditions can be specified using the AND or the OR operators in the WHERE clause.

**Example 13.15** **Update the STUDENT table to set age of the student in class 9-B to 15. Also show the records of the table to check whether the record was updated or not.**

```
mysql> UPDATE STUDENT SET AGE = 15 WHERE CLASS = '9-B';
Query OK, 1 row affected (0.08 sec)
Rows matched: 1  Changed: 1  Warnings: 0
mysql> SELECT * FROM STUDENT;
+-------------+---------+--------------+------+-------+-------+
| ROLL_NUMBER | NAME    | PHONE_NUMBER | AGE  | MARKS | CLASS |
+-------------+---------+--------------+------+-------+-------+
|           1 | RAHUL   |   9876543210 |   18 |    89 | 12-D  |
|           2 | SARFARAZ|   9823416790 |   17 |    97 | 11-A  |
|           3 | RIA     |   7825516230 |   16 |    67 | 10-C  |
|           4 | PALAK   |   9999123456 |   15 |    75 | 9-B   |
|           5 | KRISH   |   9807126534 |   14 |    90 | 8-D   |
+-------------+---------+--------------+------+-------+-------+
5 rows in set (0.00 sec)
```

**Example 13.16** **Let us update the class of all the students to 6-A.**

Note that in this case, we do not need the WHERE clause. We will simply write,

```
mysql> UPDATE STUDENT SET CLASS = '6-A';
```

## 13.21 DELETING ROWS FROM A TABLE

The DELETE query in SQL is used to delete existing record(s) from a table in the database. To delete only selected rows from the table, we can even use WHERE clause with DELETE query; otherwise all the records would be deleted. The basic syntax of the DELETE query, when used with WHERE clause, can be given as,

```
DELETE FROM table_name
WHERE [condition];
```

In the `condition` field any number of conditions can be specified using AND or OR operators.

**Example 13.17** **Let us delete the record of the student having roll number 6.**

Note that in this case, we do not need the WHERE clause. We will simply write,

```
mysql> DELETE FROM STUDENT WHERE ROLL_NUMBER = 6;
```

**Example 13.18** **Let us delete all the records from the STUDENT table.**

Note that in this case, we do not need the WHERE clause. We will simply write,

```
mysql> DELETE FROM STUDENT;
```

Now, the STUDENT table does not have any record.

## 13.22 THE WHERE LIKE CLAUSE IN SQL

The WHERE LIKE clause determines if a character string matches a pattern. It is usually used when only a fragment of a text value is known. That is, the SQL LIKE clause is used with the WHERE clause to compare a value to find similar values using wildcard characters. The two wildcard characters that are extensively used with the LIKE clause include % and _.

Here, % represents zero, one or multiple characters. And the underscore represents a single number or character. These two characters can also be used in combinations. The basic syntax of LIKE clause can be given as,

```
SELECT FROM table_name
WHERE column LIKE 'XXXX%'
or
SELECT FROM table_name
WHERE column LIKE '%XXXX%'
or
SELECT FROM table_name
WHERE column LIKE 'XXXX_'
or
SELECT FROM table_name
WHERE column LIKE '_XXXX'
or
SELECT FROM table_name
WHERE column LIKE '_XXXX_'
```

Here, xxxx mean any numeric or string value.

**Example 13.19** Let us select details of all the students whose name starts with 'R'.

```
mysql> SELECT * FROM STUDENT WHERE NAME LIKE 'R%';
+-------------+--------+--------------+------+-------+-------+
| ROLL_NUMBER | NAME   | PHONE_NUMBER | AGE  | MARKS | CLASS |
+-------------+--------+--------------+------+-------+-------+
|           1 | RAHUL  | 9876543210   |  18  |  89   | 12-D  |
|           3 | RIA    | 7825516230   |  16  |  67   | 10-C  |
+-------------+--------+--------------+------+-------+-------+
2 rows in set (0.03 sec)
```

**Example 13.20** Let us display details of all the students who study in the 'D section.

```
mysql> SELECT * FROM STUDENT WHERE CLASS LIKE '%D';
+-------------+--------+--------------+------+-------+-------+
| ROLL_NUMBER | NAME   | PHONE_NUMBER | AGE  | MARKS | CLASS |
+-------------+--------+--------------+------+-------+-------+
|           1 | RAHUL  | 9876543210   |  18  |  89   | 12-D  |
|           5 | KRISH  | 9807126534   |  14  |  90   | 8-D   |
+-------------+--------+--------------+------+-------+-------+
2 rows in set (0.00 sec)
```

**Example 13.21** Display the details of all the students whose phone number start with a '9' and has a '7' in it.

```
mysql> SELECT * FROM STUDENT WHERE PHONE_NUMBER LIKE '9%7%';
+-------------+----------+--------------+------+-------+-------+
| ROLL_NUMBER | NAME     | PHONE_NUMBER | AGE  | MARKS | CLASS |
+-------------+----------+--------------+------+-------+-------+
|           1 | RAHUL    | 9876543210   |  18  |  89   | 12-D  |
|           2 | SARFARAZ | 9823416790   |  17  |  97   | 11-A  |
|           5 | KRISH    | 9807126534   |  14  |  90   | 8-D   |
+-------------+----------+--------------+------+-------+-------+
3 rows in set (0.00 sec)
```

**Example 13.22** Select details of all the students who are not in classes 10, 11 or 12.

```
mysql> SELECT * FROM STUDENT WHERE CLASS LIKE '_-_';
+-------------+--------+--------------+------+-------+-------+
| ROLL_NUMBER | NAME   | PHONE_NUMBER | AGE  | MARKS | CLASS |
+-------------+--------+--------------+------+-------+-------+
|           4 | PALAK  | 9999123456   |  15  |  75   | 9-B   |
|           5 | KRISH  | 9807126534   |  14  |  90   | 8-D   |
+-------------+--------+--------------+------+-------+-------+
2 rows in set (0.00 sec)
```

*Note that here, we want a single digit only after '-'.*

### Example 13.23 Display details of all the students who are in class 10, 11 or 12.

```
mysql> SELECT * FROM STUDENT WHERE CLASS LIKE '__-%';
+-------------+----------+--------------+------+-------+-------+
| ROLL_NUMBER | NAME     | PHONE_NUMBER | AGE  | MARKS | CLASS |
+-------------+----------+--------------+------+-------+-------+
|           1 | RAHUL    | 9876543210   |   18 |    89 | 12-D  |
|           2 | SARFARAZ | 9823416790   |   17 |    97 | 11-A  |
|           3 | RIA      | 7825516230   |   16 |    67 | 10-C  |
+-------------+----------+--------------+------+-------+-------+
3 rows in set (0.00 sec)
```

### Example 13.24 Display the details of all the students whose name does not have an 'I'.

```
mysql> SELECT * FROM STUDENT
    -> WHERE NAME NOT LIKE '%I%';
+-------------+----------+--------------+------+-------+-------+
| ROLL_NUMBER | NAME     | PHONE_NUMBER | AGE  | MARKS | CLASS |
+-------------+----------+--------------+------+-------+-------+
|           1 | RAHUL    | 9876543210   |   18 |    89 | 12-D  |
|           2 | SARFARAZ | 9823416790   |   17 |    97 | 11-A  |
|           4 | PALAK    | 9999123456   |   15 |    75 | 9-B   |
+-------------+----------+--------------+------+-------+-------+
3 rows in set (0.01 sec)
```

## 13.23 SQL SELECT MIN, MAX STATEMENT

As the name suggests, the SELECT MIN statement in SQL returns the minimum value for a column. Correspondingly, the SELECT MAX statement returns the maximum value for a column.

The general MIN syntax is:

**SELECT MIN(column-name)**
**FROM table-name**

and the general MAX syntax can be given as,

**SELECT MIN(column-name)**
**FROM table-name**
mysql> SELECT MIN(MARKS) FROM STUDENT;

### Example 13.25 Display the minimum marks obtained by a student.

```
+------------+
| MIN(MARKS) |
+------------+
|         67 |
+------------+
1 row in set (0.04 sec)
```

**Example 13.26** Display the maximum marks obtained by a student.

```
mysql> SELECT MAX(MARKS) FROM STUDENT;
+------------+
| MAX(MARKS) |
+------------+
|         97 |
+------------+
1 row in set (0.04 sec)
```

**Example 13.27** Display the details of students scoring maximum marks.

```
mysql> SELECT * FROM STUDENT
    -> WHERE MARKS = (SELECT MAX(MARKS) FROM STUDENT);
+-------------+----------+--------------+------+-------+-------+
| ROLL_NUMBER | NAME     | PHONE_NUMBER | AGE  | MARKS | CLASS |
+-------------+----------+--------------+------+-------+-------+
|           2 | SARFARAZ | 9823416790   |   17 |    97 | 11-A  |
+-------------+----------+--------------+------+-------+-------+
1 row in set (0.00 sec)
```

**Example 13.28** Display the maximum marks obtained by students in classes 8 and 9.

```
mysql> SELECT MAX(MARKS) FROM STUDENT WHERE CLASS LIKE '_-_';
+------------+
| MAX(MARKS) |
+------------+
|         90 |
+------------+
1 row in set (0.00 sec)
```

**Example 13.29** Display the maximum marks obtained by students in classes 10, 11 and 12.

```
mysql> SELECT MAX(MARKS) FROM STUDENT WHERE CLASS LIKE '__-_';
+------------+
| MAX(MARKS) |
+------------+
|         97 |
+------------+
1 row in set (0.00 sec)
```

**Example 13.30** Display the maximum marks obtained by a student having roll number greater than 3.

```
mysql> SELECT MAX(MARKS) FROM STUDENT WHERE ROLL_NUMBER >3;
+------------+
| MAX(MARKS) |
+------------+
|         90 |
+------------+
1 row in set (0.00 sec)
```

## 13.24 SELECT COUNT, SUM, AVG

The SELECT COUNT statement returns a count of the number of data values. The SELECT SUM returns the sum of the data values. And the SELECT AVG returns the average of the data values.

The general COUNT syntax is:

**SELECT COUNT(column-name)**
**FROM table-name**

| Example 13.31 | Let us find out number of rows in our STUDENT table. |
|---|---|

```
mysql> SELECT COUNT(ROLL_NUMBER)
FROM STUDENT;
+--------------------+
| COUNT(ROLL_NUMBER) |
+--------------------+
|                  5 |
+--------------------+
1 row in set (0.03 sec)
```

The general SUM syntax is:

**SELECT SUM(column-name)**
**FROM table-name**

| Example 13.32 | Let us display the total marks obtained by all the students in the STUDENT table where age is less than or equal to 15. |
|---|---|

```
mysql> SELECT SUM(MARKS) FROM STUDENT
    -> WHERE AGE <= 15;
+------------+
| SUM(MARKS) |
+------------+
|        165 |
+------------+
1 row in set (0.03 sec)
```

The general AVG syntax is:

**SELECT AVG(column-name)**
**FROM table-name**

| Example 13.33 | Find out the average age of students scoring at least 90 marks. |
|---|---|

```
mysql> SELECT AVG(AGE) FROM STUDENT
    -> WHERE MARKS >= 90;
+----------+
| AVG(AGE) |
+----------+
|  15.5000 |
+----------+
1 row in set (0.00 sec)
```

## 13.25 COLUMN ALIASES

By default, SELECT statement displays the column heading(s) in the result set as the name of that column in the table. However, we can use a column alias to change the name of the column heading in the result set. The syntax of creating a column alias is,

**SELECT column_name AS column_alias**
**FROM table_name.**

Consider the Employee table given below. And observe how the AS keyword can be used to create a column alias.

```
mysql> select * from Employee;
+-------+-------+
| EmpNo | Sal   |
+-------+-------+
|   123 | 35000 |
|   234 | 50000 |
|   345 | 75000 |
+-------+-------+
3 rows in set (0.00 sec)
```

```
mysql> select EmpNo, Sal AS Salary from Employee;
+-------+--------+
| EmpNo | Salary |
+-------+--------+
|   123 |  35000 |
|   234 |  50000 |
|   345 |  75000 |
+-------+--------+
3 rows in set (0.00 sec)
```

Thus, we see that we can use column alias if the original column name does not meet our requirements or clearly define its purpose. In such a case, column alias can be used to define a meaningful name for the column.

We can also use column alias to give name to a column that is dynamically created by applying an expression to an existing column in the table.

```
mysql> SELECT EmpNo, Sal, Sal + Sal * 0.10 As NEW_SAL FROM EMPLOYEE;
+-------+-------+---------+
| EmpNo | Sal   | NEW_SAL |
+-------+-------+---------+
|   123 | 35000 |   38500 |
|   234 | 50000 |   55000 |
|   345 | 75000 |   82500 |
+-------+-------+---------+
3 rows in set (0.00 sec)
```

> An alias only exists for the duration of the query.

From the above discussion, it can be seen that SQL aliases are used to give a table, or a column in a table, a temporary name. They are often used to make column names more readable.

## 13.26 HANDLING NULL VALUES

We know how to retrieve data from a table using the SQL SELECT command along with the WHERE clause. But there is something more that has to be discussed. When we use a condition that compares a column value to NULL, it does not work properly. To handle such a situation, MySQL provides three operators:

**IS NULL** which returns True, if the column value is NULL. The basic syntax of using IS NULL operator is, column_name IS NULL.

**IS NOT NULL** which returns True, if the column value is not NULL. The basic syntax of using IS NOT NULL operator is, column_name IS NOT NULL.

<=> which compares values and gives true even for two NULL values.

Since conditions involving NULL values are special, we cannot use = NULL or != NULL to check for NULL values in columns. The code given below illustrates this concept.

```
mysql> SELECT * FROM EMPLOYEE;
+-------+-------+
| EmpNo | Sal   |
+-------+-------+
|   123 | 35000 |
|   234 | 50000 |
|   345 | 75000 |
|   456 |  NULL |
|   567 |  NULL |
|   678 |  NULL |
+-------+-------+
6 rows in set (0.00 sec)
```

```
mysql> SELECT * FROM EMPLOYEE WHERE Sal = NULL;
Empty set (0.00 sec)
```

We see that = does not work with NULL values. Therefore, we must re-write our SQL query as given below.

```
mysql> SELECT * FROM EMPLOYEE            mysql> SELECT * FROM EMPLOYEE
    -> WHERE Sal IS NOT NULL;                -> WHERE Sal IS NULL;
+-------+-------+                        +-------+------+
| EmpNo | Sal   |                        | EmpNo | Sal  |
+-------+-------+                        +-------+------+
|   123 | 35000 |                        |   456 | NULL |
|   234 | 50000 |                        |   567 | NULL |
|   345 | 75000 |                        |   678 | NULL |
+-------+-------+                        +-------+------+
3 rows in set (0.00 sec)                 3 rows in set (0.00 sec)
```

From the above discussion, we can conclude that the SQL NULL is both a value as well as a keyword. In simple terms, NULL is a place holder for data that does not exist or whose value is not known.

**Key points to remember**
- NULL is not a data type in SQL.
- Arithmetic operations involving NULL always return NULL. For example, 10 + NULL = NULL.
- All aggregate functions affect only rows that do not have NULL values.
- Comparison operations can be used with NULL values. For example,

```
mysql> select 10 = NULL;
+-----------+
| 10 = NULL |
+-----------+
|      NULL |
+-----------+
1 row in set (0.00 sec)
mysql> SELECT NULL > NULL;
+-------------+
| NULL > NULL |
+-------------+
|        NULL |
+-------------+
1 row in set (0.00 sec)
mysql> SELECT NULL <=> NULL;
+---------------+
| NULL <=> NULL |
+---------------+
|             1 |
+---------------+
1 row in set (0.00 sec)
```

**The IFNULL() Function:** The IFNULL() function is used for replacing NULL values in MySQL. The function accepts two arguments. The first argument is returned only if it is not NULL. If it is NULL, then the second argument is returned instead. The code given below demonstrates the use of IFNULL() function.

```
mysql> SELECT * FROM EMPLOYEE;
+-------+-------+
| EmpNo | Sal   |
+-------+-------+
|   123 | 35000 |
|   234 | 50000 |
|   345 | 75000 |
|   456 | NULL  |
|   567 | NULL  |
|   678 | NULL  |
+-------+-------+
6 rows in set (0.00 sec)
```

```
mysql> SELECT EmpNo, IFNULL(Sal,0) FROM EMPLOYEE;
+-------+-------------------+
| EmpNo | IFNULL(Sal,00000) |
+-------+-------------------+
|   123 |             35000 |
|   234 |             50000 |
|   345 |             75000 |
|   456 |                 0 |
|   567 |                 0 |
|   678 |                 0 |
+-------+-------------------+
6 rows in set (0.00 sec)
```

**The IF() Function:** As an alternative to IFNULL() function, we can use the IF() function along with the IS NULL/IS NOT NULL operators. The operators check for NULL values, and the IF() function will take a suitable course of action depending on the outcome of the operators.

**Example 13.34** Let us use the IF() function to replace NULL values with 0 in the salary column of the employee table.

```
mysql> SELECT EmpNo, IF(Sal IS NOT NULL, Sal, 0) FROM EMPLOYEE;
+-------+-----------------------------+
| EmpNo | IF(Sal IS NOT NULL, Sal, 0) |
+-------+-----------------------------+
|   123 |                       35000 |
|   234 |                       50000 |
|   345 |                       75000 |
|   456 |                           0 |
|   567 |                           0 |
|   678 |                           0 |
+-------+-----------------------------+
6 rows in set (0.00 sec)
```

## 13.27 SQL PRIMARY KEY CONSTRAINT

We know that the PRIMARY KEY constraint helps us to uniquely identify each record in the table. The primary key must contain UNIQUE values, and cannot have NULL values.

A table can have only one primary key and the primary key may consist of one or more fields. In this chapter, we have set the primary key by using the following syntax.

```
mysql>  CREATE TABLE STUDENT (
    -> ROLL_NUMBER INT NOT NULL,
    -> NAME VARCHAR(20) NOT NULL,
    -> PHONE_NUMBER CHAR(10) NOT NULL,
    -> AGE INT,
    -> MARKS INT,
    -> CLASS CHAR(10),
    -> PRIMARY KEY (ROLL_NUMBER)
    -> );
```

In the above statement, ROLL_NUMBER field has been set as the primary key. *To set more than one fields as the primary key*, we can write,

```
mysql> CREATE TABLE STUDENTS (
    -> ROLL_NUMBER INT NOT NULL,
    -> NAME VARCHAR(20) NOT NULL,
    -> PHONE_NUMBER CHAR(10) NOT NULL,
    -> AGE INT,
    -> MARKS INT,
    -> CLASS CHAR(10),
    -> CONSTRAINT STUDENTS PRIMARY KEY (NAME, PHONE_NUMBER)
    -> );
Query OK, 0 rows affected (0.38 sec)
```

Use the DESC statement to check the description of the newly created table.

```
mysql> DESC STUDENTS;
+--------------+-------------+------+-----+---------+-------+
| Field        | Type        | Null | Key | Default | Extra |
+--------------+-------------+------+-----+---------+-------+
| ROLL_NUMBER  | int(11)     | NO   |     | NULL    |       |
| NAME         | varchar(20) | NO   | PRI | NULL    |       |
| PHONE_NUMBER | char(10)    | NO   | PRI | NULL    |       |
| AGE          | int(11)     | YES  |     | NULL    |       |
| MARKS        | int(11)     | YES  |     | NULL    |       |
| CLASS        | char(10)    | YES  |     | NULL    |       |
+--------------+-------------+------+-----+---------+-------+
6 rows in set (0.01 sec)
```

The output shows that the fields NAME and PHONE_NUMBER are set as the primary keys of the table. To set PRIMARY KEY constraint on an already created table, the ALTER TABLE command is used. However, before setting any field as the primary key, you must ensure that the field has been declared to not contain NULL values (using NOT NULL constraint). The syntax for ALTER TABLE command can be given as,

**ALTER TABLE table_name
ADD PRIMARY KEY (column_name);**

**Example 13.35** Let us use the ALTER TABLE command to se ROLL_NUMBER as the primary key of an already existing table STUDENTS.

```
mysql> ALTER TABLE STUDENTS
    -> ADD PRIMARY KEY (ROLL_NUMBER);
mysql> DESC STUDENTS;
+--------------+-------------+------+-----+---------+-------+
| Field        | Type        | Null | Key | Default | Extra |
+--------------+-------------+------+-----+---------+-------+
| ROLL_NUMBER  | int(11)     | NO   | PRI | NULL    |       |
| NAME         | varchar(20) | NO   |     | NULL    |       |
| PHONE_NUMBER | char(10)    | NO   |     | NULL    |       |
| AGE          | int(11)     | YES  |     | NULL    |       |
| MARKS        | int(11)     | YES  |     | NULL    |       |
| CLASS        | char(10)    | YES  |     | NULL    |       |
+--------------+-------------+------+-----+---------+-------+
6 rows in set (0.00 sec)
```

Correspondingly, to set primary key constraint on multiple columns, the syntax is,

```
ALTER TABLE table_name
ADD CONSTRAINT table_name PRIMARY KEY (column_name1, column_name2,..);
```

**Example 13.36** Set the NAME and PHONE_NUMBER fields of already existing STUDENTS table as the primary key.

```
mysql> ALTER TABLE STUDENTS
    -> ADD CONSTRAINT STUDENTS PRIMARY KEY(NAME, PHONE_NUMBER);
```

## 13.28 DROP A PRIMARY KEY CONSTRAINT

To drop a PRIMARY KEY constraint, the DROP PRIMARY KEY statement is used with the ALTER TABLE statement. The general syntax can be given as,

```
ALTER TABLE table_name
DROP PRIMARY KEY;
```

**Example 13.37** Let us remove the primary key constraint from an already created table.

```
mysql> ALTER TABLE STUDENTS
    -> DROP PRIMARY KEY;
mysql> DESC STUDENTS;
+--------------+-------------+------+-----+---------+-------+
| Field        | Type        | Null | Key | Default | Extra |
+--------------+-------------+------+-----+---------+-------+
| ROLL_NUMBER  | int(11)     | NO   |     | NULL    |       |
| NAME         | varchar(20) | NO   |     | NULL    |       |
| PHONE_NUMBER | char(10)    | NO   |     | NULL    |       |
| AGE          | int(11)     | YES  |     | NULL    |       |
| MARKS        | int(11)     | YES  |     | NULL    |       |
| CLASS        | char(10)    | YES  |     | NULL    |       |
+--------------+-------------+------+-----+---------+-------+
6 rows in set (0.01 sec)
```

From the output, it is clear that now no field is set as the primary key of the table.

## 13.29 ADDING FOREIGN KEY CONSTRAINT

In the last chapter, we read that a FOREIGN KEY is a key used to link two tables. FOREIGN KEY is basically a field (or collection of fields) in one table that refers to PRIMARY KEY in another table.

The FOREIGN KEY constraint prevents actions that would destroy links between tables. It also ensures that invalid data is not inserted into the foreign key column. Only the values given in the primary field column can be used as foreign key values. The general syntax of adding foreign key constraint can be given as,

```
CREATE TABLE table_name (
Column_1 data type,
Column_2 data type,
Column_J data type,
Column_N data type,
PRIMARY KEY (Column_I),
FOREIGN KEY (Column_J) REFERENCES Persons(Column_J)
);
```

## Example 13.38  Create a table STUDENTS with Teacher_ID as foreign key.

Note that before creating table STUDENTS, we must create a table TEACHER.

```
mysql> CREATE TABLE TEACHER(
    -> TEACHER_ID INT NOT NULL,
    -> TEACHER_NAME VARCHAR(20),
    -> PRIMARY KEY(TEACHER_ID)
    -> );
Query OK, 0 rows affected (0.37 sec)
mysql> CREATE TABLE STUDENTS(
    -> ROLL_NO INT NOT NULL,
    -> SNAME VARCHAR(20),
    -> MARKS INT,
    -> TEACHER_ID INT,
    -> PRIMARY KEY(ROLL_NO),
    -> FOREIGN KEY (TEACHER_ID) REFERENCES TEACHER(TEACHER_ID)
    -> );
Query OK, 0 rows affected (0.40 sec)
```

To create a FOREIGN KEY constraint on an already existing table, we must use the ALTER TABLE command as given below.

```
ALTER TABLE STUDENTS
ADD FOREIGN KEY (TEACHER_ID) REFERENCES TEACHER(TEACHER_ID);
mysql> DESC STUDENTS;
```

| Field | Type | Null | Key | Default | Extra |
|---|---|---|---|---|---|
| ROLL_NO | int(11) | NO | PRI | NULL | |
| SNAME | varchar(20) | YES | | NULL | |
| MARKS | int(11) | YES | | NULL | |
| TEACHER_ID | int(11) | YES | MUL | NULL | |

4 rows in set (0.00 sec)

## Key Terms

**SQL:** A database query language.

**Clients:** Computers that install and run RDBMS software are called clients.

**Servers:** To access data, clients connect to powerful machines called servers.

**Metadata:** Data describing data stored in database.

**Data Definition Language (DDL):** SQL statements used to create or modify database objects (like tables, views, indexes, users, etc.).

**Data Manipulation Language (DML):** SQL statements used to manipulate data (like inserting, updating, deleting data).

**Operator:** A reserved word or a character in SQL statement that is extensively used in WHERE clause of the query to perform arithmetic or comparison operations.

**Database:** A collection of related tables.

**Conjunctive operators:** The SQL AND and OR operators that are used to combine multiple conditions to specify a criterion for fetching data from a table are called as the conjunctive operators.

**Foreign key:** A field (or collection of fields) in one table that refers to PRIMARY KEY in another table.

## Chapter Highlights

- MySQL is an open-source software; so users do not have to pay to use it.
- SQL queries (or statements) can be used to perform operations like retrieving, inserting, updating and deleting data. They can be also used to create tables or modify the structure of existing tables. However, to use SQL queries, you must first install a database, like Oracle, MySQL, MongoDB, PostGres SQL, SQL Server, DB2, etc.
- In MySQL, every client can make a request to a server, which then responds with the desired output.
- We can use the SQL SELECT statement to perform mathematical calculations.
- Numeric Functions are used to perform operations on numbers and return numbers.
- The string functions in MySQL are used to manipulate textual data stored in tables.
- A database is created using the CREATE DATABASE statement.
- To select a particular database and start using it, we need to use the database command.
- In SQL, the CREATE TABLE statement is used to create a table.
- A table can be deleted using the DROP TABLE statement. When a table is deleted, all its definition, data, indexes, views, triggers, constraints and permission specifications are removed from the database.
- INSERT INTO statement is used to add new rows of data in a table that exists in the database
- The SELECT statement in SQL is used to fetch or retrieve data from one or more tables in the database.
- SELECT DISTINCT statement eliminates duplicate entries while displaying data from the table.
- The WHERE clause is used in the SELECT statement to specify a condition for retrieving data from one or more tables.
- The ORDER BY statement in SQL is used to sort the retrieved data in either ascending or descending order.
- The SQL UPDATE statement is used to modify the existing data in a table.
- The DELETE query in SQL is used to delete existing record(s) from a table in the database.
- Column alias are used to change the name of the column heading in the result-set.
- The SQL NULL is both a value as well as a keyword. In simple terms, NULL is a place holder for data that does not exist or whose value is not known.
- PRIMARY KEY constraint helps us to uniquely identify each record in the table. The primary key must contain UNIQUE values, and cannot have NULL values.
- A table can have only one primary key which, in turn, consist of one or more fields.
- To set PRIMARY KEY constraint on an already created table, the ALTER TABLE command is used.

## Review Questions

1. What is SQL? Why is it used?
2. MySQL and SQL are the same. Comment on this statement.
3. Explain the working of MySQL.
4. Differentiate between DDL and DML.
5. Why do we need to specify data type? List some data types used in SQL.
6. Differentiate between `char` and `varchar`.
7. How can we create a database in SQL?

8. Write the SQL statements that you will use for the following:
   a. Create a database
   b. View a list of all the databases present in MySQL
   c. Change to another database
   d. Delete a database
   e. Create table
   f. To return values that match values in a list or a sub-query
   g. To sort the retrieved data in either ascending or descending order
   h. To remove records from a table
   i. To return the maximum value for a column
   j. To return the minimum value for a column
   k. To return a count of the number of data values
   l. To return the sum of the data values
   m. To return the average of the data values
   n. To set PRIMARY KEY constraint on an already created table
   o. To drop a PRIMARY KEY constraint.
9. Differentiate between DROP TABLE and DROP DATABASE statements.
10. Explain the syntax of the SELECT statement.
11. What are conjunctive operators? Explain with the help of an example.
12. With the help of an example, explain how you will use the ORDER BY clause to sort data based on multiple columns.
13. What are column aliases?
14. Explain some operators that are used to handle NULL values in SQL.
15. What does primary key constraint state? How can we enforce such a constraint in SQL?
16. Consider the tables given below and write instructions for the following:

| CID | First_name | Last_name | Email | Address | City | State | Zipcode |
|---|---|---|---|---|---|---|---|
| 1 | Girish | Patel | gpatel@gmail.com | 3200 Ki rti Nagar | Merrut | UP | 22121 |
| 2 | John | Samuel | John.s@gmail.com | 1250 Windsor | Lansdowne | UK | 02169 |
| 3 | Tina | Bhargava | Bhargava.tina@gmail.com | 931 Thomas Jefferson Road | Trichy | TN | 22902 |
| 4 | Jamat | Ali | alij786@gmail.com | 11350 Indira Nagar | Bangalore | KA | 22960 |
| 5 | Nick | Jones | nickjones@gmail.com | 2050 Jammu Highway | Katra | JK | 22902 |

| Order_id | Order_Date | Amount | CID |
|---|---|---|---|
| 1 | 07/04/1776 | 234.56 | 1 |
| 2 | 03/14/1760 | 78.50 | 3 |
| 3 | 05/23/1784 | 124.00 | 2 |
| 4 | 09/03/1790 | 65.50 | 3 |
| 5 | 07/21/1795 | 25.50 | 10 |
| 6 | 11/27/1787 | 14.40 | 9 |

a. Get a list of those customers who placed an order and the details of the order they placed.
b. Append Orders information with customer information.
c. Get a list of all orders for which we failed to record information about the customers who placed them:

17. Consider the tables and write the queries for listing all orders with given product names, quantities, and prices.

| Product | Order Item |
|---|---|
| Id | Id |
| ProductName | OrderId |
| SupplierId | ProductId |
| Unit Price | UnitPrice |
| Package | Quantity |
| IsDiscontinued | |

18. Consider the table given below and write the following queries.
    a. Select the name and age of Students.
    b. fetch data for students with age more than 17.
    c. Student with information of male students, of age more than 17.

| ID | Name | Subject | Age |
|---|---|---|---|
| 100 | Ashish | Maths | 19 |
| 200 | Rahul | Science | 20 |
| 300 | Naina | Physics | 20 |
| 400 | Sameer | Chemistry | 21 |

## Programming Exercises

1. **Create a database having two tables with the specified fields, to computerize a library system of a Delhi University College.**
   LibraryBooks (Accession number, Title, Author, Department, PurchaseDate, Price)
   IssuedBooks (Accession number, Borrower)
   a. Identify primary and foreign keys. Create the tables and insert at least 5 records in each table.
   b. Delete the record of book titled "Database System Concepts".
   c. Change the Department of the book titled "Discrete Maths" to "CS".
   d. List all books that belong to "CS" department.
   e. List all books that belong to "CS" department and are written by author "Navathe".
   f. List all computers (Department = "CS") that have been issued.
   g. List all books which have a price less than 500 or purchased between "01/01/1999" and "01/01/2004".

2. **Create a database having three tables to store the details of students of Computer Department in your college.**
   Personal information about Student (College roll number, Name of student, Date of birth, Address, Marks(rounded off to whole number) in percentage at 10 + 2, Phone number)
   Paper Details (Paper code, Name of the Paper) Student's Academic and
   Attendance details (College roll number, Paper code, Attendance, Marks in home examination).
   a. Identify primary and foreign keys. Create the tables and insert at least 5 records in each table.
   b. Design a query that will return the records (from the second table) along with the name of student from the first table, related to students who have more than 75% attendance and more than 60% marks in Paper 2.

c. List all students who live in "Delhi" and have marks greater than 60 in Paper 1.
   d. Find the total attendance and total marks obtained by each student.
   e. List the name of student who has got the highest marks in Paper 2.

3. **Create the following tables and answer the queries given below.**
   Customer (CustID, email, Name, Phone, ReferrerID)
   Bicycle (BicycleID, DatePurchased, Color, CustID, ModelNo)
   BicycleModel (ModelNo, Manufacturer, Style)
   Service (StartDate, BicycleID, EndDate)
   a. Identify primary and foreign keys. Create the tables and insert at least 5 records in each table.
   b. List all the customers who have the bicycles manufactured by manufacturer "Honda".
   c. List the bicycles purchased by the customers who have been referred by customer "C1".
   d. List the manufacturer of red colored bicycles.
   e. List the models of the bicycles given for service.

4. **Create the following tables, enter at least 5 records in each table and answer the queries given below.**
   EMPLOYEE (Person_Name, Street, City)
   WORKS (Person_Name, Company_Name, Salary)
   COMPANY (Company_Name, City)
   MANAGES (Person_Name, Manager_Name)
   a. Identify primary and foreign keys.
   b. Alter table employee, add a column "email" of type `varchar(20)`.
   c. Find the name of all managers who work for both Samba Bank and NCB Bank.
   d. Find the names, street addresses and cities of residence and salary of all employees who work for "Samba Bank" and earn more than $10,000.
   e. Find the names of all employees who live in the same city as the company for which they work.
   f. Find the highest salary, lowest salary and average salary paid by each company.
   g. Find the sum of salary and number of employees in each company.
   h. Find the name of the company that pays the highest salary.

5. **Create the following tables, enter at least 5 records in each table and answer the queries given below.**
   Suppliers (SNo, Sname, Status, SCity)
   Parts (PNo, Pname, Colour, Weight, City)
   Project (JNo, Jname, Jcity)
   Shipment (Sno, Pno, Jno, Qunatity)
   a. Identify primary and foreign keys.
   b. Get supplier numbers for suppliers in Paris with status>20.
   c. Get supplier details for suppliers who supply part P2. Display the supplier list in increasing order of supplier numbers.
   d. Get supplier names for suppliers who do not supply part P2.
   e. For each shipment get full shipment details, including total shipment weights.
   f. Get all the shipments where the quantity is in the range 300 to 750 inclusive.
   g. Get part nos. for parts that either weigh more than 16 pounds or are supplied by suppliers S2, or both.
   h. Get the names of cities that store more than five red parts.
   i. Get full details of parts supplied by a supplier in Delhi.
   j. Get part numbers for part supplied by a supplier in Allahabad to a project in Chennai.
   k. Get the total number of project supplied by a supplier (say, S1).
   l. Get the total quantity of a part (say, P1) supplied by a supplier (say, S1)

## Fill in the Blanks

1. MySQL works on _____ model.
2. _____ describes data stored in database.

3. _____ Language is used to create or modify database objects (like tables, views, indexes, users, etc.).
4. Data type _____ is used to define fixed length strings.
5. _____ is a reserved word or a character in SQL statement that is extensively used to perform arithmetic or comparison operations.
6. _____ keyword ensures no duplicate values.
7. _____ function displays a sub-string of given length starting from the specified position.
8. _____ statement is used to see a list of all the databases present in MySQL.
9. The DROP DATABASE statement is used to _____ an existing database.
10. In SQL, the _____ statement is used to create a table.
11. Once the table is created, we can use the _____ command to see the description of the newly created table.
12. _____ statement is used to add new rows of data in a table that exist in the database.
13. The _____ statement in SQL is used to fetch or retrieve data from one or more tables in the database.
14. _____ statement eliminates duplicate entries while displaying data from the table.
15. The _____ clause returns values that fall within a given range.
16. The _____ keyword can be used to create a column alias.
17. _____ operator returns True, if the column value is NULL.
18. _____ KEY is a key used to link two tables.
19. The _____ constraint ensures that invalid data is not inserted into the foreign key column.

## State True or False

1. MySQL is a proprietary software.
2. MySQL satisfies ACID property.
3. MySQL is a database query language.
4. The server application responds with the requested information that is displayed on the client machine.
5. DDL is used to manipulate data.
6. `Char` performs faster than `varchar`.
7. The ALL keyword is used to compare any applicable value in the list.
8. The `strcmp()` function returns 1, if the first string is smaller than the second.
9. When we delete a database, all the information stored in it is lost.
10. The WHERE clause can be used retrieve data only from a single table.
11. The WHEREIN clause returns values that match values in a list or a sub-query.
12. The ORDER BY clause can be used to sort data according to multiple columns.
13. An underscore represents zero, one or multiple characters.
14. A column alias permanently changes the heading of the column.
15. Equality operator does not work with NULL values.
16. NULL is a data type in SQL.

17. All aggregate functions affect only rows that do not have NULL values.
18. Comparison operations cannot be performed on NULL values.
19. The primary key must contain NULL values.
20. A table can have only one primary key and the primary key may consist of one or more fields.

## Multiple Choice Questions

1. We cannot _____ data using SQL statements.
   a. delete   b. update   c. retrieve   d. None of these.

2. Which of the following is not an example of a database?
   b. MySQL   b. SQL   c. PostGres SQL   d. SQL Server

3. Which function returns the smallest integer value that is greater than or equal to a number?
   a. Ceil()   b. floor()   c. round()   d. abs()

4. Which function is used to remove leading and trailing white spaces from the given string?
   a. TRIM()   b. LTRIM()   c. RTRIM()   d. RPAD()

5. Which clause is used with SELECT statement to filter the records in the table and fetch only those that meet the specified criteria?
   a. ORDER BY   b. WHERE   c. DISTINCT   d. UPDATE

6. Which SQL statement is used to modify the existing data in a table?
   a. ORDER BY   b. WHERE   c. INSERT INTO   d. UPDATE

7. Which clause is used with the WHERE clause to compare a value to find similar values using wildcard characters?
   a. IN   b. BETWEEN   c. LIKE   d. DISTINCT

8. Which operator compares values and gives True even for two NULL values?
   a. IS NULL   b. IS NOT NULL   c. <=>   d. All of these.

9. The SQL NULL is _____.
   a. value   b. keyword   c. Both of these.   d. None of these.

10. Which function is used for replacing NULL values in MySQL?
    a. IS NULL   b. IFNULL()   c. IS NOT NULL   d. <=>

11. Which command is used to create a FOREIGN KEY constraint on an already existing table?
    a. ALTER TABLE   b. CREATE TABLE   c. INSERT INTO   d. UPDATE TABLE

## Give the Output

1. SELECT 20 + 5 - 10 * 3
2. SELECT 100/20 *2 + 8 -4;
3. SELECT (50 > 10) AND (50 <= 100);
4. SELECT POW(CEIL(ABS(-12.34)),2);
5. SELECT LOG10(MOD(110,FLOOR(100.89)));
6. SELECT CHAR_LENGTH(CONCAT('PYTHON','PROGRAMMING'));
7. SELECT LCASE(RIGHT('PYTHON PROGRAMMING',10));
8. SELECT LPAD(LTRIM('         PYTHON PROGRAMMING'),25,'#');

9. `SELECT REPEAT(MID('PYTHON PROGRAMMING',7,7),3);`
10. `SELECT RPAD(REVERSE('PYTHON'),15,'@');`

# Answers

## Fill in the Blanks
1. client-server
2. Metadata
3. Data Definition
4. char
5. Operator
6. UNIQUE
7. MID()
8. show databases;
9. remove
10. CREATE TABLE
11. DESC
12. INSERT INTO
13. SELECT
14. SELECT DISTINCT
15. WHERE BETWEEN
16. AS
17. IS NULL
18. FOREIGN
19. FOREIGN KEY

## State True or False
1. False
2. False
3. False
4. True
5. False
6. True
7. False
8. False
9. True
10. False
11. True
12. True
13. False
14. False
15. True
16. False
17. True
18. False
19. False
20. True

## Multiple Choice Questions
1. d
2. b
3. a
4. a
5. b
6. d
7. c
8. c
9. c
10. b
11. a

## Give the Output
1. -5
2. 14
3. 1
4. 169
5. 1
6. 17
7. rogramming
8. #######PYTHON PROGRAMMING
9. PROGRA PROGRA PROGRA
10. NOHTYP@@@@@@@@@

# Introduction to Emerging Trends

## 14

### Chapter Objectives

An *emerging trend* is a topic area that is growing in interest and utility over time. Researchers, academicians and industry experts, all pitch their knowledge to delve into upcoming technologies to gain maximum benefit out of these areas. In the field of Information Technology, some recent trends that we will be covering in this chapter include:

- Artificial intelligence and machine learning
- Natural language processing
- Immersive experience of Augmented Reality (AR) and Virtual Reality (VR)
- Robotics
- Big data and its characteristics
- Internet of Things (IoT), sensors and smart cities
- Cloud Computing and Cloud Services (SaaS, IaaS, PaaS)
- Grid computing and blockchain technology.

## 14.1 ARTIFICIAL INTELLIGENCE

Artificial Intelligence (AI), in simple terms, aims to create intelligent machines that think and act like humans. This would enable machines to perform tasks like speech recognition, learning, planning, reasoning and problem solving. AI makes it possible for machines to learn from experience, adjust to new inputs and perform tasks by processing large amounts of data and recognizing patterns in it.

For example, a program using AI may keep a check on whether certain parameters within a program are behaving normally. For example, the machine may raise an alarm if a parameter crosses a certain threshold which might, in turn, affect the outcome of the related process.

## 14.2 MACHINE LEARNING

Machine learning is an application of artificial intelligence that enables machines to automatically learn and improve from experience without being explicitly programmed. It enables the computers (machines) to make data-driven decisions rather than being explicitly programmed for carrying out a certain task. These algorithms are designed to learn and improve over time when they are exposed to new data.

Machine learning algorithms include a set of programs in which the process of learning begins with data to look for patterns in data and make better decisions in the future based on the examples or experiences provided to it.

Machine learning algorithm enables computers to learn by themselves without any human intervention or assistance and adjust actions accordingly. Thus, the process of teaching the machines is a structural process that can be broken down into three steps as illustrated in Fig. 14.1.

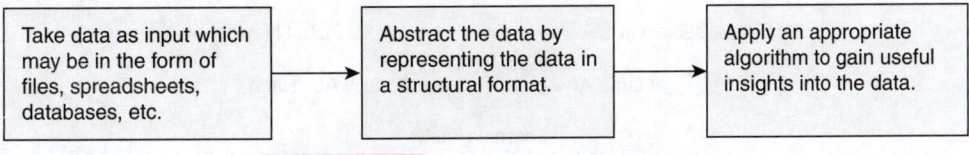

**Figure 14.1** Steps in machine learning

Machine learning algorithms are used to analyze massive amounts of data to

- identify profitable opportunities or dangerous risks
- form a recommendation engine to personalize online ad delivery in almost real time
- detect fraud
- filter spam
- detect threats to network security.

Figure 14.2 gives an insight into the vast scope of machine learning. A few examples of the applications of this emerging technology in real life are given below.

- Facebook's News Feed feature uses machine learning to personalize each member's feed. If a user frequently tags or writes on the wall of a particular friend, the News Feed changes its behavior to display more content from that friend.
- Human resource (HR) systems use machine learning algorithms to identify characteristics of effective employees and use this knowledge to select the best suitable candidate from the set of all the applicants of a particular vacant post.
- Self-driving cars use deep learning neural networks (a branch of machine learning) to identify objects and determine optimal actions for safely steering a vehicle down the road.
- Tumour detection, drug discovery, and DNA sequencing
- Predicting the price and load of electricity that will be consumed in an area
- Voice recognition system
- Diagnosis of diseases (like diabetes, cancer) based on the symptoms of patients
- Identification of frequently selling products or products that sell well together so that lucrative discounts can be given to further boost their sales.

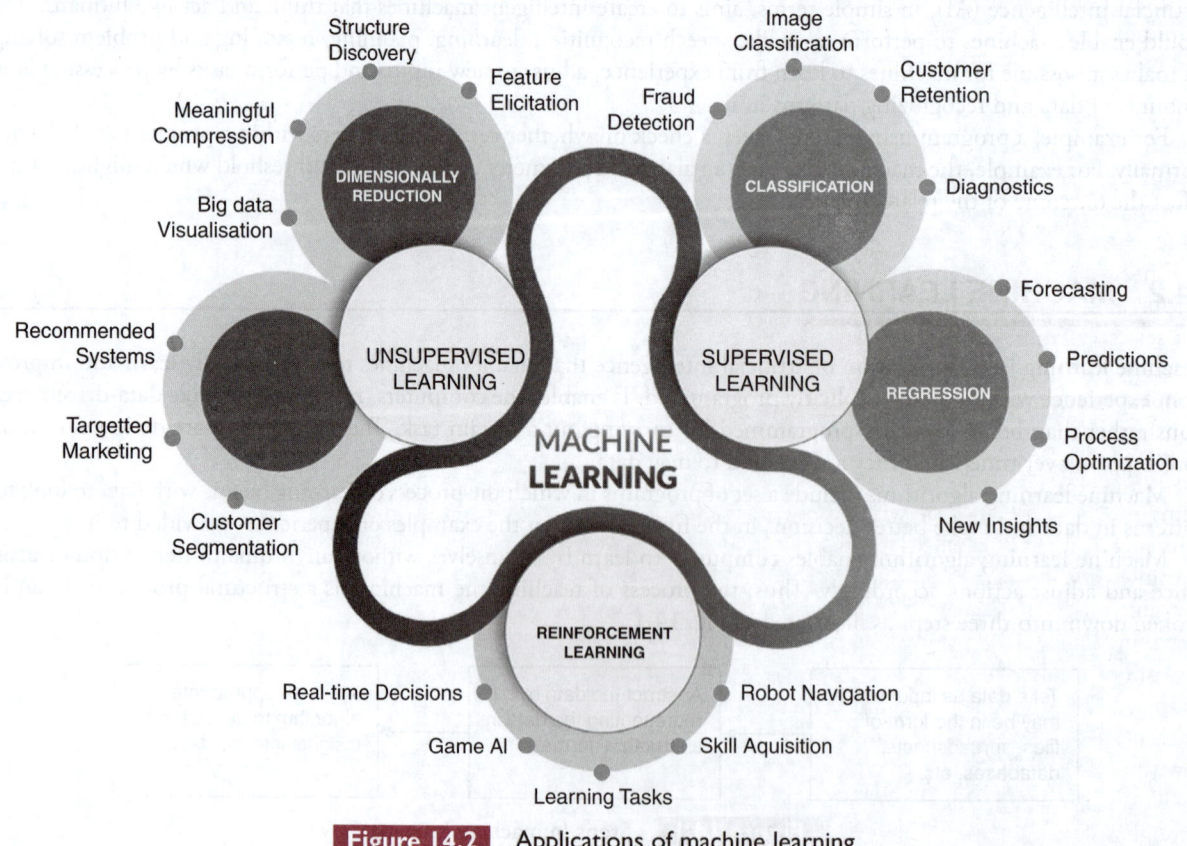

**Figure 14.2** Applications of machine learning

### 14.2.1 How Machine Learning Works

Machine learning algorithms use a training data set to create a model. When new input data is given to the algorithm, the model predicts values for it. The accuracy of these predicted values is then evaluated. If the accuracy is acceptable, the machine learning algorithm is deployed, else it is trained again with an augmented training data set.

### 14.2.2 Types of Machine Learning Algorithms

Machine learning algorithms can be categorized as supervised and unsupervised.

**Supervised machine learning algorithms:** Supervised machine learning algorithms, as the name indicates, has a supervisor as teacher. These algorithms apply learning from past data (or experiences) to new data using labelled examples.

> Supervised learning should be used when output of data in the training set is known.

These algorithms start with analyzing a known training dataset, to produce an inferred function that can be used to predict future data values. The learning algorithm then compares the predicted output with actual output to find errors and modify the model accordingly.

For example, if we have a basket filled with different varieties of fruits then the first step is to train the machine to identify a fruit. Now, our machine can easily identify an apple and a banana. Supervised learning algorithms can be further classified into two categories:

*Classification Algorithm:* A classification algorithm classifies data into a particular group. Classification techniques predict discrete categories. For example, a fruit can be classified as either an apple or a banana or an orange or any other one. In real-world applications, classification can be used in medical imaging, speech recognition, hand-writing recognition, credit scoring, predicting if an incoming email is authentic or spam, or whether a tumour is cancerous or benign.

Classification algorithms are best used if data can be tagged, categorized, or separated into specific groups or classes. Commonly used classification algorithms include support vector machine (SVM), decision trees, *k*-nearest neighbour and Naïve Bayes, discriminant analysis, to name a few.

*Regression:* A regression algorithm predicts a real value. In contrast to classification algorithms, regression predicts continuous values. For example, the cost of a product, the value of a stock, changes in temperature or fluctuations in power demand. Commonly used regression analysis algorithms include logistic regression, neural networks, etc.

> In supervised learning, clear instructions are given specifying what needs to be learnt and how it needs to be learnt.

Thus, in supervised machine learning algorithm, data input and desired output, along with a feedback about the accuracy of predictions during algorithm training are provided. Data scientists can select variables or features that can be used by the model to analyse data and make predictions. For example, supervised learning can be used by a company to identify customers who are likely to churn (that is, stop using the company's products or services). It can also be used by insurance companies to predict the likelihood of occurrence of a mishap and determine the Total Insurance Value.

**Unsupervised learning:** Unsupervised learning trains the machine to deal with information that is neither classified nor labelled. In this case, the machine learning algorithm works on that information without any guidance. The unsorted information is grouped based on similarities, patterns and differences without any prior training of data. For example, if we give an image of mango and an orange, then initially the machine has no idea about how a mango looks and how the orange looks.

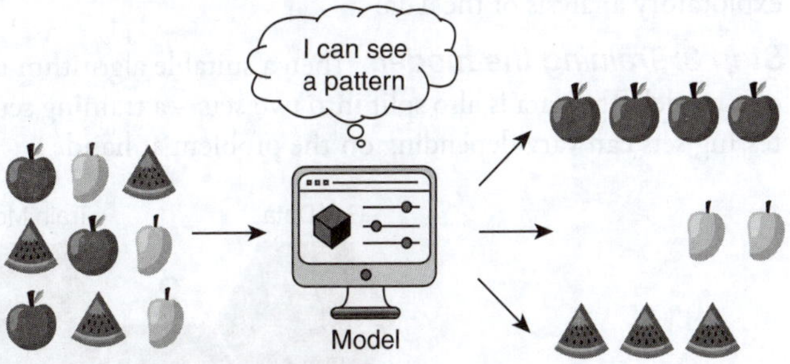

Unsupervised machine learning algorithm learns through observation and finding structures in the data. That is, the model automatically finds patterns and relationships in the dataset by creating clusters in it (Fig. 14.3). For example, if given a dataset of pictures of both mangoes and oranges, the algorithm can make two clusters – one containing only pictures of oranges and the other of mangoes. What an unsupervised machine learning cannot do is

**Figure 14.3** Classifying fruits

specifying labels to the clusters. That is, it can only segregate the pictures but cannot tell that this is a real-world orange and that is a mango.

Unsupervised learning can be categorized into two sets of algorithms:

***Clustering:*** In clustering, the aim is to discover inherent groupings in the data or discover hidden patterns. For example, a company may like to group its customers by their purchasing behavior, a cell phone company can use clustering to optimally decide the locations where they can build cell phone towers (these clusters can depict the number of people relying on their towers). Other applications include gene sequence analysis, market research, and object recognition. Commonly used clustering algorithms include k-means, k-medoids, hierarchical clustering, etc.

**Figure 14.4** Different approaches of supervised and unsupervised learning

***Association Analysis:*** In association mining (or analysis), the aim is to discover rules that describe large portions of data. For example, a company can use association analysis to conclude that a customer who buys X also buys product Y.

Thus, unsupervised machine learning algorithms (also called neural networks) are used when the information used to train is neither classified nor labelled. These algorithms use an iterative approach called deep learning to review data and arrive at conclusions. Unsupervised learning algorithms are more used for complex tasks than supervised learning systems. For example, these algorithms are used in image recognition, speech-to-text and natural language processing applications, and to predict the probability of presence of a particular disease. A retailer can use unsupervised learning technique to find out products that customers tend to buy more frequently.

> Semi-supervised machine learning algorithm fall somewhere between supervised and unsupervised algorithms since they use both labelled and unlabelled data for training. These algorithms improve accuracy.

### 14.2.3 Steps in Machine Learning

Irrespective of the algorithm used, the steps to perform machine learning remain the same. These steps (given in Fig. 14.5) include:

***Step 1: Collecting data:*** We first need to gather raw data which may be available in Excel sheets, Access/MySQL or any other database, text files, etc. This step forms the foundation of other subsequent steps. More the variety and quantity of the data, better are the learning prospects for the machine.

***Step 2: Preparing the data:*** The gathered data may not be of acceptable quality. So, our second task is to improve data quality (if required) by fixing issues such as dealing with missing data and treatment of outliers. This is done by exploratory analysis of the data.

***Step 3: Training the model:*** Then a suitable algorithm is selected and the cleaned data is represented in the form of a model. The data is also split into two sets – a training set and a testing set. The ratio of the records in training and testing sets can vary depending on the problem at hand.

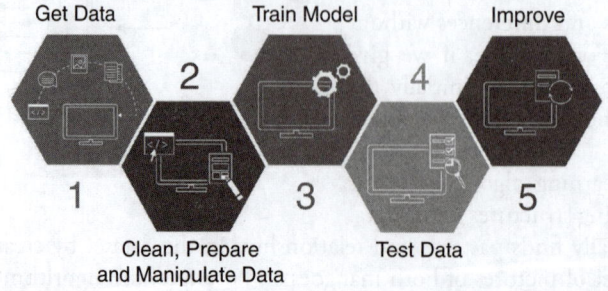

**Figure 14.5** Detailed steps in machine learning algorithms

As the name suggests, training data set is used for developing or training the model and the testing data set is used as a reference for checking the accuracy of output of the model.

***Step 4: Evaluating the model:*** In this step, the testing data set is used to evaluate the accuracy of the model formed in Step 3.

***Step 5: Improving the performance:*** After evaluating the model, there may be a need to modify the existing model by adding/deleting variables to enhance its accuracy or choose a different model altogether. This step may involve significant time and effort of the data scientist.

## 14.3 NATURAL LANGUAGE PROCESSING

Natural Language Processing or NLP is a field of Artificial Intelligence that gives the machines the ability to read, understand and derive meaning from human languages. NLP is a multi-disciplinary field that includes knowledge from many disciplines including computer science and computational linguistics, which aims to fill the gap between human communication and computer understanding.

With increased access to data and computational power, NLP can be successfully applied in areas like healthcare, media, finance, human resources and others.

NLP techniques are specifically designed to automatically handle natural human language in the form of speech or text.

NLP can help you with lots of tasks and the fields of application just seem to increase on a daily basis. Let us mention some examples:

- NLP is used to recognize and predict diseases based on electronic health records and the patient's own speech. For example, Amazon Comprehend Medical is a service that uses NLP to identify the condition of a patient, learn about medications and treatment based on patient notes, clinical trial reports and other electronic health records.
- Organizations use NLP to analyze the customer's feedback about a service or product. This can be done by collecting and analysing reviews and comments that they write on social media.
- Companies also use NLP to reduce customer complaints. For example, Royal Bank of Scotland uses text analytics (an NLP technique) to analyze customers' reviews from feedback forms, emails, surveys and call centre conversations to identify the root cause of customer dissatisfaction and improve the business process.
- IBM has developed a cognitive assistant tool that works like a personalized search engine. It automatically learns everything about the users and then remind them of a name, a song, or anything that they are unable to recall at that moment.
- NLP is used by email service providers like Yahoo and Google to filter and classify emails as spams. For this, they analyze words in the text to know whether the email is a spam email or not.
- MIT has developed an NLP-based tool to identify fake news by analyzing if its source is accurate or politically biased. This helps to determine if the source of the news is to be trusted or not.
- Amazon's Alexa and Apple's Siri use NLP to respond to voice instructions. For example, we often use voice-search on Google to find information on weather forecast, best route to a particular destination, or turn on the lights at home.
- Financial traders use NLP to track and analyze news, reports, comments about possible mergers between companies, and other sources information to know the trends in the market.
- Companies are using NLP to select most suitable candidates for recruitment and automating routine litigation that helps them save time and cut down the costs involved.
- NLP helps in investigative discovery that identify patterns and clues in emails or written reports to help detect and solve crimes.
- Email service providers are using NLP for spam filtering. They compare the words in spam to valid emails to identify junk mail.
- Word Processors such as Microsoft Word uses NLP to check the grammatical accuracy of texts.
- Interactive Voice Response (IVR) applications use NLP in call centres to respond to certain users' requests.

A few years back, Microsoft analyzed large samples of search engine queries to identify internet users who were suffering from a particular disease.

### 14.3.1 Importance of NLP

**NLP is becoming increasingly important due to following reasons in today's scenario:**
- Availability of massive volumes of textual data
- Increasing demand for a rich set of applications that allows computers to communicate with humans in their own language. For example, NLP enables computers to read text, hear speech, interpret it, measure sentiment and separate the important part from non-important parts.
- Enhanced capability of machines to analyze more language-based data than humans. Computers do this work in a consistent and unbiased way without getting bored or tired.
- With huge amounts of unstructured data generated every day, NLP is the only way to analyze the text and speech data efficiently.
- Natural language processing uncovers the insights hidden in word streams.

> Natural language processing uncovers the insights hidden in the word streams.

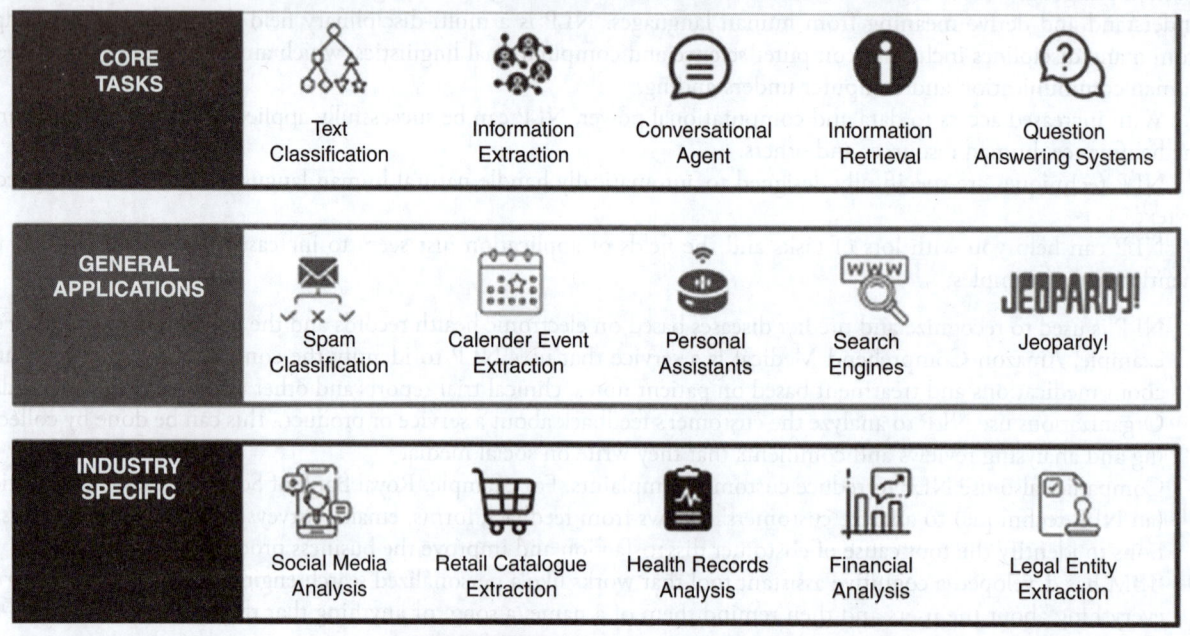

**Figure 14.6** Applications of NLP

### 14.3.2 Challenges in NLP

- Human language is diverse and complex. There are infinite ways – both verbally and in writing – by which we can express ourselves.
- Every language has a unique set of grammar and syntax rules, terms and slang.
- We often misspell words or intentionally abbreviate them, or omit punctuation marks. Sometimes, this makes the text very difficult to be understood or analyzed correctly.
- When we speak, we have regional accents, and we mumble, stutter and borrow terms from other languages.
- We often use same words but with a different meaning. For example, consider: Slow, children and Slow, children? or Slow children. The three sentences are with same words but with different meanings.
- Languages are often ambiguous. For example, in English, a word can be used as a noun as well as a verb. Pronouns makes the task even tougher. For example, Goransh went to Pranay. He said, "I am very happy." Here, it is difficult to say who is I.

### 14.3.3 How NLP works

The basic tasks performed for NLP operations include:

***Document summarization:*** Generate a document summary (including search and indexing, duplication detection).

*Topic discovery:* Identify the meaning and theme in text.

*Contextual extraction:* Automatically pull structured information from text-based sources.

*Sentiment analysis:* Identify the mood or subjective opinions within large amounts of text.

*Speech-to-text and text-to-speech conversion:* Transforming voice commands into written text, and vice versa.

For example, to analyze a long paragraph,

*Step 1:* We first perform tokenization, i.e., break it into individual words.
*Step 2:* Remove the stop words. These stop words can be words in the language like "and", "the" or "to" in English. This is important as they provide little or no value to the NLP objective.
*Step 3:* Stemming the remaining words. This process involves slicing the end or the beginning of words to remove affixes – prefixes or suffixes. This helps us to get the root words.
*Step 4:* Lemmatization: The number of words is further reduced by grouping together different forms of the same word. For example, went and go, best and good, run and ran, and words that sound similar when grouped together.

Once this is done, sentiment analysis can be done to understand the meaning of the text and identify the mood (positive or negative) in which it was said/written.

From the above discussion, we see that NLP heavily relies on the syntax and the semantics of the language for analysis. Syntax is the arrangement of words in a sentence to make grammatical sense and Semantics is the context in which those words are used.

## 14.4 IMMERSIVE EXPERIENCE

Immersive Experience is any technology that extends reality or creates a new reality by leveraging the 360-space. While some types of Immersive Experience extend reality by overlaying digital images on a user's environment, others create a new reality by completely immersing users in a digital environment, shutting them out from the rest of the world (Fig. 14.7).

The simplest tool to enjoy immersive content is through smartphones or specialized headsets. On the software side, although a web app or a desktop application can be used, web app is more popular.

### 14.4.1 Types of Immersive Experiences

**360-degree content:** 360-degree content is an interactive photo or a video recording shot in every direction at the same time. This allows users to change the viewing direction at any moment. Digital twin is a precise virtual model of a real-life object, process, or system. We can even create a digital twin of an object that does not exist. Such models can be used to display textual details or to monitor, control, and run simulations.

**Virtual reality (VR):** Virtual reality (VR) is a computer simulation that immerses the user inside a virtual world and allows him/her to interact with the environment. VR stimulates users' senses to make them feel as if they are actually present in that environment.

**Figure 14.7** Experiencing immersive experiences

VR shuts a user completely from the rest of the world while being surrounded by content. Through a head-mounted display (HMD), whatever content the user experiences in the headset becomes the reality for him.

**360 vs. 360 VR:** Though the two terms are same, 360 VR is a combination of 360-content with VR mode. It allows users to view the 360-content in a cardboard headset, or sometimes even a mobile 360 VR headset. Users can experience 360-content without the help of an HMD and is best experienced on mobile.

***Mobile VR*** leverages HMDs that are connected to smartphones. Examples of these are the Samsung Gear VR, Google's Daydream or even Google Cardboard.

***True VR*** uses headsets with powerful computers or consoles. Examples include HTC Vive, Oculus Rift, Playstation VR, etc. These powerful HMDs use sensors (separate from the HMD) to keep a track of a person's movement and his surroundings. The sensors would then adjust the VR content to whatever is within a user's environment. True VR uses CGI and 3D modelling for content.

***360 VR vs. In-VR:*** With 360 VR, users can use their device to explore content by looking in any direction but it does not change the content that surrounds the objects. In-VR content takes depth into consideration. This means that when a person is viewing an object, he can move closer to the object or move further away from it. The entire content is adjusted accordingly.

***Augmented Reality:*** Augmented Reality (AR) enhances the user's perception of the real world by adding a computer-simulated layer of information on top of it. While AR adds or hides data from the environment, VR completely replaces the user's perception of the real world.

Using AR, digital images are presented on top of the real world. This means that users who leverage AR are not completely shut off from the world. Instead, AR extends their reality.

For example, Snapchat Filters that overlay digital images onto your face is an application of AR. Another example of AR is Pokemon Go where users can walk around with their mobile phones and find Pokemon that are overlaid on the environment around the user.

Many stores like Target and Ikea have their own AR apps where users can choose a product and place it virtually on anything to see how it looks. For example, you can choose a dress and see how it looks on you. This allows consumers to "try out" a product before even buying it.

***Mixed Reality:*** Mixed Reality (MR) brings together VR and AR into an enhanced version of AR. Mixed Reality is also referred to as AR 2.0 because it achieves better immersion than AR. MR integrates virtual objects to the real world. It responds to changes in the environment and to user interaction in real-time.

Unlike VR, MR does not shut out users from the rest of the world. Instead, the HMD is more like a pair of glasses that overlays digital images on top of your environment (just like AR).

***Extended Reality (ER)*** is used to enhance or completely replace reality.

## 14.4.2 Applications of Immersive Experiences

Immersive Technology is not a new term for those who read Sci-Fi books or watch Sci-Fi movies.

***Business:*** Every business generates a number of reports using ERP software. These reports are, at times, difficult to understand. In such cases, AR headset is used to see only the most important bits of data in the report. The headset will show all the details when the user looks at specific parts of the report.

Using a VR headset can make remote business meetings through tele or video conferencing more authentic.

***E-commerce*** uses 360-degree technologies to provide better visualizations. It allows users to look at the product from every possible angle (Fig. 14.8). Many websites have made the 360-degree content even more interactive. It can react to changes in options in real-time, giving the user an immediate preview.

These websites also use MR to show how the product will look like in a real-life environment.

***Architecture and design*** fields make extensive use of immersive technology. With VR, we can explore building designs in a 1:1 scale. AR is used to show additional relevant information. MR allows architects to edit 3D models created by them as per the user's requirements. Any small changes and adjustments in the simulation are reflected instantly.

***Engineering, maintenance, and repair*** of complex equipment can be easily done using immersive techniques. While repairing, engineers use AR headsets to get useful data right away. Artificial intelligence can help them by giving suggestions about the best action that can be taken.

In the design phase, a digital twin is used by engineers to see their creations in a virtual environment. They no longer need to build prototypes. Similarly, during testing phase, a digital twin can be used for running simulations and collecting analytical data.

**Figure 14.8** Using immersive experiences for shopping

*Healthcare* is another area that extensively uses immersive experiences. Augmented and virtual reality, both can make the current state of medical training more effective. While AR provides useful information to healthcare employees when learning how to use new equipment, VR can help them to practice complex medical procedures in a virtual environment before actually performing them on a live patient.

*Telemedicine* uses VR or MR to break the distance barriers between patients and practitioners. Patients can now get themselves diagnosed in a more comfortable setting and having more accessible medical services. AR headset can be used to give important information to every patient in a hospital, keep their minds busy and divert them from all their worries.

VR solutions are also used to reduce anxiety in patients by helping them with sleep or just serving as a positive distraction. AR can be used to visualize patient data and treatment assistance. An AR headset can directly show only the relevant information on the patient's body or give suggestions regarding the medicine to be prescribed. Moreover, during surgeries, immersive technologies can be used to outline the most optimal cutting path, give warnings about potential problems and help with additional information.

*Travel industry* uses immersive technologies for selling real-life experiences. For example, 360-degree content and VR provide customers with the option to try before they buy something. Customers can have a virtual tour of the place where they intend to go, and virtually walk around in the hotel they intend to book. This will help them decide if they are making the right choice. An AR headset can serve as a 24×7 personal tour guide that provides additional information in real-time, making sightseeing easier and more informative by helping them in finding cafes, restaurants, hotels, inns and landmarks.

*Real-estate* uses immersive technologies to virtually show the property that has been let out on rent or pitched for sale. It is very inconvenient and time consuming for the buyer as well as the seller to see every property. Buyers can check out the properties remotely whenever they have time, that too without the help of a real-estate agent. Later, they can personally visit only selected properties and use MR headset to get information about the property, decoration options or furnishing suggestions.

Augmented reality in logistic centres use immersive technology to reduce warehouse costs by using AR smart glasses in the picking process. The smart glasses show a list of products to be picked (reducing lookup times) and calculate an optimal route (to lower travel time). Headsets are used to read barcodes and determine if the current location is the right one. In case the location is not correct, the headset guides the workers to the correct location.

> DHL could cut 25% cost by using AR in their logistic business. Automaker Volvo uses VR headsets in the testing process and BMW uses it for workstation planning.

*Automakers* use MR for testing automobiles in simulated extreme situations. Sensors in the headsets enable precise measurement of reaction times and other important safety factors. VR is also used in workstation planning to reduce the labour force required and assess processes completely virtually. AR headsets can be used by employees for engine assembly units training at a faster pace (approx. three times faster).

*Car industry* is also using immersive technology to create virtual showrooms where consumers can look at cars, take virtual test drives and even virtually sit in actual car seats.

*Retail Industry:* Companies like Adidas uses VR to enhance workflow by using VR as a virtual team collaboration space. They use it when different teams have to work together. VR gives employees the ability to be in the same virtual room and share 3D models and other content.

Walmart uses VR headsets for training employees. They use immersive experience to prepare their employees for different real-life situations.

*Education:* VR can help students to learn about a particular concept. For example, a VR headset can be used to take a virtual tour of a historical monument and learn about historical events of importance associated with it. Similarly, MR can be used to learn about the human body and how each part functions by overlaying digital images on an actual person and highlighting where the different parts are located.

*Gaming* was among the first applications that extensively used Immersive Technology (Fig. 14.9). The launch of the Playstation VR, Pokemon Go and VR arcades are examples of application of this technology.

**Figure 14.9** VR for game playing

## 14.5 ROBOTICS

Robotics is a branch of engineering that involves the conception, design, manufacture, and operation of robots. It is an inter-disciplinary field that includes the study of electronics, computer science, artificial intelligence, mechatronics, nanotechnology and bioengineering.

Science-fiction author Isaac Asimov, had first used the term robotics in the year 1940s. According to him, robots must,

*Rule 1:* never harm humans.
*Rule 2:* always follow instructions from humans without violating rule 1.
*Rule 3:* protect themselves without violating the other rules.

Some important aspects of robot include:

- They have electrical components for providing power and controlling the machinery.
- They have mechanical construction and their shape or design depends on the task they are intended to accomplish.
- They are programmed. Instructions fed to them help them to determine what, when and how it would do something.

These days, robots are being extensively designed as bots that explore Earth's harshest conditions and assist in almost every facet of healthcare. Though the robotics industry is still evolving, we already have robots that work in the deepest depths of our oceans to the remote heights of outer space. They are being used to do everything that humans could not dream of doing.

### 14.5.1 Types of Robots

*Pre-programmed Robots* operate in a controlled environment to perform simple, monotonous tasks. For example, a mechanical arm on an automotive assembly line that is used to weld a door, or insert a certain part into the engine. This type of robot can perform that task for longer hours, faster and more efficiently than a human.

*Humanoid Robots* look like humans and/or mimic human behavior. They can perform human-like activities (like running, jumping and carrying objects). Sophia and Atlas are two popular examples of humanoid robots.

*Autonomous Robots* operate without human operators. They are designed to perform tasks in open environments that do not require human supervision. For example, the Roomba vacuum cleaner uses sensors to roam freely throughout a home to clean it.

> Robots are also used for tasks varying from diffusing bombs and performing surgeries. VR robots are also becoming popular these days.

*Teleoperated Robots* are mechanical bots controlled by humans. They are used in extreme geographical conditions, weather, circumstances, etc. For example, human-controlled submarines used to fix underwater pipe leaks during the BP oil spill or drones used to detect landmines on a battlefield are examples of teleoperated robots.

*Augmenting Robots* either enhance current human capabilities or replace the capabilities a human may have lost. Robotic prosthetic limbs or exoskeletons used to lift hefty weights are examples of such robots.

### 14.5.2 Applications of Robotics

Over the past decade, robotics has been utilized in wide-ranging applications where they:

- help fight forest fires
- assist humans in manufacturing plants (known as co-bots)
- provide companionship to elderly people
- work as surgical assistants
- deliver food order or other packages
- perform household tasks like vacuuming and mowing the grass
- locate and transfer items in warehouses
- perform search-and-rescue missions after natural disasters
- detect landmines in war zones.

**Robots have several industrial applications:**

The **manufacturing** industry is amongst the first well-known user of robots. Robots and co-bots (bots that work alongside humans) are used in the automobile industry to efficiently test and assemble products like cars and related machinery.

Logistics **companies** use robots in their warehouses to perform tasks like shipping, handling goods and ensuring quality control. Robots are supposed to take items off the shelves, transport them across the warehouse floor and package them. They are now also used for last-mile delivery of packages for faster and efficient delivery.

**Self-driving cars** are a result of integrating data science with robotics. Automakers like Tesla, Ford, Waymo, Volkswagen and BMW are all working to provide users an ultimate experience of travel that will let them sit back, relax and enjoy the ride. Companies like Uber and Lyft are also developing autonomous rideshare vehicles that will be operated without humans.

**Healthcare industry** uses robots to perform complicated surgeries, deliver everything from medicines to clean linens.

**Space agencies** like NASA use robots in different ways (Fig. 14.10). Robotic arms on spacecraft can move large objects in space. Robotic spacecraft can visit other worlds like the Moon or Mars. For example, Mars rovers Spirit and Opportunity are robots. Cassini studies Saturn and its moons and rings. Robots like The Voyager and Pioneer spacecraft are now traveling beyond our solar system. People on Earth use computers to send messages to the spacecraft. The robots have antennas that pick up the message commands and work as per the instructions given to it. Robotic airplanes can fly without a pilot aboard. NASA is also developing Robonaut to help people in space. The upper body of Robonaut looks like a person. It has a chest, head and arms. They can work outside a spacecraft and work like an astronaut on a spacewalk.

 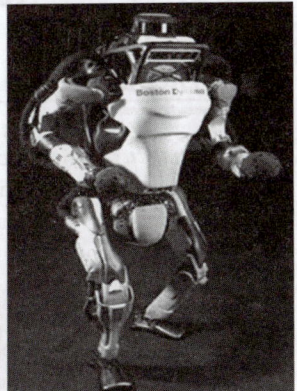

**Figure 14.10** Robots used by NASA

NASA is also working on robots that might help an astronaut in an emergency. For example, when the astronaut is seriously hurt, a doctor on Earth could use the robotic arm to perform surgery. This technology can help doctors on Earth, as well. Doctors can help people in faraway places where there are no surgeons to perform complicated surgeries.

Robots are also used as **scouts** to check out new areas to be explored. They take photographs, measure the terrain, look for dangers and find the best places to walk, drive or stop. This not only helps scientists and engineers make better plans for exploring but also helps astronauts to work more safely and quickly. Fig. 14.11 shows some poplar robots.

ASIMO is a humanoid that has the ability to recognise moving objects, postures, gestures, understand its environment, and interact with humans.

Pepper is the world's first robot capable of recognising human emotions. It is social, can converse with people, give them directions and even dance with them

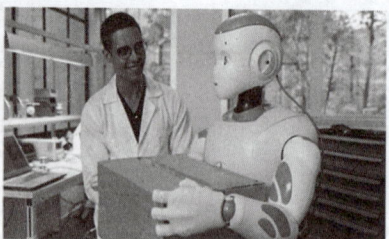

Romeo helps with everyday tasks, assists when people have fallen over, makes conversations and plays games.

Buddy is designed to entertain the family, help you with your everyday activities, offer reminders, provide recipes in the kitchen, make video calls, keep an eye on your home while you are not at home, connect all your smart home devices togaher and even help your children learn.

Panasonic Robot Egg uses NLP to communicate and can be controlled by your voice. It plays video footage via a built-in projector and even engages in interactive games. This robot is Wi-Fi connected and promises software updates in future to improve it futher.

REEM is a full-size humanoid service robot that can act as a receptionist, provide entertainment for guests, make presentations and give speeches in different languages and help with a variety of different chores. REEM is able to self-navigate, interact with people it encounters and keep on running for up to eight hours.

**Figure 14.11** Popular robots that are commonly used today

## 14.6 BIG DATA

*Big data analytics* is the process of collecting, organizing, and analyzing large sets of data (called *big data*) to discover patterns and other useful information. It can help organizations to better understand the information contained within the data. Big data analysis allows users to evaluate large volumes of transaction data and other data sources that traditional systems would not be able to handle.

Big data is a term used for analyzing data sets whose size or type is beyond the ability of traditional relational databases to capture, manage, and process with low latency (less delay). The special features of data sets used in big data analysis include high volume (large amount), high velocity (frequently changing), or high variety (different types). This data comes from sensors, devices, video/audio, networks, log files, transactional applications, and web and social media. Much of the data is generated in real time and on a very large scale.

Analyzing this big data allows data scientists or business users to make better and faster decisions using data that was previously inaccessible or unusable. Big data analytics uses advanced analytics techniques such as text mining, data mining, machine learning, predictive analytics, forecasting, data optimization, and natural language processing. Although these processes are separate, they are integrated for high-performance analytics (Fig. 14.12).

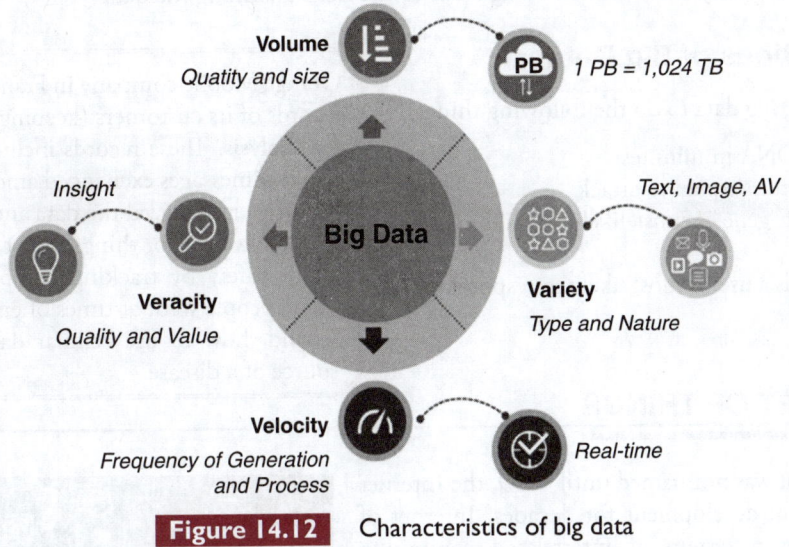

**Figure 14.12** Characteristics of big data

Sophisticated software tools are used for big data analytics. Big data analysis outperforms data warehousing as it can easily handle large amount of unstructured and semi-structured data efficiently. Furthermore, data warehouses may not be able to handle the processing demands posed by sets of big data that are updated frequently or even continually. This is especially important in the case of real-time data on stock trading or online activities of website visitors or the performance of mobile applications.

Big data analytics environments and technologies including Hadoop, MapReduce, and NoSQL databases can process huge data sets over clustered systems. Big data analysis techniques can analyze large data sets of size ranging from a few terabytes to zettabytes.

### 14.6.1 History and Evolution of Big Data Analytics

The history of big data analysis can be traced back to 1950s when people were not even aware of the term *big data*. In those days, people were analyzing business numbers in a basic spreadsheet software to uncover insights and trends in the business.

Later, businesses switched to data warehousing and data mining techniques to gather information, run analytics, and unearth information that could be used for future decisions. However, today, businesses have grown to an extent that they are seeking to identify insights for immediate decisions. The ability to work faster and stay agile gives organizations a competitive edge like never before.

### 14.6.2 Benefits of Big Data

Big data analytics helps organizations to harness their data and identify new opportunities. This leads to smarter business moves, more efficient operations, higher profits, and happier customers. Big data analysis helps business in the following ways:

*Cost reduction* Big data technologies such as Hadoop and cloud-based analytics give significant cost advantages when it comes to storing large amounts of data. This data can be analyzed to identify more efficient ways of doing business.

*Faster and better decision-making* Because of the speed at which new data sources and types of data can be analyzed, businesses are able to process information immediately and make decisions based on what they have learned.

***New products and services*** The ability to map customer needs and satisfaction through analytics gives customers what they exactly want. Therefore, businesses are using big data analysis techniques to meet customer needs.

Big data analysts typically want the knowledge that comes from analyzing the data.

### 14.6.3 Applications of Big Data

Researchers are using big data to do the following things:

- Decode human DNA in minutes
- Predict where terrorists plan to attack
- Determine which gene is most likely to cause certain diseases
- Determine the ads a user is most likely to respond to on Facebook

> Orange Mobile company in France used 2.5 billion records of its customers (keeping them anonymous) for analysis. These records included details on calls and text messages exchanged among 5 million users. Researchers analyzed the data and proposed projects that showed two things. First, how to improve public safety by tracking cell phone data to map where people went at times of emergencies.
> Second, how to use cellular data to find out the source of a disease.

## 14.7 INTERNET OF THINGS

Although the concept was not named until 1999, the Internet of Things has been in development for decades. Internet of Things (IoT) means a system of interrelated computing devices, machines, objects, animals or people that have unique identifiers for identification and also the ability to transfer data over a network without requiring human-to-human or human-to-computer interaction.

If the thing, in the Internet of Things, is a person, then he/she can have heart monitor implant; if it is an animal, it can have a biochip transponder; if it is an automobile, it can have sensors to generate alert alarms (example, when the pressure in tyre is too low) and if it is any other natural or man-made object, then it is assigned an IP address and provided with the ability to transfer data over a network (Fig. 14.13).

**Figure 14.13** IoT

The huge availability of address space in IPv6 has led to the development of the Internet of Things. With more IP addresses available, more number of devices can be connected to exchange information with each other.

Today, IoT is being widely used for precision agriculture, building management, healthcare, energy and transportation. The first internet appliance was a Coke machine at Carnegie Melon University in the early 1980s when the programmers succeeded in connecting the machine over the internet to check the status of the machine and determine the availability of a cold drink. This check helped them to save their time as they did not have to go to the machine to buy Coke when it was not available in the machine.

> In simple terminology, IoT is the concept of connecting any devices over the Internet.

Later, other devices like cell phones, coffee makers, washing machines, headphones, lamps, wearable devices and almost anything you can think of could be connected. It is interesting to know that the analyst firm Gartner has said that by 2025, there will be over 25.1 billion connected devices. Other analysts have said that this number will be over 100 billion. So we can conclude that IoT is a giant network of connected "things" (including people), which links people-people, people-things, and things-things.

### 14.7.1 Examples of Applications of IoT

***Whenever we read about a new technology, the first question that comes to our mind is how this technology is going to help us?*** With IoT, where anything that can be connected will be connected, the question is why should we want these devices to be connected? There are many examples to justify the need for such connections.

***Case 1:*** Imagine you are going for a meeting and your car tells you the best route to take. If there is traffic jam then your car sends a text message to the other party notifying them that you will be late.

*Case 2:* Imagine that the moment your alarm rings to wake you, a message is sent to the coffee machine to start brewing coffee for you.
*Case 3:* The smart watch that your wear in office tells you when and where you were most active and productive.
*Case 4:* You have a self-driving car with complex sensors to detect objects in their path,
*Case 5:* A smart football that can track how far and fast it is thrown and record those statistics via an app for future training purposes.
*Case 6:* You have a smart refrigerator that can text message you that milk packets are over in the fridge and you need to buy them before you come home. Or, your fridge checking the expiry date of an ice-cream and notifying you that you should not eat it now.
*Case 7:* Imagine that you have an AC installed in your residence which is connected with your smartphone. On a very hot day, you can instruct your AC to start and set the room temperature to 18 degrees before you finally reach home.

In an article, Ashton wrote that if computers knew everything about things (using data gathered by them) without any help from us then we would be able to track and count everything. It would also reduce waste, loss and cost. We would know exactly when things need to be replaced, repaired or recalled, and whether they were fresh or past their best.

In this way, IoT can help organizations to save a lot of money through improved process efficiency, asset utilization and enhanced productivity. With improved tracking of objects using sensors and connectivity, companies can better analyze them and make smart decisions. For example, if you own a car manufacturing company, then you can know which accessories are the most popular by using sensors to detect which areas in the showroom are the most popular, and where customers linger longest. You can even use the available sales data to identify which components are selling fastest and then automatically align sales data with supply, so that the popular items never goes out of stock.

> The information collected by IoT devices can be used to detect patterns, make recommendations, and detect possible problems before they occur.

We all have heard that the Indian government is working hard to develop smart cities. Do you know that smart cities use IoT for efficient utilization of resources? Figure 14.14 gives an overview of such a city. IoT has the potential to transform entire cities by solving real problems faced by the people every day. With the proper connections and data, the IoT can solve traffic congestion issues and reduce noise, crime, and pollution.

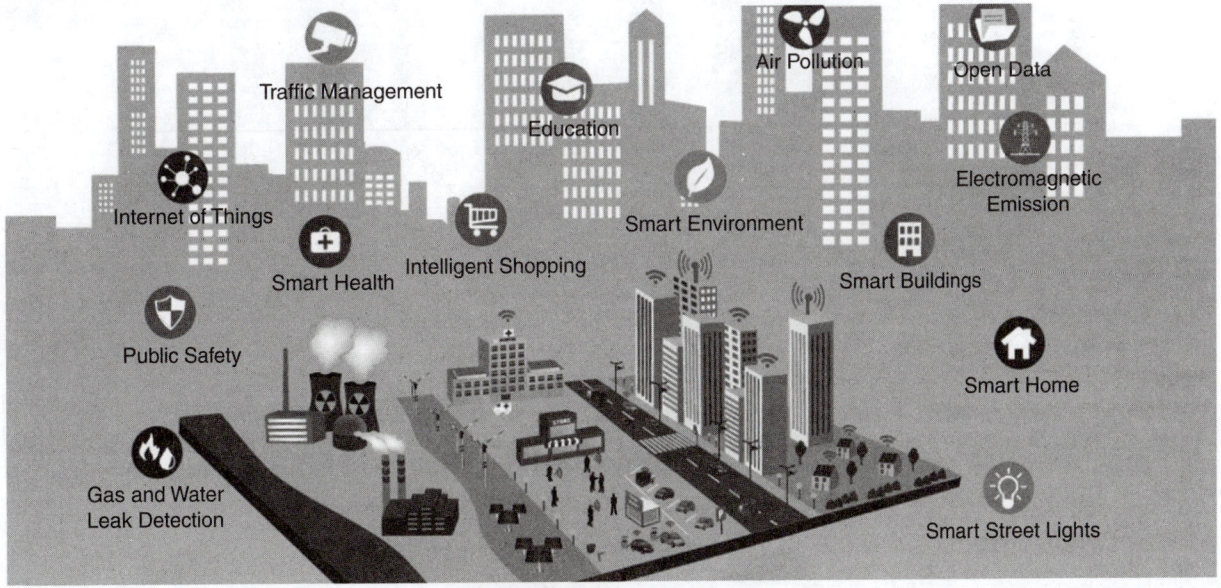

**Figure 14.14** A smart city

Source: https://aliga.sk/en/what-the-heck-is-a-smart-city/

## 14.7.2 IoT Products

Big companies like Honeywell, Hitachi, GE, Cisco, AT&T, Apple, Google, IBM, Microsoft, Skyworks, Iridium Communications, Red Hat, Zebra Technologies and InterDigital are already playing in the market to realize the benefits of IoT. A few examples are given here:

***Amazon Echo for Smart Home*** works through its voice assistant, Alexa. Users can talk to Alexa and order it to perform a variety of functions. For example, users can tell Alexa to play music, provide a weather report, get sports scores, order an Uber, and do much more.

***Fitbit One – Wearables*** tracks your steps, floors climbed, calories burned, and quality of sleep. The device wirelessly connects with computers and smartphones to transmit your fitness data in understandable charts to monitor your progress.

***Barcelona – Smart Cities:*** The Barcelona city in Spain is one of the foremost smart cities in the world. It has implemented several IoT initiatives that have helped to enhance smart parking and the environment.

***AT&T - Connected Car:*** AT&T added 1.3 million cars to its network in the second quarter of 2016. With this, the count of total number of connected cars rose to 9.5 million.

> Amazon Web Services, Microsoft Azure, IBM's Watson, Cisco IoT Cloud Connect, Salesforce IoT Cloud, Oracle, Integrated Cloud and GE Predix are popular IoT platforms.

Thus, we see that IoT allows for virtually endless opportunities and challenges thereby making it a hot topic for research. According to a report, nearly $6 trillion will be spent on IoT solutions over the next five years. Figure 14.15 shows the advantages of implementing and using IoT in manufacturing and industries. *Source*: Morgan Stanley-Automation World Industrial Automation Survey, AlphaWise.

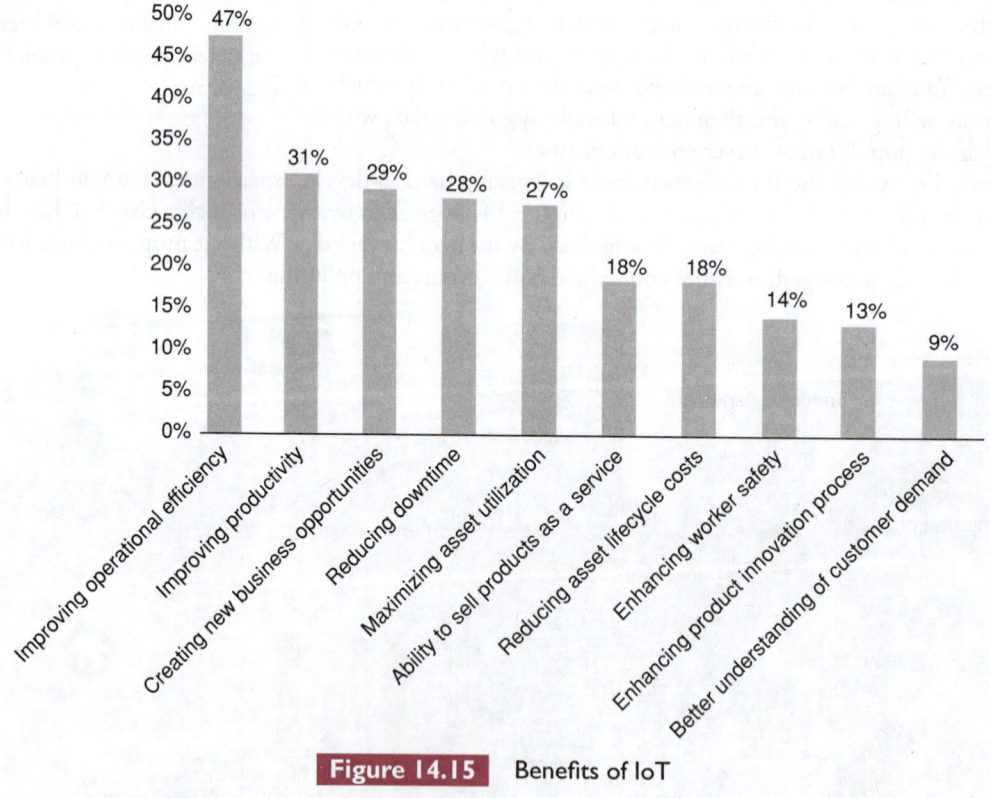

**Figure 14.15** Benefits of IoT

## 14.7.3 Challenges

Security is the biggest issue that we often come across while talking about IoT. With billions of devices connected together, concerns of privacy and data sharing always haunt our minds.

In fact, the protection of sensitive data was ranked as the top concern among enterprises according to the 2016 Vormetric Data Threat Report. Hackers try to penetrate connected cars, critical infrastructure, and even people's homes. Therefore, the main focus of the companies is to ensure security of all the data generated by these devices.

Another issue with IoT is that massive amounts of data is being generated by these devices. So, companies need to figure out how they would store, monitor, analyze and deduce results from this vast amount of data that is continuously being generated.

However, despite all odds, IoT is being used by several industries including manufacturing, defence, transportation, banks, retail, oil and gas mining, health care, connected homes and banks, to name a few.

## 14.8 SENSORS

A sensor is a device that detects and responds to some type of input that it receives from the physical environment. This input could be heat, light, motion, pressure, moisture, or any other environmental phenomena. As the output, sensors usually generate a signal that is converted to human-readable form and then displayed at the sensor location or transmitted electronically over a network for reading or further processing. Figures 14.16 and 14.17 show the different types of sensors.

For example, an oxygen sensor in a car's emission control system detects the gasoline/oxygen ratio. If the mixture is not optimal, the balance is readjusted.

Another example is motion sensors in home security lights, automatic doors and bathroom fixtures, which send out microwaves, ultrasonic waves or light waves and detect when the flow of energy is interrupted by something entering its path.

*Vision and Imaging Sensors* detect the presence of objects or colours within their fields of view. They display a visual image of whatever it detects.

*Temperature Sensors* detect thermal parameters and provide signals to the inputs of control and display devices. They are used to measure the thermal characteristics of gases, liquids, and solids in many industrial processes.

*Radiation Sensors* sense the presence of alpha, beta, or gamma particles and provide signals to counters and display devices. They are usually used for surveys and sample counting.

*Proximity Sensors* detect the presence of nearby objects through non-contacting means within a range of up to several millimetres. They are used in manufacturing operations to detect the presence of parts and machine components.

*Pressure Sensors* detect forces per unit area in gases or liquids and provide signals to the inputs of control and display devices.

*Position Sensors* sense the positions of valves, doors, throttles, etc. and supply signals to the inputs of control or display devices.

*Photoelectric Sensors* sense objects passing within their field of detection. They can even detect color, cleanliness, and location, if required. Photo sensors are commonly used in manufacturing and material-handling automation. For example, they are used for counting, robotic picking, and automatic doors and gates.

*Particle Sensors* sense dust and other airborne particulates and supply signals to the inputs of control or display devices. Particle sensors are common in bin and baghouse monitoring.

*Motion Sensors* sense the movement or stoppage of parts, people, etc. and supply signals to the inputs of control or display devices. They are usually used for detecting the stalling of conveyors or the seizing of bearings.

*Metal Detectors* sense the presence of metal in a variety of situations ranging from packages to people.

*Level Sensors* are used to determine the height of gases, liquids, or solids in tanks or bins. The information is then passed as signals to the inputs of control or display devices.

**Figure 14.16** Different types of sensors

***Leak Sensors*** are used to identify or monitor the unwanted discharge of liquids or gases. Some leak detectors are used to measure the effectiveness of the seals in vacuum packages.

***Humidity Sensors*** measure the amount of water in the air and convert these measurements into signals that can be used as inputs to control or display devices.

***Gas and Chemical Sensors*** sense the presence and properties of various gases or chemicals and relay signals to the inputs of controllers or visual displays.

***Force Sensors*** measure various parameters related to forces such as weight, torque, load, etc. and provide signals to the inputs of control or display devices.

***Flow Sensors*** sense the movement of gases, liquids, or solids and provide signals to the inputs of control or display devices. They are used extensively in the processing industries.

***Flaw Sensors*** detect inconsistencies on surfaces or in underlying materials such as welds. They are used in a variety of manufacturing processes.

***Flame Detectors*** sense the presence and quality of fire and provide signals to the inputs of control devices. They are used in many combustion control applications like burners.

***Electrical Sensors*** sense current, voltage, etc. and provide signals to the inputs of control devices or visual displays.

***Contact Sensors*** detect physical touch or contact between the sensor and the object being observed or monitored. They are often used in alarm systems to monitor doors, windows, and other access points. For example, when a door or window is opened/closed, a magnetic switch provides an indication to the alarm control unit so that the status of that entry point is known. They are also used as proximity sensors in robotics applications and automated machinery.

***Non-contact Sensors*** do not require a physical touch between the sensor and the object being monitored in order to function. Radar guns used by law enforcement to monitor the speed of vehicles is an example of a non-contact sensor.

***Speed Sensor*** detects the speed of an object or vehicle.

***Ultrasonic Sensor*** detects noise and measures distance between two objects. For this, high-frequency sound waves generated by active ultrasonic sensors are received back by the ultrasonic sensor for evaluating the echo. The time delay between transmitting and receiving the echo is used to calculate the distance to an object. Passive ultrasonic sensors are used for detecting ultrasonic noise present under specific conditions.

**Figure 14.17** (a) Temperature sensor, (b) Ultrasonic sensor and (c) Speed sensor

## 14.9 SMART CITIES

A smart city is a framework that makes extensive use of Information and Communication Technologies (ICT), to develop, deploy, and promote sustainable development practices to cater to growing urbanization issues. ICT increases operational efficiency, share information with the public and improve both the quality of government services and citizen welfare. This ICT framework is basically an intelligent network of connected objects and machines that transmit data using wireless technology over the cloud.

Cloud-based IoT applications receive, analyze, and manage data in real-time to help municipalities, companies and citizens make better decisions that improve quality of life.

In a smart city, citizens are connected using smartphones, mobile devices, smart cars and smart homes. Sharing data with a city's physical infrastructure and services can help service providers improve energy distribution, streamline trash collection, decrease traffic congestion and improve air quality. The primary goal of a smart city is to create an urban environment that provides its citizens a high quality of life while also generating overall economic growth. Smart city technologies aim at optimizing infrastructure, mobility, public services, and utilities. For example,

- Connected **traffic lights** receive data from sensors and cars (adjusting light cadence and timing to respond to real-time traffic) to reduce congestion on roads.
- Connected **cars** can share data with parking meters and electric vehicle (EV) charging docks and direct drivers to the nearest available spot.
- Smart **garbage cans** send data to waste management companies so that they can schedule a pick-up.
- Citizens can use their smartphone as driver's license and other digital credentials to speed-up and simplify access to the city and local **government services**.
- Smart city initiatives also address **environmental concerns** such as climate change and air pollution.
- Sensors are used to measure water parameters and guarantee the quality of drinking water. A smart city also has proper **wastewater removal** and drainage system.
- Smart city improves **public safety** by monitoring areas of high crime through sensors. Sensors can also be used to issue an early warning before droughts, floods, landslides or hurricanes.
- **Smart buildings** with sensors monitor the structural health of buildings. They can detect wear and tear and notify officials when repairs are needed.
- Sensors are used to **detect leaks** in water mains and other pipe systems. This reduces costs and improves the efficiency of public workers.
- Smart city also provides **efficiency** to tasks related to urban manufacturing, urban farming, including job creation, energy efficiency and space management.

**Figure 14.18**  Wi-Fi connectivity in smart cities

## 14.9.1 Need for Smart Cities

Today, 54% of people across the globe live in cities. This number would reach to 66% in around the year 2050. This means that considering the overall population growth and movement of people from rural to urban areas, another 2.5 billion people will be added to cities over the next three decades. Hence, environmental, social, and economic sustainability has to be ensured to deal with such rapid urbanization. Smart city is one such initiative in this direction.

Secured wireless connectivity and IoT technology have transformed our cities. For example, streetlights are being installed with intelligent lighting system that works on solar power and connects to a cloud-based central control system. Their high-power embedded LEDs alert commuters about traffic woes, provide severe weather warnings, detect free parking spaces and even work as EV charging docks.

With the introduction of 5G technology, smart cities project will get a boost due to more and better connectivity with devices.

### 14.9.2 Examples of Smart Cities

A smart city supports a technology-based infrastructure that takes environmental initiatives, performs urban planning, has a high-functioning public transportation system and allows humans to live and work within the city and utilize its resources.

*New York City:* The New York City Department of Transportation uses a congestion management system that has improved travel times by 10%. The NYCx Challenges initiative invites entrepreneurs, technologists, and tech professionals to participate in open competitions and propose ideas that can solve problems related to urban areas (like pollution, income inequality, and transport).

Automated water meters in New York consist of small devices connected to individual water meters that sends daily readings to a computerized billing system.

*Amsterdam Smart City:* Amsterdam is a smart city that shares traffic and transportation data with interested parties such as developers for creating mapping apps that connect to the city's transport systems.

The city has autonomous delivery boats called **'roboats'** to keep things moving in a timely fashion. It also supports a floating village of houses, solving the city's overcrowding problem with sustainable, energy-efficient technology. In this city, power is generated within communities, and homes receive water from the river after it is filtered within their tanks.

*Copenhagen Smart City:* Copenhagen is known as one of the smartest cities in the world. The city uses open data in its collaboration with the Massachusetts Institute of Technology (MIT) to develop an innovative smart bike system.

The city is embedded with sensors that provide real-time information that is shared to monitor and manage air quality and traffic congestion.

*Singapore Smart City:* Singapore uses sensors and IoT-enabled cameras to monitor the cleanliness of public spaces, crowd density and the movement of locally registered vehicles. Companies monitor energy use, waste production and water use in real time. Singapore is also working on autonomous vehicles including robotic buses, and an elderly monitoring system to ensure the health and well-being of its senior citizens.

> According to Forbes 21 May 2019, the top 10 smart cities in the world are London, New York, Amsterdam, Paris, Reykjavik, Tokyo, Singapore, Copenhagen, Berlin, Vienna.

*Dubai Smart City:* Dubai has smart buildings, smart utilities, smart education, telemedicine, smart healthcare and smart tourism. It also uses smart systems for traffic routing, parking, infrastructure planning and transportation.

*Barcelona Smart City:* This smart city has smart transportation system and smart bus systems with smart bus stops that provide free Wi-Fi, USB charging stations and bus schedule updates for riders. Barcelona has an app-based bike-sharing and smart parking system that includes online payment options. Sensors are used to monitor temperature, humidity, amount of rainfall, pollution and noise.

### 14.9.3 Security Objectives

*Availability* ensures actionable, real-time, and reliable access to data without which the smart city cannot thrive.

*Integrity* is an important feature as smart cities rely on reliable and accurate data. Stored data should be accessed and modified only by authorized persons.

*Confidentiality* refers to sensitivity of the data collected, stored, and analyzed. Due care must be taken to prevent unauthorized disclosure of sensitive information.

*Accountability* makes the users of the data responsible for their actions. In whatever way they access and interact with the system, it is recorded (also referred to as logged). These logs or records should be difficult to forge.

The above security features call for strong authentication and ID management systems that must be integrated into the ecosystem to ensure that data is shared, accessed and manipulated only by authorized parties.

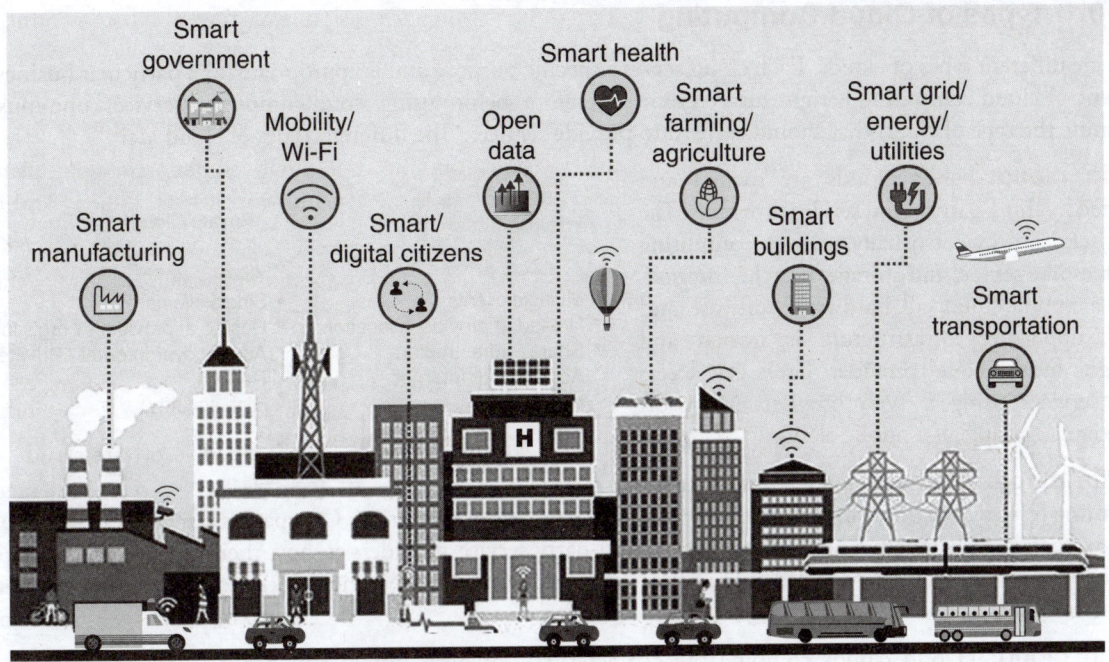

**Figure 14.19** Smart city components

## 14.9.4 How a Smart City Works

Smart cities utilize their web of connected IoT devices and other technologies to achieve their goals of improving the quality of life and achieving economic growth. Figure 14.19 shows the components of a smart city. Successful smart cities follow four steps:

*Collection:* Smart sensors throughout the city gather data in real time.

*Analysis:* Data collected by the smart sensors is assessed in order to draw meaningful insights.

*Communication:* The insights obtained in the analysis phase are communicated with decision makers through strong communication networks.

*Action:* Cities use the insights pulled from the data to create solutions, optimize operations and manage assets to improve the quality of life for residents.

## 14.9.5 Challenges

Data privacy and **security** are top concerns in a smart city. There is always a fear of data being hacked and misused.

Presence of sensors and cameras everywhere may be perceived as an **invasion of privacy** or government surveillance by the citizens.

Another issue is **connectivity**. IoT devices scattered across the city would not work in the absence of a powerful network connection.

> To address privacy issues, data collected should be anonymized and not be personally identifiable information.

## 14.10 CLOUD COMPUTING

Cloud computing, in simple terms, means delivering computing services including servers, storage, databases, networking, software, analytics, and intelligence over the Internet ("the cloud"). However, users pay for only the cloud services they use. This helps them to lower operating costs of their business, run infrastructure more efficiently with scaling (or changing as sometimes business needs more services and at other times less) needs of the business.

### 14.10.1 Types of Cloud Computing

There are different types of clouds. Each cloud serves a specific purpose and is appropriate for a particular business. No one type of cloud computing is right for everyone. Therefore, before using cloud computing services, one must first determine the type of cloud that should be used to provide services. The different types of cloud are:

**Public cloud:** Public clouds are owned and operated by third-party cloud service providers. The cloud service provider usually delivers computing resources like servers and storage over the Internet. With a public cloud, all hardware, software and other supporting infrastructure is owned and managed by the cloud provider. Users can access these services using a Web browser. Microsoft Azure is an example of a public cloud.

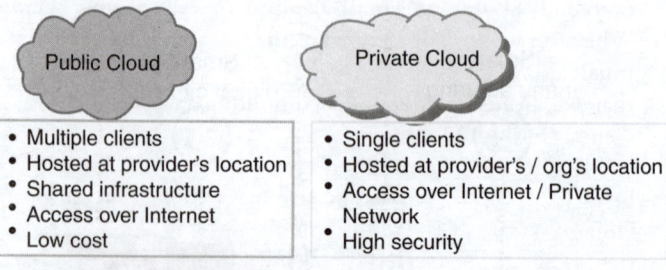

**Figure 14.20** Public cloud vs. private cloud

**Private cloud:** A private cloud refers to cloud computing resources to be exclusively used by a single business or organization. Companies can either deploy a private cloud in their own company's head office or pay third-party service providers to host their private cloud. The cloud services of a private cloud are provided over a private network (company's own network) and not over a public network like the Internet.

**Hybrid cloud:** Hybrid clouds combine the characteristics of both public and private clouds. Now, data and applications can be shared between the two clouds. And due to this, a hybrid cloud gives business more flexibility, more deployment options and helps to better use existing infrastructure with greater security and control.

### 14.10.2 Types of Cloud Services: IaaS, PaaS, Serverless and SaaS

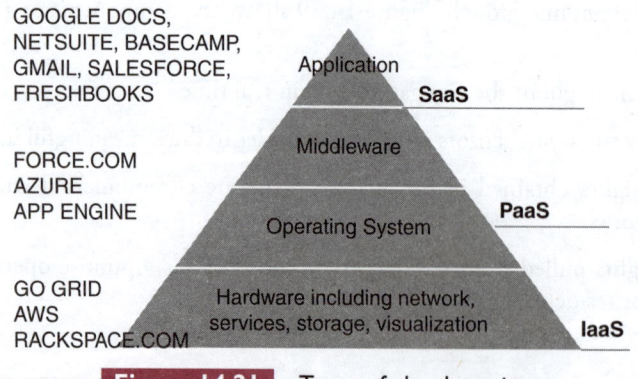

**Figure 14.21** Types of cloud services

Most cloud computing services fall into one of three broad categories (Fig. 14.21) which are given below:

***Infrastructure as a service (IaaS):*** The most basic category of cloud computing services is the IaaS. IaaS provides IT infrastructure like servers, storage, networks and operating systems as a service from a cloud provider.

***Platform as a service (PaaS):*** PaaS refers to cloud computing services that supply on demand, the platform or the environment for developing, testing, delivering and managing software applications. PaaS makes it easier for developers to quickly create applications, without having the need to set up or manage the underlying infrastructure of servers, storage, network and databases needed for development.

***Software as a service (SaaS):*** Software as a service is a method for delivering software applications over the Internet. They are basically provided on demand and on a subscription basis. Cloud providers not only provide software applications but also provide the infrastructure requires for the software. Software maintenance, upgrades and security are taken care of by the cloud provider. Users access the applications over the Internet, usually with a web browser on their phone, tablet or computer.

> Cloud computing is a more efficient way of delivering computing resources.

### 14.10.3 Uses of Cloud Computing

Before the cloud computing era started, companies had to invest a lot to set up, maintain and upgrade the required hardware and software. However today, cloud computing is used by everybody having an **email account** or even a smart phone. Whenever we send or receive an email, **watch movies, listen to music, play games or store pictures and other files**, it is likely that we are using the cloud computing facilities behind the scenes. (Fig. 14.22)

Though cloud computing is only a few years old, it is now being used by organizations varying from tiny start-ups to global corporations. Cloud computing is extensively used in the **creation and testing of new applications**. It is also used to store, back up and recover data. For example, in your smart phones you must have seen an app with name cloud. When you save your files on the cloud using your phone, then even if you delete those files from your phone, they can still be recovered from the cloud.

**Figure 14.22** Applications of cloud computing

Some cloud computing services are available free of cost for users. Google Drive, which offers 15 GB of storage space to all users who have a Gmail account is an example (Fig. 14.23). Users can upload their important files, pictures and other documents on the Google Drive. Users just have to type the URL https://www.google.com/drive/ and enter their Gmail username and password to upload their files and folders, share them with others and do lots more.

**Figure 14.23** Cloud providers

Similarly, OneDrive from Microsoft offers 5GB storage space to all users having a Microsoft account.

### 14.10.4 Advantages

**Cost:** Cloud computing eliminates the need of buying hardware and software. Moreover, there is no need for a dedicated IT team and other infrastructure to maintain, upgrade, backup, and secure the hardware or software.

**Speed:** Most cloud computing services are provided on demand; so even large amounts of computing resources can be made available in minutes, with just a few mouse clicks.

**Global scale:** A company can avail services anywhere from the best suitable geographic location. Applications and data are not tied to a device but can be accessed from anywhere.

**Productivity:** Instead of setting up and maintaining hardware and software and performing other time-consuming activities, the employees of the company can spend their time on achieving more important business goals.

> Gmail uses cloud to store and backup the user's data, emails, pictures and other files. Netflix also uses cloud computing services to run its video streaming service.

**Performance:** The cloud computing service providers regularly upgrade to the latest, fastest and most efficient computing hardware. This not only provides services at an extremely fast speed but also is beneficial for a business that can never invest money to buy the latest hardware for its use.

**Reliability:** Cloud computing takes data backup, keeps redundant copies of data at multiple locations within the cloud provider's network and performs disaster recovery techniques so that even in case of failure of one or more computers, the business can remain operational.

**Security:** Cloud computing service providers use a broad set of technologies and controls to protect data, applications and infrastructure from potential threats.

**Flexible and scalable:** Cloud-based applications can be easily customized to increase or decrease power, storage, and usage of other hardware as users' needs change.

## 14.11 GRID COMPUTING

Normally, a computer performs user-defined operations with its own set of limited resources. The computers we have has an upper limit to how fast it can complete an operation or how much data it can store. These computers are good for small operations but inefficient for high computational tasks.

To better understand the concept of grid computing, imagine several million computers of different type (laptops, desktops, super computers, mobile phones) from all over the world being connected together to form a single, huge and super-powerful computer (Fig. 14.24). This huge super powerful and global computer is called the grid. The name grid is analogous to the power grid as it has some similarity with the power grid. For example, as in a power grid, in grid computing the user never knows from where he is getting the computer power – from a supercomputer in the U.S., a laptop in China, or from a desktop in

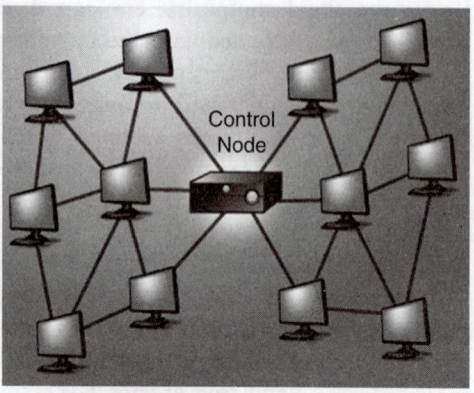

**Figure 14.24** Grid Computing

New Zealand. The user just knows that when he plugs in his computer to the Internet, he will get sufficient power to do his job and that he will have to pay for what he gets.

As of now, there are already hundreds of smaller grids around the world which are specifically created to help a particular group of users (like researchers or scientists). Efforts are being done to combine all the smaller grids to form a single powerful grid. This one grid will be a global network of computers operating as a vast computational resource. A grid computing system can be as simple as a collection of similar computers using the same operating system (homogeneous system) or as complex as an inter-networked system in which each computer runs on a different operating system (heterogeneous system). However, with a well-defined interface, accessing a grid computing system would be similar to accessing a local machine's resources.

Grid computing can be used by different types of users for a wide range of applications. For example, a scientist studying proteins can use it to analyze data; a businessman can tap into the grid through his PDA to access his company's network to forecast the future of a particular stock; an army officer can use the grid to coordinate between $n$ different military networks to formulate a battle strategy. However, the users must have special software that is unique to the computing project for which the grid is being used.

> Grid computing uses the Internet to share computer resources. It is however different from the World Wide Web as the WWW uses Internet to share information and not resources.

### 14.11.1 Components of Grid Computing

A grid computing system consists of:

A **central server** to prioritize and schedule tasks across the network; determine resources that each task will be authorized to access; monitor the system to check that the system is not overloaded; and ensure that performance of any individual node connected to the network does not drop.

A special **grid computing software** that acts as an interface for the users as well as for the resources the system will tap into for different applications.

A **middleware software** to enable heterogeneous computers to run different applications across the grid. Without middleware, communication across the system would be impossible.

Basically, in a grid computing system a major concern is security. Hence, the central server and the middleware application work together to protect the system from malicious hackers and provide authorized and authenticated access to the users. The server and middleware control how much access each computer has to the network's resources.

The control server and middleware application together ensure that any one computer does not dominate the network and simultaneously not allow network applications to take up all the resources of any one computer.

## 14.11.2 Grid Computing Applications

Grid computing is an emerging technology and its use for academic and research projects are on a constant rise (Fig. 14.25). The two most popular applications of grid computing are:

***The Search for Extra-terrestrial Intelligence (SETI) project:*** The project analyzes data collected by radio telescopes to search for evidence of intelligent alien communications. It is beyond the capacity of an individual computer to analyze the massive amount of data. So a grid of computers has been formed to create a virtual supercomputer.

***The Folding Project:*** The project is undertaken to study how proteins take certain shapes (called folds), and what effect these folds have on the functioning of the proteins. Scientists believe that several diseases like Parkinson's or Alzheimer's are caused due to mis-folding of the proteins. Once they are able to derive the relationship between folding patterns and functioning of the protein, they may be able to discover new ways to treat or even cure these diseases.

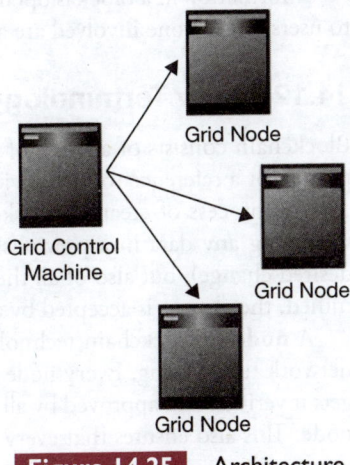

**Figure 14.25** Architecture of grid computing service

## 14.11.3 Running an Application in Grid Computing

Once the grid computing system is installed, the control server sends a part of the huge amount of data to the user's computer for analysis. Powered by untapped CPU resources, the software analyses the data. The project's software running on the grid system has a very low resource priority. If the user runs an application that demands enormous processing power, the execution of project software is suspended temporarily until the CPU usage returns to normal. From that point, the software again starts analyzing the data.

Eventually, when data analysis is complete, the project software will send the data back to the central server, which relays it to the appropriate database. After relaying the analyzed data, the central server will then send the next chunk of data to the user's computer, and the cycle repeats itself.

## 14.11.4 Major Concern

There are no constraints on the limits of grid computing provided all devices connected on the grid follow a standardized set of rules. Without standardization, it will be very time consuming and difficult for application programmers to create applications that work on different systems.

As of now, many existing grid computing systems work on proprietary software and tools. However, if every grid system uses a mutually agreed upon and reliable set of standards then it will be easier and more efficient for organizations to adopt the grid computing model.

Thus, an effective and efficient grid computing system will enable users to complete ambitious goals in relatively less time. The future will see more organizations creating versatile networks to solve computational problems that were once thought of as impossible.

## 14.12 BLOCKCHAIN TECHNOLOGY

To understand blockchain technology let us take an analogy. You have worked with simple MS Word document and Google Doc. Like MS Word document, Google Doc is also a word processing software. However, Google Doc allows users to share the document with other people. Users working on the same document need not copy it or transfer it to each other. They can simply share it. This sharing creates a decentralized distribution chain that gives everyone access to the document simultaneously. No user has to wait for other users to complete their piece of work in that document. Another big advantage here is that all changes made in the Google Doc are recorded in real-time, making the changes completely transparent.

A similar principle is used in blockchain technology. A blockchain is a time-stamped series of immutable records of data that is managed by a network of computers (not by any single device). Each block is secured and linked to other blocks in a chain.

Information in a block is open so that it can be viewed by everyone. This makes blockchain technology transparent to users as everyone involved are accountable for their actions.

### 14.12.1 Key Terminology

Blockchain consists of a chain of **blocks** where each block stores data and a hash value. Moreover, every block has a pointer or a reference to the previous block in the chain.

The process of creating blocks is known as **mining**. Correspondingly, people mining blocks are called **miners**. Changing any data in a previously created block will require re-mining of not just that particular block (with the desired change), but also of all the blocks in the chain that were mined after that block. When a block is successfully mined, the change is accepted by all of the nodes on the network.

A **node** in blockchain technology is any electronic device that maintains copies of the blockchain and keeps the network functioning. Every node has its own copy of the blockchain. When a new block is mined, the network first gets it verified and approved by all the nodes thereby making the process of updating a blockchain transparent to every node. This also ensures that every node has the updated copy of blockchain and maintains integrity and trust among users.

In blockchain technology, **tokens** are created to represent any kind of digital asset (which may include music files, contracts, tickets, a patient's medical records, or any other document), track its ownership and execute its functionality according to a set of programming instructions.

### 14.12.2 Success Factors

Reasons for the success of blockchain include the following unique features of this technology:

- It is decentralized and not owned by a single device.
- The data is stored in encrypted form.
- Every block is immutable; so no one can modify the data that is already stored within a blockchain.
- The blockchain is transparent; so anyone can view the data stored in a block.

### 14.12.3 Applications

Blockchain technology has infinite number of applications across almost every industry. Apart from bitcoin, it can be used in finance industry to track fraud, in medical field to securely share patient medical records between healthcare professionals and to track the usage of any digital asset, especially intellectual property, to prevent its misuse.

Blockchain can be used by artists for selling recorded **music** directly, thereby by cutting out commission paid by music companies and distributors like Apple or Spotify. Authors can even sell their **Ebooks to avoid costs charged by online shopping companies like Amazon and credit card processing companies.**

In future, blockchains may even eliminate bank accounts and practically all services offered by banks.

### 14.12.4 Use of Blockchain Technology for Online Purchase

The word blockchain is made up of two words – block and chain. Here, block means any digital information stored in a chain where chain is usually a public database.

An online shopping website uses blocks to store information about transactions like the date and time of your most recent purchase from the website as well as the amount for which the purchase was made. It also stores information about who is participating in the transaction. But, instead of using the user's actual name, a unique "digital signature," that works as a username is stored.

Every block also stores a unique cryptographic code called a "hash" that sets it apart from the other blocks in the chain.

For example, if you have made a purchase and after paying for your order, you want to buy another product then a separate block will be created with another unique code.

When a purchase is done and a **block is created, the transaction is verified**. This verification is automatically done by a network of computers. During this process, nodes confirm the details of the purchase, including the transaction's time, amount, and participants.

If the transaction is verified as accurate, then all its details like the amount, the user's digital signature, and digital signature of the shopping website are **stored in the block.**

The block is then assigned a unique code for identification. This code is known as a **hash. Once hashed, the block is added to the blockchain.**

Any block in the blockchain, then becomes publicly available for anyone to view (Fig. 14.26).

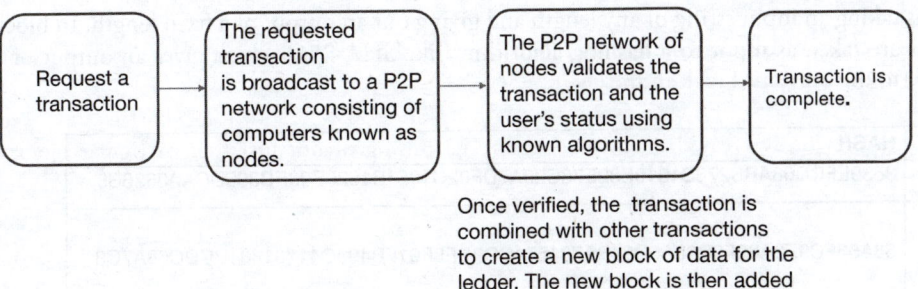

Figure 14.26   Process of adding a new node in the existing block chain

### 14.12.5 Pillars of Blockchain

Blockchain is a new technology on which extensive research is being done, especially because it helps to reduce risk, eliminate fraud and maintain transparency in all transactions involving digital assets. The three main properties of Blockchain Technology which have helped it gain widespread acclaim are as follows:

**Decentralization** The traditional client-server model is an example of a centralized system in which one entity controls all data transactions. However, some issues with this system are:

- All data is stored in one place; so, it is vulnerable to be attacked by hackers.
- If the software of the centralized system is being updated, the entire system halts.
- If the software of the centralized system shuts down due to some error, malicious software or an attack, the entire system halts.

In a decentralized system, the information is not stored by one device. Rather, every device in the network owns the information.

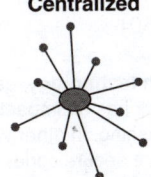

Centralized systems have a core authority that **dictates the truth** to the other participants in the network.

Only **priveleged users** or institutions can confirm new transactions

Decentralized systems have **no core authority** to dictate the truth to the other participants in the network.

**Every participant** in the network can access the history of transactions or confirm new transactions.

Figure 14.27   Centralized vs. decentralized authority

**Transparency** Transparency ensures integrity of the document, which creates trust in the asset. A user's identity is hidden via complex cryptography and represented only by his/her public address. For example, a message "Kiara sent 1 BTC" will be stored as "4TC5bhsFGkDwyz7voFXEmQwT2KbySt7CZO sent 1 BTC".

Here, the person's real identity is secure. Anyone can see the transactions that were done by Kiara, though not with her real name but with her public address. This level of transparency was never there in financial systems before.

**Immutability** Immutability here means that once data is entered in a block, it cannot be changed or deleted.

Decentralization, immutability and transparency are the key pillars that are applicable for any digital asset.

## 14.12.6 Hashing in Blockchain

The term hashing means taking an input string of any length and giving out an output of a fixed length. In blockchain technology, transactions are taken as input to a hashing algorithm (like SHA-256) which gives an output of a fixed length as shown in Fig. 14.28.

| INPUT | HASH |
|---|---|
| Hi | 3639EFCD08ABB273B1619E82E78C29A7DF02C1051B1820E99FC395DCAA3326B8 |
| Welcome to blockgeeks. Glad to have you here. | 53A53FC9E2A03F9B6E66D84BA701574CD9CF5F01FB498C41731881BCDC68A7C8 |

**Figure 14.28** Input value and its hash value

In the hash generated, we can see that no matter how big or small the input is, the output will always have a fixed 256-bits length.

The best part of the hash function is that even if a single change is made to the input, the hash changes drastically with no resemblance to its prior value. Consider, the two hash values given in Fig. 14.29. Though there is a change in case of just one character, the hash code varies considerably.

| INPUT | HASH |
|---|---|
| This is a test | C7BE1ED902FB8DD4D8997C6452F5D7E509FBCDBE2808B16BCF4EDE4C07D14E |
| this is a test | 2E99758548972A8E8822AD47FA1017FF72F06F3FF6A016851F45C398732BC50C |

**Figure 14.29** Modified input value and its hash value

Now if this was, say, the third block in the blockchain, then any chain in one block will also change the hash of the other blocks in the block chain (Fig. 14.30).

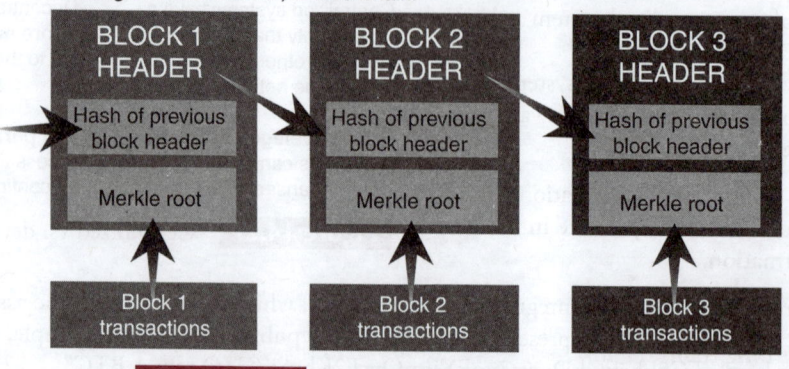

**Figure 14.30** Simplified bitcoin block chain

## Key Terms

**Artificial Intelligence:** Technology that aims to create intelligent machines that think and act like humans.

**Machine Learning:** An application of artificial intelligence that enables machines to automatically learn and improve from experience without being explicitly programmed.

**Natural Language Processing:** A field of artificial intelligence that gives machines the ability to read, understand and derive meaning from human languages.

**Stemming:** The process of slicing the end or the beginning of words to remove affixes – prefixes or suffixes. This helps us to get the root words.

**Lemmatization:** The process that involves reducing the number of words by grouping together different forms of the same word.

**360-degree content:** An interactive photo or a video recording shot in every direction at the same time. This allows users to change the viewing direction at any moment.

**Digital twin:** A precise virtual model of a real-life object, process, or system. We can even create a digital image of an object that does not exist.

**Virtual Reality (VR):** A computer simulation that immerses the user inside a virtual world and allows him/her to interact with the environment.

**Robotics:** A branch of engineering that involves the conception, design, manufacture and operation of robots.

**Big data analytics:** The process of collecting, organizing, and analysing large sets of data (called *big data*) to discover patterns and other useful information.

**Internet of Things (IoT):** A system of interrelated computing devices, machines, objects, animals or people that have unique identifiers for identification and also the ability to transfer data over a network without requiring human-to-human or human-to-computer interaction.

**Sensor:** A device that detects and responds to some type of input that it receives from the physical environment.

**Smart city:** A framework that makes extensive use of Information and Communication Technologies (ICT), to develop, deploy, and promote sustainable development practices to cater to growing urbanization issues.

**Cloud Computing:** Delivering computing services including servers, storage, databases, networking, software, analytics, and intelligence over the Internet ("the cloud").

**Infrastructure as a Service (IaaS):** Cloud computing services that provide IT infrastructure like servers, storage, networks and operating systems as a service from a cloud provider.

**Platform as a Service (PaaS):** Cloud computing services that supply on demand, the platform or the environment for developing, testing, delivering and managing software applications.

**Software as a Service (SaaS):** Software as a service is a method for delivering software applications over the Internet. They are basically provided on demand and on a subscription basis.

**Blockchain:** A time-stamped series of immutable records of data that is managed by a network of computers. Each block is secured and linked to other blocks in a chain.

**Mining:** The process of creating blocks is known as **mining**. Correspondingly, people mining blocks are called **miners**.

## Chapter Highlights

- Supervised machine learning algorithms learn from past data (or experiences) to create new data using labelled examples.
- Unsupervised learning trains the machine to use information that is neither classified nor labelled.
- Immersive Experience: Technology that extends reality or creates a new reality by leveraging the 360 space.
- While AR adds or hides data from the environment, VR completely replaces the user's perception of the real world.
- Public clouds are owned and operated by third-party cloud service providers. The cloud services of a private cloud are provided over a private network.

- Changing any data in a previously created block will require re-mining of not just that particular block (with the desired change), but also of all the blocks in the chain that were mined after that block.
- A node in blockchain technology is any electronic device that maintains copies of the blockchain and keeps the network functioning. Every node has its own copy of the blockchain.

## Review Questions

1. What do you understand by the term AI?
2. How can a machine learn?
3. Differentiate between supervised and unsupervised learning.
4. Give some applications of NLP.
5. Explain the reasons for popularity of NLP.
6. List any five issues encountered while translating human language into computer language.
7. Explain the different techniques of immersive experience.
8. Differentiate between AR and VR.
9. List some applications of immersive experience.
10. Write a note on the different types of robots that are available today.
11. Give a few industry-wise applications of robots.
12. Write a short note on IoT.
13. Is there any way Cloud Computing, IoT and Sensors can be connected to each other? If yes, how?
14. With help of examples, give the applications of sensors in smart cities.
15. Explain the different types of sensors highlighting their utility.
16. Differentiate between contact and non-contact sensors.
17. When will you call a city as a smart city?
18. Discuss the security concerns in smart cities.
19. Explain the different types of clouds that are used to provide services in cloud computing technology.
20. Write a detailed note on the different types of cloud services.
21. Write a short note on the components and utility of grid computing.
22. Explain the key pillars of blockchain technology.

## Fill in the Blanks

1. Machine Learning algorithms use a _____ data set to create a model.
2. _____ techniques predict discrete categories.
3. _____ learning trains the machine to use information that is neither classified nor labelled.
4. _____ means identifying the mood or subjective opinions within large amounts of text.
5. _____ is the process of slicing the end or the beginning of words to remove affixes.
6. _____ is an interactive photo or a video recording shot in every direction at the same time.
7. We can even create a digital _____ of an object that does not even exist.
8. Snapchat is an example of _____.
9. _____ look like humans and/or mimic human behavior.
10. _____ are created to help people in space.
11. _____ is the process of collecting, organizing, and analysing large sets of data to discover patterns and other useful information.
12. Big data analysis techniques can analyse large data sets of size ranging from few terabytes to _____.
13. IoT uses _____ addresses.
14. _____ detects and responds to some type of input that it receives from the physical environment.
15. _____ sensor detects noise and measures the distance between two objects.
16. With the introduction of _____ technology, smart cities project will get a boost due to more and better connectivity with devices.

17. _____ is a time-stamped series of immutable records of data that is managed by a network of computers.
18. Each block stores _____ and a _____ value.
19. In blockchain technology, _____ are created to represent any kind of digital asset.
20. The three key pillars of blockchain technology that are applicable on any digital asset are _____, _____ and _____.

## State True or False

1. Machine Learning enables computers to make instruction-driven decisions.
2. Unsupervised learning is used when output of data in the training set is known.
3. NLP can analyze only structured data.
4. Stemming is the process that involves reducing the number of words by grouping together different forms of the same word.
5. Digital twin is a precise virtual model of a real-life object, process, or system.
6. Autonomous robots operate with human assistance and instructions.
7. Ultrasonic sensors are used to calculate the distance to an object.
8. Data logs are created to ensure the accountability of data.
9. Microsoft Azure is an example of a private cloud.
10. Changing any data in a previously created block will require re-mining of not just that particular block but also of all the blocks in the chain that were mined after that block.
11. Every node has its own copy of the blockchain.

## Multiple Choice Questions

1. Which of the following is not a classification algorithm?
   a. Decision trees    b. k-means    c. *k*-nearest neighbour    d. Naïve Bayes
2. _____ is used when the information used to train is neither classified nor labelled.
   a. Decision trees    b. *k*-nearest neighbour    c. Neural Networks    d. Naïve Bayes
3. Interactive Voice Response (IVR) applications used in call centres to respond to certain users' requests is an example of _____.
   a. NLP    b. Decision Trees    c. Classification    d. Clustering
4. Pulling structured information from text-based sources means _____.
   a. topic discovery    b. document summarization
   c. contextual extraction    d. sentiment analysis
5. _____ allows users to move closer to the object or move further away from it.
   a. In-VR    b. True VR    c. Mobile VR    d. 360 VR
6. Which of the following is not a humanoid?
   a. REEM    b. PEPPER    c. SOPHIA    d. GITA
7. Which type of robots either enhance current human capabilities or replace the capabilities a human may have lost?
   a. Teleoperated    b. Autonomous    c. Augmenting    d. Humanoids
8. The special feature(s) of data sets used in big data analysis include high _____.
   a. variety    b. velocity    c. volume    d. All of these.
9. Big data technology does not include _____.
   a. Hadoop    b. MapReduce    c. NoSQL    d. SQL
10. Unauthorized disclosure of sensitive information affects the _____ of information.
    a. accessibility    b. confidentiality    c. accountability    d. integrity
11. Storage, networks, and operating systems are provided using _____.
    a. PaaS    b. SaaS    c. IaaS    d. All of these.
12. Every block also stores a unique cryptographic code called a _____.
    a. Hash    b. token    c. node    d. block

# Answers

## Fill in the Blanks
1. training
2. Classification
3. Unsupervised
4. Sentiment analysis
5. Stemming
6. 360-degree content
7. twin (or virtual model)
8. AR
9. Humanoid robots
10. Robonauts
11. Big data analytics
12. zettabytes
13. IPv6
14. Sensor
15. Ultrasonic
16. 5G
17. Blockchain
18. data, hash
19. tokens
20. distribution, decentralization, transparency.

## State True or False
1. False
2. False
3. False
4. False
5. True
6. False
7. True
8. True
9. False
10. True
11. True

## Multiple Choice Questions
1. b
2. b
3. a
4. c
5. a
6. d
7. c
8. d
9. d
10. b
11. c
12. a